Medieval Liturgy

GARLAND MEDIEVAL CASEBOOKS
VOLUME 18
GARLAND REFERENCE LIBRARY OF THE HUMANITIES
VOLUME 1884

GARLAND MEDIEVAL CASEBOOKS

JOYCE E. SALISBURY AND CHRISTOPHER KLEINHENZ, *Series Editors*

SEX IN THE MIDDLE AGES
A Book of Essays
edited by Joyce E. Salisbury

MARGERY KEMPE
A Book of Essays
edited by Sandra J. McEntire

THE MEDIEVAL WORLD OF NATURE
A Book of Essays
edited by Joyce E. Salisbury

THE CHESTER MYSTERY CYCLE
A Casebook
edited by Kevin J. Harty

MEDIEVAL NUMEROLOGY
A Book of Essays
edited by Robert L. Surles

MANUSCRIPT SOURCES OF
MEDIEVAL MEDICINE
A Book of Essays
edited by Margaret R. Schleissner

SAINT AUGUSTINE THE BISHOP
A Book of Essays
edited by Fannie LeMoine and
Christopher Kleinhenz

MEDIEVAL CHRISTIAN
PERCEPTIONS OF ISLAM
A Book of Essays
edited by John Victor Tolan

SOVEREIGN LADY
*Essays on Women in
Middle English Literature*
edited by Muriel Whitaker

FOOD IN THE MIDDLE AGES
A Book of Essays
edited by Melitta Weiss Adamson

ANIMALS IN THE MIDDLE AGES
A Book of Essays
edited by Nona C. Flores

SANCTITY AND MOTHERHOOD
*Essays on Holy Mothers
in the Middle Ages*
edited by Anneke B. Mulder-Bakker

MEDIEVAL FAMILY ROLES
A Book of Essays
edited by Cathy Jorgensen Itnyre

THE MABINOGI
A Book of Essays
edited by C.W. Sullivan III

THE PILGRIMAGE TO COMPOSTELA
IN THE MIDDLE AGES
A Book of Essays
edited by Maryjane Dunn and
Linda Kay Davidson

MEDIEVAL LITURGY
A Book of Essays
edited by Lizette Larson-Miller

MEDIEVAL LITURGY
A BOOK OF ESSAYS

EDITED BY
LIZETTE LARSON-MILLER

GARLAND PUBLISHING, INC.
NEW YORK AND LONDON
1997

Library of Congress Cataloging-in-Publication Data

Medieval liturgy : a book of essays / edited by Lizette Larson-Miller.
     p.   cm. — (Garland reference library of the humanities ; vol.
1884. Garland medieval casebooks ; vol. 18)
    Includes bibliographical references and index.
    ISBN 0-8153-1919-3 (alk. paper)
    1. Catholic Church—Liturgy—Texts—History and criticism.   2. Church
history—Middle Ages, 600–1500.   I. Larson-Miller, Lizette.   II. Series:
Garland reference library of the humanities ; vol. 1884.   III. Series: Garland
reference library of the humanities. Garland medieval casebooks ; vol. 18.
BX1973.M35   1997
264'.02'00902—dc21   97–6824
                                                CIP

CONTENTS

CONTRIBUTORS

MICHAEL S. DRISCOLL holds an STD from the Institut Catholique of Paris and a Ph.D. from the University of Paris IV (Sorbonne). He is currently assistant professor of sacramental theology and liturgy at the University of Notre Dame and is working as a consultant to the Bishop's Committee on Liturgy, a standing body of the National Council of Catholic Bishops. His current projects include a book to accompany the revised English language sacramentary as well as topics dealing with liturgy and sacraments in the Carolingian period.

EDWARD FOLEY, Ph.D. is a Capuchin-Franciscan priest, professor of liturgy and music at Catholic Theological Union, founding director of the joint Doctor of Ministry program, and president of the North American Academy of Liturgy. His most recent book is *Mighty Stories, Dangerous Rituals*, co-authored with Herbert Anderson and published by Jossey Bass.

PAUL A. JACOBSON, Ph.D. is director of music, First Unitarian Universalist Society of San Francisco and assistant to the president, Jesuit School of Theology at Berkeley. His current research topics include Carolingian *expositiones missae*, the singing of the Our Father in Carolingian Gaul, and Beguines and the Eucharist.

JAN MICHAEL JONCAS, S.L.D. is assistant professor of theology, University of St. Thomas, St. Paul, Minnesota. His current research interests include Carolingian baptismal and ordination commentaries.

LIZETTE LARSON-MILLER holds a Ph.D. in theology from the Graduate Theological Union in Berkeley, California. She is assistant professor of sacramental and liturgical theology at Loyola Marymount University in Los Angeles, California, and liturgical consultant to the Roman Catholic Archdiocese of Los Angeles. Her current research interests include Syrian church architecture and its relationship to theological issues in the fourth through eighth centuries, and eucharist and reconciliation.

JOHN K. LEONARD holds the Ph.D. in liturgical studies from the University of Notre Dame. He is currently assistant professor and chair of the Department of Religious Studies at Edgewood College, Madison, Wisconsin. Current research interests include investigating the relationship between liturgical and mystical prayer in the experience of medieval mystics.

GARY MACY holds a Ph.D. from the University of Cambridge. He is professor and chair at the Department of Theological and Religious Studies, University of San Diego, California, and secretary of the College Theology Society. His current research interests include medieval theology of the eucharist, an area in which he has published widely.

MARIE ANNE MAYESKI holds a Ph.D. in theology from Fordham University in New York City and is presently professor of theology at Loyola Marymount University. She is the author of *Dhuoda: Ninth Century Mother and Theologian*, and is currently working on the use of bible in homilies, saints *vitae* and similar texts of the ninth to twelfth centuries.

JOANNE M. PIERCE received her Ph.D. in theology (liturgical studies) from the University of Notre Dame. She is presently assistant professor in the Department of Religious Studies at the College of the Holy Cross (Worcester, Massachusetts) and serves as a member of ARC-USA, the official ecumenical consultation between Anglicans and Roman Catholics in the United States. Her most recent publications include "Early Medieval Vesting Prayers in the *ordo missae* of Sigebert of Minden (1022-1036)" in Nathan D. Mitchell and John F. Baldovin, eds. *Rule of Prayer, Rule of Faith: Essays in Honor of Aidan Kavanagh, O.S.B.* and "Early Medieval Prayers Addressed to the Trinity in the *ordo missae* of Sigebert of Minden (1022-36)," to appear in *Traditio* 51 (1996). Her current research interests include: the medieval eucharist, the ritual for the "churching" of women after childbirth, liturgical inculturation (historical perspectives), and liturgy and ecumenism.

SUSAN A. RABE, Ph.D. is associate professor of history, Loyola Marymount University. She is currently writing a book examining Spanish religio-political culture in the tenth and eleventh centuries, entitled *The Dragon and the Lamb: New Perspectives on the* Beatus *Apocalypses*.

INTRODUCTION

The remembrance and celebration of Christian faith made manifest in liturgical action has been one of the primary elements in the maintenance and development of the Christian church. Liturgy, in the broadest Western Christian sense of the word, encompasses all of the official, communal, ritual activity of the Christian community, including the celebrations of the sacraments, the daily office, and rituals which marked the changing of status of historical leaders, persons who, in their position, wove together the various strands of society to create what has been historically called Christendom. The continuing development of liturgy[1] since its normative formation in the early church was often a cultural action and reaction, allowing the contemporary study of historical liturgy to provide a mirror into what a particular society and its leaders saw as most important and most central to the meaning of life. Nowhere is this marriage of culture and liturgy more evident than in the church of the medieval West. The roles that liturgical celebrations and calendars played in the everyday lives of medieval Christians created a web of meaning and structure through both the centuries of rapid change and hardship and the decades marked by peaceful growth. The patterns of fast and feast which gave impetus and rest to people's lives provided part of the grid of space and time through which liturgy bridged earth and heaven.

If "liturgy's job is to maintain the tension between time and eternity,"[2] the elaboration of the liturgical year in the medieval church wallowed in this tension, filling the calendar with the universal feasts of Christ's life, the commemorations of martyrs, saints, and holy people, and local events elevated to sacred status, such as military victories and monastic dedications. The other part of the grid, space, was also pivotal to the medieval celebration of liturgy. If the temporal and the eternal were held in tension by common prayer and sacramental action, so too was the tension of place maintained by the juxtaposition of the local church, particularly in its combination of holy grave and holy altar, and the theological reality of a God who was always in all places, beyond the manipulation of place and time.

In the medieval Western church, this tension of the *loca sanctorum* and the limitless quality of the divine was often focused at the graves of those mortals who died in Christ and were recognized as the special holy by the earthly church. The tomb inscription of Martin of Tours reveals this spatial tension:

> Here lies Martin the bishop, of holy memory, whose soul is in the hand of God; but he is fully here, present and made plain in miracles of every kind.[3]

Medieval liturgy made much of both these dimensions, time and space. The organization of the liturgical year was as much about the present (and therefore timeless) reality of the events in the life of Christ as it was about the cyclical nature of human life and the natural year, with its seasons of death and life. The medieval church building, constructed with a profoundly symbolic design and the weight of tradition and culture already dictating certain elements, mirrored the hope of heaven and the accepted structures of the society in its arrangements. Liturgical space, however, was not limited to the church building. Whole towns, and indeed geographical areas, became the space of liturgies as processions and pilgrimages changed the ordinary landscape into the sacred at certain times of the year.

It was this integration of liturgy into every aspect of daily life and into every spatial and temporal reality which made ritual, official and devotional, so much a vehicle for interpreting all aspects of life in the medieval era, and in many cultures well into the late twentieth century.

Liturgy could also be used for political ends too, and here again, the medieval Western church exemplified this, using liturgy as a "glue" to hold together various feudal kingdoms by giving a rare common expression to common Christian faith. This "glue" was a necessity in the diverse society which Charlemagne inherited in the eighth century.

The Carolingian endeavor to articulate and strengthen Frankish identity and influence in the world reached a certain high point with the Council of Frankfurt in 794. At that local synod, many decisions made in the Eastern churches regarding the iconoclastic controversy and other matters were denounced or pronounced irrelevant. Behind the focus on iconoclasm and various heretical discussions, however, lay the self-conscious emergence of a regional and cultural church coming of age.

The European church, alpine and ultramontane, was both convinced of its own importance and aware of its exclusion from consultation at the II Nicene Council (787). Two characteristics of the Frankish responses to this council, recorded in the *Libri Carolini,* reveal these sentiments. The first is the markedly different world view of the Frankish court and its theological advisors from that of the Mediterranean world of late antiquity. The separation from the relatively homogeneous Mediterranean world of late antiquity, with its basis in "classical philosophy and Greek mystical expression,"[4] is revealed in the concern that the foundation of theological decisions be Latin scriptural interpretation, and that this school of interpretation be used to achieve the ultimate goal of correct faith. The second characteristic is the Frankish view that Rome was not Gaul. Not only did the Carolingian court feel that their political importance was slighted by a lack of consultation, but more sharply, they felt that Roman papal delegates did not speak for their own Church's concerns, even though Rome was the patriarchal see of the Western Church.[5] Thus, the growing pains of separation were from both the Eastern Church and the Church in Rome, in spite of a continued respect for Roman Church traditions.

Into this political and ecclesiological ferment came waves of liturgical renewal, beginning in earnest with the work of Charlemagne's advisors, and continuing through the Middle Ages. It was at this historical point that the potential which liturgy could possess as a unifying force for the disparate kingdoms of eighth-century Europe became apparent.[6] A contemporary comparative observation exemplifies this well. By looking at the use of historical documents and stories as vehicles for creating a tradition, Judith Herrin compares similar styles of creating a "tradition" between Islamic centers around the Mediterranean and the Frankish Catholic church in the eighth century:

> Islamic and Christian types of tradition . . . were . . . very different, but they all served a similar function in eighth-century society. Each helped religious authorities to systematise their history in a more favourable light, to establish their own supremacy against other interpretations of the faith or against rival political forces. Each represents "the invention of tradition"—a necessary stabilisation at a time of extreme uncertainty and rapid change.[7]

Liturgical adaptation and uniformity played a big part in this "invention of a tradition" which stabilized the culture and the institutional structure of the church in the new Western empire under Charlemagne. In redefining the relationship between Western Europe and the Papacy after several key military conquests, Charlemagne himself defined the roles of each party:

> It is our part with the help of Divine holiness to defend by armed strength the holy Church of Christ everywhere from the outward onslaught of the pagans and the ravages of the infidels, and to strengthen within it the knowledge of the Catholic Faith. It is your part, most holy Father, to help our armies with your hands lifted up to God like Moses, so that by your intercession and by the leadership and gift of God the Christian people may everywhere and always have the victory over the enemies of His Holy Name. [8]

This arrangement made between two powers confirmed an arrival of status for the Court of Charlemagne, and having thus established themselves in Christian and Islamic political circles, [9] the internal work of consolidating the Frankish lands could begin to take precedence. This consolidation included the use of liturgy as a common denominator.

The earlier work of Paul the Deacon, [10] who spent the mid-780s at Charlemagne's court, laid the ground work for the role which liturgy would play as a form of self-identification and unification within the Frankish realm. Paul played the important role of intermediary in obtaining a new set of liturgical texts for the Carolingian court in 786–787, [11] texts which formed the basis for the adaptation and dissemination of liturgy, first under the watchful eye of Alcuin of York and later by Benedict of Aniane and his students.

Alcuin (c. 735–804) would play a crucial role in the development of a European liturgy. A Northumbrian, well schooled in the liturgical customs of his native land, Alcuin arrived at the Frankish court in the mid-780s with skills in grammar which particularly appealed to the educationally minded Charlemagne, [12] and which would prove helpful in constructing a supplement to the inadequate sacramentary sent by Pope Hadrian. [13] Alcuin's limited time in Charlemagne's employment was divided between his theological defense of "orthodox" belief against the Adoptionist tendencies of some Spanish bishops and the development of solutions to liturgical needs.

The bases for his theological arguments were consistent with the times and reflective of the state of liturgy.[14] Although he did use some Roman liturgical prayers as a defense against the Spanish use of the liturgy of Toledo, his primary sources were his interpretation of scripture (from the Vulgate) and his use of the Fathers; particularly Augustine, Ambrose, Jerome, Marius Victorinus and others. Occasionally Greek Fathers in translation were also called to the task of countering what Alcuin considered Nestorian tendencies in the Spanish writings.

Within the realm of liturgical work, Alcuin's skills were put to use in two different categories: the development of private devotional material for members of the court (particularly the female members of Charlemagne's extended family) and adaptation of different liturgical sources for public liturgy. The thrust of his writing for private devotional use was penitential. Alcuin was one of the first to consolidate penitential prayers and psalm texts, particularly focusing on the seven penitential psalms.[15] These devotional exercises played an important role for the conscientious Christian at a time when the official penitential practices of the church were in a state of flux and when expectations of preparation for reception of communion remained almost unobtainably high.

Alcuin's liturgical adaptation of the *Hadrianum* was motivated by several factors. The development of necessary additions to the inadequate sacramentary was a primary reason for Charlemagne's request that Alcuin come to the Frankish royal court. But Alcuin, once at the court, was also motivated by an immediate pastoral situation centered on the ritual initiation of converts into the church. The normative pattern of initiation by the eighth century had become infant baptism, but the conquest of non-Christians, such as the Saxons and the Avars, presented the Frankish church with an opportunity to return to adult initiation. It was with regard to this situation that Alcuin was taken up with consultations on the proper prayers, rituals, and preliminary catecheses of adults.[16] His work in this area probably delayed his contributions to the supplement of the *Hadrianum* and necessitated the delegation of the *Hadrianum's* supplement to others.[17] Whatever the extent of Alcuin's actual compositional work on eucharistic liturgical texts and rubrics was, however, it laid the groundwork for the more extensive liturgical structures and texts compiled in the ninth century, and the fruits of this work are traceable into the *ordines* of the ninth through eleventh centuries.

The bulk of the work on the supplement seems to have fallen to Benedict of Aniane (c. 750–821) and other scholars surrounding the Frankish court. Charlemagne's death in 814, and the raising of his son Louis the Pious to power before, during and after Charlemagne's death, did not bring a halt to the work of creating a Frankish liturgy book to serve as a model for liturgical celebration. On the contrary, Benedict's work of compiling the pre-existing prefaces and benedictions,[18] adding missing pieces from the work of Alcuin and other sources, (including a number from the Mozarabic liturgy)[19] and uniting them with an introduction under the name *Hucusque,* took place primarily during the early years of Louis' reign.[20] The dissemination of this liturgical model was assisted by the systematization of the Benedictine Rule under Benedict of Aniane, receiving official approval as the monastic rule of the land at the Synod of Aachen in 817. With a monastic system in place, the liturgy as contained in the *Hadrianum* and its official supplement was extended beyond the Court at Aachen and into the abbeys and chapels of the "counts" loyal to the vision of a unified Frankish empire. Ironically, as the political and legal unification dreamed of by Louis the Pious unraveled under his sons,[21] the liturgy, while never completely uniform in any century, did achieve a degree of uniformity which allowed it to function as the common European "language" for several centuries to follow.

It is this ninth-century starting point, partially rooted in a political desire to use a unified liturgy to promote a unified kingdom, that led to the tremendous outpouring of liturgical renewal and consolidation which continued through the thirteenth century. This flurry of liturgical work forms the material on which the majority of essays in this volume are based. Gathered together in this collection is a wide range of topics, but they represent some of the most important dimensions of liturgical study for students of medieval history.

The book is structured in three groups of three, a numerological scheme which would have delighted the medieval mind convinced of the mystical import of the number three. The first three essays focus on eucharistic liturgy, now and then "the summit toward which the activity of the Church is directed . . . and the fount from which all her power flows."[22] The first essay, by Joanne Pierce, functions as an informative introduction to medieval eucharistic practice by tracing the development of the very documents, the *ordines*, which described how the ritual of the Eucharist was structured. Her historical focus on the ninth to eleventh centuries is then augmented by Gary Macy, who focuses on commentaries on the Mass in the twelfth and thirteenth centuries to discern, not so much how the liturgy was done as to interpret what the liturgy meant to various participants. Finally, concluding the first section, Marie Anne Mayeski addresses the importance of the liturgy as theological source and context by exploring the scriptural and liturgical exegesis behind medieval preaching.

In the second section, three essays look at the ecclesial, canonical and cultural impact on medieval society that liturgical rites other than the Eucharist were able to wield. Jan Michael Joncas addresses the importance of ordination rites in the eleventh century and how shifting understandings of the position of the ordained person influenced perceptions of medieval church structure and built on the importance of symbolic images and numbers. The transitional nature of penance, how forgiveness is ritualized, is evaluated by Michael Driscoll, who calls attention to the pivotal nature of the changes to this sacrament made within the narrow time frame of the early medieval church and their implications for future understandings of sin and forgiveness. John Leonard, on the other hand, takes a sweeping look at the rituals surrounding marriage from the fourth to the thirteenth centuries, revealing a gradual assumption of cultural patterns into the realm of church law.

The third part of the collection deals with issues supporting and surrounding liturgy. Edward Foley examines the role of music in the medieval eucharistic liturgy, not from the usual perspective of a moment in the development of Western music history but from the view of the congregation and what liturgical music may have been sung by the entire community. Susan Rabe looks at the architectural space of liturgy and the monumental role that the symbolic interpretation of space played in the medieval imagination, paying particular attention to the relationship of theological controversy and architectural symbolism in the eighth and ninth centuries. Finally, Paul Jacobson explores the possible sources for the ritual and theology of royal anointing as it develops in the Holy Roman Empire of Carolingian times. By proposing a liturgical, and specifically initiatory source for the royal anointings, light is shed on the theological understanding of ritual anointings in both medieval initiation and in the making of kings.

It is with the firm belief that to understand medieval history one must understand something of the liturgy that this volume is offered. All of the authors bring fine research, fine writing and invaluable bibliographical sources to their tasks, and all of the essays contribute to a greater understanding of the role of liturgy in the medieval world; may this be part of the stream of continuing conversation between the disciplines of theology, liturgy and medieval history.

Notes

1. *Liturgia semper reformanda* as a subcategory of *Ecclesia semper reformanda* is based on the *Decree on Ecumenism* Chapter II, n. 6 of the *Documents of Vatican II. Documents on the Liturgy: 1963–1979—Conciliar, Papal, and Curial Texts* (Collegeville: The Liturgical Press, 1982). See commentary in Dennis Smolarski, *Sacred Mysteries: Sacramental Principles and Liturgical Practice* (New York: Paulist Press, 1994), chapter 1.

2. James A. Wilde, *"Epilogue"* in *At That Time: Cycles and Seasons in the Life of a Christian* (Chicago: LTP, 1989), 95.

3. "Hic conditus est sanctae memoriae Martinus episcopus. Cuius anima in maju Dei est, sed hic totus est praesens manifestus omni gratia virtutum." E. LeBlant, Les inscriptions chrétiennes de la Gaule (Paris: Imprimerie Impériale, 1856), 1:240. Cited and translated in Peter Brown, *The Cult of the Saints: Its Rise and Function in Latin Christianity* (Chicago: The University of Chicago Press, 1981), 4.

4. Judith Herrin, *The Formation of Christendom* (Princeton, NJ: Princeton University Press, 1987), 458.

5. Ibid., 436.

6. ". . . just as there is but one zeal in belief, so there is but one way of singing. Churches united by the holy reading of the one holy law should also be united by the venerable practice of a unified modulation of voices; differences in celebration must not separate those who religiously adhere to one faith." "Charlemagne on Roman Unity," *Libri Carolini* I.1, ch. 6. Cited in Robert Cabié, *History of the Mass,* trans. by Lawrence Johnson (Washington, DC: The Pastoral Press, 1992), 63.

7. Herrin, *Formation of Christendom,* 304.

8. "Charlemagne's Letter to Pope Leo III (796)." Cited in Brian Tierney, *The Middle Ages. Volume I: Sources of Medieval History* (New York: Alfred A. Knopf, 1978, 3rd ed.), 102.

9. In 797–798, the Court at Aachen received diplomatic missions from "a claimant to the caliphate of Cordova"; maintained contact with the caliphate in Baghdad; and exchanged gifts with King Alfonso II of the Asturias. cf. Herrin, p. 299.

10. Paul the Deacon was a well-educated Lombardian who was banished to the monastery of Monte Cassino when Lombardy was conquered by the Franks under Charlemagne in 774. His historical writing on the Lombards, *Historia Langobardorum* is invaluable in covering the sixth to eighth centuries in that region and the ongoing relationship between the Franks and the Lombards before and after the conquest. He went to the court of Charlemagne to ask for freedom for his brother who was captured during the conquest. See Chapter IV "*Aula Renovata:* the Carolingian Court before the Aachen Palace" in D.A. Bullough, *Carolingian Renewal: Sources and Heritage* (Manchester: Manchester University Press, 1991), particularly pages 137–147.

11. "As to the sacramentary arranged by our predecessor Pope Gregory, you have asked us through the grammarian Paul for an authentic copy that conforms to the tradition of our holy church; we have sent this to your royal excellency by the Monk John, abbot from the city of Ravenna." *Letter 69, Pope Hadrian I to Charlemagne.* Cited in Cabié, *History of the Mass,* p. 63.

12. Bullough, *Carolingian Renewal,* p. 145.

13. The sacramentary of Hadrian I was a book intended for papal liturgy and therefore contained few of the liturgical texts and rubrics for pastoral situations such as those needed by the various Frankish churches. The addition of these extra liturgies, as they are found in the *Supplement,* were primarily the work Benedict of Aniane with some earlier groundwork done by Alcuin himself. Both Benedict and Alcuin borrowed from existing local practices, other Roman books and *ordines,* Celtic prayer and tradition, in addition to composing original prayers themselves. See Cyrille Vogel, *Medieval Liturgy: An Introduction to the Sources,* trans. and revised by William Storey and Neils Rasmussen (Washington, DC: The Pastoral Press, 1986), especially pages 79–82.

14. The early church use of liturgy as a primary basis for forming theology was no longer viable considering the "liturgical disarray" which existed prior to the ninth century's more successful attempts at liturgical uniformity. See Bullough, *Carolingian Renewal,* p. 188.

15. Alcuin seems to have been one of the first people to write on the seven psalms as a unit (Psalms 6, 31, 37, 50, 101, 128 and 142), ibid., 173.

16. See Gerald Ellard, *Master Alcuin: Liturgist* (Chicago: Loyola University Press, 1956), chapter IV especially.

17. The authorship of these votive masses is debated, as is the role of Alcuin in the composition of the supplement at all. Earlier scholarship, particularly that of E. Bishop, H. Lietzmann, and E. Bourque, credited Alcuin as the author because of his position at the court of Charlemagne. The next round of scholarship was not so clear, and particularly Jean Deshusses has made a strong argument for Benedict of Aniane as the primary author and compiler. Jean Deshusses, "Le 'Supplément' au sacramentaire grégorien: Alcuin ou Saint Benoît d'Aniane?" *Archiv für Liurgiewissenschaft* 9 (1965), 48–71.

18. Here is a clue to Benedict of Aniane being the author of the *Hucusque* (the introduction) and the supplement. The presence of additional benedictions was very much part of the monastic structure of liturgy with which Benedict would be both familiar and responsible for. See Deshusses, pages 60–71.

19. See Deshusses, pages 60–65.

20. Bullough, *Carolingian Renewal,* p. 245.

21. See the interesting analysis of Geoffrey Barrachough in Chapter 3 of *The Crucible of Europe: The Ninth and Tenth Centuries in European History* (Berkeley: University of California Press, 1976), especially pages 58–68.

22. *Sacrosanctum concilium,* 10. Documents of the II Vatican Council. Edited and translated in *Vatican Council II: The Conciliar and Post-Conciliar Documents,* ed. Austin Flannery (Collegeville: Liturgical Press, 1975), 6.

EUCHARISTIC LITURGY

THE EVOLUTION OF THE *ORDO MISSAE* IN THE EARLY MIDDLE AGES

Joanne M. Pierce

INTRODUCTION

The celebration of the Eucharist, or Mass (*missa*, to use the Western medieval term), was by far the most important component of the medieval liturgical life. The essays in this volume by Gary Macy and Marie Anne Mayeski will address significant approaches to the study of the Mass, particularly in the "high" and later Middle Ages. This essay, however, will deal with the structure of the Mass in the earlier medieval period (ninth through eleventh centuries), before the time of the liturgical reform undertaken by Gregory VII (Hildebrand; 1073–1085).

During the early centuries of Christianity, a set order of service for the celebration of the Eucharist was established (with a fair degree of local variation) and became gradually more complex and elaborate.[1] In the West, this structure, or *ordo missae*, came to include a number of different elements which were to become standard in the medieval period, as the Romano-Frankish/Germanic liturgy was established in most of western Europe.[2]

The components of the *ordo missae* can be grouped in two different ways: either as smaller segments of ritual action, like the entrance rite, introductory rites, readings, offertory rite, communion rite; or as individual prayer units, such as the opening prayer (*oratio* or *collecta*), the *Gloria*, or the *Agnus Dei*. An incredible amount of work has been done on dating the additions of various parts of the *ordinary* of the Mass (components which are, with some exceptions, fixed and do not change according to the liturgical season), most of which had been set in place in the "Roman" rite since late antiquity[3]: examples[4] include the *Kyrie*,[5] the *Gloria*,[6] the *Sanctus*,[7] the *canon missae*[8] (or Roman Canon), the Lord's Prayer, the *Agnus Dei*, and the communion rite.[9] This essay will not discuss how the various sections of the Mass *ordo* came to be set before the ninth century. Instead, the focus here will be on the evolution of the *ordo missae* as a unit in the early medieval period, following a theory proposed by liturgical historian Boniface Luykx, O. Praem.[10]

EARLY MEDIEVAL LITURGICAL SOURCES

Some of the structure of the early medieval Mass can be outlined by a study of the various early medieval sacramentaries, books which contained the official, public prayers for the celebrant or presider to be used during the celebration of Mass. The earliest examples[11] of those used in the Roman rite[12] (albeit in more-or-less "Gallicanized" manuscript witnesses[13]) are the "Old" Gelasian sacramentary (or GeV)[14] and the Gregorian sacramentary (or GrD).[15] The GeV seems to date from the mid- to late-seventh century, and to derive from two different and earlier strata of Roman presbyteral liturgy,[16] while the GrD reflects various versions of papal liturgy dating from the late seventh and eighth centuries.[17]

The prayer texts of the Mass formularies (or sets of prayers for the celebration of Mass) are instructive; one can study clearly the major *orationes* of the Mass, as well as preface texts and (in the GeV, and in the GrD during Lent) final blessings *super populum*.[18] Mass formularies found in these early sacramentaries would vary according to day of the week and season of the liturgical year (the *temporale*); other prayers would be assigned to various feasts of the saints (the *sanctorale*),[19] and Masses for other occasions (e.g., requiem Masses, nuptial Masses) or "various needs" (votive Masses, such as a Mass for sailors,[20] in time of war,[21] or to repel a storm[22]). Sacramentaries could also contain certain collections of prayers for other occasions, for example, "morning" and "evening" prayers,[23] and penitential prayers.[24] Most crucial to this study, however, is the addition (at the end of the seventh century) of an abbreviated, almost proto-*ordo missae* at the beginning of some of the Gregorian *codices*.[25]

Roughly contemporary with this brief, early form of the *ordo missae* are the earliest medieval liturgical sources which comprehensively attest to the structure of the celebration of Romano-

Frankish or Romano-Germanic Mass: the *ordines romani*. As Vogel puts it:

> Strictly speaking, an *ordo* is a description of a liturgical action (*actio liturgica*), a directory or guide for the celebrant and his ministers setting forth in detail the arrangement of the entire ritual procedure and how to carry it out.[26]

These *ordines romani* seem to have been rather early liturgical "booklets" (*libelli*) which circulated independently from each other and from the sacramentary texts;[27] they combined both an *ordo* strictly speaking as well as what would later be termed rubrics ("stage directions" or descriptions of step-by-step liturgical actions) for the celebration of various liturgical services.[28]

The *ordines romani* "survive only in collections . . . [which] . . . can differ widely in both size and scope."[29] The best edition available is that published by Michel Andrieu,[30] who categorized them into a number of distinct "collections": one (collection A), showing clear Roman origin; and others which have been "Gallicanized," or adapted to the needs of the Frankish (and Germanic) churches north of the Alps (collection B, a "Gallicanized" collection, and "Gallican" collections, such as the Saint Armand collection, the St. Gall collection, and two smaller collections).[31]

Perhaps the most crucial of these *ordines romani* is *ordo romanus primus*, or OR I, the "first surviving *ordo* of the solemn papal Mass."[32] Composed in all probability just after the turn of the eighth century, OR I sets the stage as it were for both the formal celebration of Mass by bishops north of the Alps, as well as the simpler presbyteral celebration and the *missa privata* which was to become so important during the Middle Ages.[33] When compared with the *ordo missae* which becomes standard by the thirteenth century,[34] OR I contains some notable additions[35] (e.g., the "greeting" of the *sancta*, or reserved Eucharist, during the entrance procession, and the *fermentum* rite, in which pieces of the consecrated bread are distributed to acolytes to be taken to the *tituli*, or presbyteral churches in the city[36]) and some notable omissions (for example, the Creed, which was not added to the Roman liturgy until 1014, at the specific request of the Emperor Henry II).[37]

The most important general production and elaboration[38] of the *ordo missae* (OM), however, seems to occur somewhat later:

> It is only in the ninth century that the first example of a written *ordo missae* or "order of Mass" appears. Thus, the presider at an early medieval Mass would have available for his use not only a sacramentary . . . but also a separate booklet containing an outline of the Mass itself (an order of service) along with a number of private prayers and responses for the use of the presider alone.[39]

There are several examples of the OM which date from the ninth through the eleventh centuries. These texts are the foundation on which rests the theory covering the evolution of the OM to the eve of the Gregorian liturgical reform. Some of these *ordines missae*, as will be seen, have been published in modern critical editions; several others can be found in an eighteenth-century collection of early liturgical texts compiled by Dom Edmond Martène.[40] Among the most important of these modern edited texts are:

1. Amiens (ninth or tenth century): this early medieval sacramentary contains the earliest example of a separate *ordo missae*; edition by Victor Leroquais, "L'*ordo missae* du sacramentaire d'Amiens," *EL* 41 (1927), 435–445.

2. Nonantola (tenth century): this OM is found in an *Enchiridion sacerdotale*, not a missal or sacramentary; edition by Pierre Salmon, "L'*Ordo missae* dans dix manuscrits du Xe au XVe siècle," in *Analecta Liturgica: Extraits des manuscrits liturgiques de la Bibliothèque Vaticane* (Città del Vaticano: Biblioteca Apostolica Vaticana, 1974; *Studi e Testi* 273), 196–221, here, 198–200.[41]

3. Hamburg (eleventh century): this Ritual-Votive Missal was edited by Niels K. Rasmussen, O.P., "An Early *ordo missae* from Hamburg with a *litania abecedaria* addressed to Christ (Rome, Bibl. Vallicelliana, Cod. B 141, XI cent.)," *EL* 98 (1984), 198–211.

4. Salins (eleventh century): this OM is found in the well-known pontifical of Hughes of Salins; edited by Jean Lemarié, "Le pontifical d'Hugues de Salines, son 'ordo missae' et son 'libellus precum'," *Studi Medievali*, ser. 3, 19 (1978), 363–425.

5. Minden (*circa* 1030): this important OM is found in a *libellus precum* prepared for Bishop Sigebert of Minden; edited by Joanne Pierce, *Sacerdotal Spirituality at Mass: Text and Study of the Prayerbook of Sigebert of Minden (1022–1036)* (University of Notre Dame: unpublished Ph.D. dissertation, 1988).[42]

6. Reichenau (beginning of the eleventh century): also a key text; the OM was edited by Joaquim Bragança, "O 'Ordo Missae' de Reichenau," *Didaskalia* 1 (1971), 137–161.

7. Ivrea (later tenth or early eleventh century): another important OM from a pontifical source; edited by Bonifacio Baroffio and Ferdinand Dell'Oro, "L'*Ordo Missae* del vescovo Warmundo d'Ivrea," *Studi Medievali*, ser. 3, 16 (1975), 795–824.

8. Volturno 2 (end of the eleventh century): this OM is found in a manuscript once thought to be a sacramentary from Monte Cassino, but which is actually the (slightly) more recent of two liturgical manuscripts from San Vincenzo al Volturno; edited by Virgil Fiala, "Der Ordo missae im Cod. Vat. lat. 6082," in *Zeugnis des Geistes. Gabe zum Benedictus-Jubilaeum 547–1947* (Beuron/Hohenzollern: Beuroner Kunstverlag, 1947; *Benediktinschen Monatschrift* XXIII), 180–224.

Other important texts, available only in the Martène edition, include:

9. Corbie (second half of the tenth century): this OM comes from the sacramentary of Ratoldus of Corbie; Martène, DAER, *Lib.* I., *Cap.* IV, *Art.* XII, *Ordo* XI, cols. 562–568 (Martimort, nos. 106, 986).[43]

10. Moissac (eleventh century): this OM comes from a sacramentary of Figeac used at the Abbey of Moissac; Martène, *Ordo* VIII, cols. 537–541 (Martimort, nos. 191, 552).

11. Reims (or Saint-Thierry 1; end of the ninth century): this text is a very early list of prayers to be recited at certain points in the OM, from the sacramentary of Reims (later used at Saint-Thierry); Martène, DAER, *Lib.* I., *Cap.* IV, *Art.* XII, *Ordo* IX, cols. 541–548 (Martimort, nos. 354, 553).

12. Stavelot (eleventh century): Martène, *Ordo* XV, cols. 582–594 (Martimort, no. 303).

13. St.-Denis (mid-eleventh century): Martène, *Ordo* V, cols. 518–528 (Martimort, nos. 109, 548).

14. Saint-Thierry (2; end of the tenth century): another early list of prayers for use at certain points in the OM (with attached Mass formularies), from a sacramentary of Saint-Thierry; Martène, *Ordo* X, cols. 548–562 (Martimort, nos. 355, 554).

15. Salzbourg-Séez (mid-eleventh century): Martène, *Ordo* XIII, cols. 574–580 (Martimort, no. 153).

16. Tours (beginning of the eleventh century): from the Missal of St. Martin of Tours; Martène, *Ordo* VII, cols. 534–537 (Martimort, no. 323).

17. Troyes (*circa* 1060): Martène, *Ordo* VI, cols. 528–534 (Martimort, nos. 549–550).

18. Volturno 1 (eleventh century): the older of the two Volturno manuscripts, known earlier as the "Chigi" *ordo*; Martène, *Ordo* XII, cols. 568–574 (Martimort, no. 556).

SACERDOTAL APOLOGIAE

Before moving to a description of the proposed evolution of the OM, some brief mention must be made of the importance of sacerdotal *apologiae*, or "apology-type" prayers. These *apologiae* are prayer texts written for individual recitation by a bishop or priest during the celebration of Mass; they express the presider's sense of sinfulness and unworthiness, and may also contain actual confessions consisting of lists of sins.[44] The increased popularity of these prayers in areas of Europe north of the Alps can also be attributed to a process of liturgical inculturation, an expression of "northern European spirituality"[45] which stressed "a special preference for the dramatic, the verbose, and the moralizing."[46] Indeed, the stylistic contrast between the older, Roman "collect" style of prayer found in the early sacramentaries and these rather florid compositions could hardly be more striking:

> Roman collects . . . are always plural, communally oriented, spare and almost terse in their address to God and expression of petitions.

> The apologies (and other related prayers) . . . are, in contrast, highly
> individualistic, almost solely presider-oriented, fulsome of
> expression, and imbued with a spirituality of "rejection of the world
> and worldly things."[47]

Sources for these prayers included early medieval collections of
devotional prayers, or prayer books (*libelli precum*) prepared for
various individuals.[48]

One particular form of penitential prayer text eventually evolved
into the *Confiteor* prayer which becomes part of the Tridentine OM.[49]
At this point in time, the text of the prayer was quite fluid; although
confession-type prayers had been inserted into the OM since the ninth
century; a response (the *Misereatur*) was only centuries later attached
to the prayer.[50]

There are several characteristics of these *Confiteor*-type prayers
which distinguish them from *apologia*-type prayers in general:
acknowledgment of sin before God and a priest (or assistants); petition
for his/their intercession (i.e., the intercession of the Church); mention
of the saints; in older forms, reference to the altar; and, by the eleventh
century, augmentation of the statement of sin (usually by including lists
of sins) and of the intercessory formula.[51]

A very complete study of the textual history of one particular form,
the *Suscipe confessionem meam*, has been published by the Portuguese
liturgist (and editor of the Reichenau OM), Joaquim Bragança.[52] In this
work, he attempts to pull together the various theories which attempt to
explain why these types of prayers are added to the *ordo missae* in the
first place. He finally concludes that several factors are at work: a new
spiritual attitude (possibly stronger North of the Alps), one of awe
before the great mystery of the Eucharist; the influence of the practice
of the private Mass on other, more public solemn celebrations
(apologies are to be recited during the sung sections of the Mass, for
example); and the need for more frequent internal purification, often
unfilled due to the still-strenuous penances imposed (a remnant of the
earlier practice of public penance, which had not yet been replaced by
private confessional penance and milder, commutable, tariff
penalties).[53] The extreme number of these prayers was to be cut back
later by the liturgical reforms of Gregory VII, anxious to purify the
Roman liturgy from "Germanic" influences.[54]

The increase in the number of *apologiae* included as part of the so-called "unchangeable" part of the Mass (*ordinarium missae*) can be seen not only as a "marker" for certain stages of liturgical evolution (as will be discussed further below), but also as an indication of the increased privatization and clericalization of the liturgy[55] in these centuries.[56] Certain "soft spots" (that is, points of "action without words"[57]) in the *ordo missae* are the *loci* for these prayers in the earliest stages of this evolution process. Examples include communion prayers, certain types of offertory prayers[58] (such as the *Suscipe sancte Trinitas* series), and forms of the *Memento* prayer within the Canon.[59] Another custom also seems to begin at this time, that is, the attribution of authorship of some apology-type prayers to important Church Fathers (e.g., Augustine, Ambrose).[60]

LUYKX'S THEORY

Luykx's work attempts to delineate several phases in the evolution of the *ordo missae* in the west. Several of the *ordines* discussed above, in particular the Minden *ordo*, play a crucial role in his theory. Luykx's hypothesis is this: one factor in distinguishing stages in the development of the *ordo missae* is the number and placement of certain types of prayers (among the most important being the so-called *apologiae*) present in individual examples of *ordines missae*.

There are three types of *ordines* in this evolutionary series. The first Luykx calls the "Apology Type" (which can be subdivided into a primitive and more a devout/developed type[61]); the second he names the "Frankish Type"; and the third, the "Rhenish *Ordo Missae*."[62] The second and third types do contain elements of the earliest form.[63]

The Apology Type contains three clusters of apologies at three important "soft spots" in the Mass liturgy: at the beginning of Mass (*orationes ante altare*); at the offertory (*orationes ad munus offerendum*); and at communion.[64] Two examples of this relatively simple structure can be found among the Martène *ordines*: the Reims *ordo* and the Saint-Thierry *ordo*.[65]

The Frankish Type contains a further elaboration of prayers in these original "soft spots," as well as development in other areas. Apologies are headed and linked together by rubrics, becoming part of the structure of the OM itself. Prayers (and, in some cases, psalmody and versicles) are added to other "moments" in the *ordo*: the vesting and spiritual preparation of the celebrant in the sacristy, including the verse *Lavabo* at the washing of hands before vesting; the entrance procession; the incensing of the altar; preceding and following the proclamation of the Gospel; the offertory prayers, especially in the multiplication of the *Suscipe sancta Trinitas prayers;*[66] at the *Sanctus*; the commixtion of the eucharistic species (that is, the dropping of a piece of consecrated host into the chalice of consecrated wine before communion); before and after communion; at the end of Mass (the *Placeat*); and during the doffing of vestments in the sacristy. In addition, gestures (e.g., signs of the cross, and bows) are also multiplied as expressions of the personal piety of the priest.[67] The Amiens OM is the oldest and best example of this evolutionary stage.[68]

The third type is the Rhenish Type. This is an expanded, more elastic type of OM, originally designed for the use of a bishop at a large, formal Mass.[69] Luykx describes the characteristics of this type in great detail; in summary, these include: apologies and other added prayers tied together by longer groups of rubrics; presence of certain prayer texts (e.g., the *Largire sensibus nostris* at the handwashing), in place of others characteristic of the earlier types (in this case, the *Lavabo*); elaboration of vesting and preparatory actions with psalmody, versicles, and other short prayers; elaboration of a new "Eingangsritus" or entrance rite; multiplication of kissing and confession rituals; increasing clericalization of the offertory (e.g., multiple handwashings); elaboration of private prayers/psalms during the *Sanctus*; reorganization and elaboration of the prayers during the Communion rite; and the detailing of a thanksgiving rite after Mass.[70] It should be noted that assistants, servers, and other clerics also have certain prayers and actions prescribed for them, as well. Luykx cites the Minden *ordo* as an outstanding example of this third, "Rhenish" type of early medieval OM.[71] He conjectures that this type originated at the Abbey of St. Gall,[72] spreading perhaps through the intermediaries of Reichenau and Mainz.[73] Luykx cites Sigebert of Minden and his manuscripts as an example, stating that Sigebert ordered his liturgical books through his metropolitan in Mainz, and that they were actually manufactured (in the original sense of the word) at Reichenau.[74] In fact, more recent scholarship holds that the Minden books were prepared at St. Gall, with perhaps some Reichenau influence.[75]

Luykx's work did not go unnoticed by others. For example, one of the most important liturgical historians of the twentieth century, Joseph Jungmann, incorporated Luykx's hypotheses in the later editions of his classic work on the history of the Roman Mass, *Missarum Sollemnia*. A comparison of the second edition (1949, *MRR*, English translation 1950) with the fifth and last edition (*MS⁵* 1962) is instructive in noting Luykx's influence.

The most important effect of Luykx's article can be seen in a comparison of the indices which close each edition. In *MS⁵*, a completely new category is introduced in the index of sources: that of the "Rheinischer Messordo."[76] Manuscripts listed under this category,[77] are found in *MRR²* under the general title of "Séez group."[78]

A comparison of the texts of the two editions shows that most of the changes made involve a simple substitution of the term "Rheinischer Messordo" (or various forms thereof) for the older term "Séez group."[79] The major point at which Jungmann introduces Luykx's theories comes at the beginning of his discussion of the Franco-Roman Mass and its development from the ninth century.[80] He adds an extra paragraph after his description of what had been known as the "Séez group," introducing Luykx's terminology, and summarizes Luykx's theory briefly in a new footnote;[81] it appears in an earlier section[82] of Volume I, and is included in a more general discussion of sacerdotal *apologiae* in the *ordo missae*.[83] Interestingly, Jungmann singles out the Minden OM for special attention: he finds it to be "the zenith in the development of the *apologiae*," which "assembles practically all the prayer formulas to be gotten anywhere at that time."[84]

Later, Joseph Lemarié partially synthesized the state of the question as it stood in 1979, in his discussion of the Salins OM as a Rhenish-Type OM.[85] Building on the work done by both Bragança and Baroffio with Dell'Oro,[86] he summarized pertinent characteristics of the Rhenish OM[87] as follows:

1. The washing of the hands with the *Largire clementissime* Pater prayer;

2. Psalms 83 (*Quam delicta*), 84 (*Benedixisti*), and 85 (*Inclina Domine*) during the priest's preparation;

3. During the entrance procession, Ps 42 (*Inclina me*), the antiphon *Introibo ad altare,* followed by the prayer *Aufer a nobis;*

4. Prayers prescribed for private recitation during the *Gloria;*

5. Similar prayers during the presentation of the gifts, among which is placed the prayer *Facturus memoriam;* [88]

6. Psalmody recited by deacons and subdeacons (Pss 19, 24, 50, 89, 90) during the Canon, followed by versicles and two prayers: Gaudeat and *Precibus nostris;*

7. The "formulas" *Habete uinculum caritatis and Pax Christi et ecclesiae* used during the Pax, or greeting of peace before communion;

8. Another "formula," the *Meritis et intercessionibus,* used during communion;

9. A short rite in the sacristy after Mass, consisting of the *Benedicite omnia opera* (the Canticle of the Three Young Men, Dan 3:57–88) with two accompanying prayers, *Deus qui tribus pueris,* and *Actiones nostras.* [89]

In a more intensive comparison of the Salins OM with those of Reichenau and Minden, he finds that, despite similarities in content and structure, there is no direct dependence on either. The Salins OM has "son originalité propre."[90]

Perhaps the conclusions of the late Niels Rasmussen, in his edition of the Hamburg OM, can serve to indicate some underlying issues in any continuing study of the evolution of the OM. He agrees with Luykx and Bragança on narrowing down the date (tenth century) and possible place of composition (Saint Gall, Reichenau, and Mainz[91]) of the Rhenish Type of OM;[92] however, he notes:

> That much still remains to be done is shown by the fact that scholars have not yet been able to establish more than a very simple typology for the mass orders. . . . But before pursuing this task of establishing a more exact typology it is important to make the texts available.[93]

This is a key point; it is impossible to build a solid theoretical structure without first examining closely the bricks which will be used in the construction.

CONCLUSION

Piecing together the evolutionary stages in the development of the early medieval OM is painstaking work. Clearly, a great deal has been done since mid-century, especially in the preparation of modern critical editions of several important *ordines*. However, more still needs to be done: several important *ordines* are still available only in reprints of Martène's eighteenth-century transcriptions, and some key *libelli precum* are also found only in transcriptions several centuries old; the full texts of the prayers found in the *libelli precum* and the *ordines missae* studied by Salmon and Ebnet should be published and made available for analysis; and a complete study of the *apologiae* (updating Cabrol) has yet to be made. Such a study would be more difficult than it seems at first glance: *apologiae* are "very plastic prayer forms; compilers [of *libelli precum* and *ordines missae*] seem to have had few qualms about 'mixing and matching' *incipits* with different sections or bodies of text."[94]

While the technical details of working out the evolutionary process may be of interest only to liturgical historians, the implications of such studies have far-reaching implications. This early medieval elaboration of the basic OM structure, a form of liturgical inculturation from Mediterranean to northern European "world-views,"[95] provides a window into the underlying piety of the Carolingian, Ottonian, and Salian periods, since "it is clear that slowly, from the ninth century on, a kind of private devotional service is introduced into the public celebration of the Mass."[96] This private, sacerdotal devotional pattern (albeit in "a less florid form") influences not only the rest of the medieval period, but the later Tridentine *ordo missae* (1570) as well.[97] Clearly, then, the study of the early medieval *ordo missae* can be a rich source of insight for anyone interested in investigating medieval religious culture/spirituality (the individual as well as the communal dimensions) in any of its varied forms and manifestations.

Notes

1. Some useful general histories for the medievalist and graduate student include Robert Cabié, *The Church at Prayer*. Volume II: *The Eucharist*, translated by Matthew J. O'Connell (Collegeville, MN: Liturgical Press, 1986); on some topics, however, the medievalist might find the original edition of the four-volume work more helpful, edited by Aimé-Georges Martimort, Noele Maurice Denis-Boulet, and Roger Beraudy, *The Church at Prayer: The Eucharist* (New York: Herder and Herder, 1973; also available in the original French as *L'Église en prière*). Another standard work is Joseph A. Jungmann, S.J., *The Mass of the Roman Rite: Its Origins and Development,* translated by Francis A. Brunner, C.SS.R. Volumes I and II (Westminster, MD: Christian Classics, 1986; = *MRR*). This last work is a reprint of the English translation of the second edition (1949) of the original German text entitled *Missarum Sollemnia: Eine genetische Erklärung der Römischen Messe*, published by Herder; as will be seen, this German original eventually went through five editions (1962; = MS^5).

2. Between the time of Gregory the Great (d. 604) and Gregory VII (d. 1085). For more information, see the standard work in the field of medieval liturgy: Cyrille Vogel, *Medieval Liturgy: An Introduction to the Sources*, translated and revised by William G. Storey and Niels K. Rasmussen, O.P. (Washington, DC: The Pastoral Press, 1986). Other helpful works in the area of early medieval liturgy include Richard W. Pfaff, *Medieval Latin Liturgy: A Select Bibliography* (Toronto: University of Toronto Press, 1982) and Éric Palazzo, *Histoire des livres liturgiques. Le Moyen Age. Des origines au XIII e siècle* (Paris: Beauchesne, 1993).

3. The most important exception to this statement is the Creed. The Constantinopolitan form of the Nicean Creed has been used during the celebration of Mass in Spain since the late sixth century (Council of Toledo, 589), and in the Carolingian Holy Roman Empire since the end of the eighth century (794). At the insistence of the Emperor Henry II, it was incorporated at last into the *ordo missae* at Rome in 1014, to be used on Sundays and feast days. See Cabié, pp. 131–132, and Jungmann, *MRR* I, pp. 469–470. For an edition of the "ordinary" of the Roman Mass, see Bernard Botte and Christine Mohrmann, *L'ordinaire de la messe* (Paris: Cerf, Louvain: Mont César, 1953).

4. For substantial bibliography on the various sections of the ordinary of the Mass, see Cabié, Section II. The following footnotes point out either more recent publications, or highlight major references.

5. For some interesting observations on the evolution of the *Kyrie*, see John F. Baldovin, *"Kyrie Eleison* and the Entrance Rite of the Roman Eucharist," *Worship* 60 (1986), 334–347.

6. See Jean Magne, "'Carmina Christo' III Le 'Gloria in Excelsis'," *Ephemerides Liturgicae* (= *EL*) 100 (1986), 368–390.

7. Perhaps the most comprehensive work on the *Sanctus* has been done recently by Brian Spinks, *The Sanctus in the Eucharistic Prayer* (Cambridge: Cambridge University Press, 1991). See also Magne, "'Carmina Christo' I Le 'Sanctus' de la messe latine," *EL* 100 (1986), 3–27.

8. Perhaps the most accessible critical edition of the canon was published by Bernard Botte, *Le canon de la messe romaine* (Louvain: Mont César, 1935).

9. For further information, see Joseph Jungmann, *The Early Liturgy: To the Time of Gregory the Great*, Francis A. Brunner, C.SS.R, transl. (Notre Dame, IN: University of Notre Dame Press, 1959, 1976), especially Chapter 23. Paul F. Bradshaw, *The Search for the Origins of Christian Worship* (Oxford/NY: Oxford University Press, 1993), chapter 6, provides an overview of the scholarly work on the early Eucharist.

10. Luykx, *De oorsprong van het gewone der Mis,* (Utrecht-Antwerpen: Verlag Het Spectrum, 1954), *De Eredienst der kerk,* Heft 3. Citations will be taken from the German translation by Johannes Madey, which appeared as "Der Ursprung der gleichbleibenden Teile der heiligen Mess *(Ordinarium Missae),*" in *Liturgie und Mönchtum* 29 (1961), 72–119 (this issue published under the separate title *Priestertum und Mönchtum*). Fr. Luykx was more recently able to confirm that no further work has been done to test his theory of the evolution of the *ordo missae*; private conversation, April 1987.

11. An older witness, the so-called "Leonine sacramentary," or the *Veronensis*, is actually a collection of *libelli missarum*, or "Mass booklets" which contained individual Mass formularies for various days. The formularies themselves seem to date to the mid-fifth through the mid-sixth centuries; for further information, see Vogel, pp. 37–46 (with further bibliographical suggestions in the extensive notes), and D.M. Hope, *The Leonine Sacramentary: A Reassessment of Its Nature and Purpose* (Oxford, 1971). For more on the *Veronensis* and other sacramentaries, see Palazzo, pp. 47–83.

12. Other sacramentaries which witness to the existence of non-Roman Western liturgy do exist. Among the most important are: the *Missale Gothicum*, the *Missale Francorum*, and the *Missale Gallicanum vetus* (all edited by L.C. Mohlberg), the *Bobbio Missal* (edited by E.A. Lowe), and the "Mone Masses" (pp. 61–91 of Mohlberg's edition of the *Gallicanum vetus*), all from Gaul and Germany; *The Stowe Missal* (edited by G.F. Warner), representative of Celtic liturgy; *the Liber Mozarabicus sacramentorum* and the *Liber ordinum* (both edited by M. Férotin), which stem from the Mozarabic liturgy in Spain; and the *Sacramentarium Triplex* (edited by O. Heiming), the *Sacramentarium Bergomense* (edited by A. Paredi), the Sacramentary of Biasca (edited by O.

Heiming as *Das ambrosianische Sakramentar von Biasca*), and the Sacramentary of Ariberto (edited by A. Paredi as *Il sacramentario di Ariberto*), all representative of the Ambrosian/Milanese liturgy. For more information, see Vogel, pp. 107–110, W.S. Porter, *The Gallican Rite* (London, 1958), and Archdale A. King, *Liturgies of the Past* (London, 1959), and *Liturgies of the Primatial Sees* (London, 1957).

13. The stages of development of the Roman liturgy are complex; due to the "importation" of early liturgical books used at Rome to areas north of the Alps, especially during the Carolingian era, the liturgy quickly becomes "hybridized," a Romano-Frankish/Germanic mix. This "mixed" liturgy is reintroduced to Rome in Ottonian times, and becomes fixed as "the" Roman liturgy; see Vogel, p. 61.

14. Edited by L.C. Mohlberg, *Liber sacramentorum Romanae aeclesiae ordini anni circuli* (Rome, 1960; RED, series major, 4). A major study was done by A. Chavasse, *Le sacramentaire Gelasien* (Tournai, 1958); other, shorter discussions can be found in B. Neunheuser, "The 'Sacramentarium Gelasianum' (*Reg. lat.* 316) and Its Significance in Liturgical History," in *Sacramentarium Gelasianum* (Photo-typice Editum; Vatican City, 1975), 30–49. Its name comes from an early attribution to Pope Gelasius (492–496); see Vogel, pp. 64–70.

15. Critical edition by Jean Deshusses, *Le sacramentaire grégorien*, 3 vols. (Fribourg, 1971, 1979, 1982; *Spicilegium Friburgense* 16, 24, 28).

16. Vogel, 68–69; it could be as early as 628 and as late as 715. A Frankish version of the GeV, mixed with one type of the Gregorian sacramentary tradition, seems to have been the ancestor of a family of "second-generation" sacramentaries in northern Europe: the "Frankish-Gelasians" or the "Eighth-century Gelasians." Several of the major examples include: the *Sacramentary of Gellone* (edited by A. Dumas and J. Deshusses); the *Sacramentary of Angoulême* (edited by P. Saint Roch); the *Phillipps Sacramentary* (edited by O. Heiming); the *Sacramentary of St. Gall* (edited by L.C. Mohlberg); the *Sacramentary of Rheinau* (edited by A. Hänggi and A. Schönherr); and the *Sacramentary of Monza* (edited by A. Dold and K. Gamber). See Vogel, pp. 70–78.

17. Vogel, pp. 79–102. The Gregorian sacramentary that was used north of the Alps by Charlemagne in attempt to unify his realm liturgically was known as the *Hadrianum*. Since a papal sacramentary was lacking in certain Mass formularies and other texts necessary for presbyteral (i.e., "parochial") use, it was "corrected and expanded" by the Frankish monk, Benedict of Aniane (d. 821), who added additional material (and a preface, the *Hucusque*) known as the "Supplement"; see Vogel, pp. 82–88.

18. The GrD, for example, clearly lists three major collect-style prayers, or *orationes*: the *oratio*, or opening prayer; the *super oblata*, or prayer over the gifts; and the *ad completa/complendum*, the prayer after communion. The GeV refers to these two last as *secreta* and *post communionem*. See Vogel, p. 79.

19. The two cycles were listed in separate "books" in the GeV, but in the Gregorian sacramentaries were usually "merged into a single, continuous series of Sundays and festivals"; see Vogel, pp. 65–66 and 79. Note that one important "marker" in the dating of these sacramentary manuscripts is the presence or absence of Mass formularies for the Thursdays in Lent, since these were non-eucharistic or "aliturgical" days until the time of Gregory II (715–731); see Vogel, p. 69, 85.

20. GrD 1320–1322, found in the Supplement.

21   Three such Mass formularies are found in the Supplement to the Hadrianum: GrD 1330–1334; GrD 1335–1338; and GrD 1339–1342. Other general *orationes* are also listed (GrD 1328–1329), as well as a Mass for peace (GrD 1343–1345), and Masses for other forms of tribulation.

22. GrD 1375–1378.

23   A lengthy series is found in the Hadrianum, GrD 935–979, along with a series of "daily" prayers (*orationes cottidianae*, GrD 876–934). For more information, see A. Chavasse, "Les orasions pour les dimanches ordinaires," *RB* 93 (1983), 31–70, 170–244.

24. For example, a lengthy series of *orationes pro peccatis* can be found in the Hadrianum (GrD 840–875). Other such prayers can be found certain Gregorian *codices* under the title of *apologiae* (e.g., GrD 4381); these prayer texts have an important role in the evolution of the OM, see below.

25. It is entitled *Qualiter missa romana caelebratur*, and in a paragraph-length description mentions the *introit*, the *Kyrie*, the *Gloria* (on certain occasions), the *oratio* (or opening prayer), the *apostolum*, the *gradualem* or *alleluia*, the *euangelium*, the *offertorium* and the *oblationem super oblata*. The ordo also provides the complete texts for the preface and Roman canon (with the *sursum corda* dialogue), concluded by the Lord's Prayer, the *Pax*, and the *incipit* of the *Agnus Dei* (GrD 2–20). Part of the text can be found in Vogel, p. 158. See also J. Deshusses, "The Sacramentaries: a Progress Report" *Liturgy* 18 (1984), 13–60, here, p. 39; cited in Vogel, p. 125, n. 223.

26. Vogel, p. 135. For more on the *ordines Romani*, see A.-G. Martimort, *Les "Ordines," les ordinaires et les cérémoniaux* (Turnholt: Brepols, 1991; *Typologie des sources du Moyen Âge occidental*, fasc. 56), and Palazzo, pp. 187–196.

27. Vogel, p. 144–145.

28. See Vogel, 135–136, and 197–198, note 1.

29. Vogel, p. 145.

30. Michel Andrieu, *Les ordines romani du haut moyen âge*. Vol. 1: Les manuscrites; vols. 2–5: Les textes (Louvain: 1931–1961; *Spicilegium Sacrum Louvaniense* 11, 23, 24, 28, 29).

31. Vogel, pp. 144–155, and Palazzo, pp. 194–196.

32. Vogel, p. 155.

33. The term originally referred to the celebration of Mass by smaller groups outside of the major Sunday and festal settings. Only later does it refer to the "solitary" Mass celebrated privately by the priest, especially in the post-Tridentine period; see A. Häussling, *Mönchskonvent und Eucharistiefeier: Eine Studie über die Messe in der abendländischen Klosterliturgie des frühen Mittelalters und zur Geschichte der Messhäufigkeit* (Münster: Aschendorff, 1972; LQF 58).The important *Excursus* on the "Private Mass" revised by Storey and Rasmussen in Vogel's book summarizes clearly the lines of recent study on the subject; see Vogel, pp. 156–158. Their notes indicate varying points of view; see Vogel, "Une mutation culturelle inexpliquée: le passage de l'Eucharistie communitaire à la messe privée," *RSR* 54 (1980), 231–250; and Nussbaum, *Kloster, Priestermönch, und Privatmesse* (Bonn: Hanstein, 1961; Theophaneia 14). More recent work on the subject includes A. Angenendt, "Missa specialis. Zugliech ein Beitrag zur Entstehung der Privatmessen," *Frümittelalterliche Studien* 17 (1983), 153–221; see Palazzo, p. 53, n. 2. See also Cabié, pp. 136–137.

34. For an overview of the development of the Tridentine OM (1570), see Cabié, pp. 149–171. The classic study of thirteenth-century developments was done by S.J.P. van Dijk and J. Hazelden Walker, *The Origins of the Modern Roman Liturgy* (Westminster, MD: The Newman Press; London: Darton, Longman & Todd, 1960).

35. Andrieu, *Les ordines*, vol. II, pp. 65–108; a good overview can be found in Jungmann, *MRR* I, pp. 67–74. There is an English translation available, by E.G.C.F. Atchley, *Ordo Romanus Primus* (London, 1905), but it is based on an uncritical text and should be used only in conjunction with Andrieu. OR I exists in both a long and a short recension (the older of the two), and is supplemented by two other *ordines*, a Roman text (OR II) and a Frankish text (OR III). In addition, OR IV and V are Romano-Frankish and Romano-Germanic texts for the celebration of papal/solemn Mass. For a complete discussion of the individual *ordines*, see Vogel, pp. 155–190.

36. See Cabié, *Eucharist*, pp. 111–113.

37. See above.

38. Palazzo, p. 50.

39. Joanne M. Pierce, "Early Medieval Liturgy: Some Implications for Contemporary Liturgical Practice," in *Worship* 65 (1991), 509–522; here, 515.

40. Edmond Martène, *De antiquis Ecclesiae ritibus* (= DAER), *Lib.* I, *Cap.* IV (1737; reprinted Hildesheim: G. Olms, 1967). When working with these texts, one should always confer with two recent studies on Martène's sources by Aimé-George Martimort: *La documentation liturgique de Dom Edmond Martène. Étude codicologique.* (Città del Vaticano: Biblioteca Apostolica Vaticana, 1978; *Studi e Testi* 279); and "Additions et corrections à *La documentation liturgique de Dom Edmond Martène*," *Ecclesia Orans* 3 (1986), 81–105.

41. Note, however, that this edition does not include the full texts of the prayers interpolated into the structure of the OM, but is rather an outline of headings and incipits. Several other *ordines* are also included in the article, but only the Nonantola OM dates from the tenth or eleventh century. For similar partial transcriptions of other *ordines missae*, see Adalbert Ebner, *Missale Romanum im Mittelalter. Iter Italicum.* (Graz: Akademische Druck-U. Verlagsanstalt, 1957).

42. This (incomplete) manuscript, which contains an *ordo missae* as well as an *ordo* for the veneration of the Cross, and the beginning of a series of daily prayers, is actually a *libellus precum*, or book(let) of prayers. It is one of a set of nine liturgical books prepared for Sigebert about the year 1030 and, judging from the generally excellent physical condition of the manuscript, may well have been used as a source book or guide for a master of ceremonies. For a more complete discussion of its significance, see Joanne Pierce, "New Research Directions in Medieval Liturgy: The Liturgical Books of Sigebert of Minden (1022–1036)," in Gerard Austin, O.P., ed., *Fountain of Life* (Washington, DC: The Pastoral Press, 1991), 51–67. The original manuscript is held in the collection of the Herzog August Bibliothek in Wolfenbüttel, Germany, under the signature *Codex Helmstadiensis* 1151. The eucharistic section of the manuscript was edited in 1557 by Matthias Flacius Illyricus, and the *ordo missae* became known as the Missa Illyrica. This edition can most easily be found in Edmond Martène, *DAER* (1737; reprinted Hildesheim: G. Olms, 1967), *Lib.* I, *Cap.* IV, *Ordo* IV, cols. 489–528. The fresh edition of the entire manuscript done by Joanne Pierce is currently being revised for possible publication in the *Medieval Studies* series of the Medieval Institute, University of Notre Dame. For more on the Minden text, see Pierce, "Early Medieval Liturgy," and "Some Early Medieval Vesting Prayers," to appear in a *festschrift* for Aidan Kavanagh, O.S.B. (edited by John Baldovin, S.J., and Nathan Mitchell; Liturgical Press, expected 1996). The most recent description and bibliography can be found in Wolfgang Milde, "Die Handschriften des Bischofs Sigebert von Minden," in Martin Klöckner, ed, *Lectionarium. Berlin, Ehem. Preussiche Staatsbibliothek, Ms. theol. lat. qu. 1* (z. Zt. Krakow,

Biblioteka Jagiellonska, Depostium). (München: Edition Helga Legenfelder, 1993; *Codices illuminati medii aevi* 18), 7–25; here pp. 12–13.

43. All of these Martène *ordines* can be found in the same book, article, and chapter; hereafter, they will be listed only according to *ordo* and column numbers. Martimort numbers refer to the manuscript listing in *La documentation*, see above.

44. For a more complete but rather outdated discussion of *apologiae*, see Fernand Cabrol, "Apologies," *DACL* 1.2 (1907): cols. 2591–2601. See also Anselm Strittmater, "An Unknown 'Apology' in Morgan Manuscript 641," *Traditio* 4 (1946), 179–196; Pietro Borella, "Le 'apologia sacerdotis' negli antichi messali ambrosiana," *EL* 63 (1949), 27–41; Adrian Nocent, "Les apologies dans la célébration eucharistique," in *Liturgie et rémission des péchés* (Rome: Edizioni Liturgiche, 1975), 179–196; and Cabié, pp. 130–131.

45. Pierce, "Early Medieval Liturgy," p. 514.

46. Anscar Chupungco, O.S.B., *Cultural Adaptation of the Liturgy* (Mahwah, NJ: Paulist Press, 1982), 28–29. See also his articles "Greco-Roman Culture and Liturgical Adaptation," *Notitiae* 15 (1979), 202–218, and "A Historical Survey of Liturgical Adaptation," *Notitiae* 17 (1981), 28–43, as well as Pierre-Marie Gy, O.P., "L'inculturation de la liturgie chrétienne en occident," *La Maison-Dieu* 179 (1989), 15–30.

47. Pierce, "New Research Directions," p. 61; see also "Early Medieval Liturgy," pp. 512–513.

48. Among the early medieval *libelli* which have been transcribed or edited: André Wilmart, "Le manuel de prières de Saint Jean Gualbert, *RB* 48 (1936), 259–299, and *Precum libelli quattuor aevi karolini* (Rome: Ephemerides Liturgicae, 1940); A.B. Kuypers, *The Book of Cerne* (Cambridge: The University Press, 1902); the Prayerbook of Charles the Bald, transcribed by F. Ninguada, *Liber precationum quas Carolus Calvus . . .* (Ingolstadii: Davidis Sartorii, 1583); the Prayerbook of Fleury, Martène, *Lib.* IV, cols. 655–694 (Martimort, no. 1131); and the *Officia per ferias*, PL 101, 509–612. Pierre Salmon has inventoried several manuscripts, and listed their contents by heading and incipit in *"Libelli Precum* du VIIIe au XIIe siècle," in *Analecta Liturgica*, pp. 121–194.

49. See Cabié, pp. 150–151, and M. Bernard, "Un texte inédite, le *Confiteor* lyonnais," *EL* 83 (1969), 459–481.

50. Jungmann, *MRR*, I, pp. 298–300.

51. Ibid., pp. 300–301. Other later developments can be noted: the prayer is stratified, to refer to God and the Church in heaven in the first section, and in the second, the intercession by the Church on earth; and the mention of the saints is lengthened by the inclusion of specific names (Mary is always mentioned first).

52. "A apologia 'Suscipe confessionem meam'," *Didaskalia* 1 (1971), 319–334.

53. Bragança, "A apologia," pp. 321–322.

54. Ibid., p. 322. He notes also that *apologiae*, as a specific *genre* of prayer within the liturgy, are only symbols of their epoch, expressions of that spirituality. They are characterized by a simple vision, biblically inspired, which characterized all medieval prayer: a humility, a deep awareness of human sinfulness and fragility, and a total confidence in the mercy of God. See also p. 334.

55. As Luykx puts it, "Klerikalisierungserscheinung in der Liturgie," see "Ursprung," p. 79.

56. See the *Excursus* on the "Private Mass" in Vogel, pp. 156–159.

57. Robert Taft, S.J., *Beyond East and West: Problems in Liturgical Understanding* (Washington, DC: Pastoral Press, 1984), 168; for a more thorough discussion of the role of "soft spots" in liturgical evolution, see chapters 10 and 11.

58. For a more complete discussion, see P. Tirot, "Les prières d'offertoire du VIIe au XVIe siècle," *EL* 98 (1984), 148–197.

59. Luykx, pp. 79–81.

60. Luykx, p. 81; see also André Wilmart, *Auteurs spirituels et textes dévots du moyen-âge* (Paris: Bloud et Gay, 1932; reprinted by Études Augustiniennes, 1971), p. 102.

61. Luykx, p. 83.

62. Luykx, p. 83.

63. Luykx, p. 85.

64. Luykx, p. 84.

65. Luykx, pp. 83–96.

66. Including a special one on behalf of the emperor/king and his progeny (*sua venerabili prole*); see p. 88.

67. A tendency which can be seen as early as 750–800, in OR VII: *Qualiter quaedam orationes et cruces in Te Igitur agandae sunt* (directions on making the sign of the cross during the canon); see Luykx, p. 86–87, and Vogel, p. 162–163.

68. Luykx, pp. 86–91.

69. Luykx, p. 91.

70. Luykx, p. 90–93.

71. Luykx, p. 93, 97, 117.

72. Luykx, p. 101: ". . . wir müssen den Ursprung des rhenischen *Ordo Missae* in St. Gallen suchen." Interestingly, St. Gall has been found to have had no little influence on the composition and production of the Sigebert books, see Pierce, *Sacerdotal Spirituality*, pp. 51–67, 127–128, and Milde, p. 12.

73. Luykx, p. 103. Bragança notes that the Minden OM seems to use the Reichenau OM as a principal source, "Reichenau," pp. 159–161.

74. Luykx, pp. 103–104. However, it is Cologne, not Mainz, which is given a place of honor in the litanies of the Sigebert music books, see Pierce, *Sacerdotal Spirituality*, pp. 56, 65–66. It is by no means certain that Reichenau was ever the artistic center historians have claimed it to be, see Charles Reginald Dodwell and D.H. Turner, *Reichenau Revisited; A Re-assessment of the Place of Reichenau in Ottonian Art*, (London: The Warburg Institute, 1965). The influence of St. Gall is, however, undeniable.

75. Hartmut Hoffmann, *Buchkunst und Königtum im ottonischen und frühsalischen Reich* (Stuttgart: Hiesermann, 1986; *Schriften der Monumenta Germaniae Historica* 30, Bd. 1 and 2); here, Bd. 1, p. 97; see also note 72, above.

76. *MS^5*, Index B, III, 2, b, p. 590.

77. Which include the Minden OM as well as several of the above *ordines*.

78. *MRR, Index* A, III, 2, b, p. 469.

79. See, for example, *MS^5*, Volume I, p. 126 n. 21; p. 130; p. 265; p. 355 n. 6; p. 356 n. 14; p. 361 n. 8; p. 373; p. 378; p. 387 n. 7; p. 403 n. 3; p. 404 n. 8; Volume II, p. 59 n. 26.

80. *MS^5*, Volume I, pp. 122–124.

81. *MS^5*, pp. 123–124, and n. 9.

82. Entitled "Die römische Messe im Frankenreich" (the English translation reads "The Roman Mass in France").

83. *MRR*, Volume I, p.79, and notes 25 and 26; *MS^5*, Volume I, pp. 104–105, and notes 25 and 26.

84. *MRR*, Volume I, p. 79. Throughout the two volumes, he continues to cite examples from the Minden OM in the detailed footnotes which accompany and illustrate his lengthy discussions of every section of the *ordo missae*.

85. Joseph Lemarié, "A propos de l'Ordo Missae du Pontifical d'Hugues de Salins," *Didaskalia* 9 (1979), 3–9

86. He finds their analytical "synoptique" table especially valuable; see Baroffio and Dell'Oro, pp. 822–823.

87. He finds that the Salins OM also exhibits some characteristics of the Frankish Type of OM: a large number of *Suscipe sancta Trinitas* prayers; the "invitation" *Orate fratres*; prayers during the *commixtio*, the placing of a particle of the consecrated host into the chalice filed with consecrated wine before communion; and the *Placeat tibi sancta Trinitas* prayer recited at the end of Mass. See pp. 4–5.

88. In the Minden OM, placed during the *Sanctus*; see Lemarié, "A Propos," p. 6, n. 2, and Pierce, *Sacerdotal Spirituality*, pp. 232–233, no. 154,

and pp. 395. It is an apology-type prayer, intended to be used as one further text in which the presider "commends" himself to God before the canon; it is headed by the rubric/title: *Hac oratione finita antequam sacramenta incipiantur iterum sese Deo commendet dicens.*

89.   Note that the first of these two prayers was commonly connected with this OT canticle even in the early sacramentaries; the Canticle of the Three Young Men was a set part of the liturgy for Ember Saturdays, hence its penitential focus. The second prayer, too, was in wide use earlier for the same Ember Saturday liturgy (as well as on other occasions, e.g., the dedication of a church); in the *ordines missae* under study here, it occasionally is placed at the beginning of the vesting rite before Mass. See Pierce, *Sacerdotal Spirituality*, pp. 429–431.

90.   Lemarié, p. 9.

91.   However, he does note certain "Irish symptoms," or influences, in his analysis of the Hamburg litany of the saints; see pp. 209–211.

92.   Rasmussen, p. 211.

93.   Ibid., p. 200.

94.   Pierce, "New Research Directions," pp. 60–61.

95.   See the above discussion of *apologiae*, and also Pierce, "Early Medieval Liturgy," pp. 518–520.

96.   Pierce, "New Research Directions," p. 61.

97.   And thus, the modern and contemporary *ordines missae* as well, see Pierce, "New Research Directions," p. 61 and "Early Medieval Liturgy," pp. 516–519.

COMMENTARIES ON THE MASS DURING THE EARLY SCHOLASTIC PERIOD

Gary Macy

INTRODUCTION

From the late eleventh century throughout the twelfth century, and into the early years of the thirteenth century, some two dozen commentaries on the Christian ritual meal, the Eucharist, appeared in Western Christendom. They were not new phenomena, indeed such commentaries had always had a place in Christian literature and had flourished under the Carolingians. Nor did this genre die out in later centuries, although few new commentaries were written in the late thirteenth or fourteenth centuries.[1]

Still, this set of treatises has several remarkable characteristics. First, the works were extremely popular in their own time, and, secondly, they remain to a large extent, unappreciated by modern scholarship. They are nevertheless an important witness to a period which marked a turning point in eucharistic devotion. During the twelfth century, stories of miracle hosts proliferated, new forms of devotion, like the elevation of the host, appeared, and in theology the first uses and explanations of transubstantiation made their debut.[2]

It is the way in which the commentaries encode this important change that discourages modern interest, for they are written in an elaborate allegorical style that leaves most moderns cold (and frankly bored). Unfortunately, the most important studies on the commentaries remain the unpublished doctoral theses of Dennis W. Krouse,[3] David F. Wright,[4] Ronald J. Zawilla,[5] Mary Schaefer,[6] and Douglas L. Mosey.[7]

The most extensive published discussion of these works remains that of Adolf Franz, in his book *Die Messe im Deutschen Mittelalter,* published in 1902 and reprinted in 1963. The book is a storehouse of strange liturgical customs adopted during the Middle Ages and the author tips his hand early in the work regarding his opinion of medieval worship: "The praxis of the church (during this period) was most often influenced by a distorted and superstitious conception [of the liturgy], dominating both people and clerics."[8] Franz represents only the major voice in a chorus of scholars who decry the commentaries as a stage in the decay of understanding the liturgy in which the original meaning of the eucharistic rite was lost under an avalanche of meaningless and disconnected symbolism. F.M. Martineau condescendingly remarked of these works:

> The interest of these little *summae* is not in their exegesis, where the imagination gives free rein to the most fantastic interpretations, a naive symbolism which seduced contemporaries, but in that which disconcerts the best-prepared scholar to appreciate the meaning of these pious allegories.[9]

Many people, even liturgical scholars, I fear, still perceive the medieval allegorical literature much as James Thurber viewed that epitome of evil, the Todal, in his book *The Thirteen Clocks*: "[It] smells of old unopened rooms," and "feels as if it had been dead at least a dozen days."[10]

Although space does not allow for a complete analysis of all the works written during this period, a brief overview of the eucharistic devotion described in some of the less known of the commentaries may, one hopes, lift the sense of dread with which modern liturgical scholarship has cloaked this genre.[11] This article will first review the major Mass commentaries of the eleventh, twelfth and early thirteenth centuries, summarizing with an analysis of their audiences, reception and focus on the relationship between spirituality, the living of the Christian life, and the liturgy itself. In a separate appendix a tentative guide to the commentaries has been provided to those readers willing to brave unopened rooms.

MASS COMMENTARIES

Whatever might be said about Martineau's own dislike for this form of literature, he is quite right in pointing out the popularity of these works among contemporaries. The works appear not only to have survived but also to have been read and copied. A sermon on the Canon of the Mass given at Clairvaux by an unknown Premonstratensian canon named Richard has survived in some sixty manuscripts dating from the twelfth to the fifteenth centuries,[12] while the extremely popular commentaries of John Beleth and Innocent III exist in well over one hundred manuscripts each.[13]

If these commentaries were read, who read them, and to what end were these then captivating allegories produced? The first question is easier to answer than the second. Several of the commentators mention that their works were undertaken by request. Odo, bishop of Cambrai from around 1095 to 1113, wrote his commentary on the Canon of the Mass as a favor to Fulgentius, abbot of the Benedictine monastery of Affligem.[14] Isaac, abbot of the Cistercian house at Stella, wrote a similar commentary dated to the years 1162–1167 at the request of John, bishop of Poitiers.[15] Honorius Augustodunensis and Gerhoh of Reichersberg both wrote commentaries to answer the demands of the religious of their individual houses.[16] Ivo, bishop of Chartres from 1090 to 1115, and the Premonstratensian Richard both delivered sermons which expounded the allegorical meaning of the Mass; Ivo presumably addressing his clergy at Chartres and Richard delivering his sermon before the monks of Clairvaux.[17]

The works appear for the most part, to be addressed to the clergy, diocesan and religious. The fact that the commentaries were written in Latin and presumed a knowledge of the prayers of the Mass rules out the possibility that these works, at least in the form in which they have survived, were intended for an uneducated audience. Their purpose was not, then, to explain the external ritual of the Mass, something with which the intended audience was presumed to be familiar but to explain the inner meaning of the outward rituals, the invisible things understood by the visible signs.

John Beleth

The first commentator on the Mass to be studied here, John Beleth, remains a somewhat obscure figure in the history of the schools of the twelfth century. Scholars know only that he was in Chartres c. 1135, was a student of Gilbert of La Porrée, and taught in Paris in the mid-twelfth century. His commentary on the offices of the church year, *Summa de ecclesiasticis officiis*, was completed between 1160 and 1164. The work was extremely popular in the Middle Ages and reached a large audience.[18] According to Beleth, his work was intended to explain the offices of the church to those who heard, but could not understand the words of the services.[19] He seems to have intended his book for clerics, but not necessarily priests.[20] Perhaps the book was written for his students at Paris.[21] Modern scholars have praised Beleth's book for its simple, straightforward, learned style, offering a distinct change from the heavily allegorical commentaries of his predecessors.[22]

Indeed, most of Beleth's commentary on the Mass offers little more than etymologies on the words of the liturgy and a description of the action of the ceremony interspersed with canonical notes. Surprisingly enough, much of his material is borrowed from the allegorical commentary of Honorius Augustodunensis.[23] Unlike many of the commentators, Beleth offers no overall conception of the eucharistic action.[24]

In his commentary on the Offertory, he mentions three things which ought to be offered: first, ourselves; second, those things necessary for the sacrifice, that is, bread and wine; and third, the gifts of the faithful.[25]

The Canon of the Mass is obviously the most important part of the liturgy for Beleth. The section of the Mass from the Secret to the Lord's Prayer is properly called the Mass *(proprie missa dicitur).*[26] Further, Beleth argues that even the words of consecration themselves can be properly called the Mass.[27] He refuses to comment on the words of consecration, because these words should be known only by the priest.[28] In explaining the silence of the Canon, he offers the traditional story of the shepherds in the early church who recited the words of consecration over their lunch of bread and wine and were destroyed by divine wrath as proof of the danger which common knowledge of these words would incur.[29] Only a vested priest, with the proper books, on a proper altar, is allowed to offer Mass, and any deviation from this procedure is prohibited under anathema.[30]

Beleth's commentary on the Communion offers a standard history of the gradually diminishing frequency of reception in the church due to the perception of growing unworthiness in the recipients. Beleth describes three practices introduced to succor those people who cannot receive the Eucharist frequently: the kiss of peace, the prayer over the people at the end of Mass, and the distribution of the blessed bread at the end of Mass.[31]

Although Beleth offers no theology of the Eucharist as such, his position as regards the act of consecration is clear. The purpose of the Mass lies in the power of the words of consecration to make the body and blood of Christ present on the altar. He surrounds these words with mystery and power and understands the presence they bring about as a dangerous thing, never to be taken lightly, neither in the act of consecration, nor in the reception of Communion. Only in the commentary on the Offertory does his attitude of pure adoration waver, when he adjures the believer to join the offering of himself to the offerings which will bring about the divine presence.

Isaac of Étoile

Unlike the commentary on the Mass written by John Beleth, the commentary on the Canon of the Mass written by the Cistercian abbot, Isaac of Étoile, offers a rich theological and allegorical yield.[32] The commentary is contained in a letter of Isaac, written to John, bishop of Poitiers, between 1162 and 1167.[33] The short work had much influence in the twelfth century and was copied by at least two other commentators of the period.[34]

Although Isaac does not offer a commentary on the Offertory, he describes the sacrifice which ought to be offered to God. Our lives crushed by vicissitudes, mixed with the tears of remorse and devotion, and cooked in the oven of a contrite and humble heart ought to make up the bread of our first offering to God.[35]

Isaac divides the Canon into three principal actions.[36] Allegorically, these actions correspond to the three altars of the tabernacle in the desert.[37] On the first altar of bronze, animal sacrifices were offered; on the second altar of gold, incense was offered; while the third altar, the Holy of Holies, remained hidden behind the wings of the cherubim.[38]

Anagogically, this allegory corresponds to the stages by which a human becomes united to God. The bronze altar represents the contrite heart upon which the spirit of remorse offers the sacrifice of penitence. The gold altar represents the pure heart upon which the spirit of devotion offers the sacrifice of justice. The Holy of Holies represents the great heart upon which the spirit of contemplation offers the sacrifice of intelligence.[39] These three sacrifices, in turn, free us from the devil, unite us to God, and allow us to delight in God.[40]

The three actions of the Canon follow this same movement of humans towards God. The first action of the Canon, the offering of the bread and wine, represents the action of servants offering their whole lives, represented by the means of their sustenance, in order to reconcile themselves to their Lord.[41] This offering is, however, insufficient to accomplish our reconciliation with God.[42] Therefore, we beg God to accomplish what we cannot do and, in the second action of the Canon, through the words of consecration our earthly offerings become the spiritual offering of Christ, the new priest who offers his body and blood on the heavenly altar, accomplishing our reconciliation and uniting us to God.[43] Because, however, body and blood of themselves produce nothing, we hope for even greater things.[44] With this hope we proceed to the third action of the Canon, praying that in our reception of the species of bread and wine on our earthly altar, we might accept the true body and blood on the second heavenly altar, and through the power of this sacrament, be united with God.[45]

Isaac's allegory bases itself on the monastic ascent of the soul from *compunctio*, to *devotio*, to *contemplatio*.[46] The purpose of the liturgy lies in its ability to assist this process. The act of consecration and the real presence do not hold the central position here. The reception of the bread and wine take place on one level (*de primo altari*), and the receipt of the body and blood on another (*de secundo ultra velum*), but the purpose of both is spiritual union with God.[47] The purpose of the liturgy lies in its ability to assist this process. The individual in his relationship to God through Christ forms the basic movement of the Mass, which is, it should be noted, directed from the people to God.

The very different approaches to the eucharistic liturgy taken by John Beleth and Isaac of Étoile are symptomatic of the latitude of eucharistic teaching in the twelfth century. A similar diversity continues to present itself throughout this century and well into the thirteenth century.

Richardus Praemonstratensis

Another commentary on the Canon of the Mass, written in the third quarter of the twelfth century, appears to be a sermon delivered at Clairvaux by a Premonstratensian canon named Richard.[48] Too little is known of Richard and his work to judge the influence of his commentary, although at least thirty-one manuscripts of his work are known to exist.[49] His basic approach consists of a rather artificial allegory based on the seven dimensions of the cross and the seven virtues and vices which he aligns with the seven *ordines* of the Canon extending from the first prayer of the Canon to the *Agnus Dei.*

Richard, like Isaac, lays great stress on the moral regeneration of the individual. The effect of both the holy cross and the sacrament of the altar is the same: evil is removed and the church is renewed.[50] For Richard, this means that we must first discipline ourselves to drive out evil, before we can accept the newness of Christ.[51] In great detail, he lists the vices of the mind and body which must be removed, and which of the corresponding virtues must replace each of the vices. He sees this regeneration as the major virtue not only of the Mass but of the redemptive act itself.[52]

Richard's description of the moment of the eucharistic liturgy has affinities to Isaac's but a much different theology. In the first *ordo*, we pray that the gifts we offer, bread, wine and water, might be blessed.[53] In the second and third *ordines*, we pray that they might become the body and blood of Christ.[54] In the fourth *ordo*, we pray that Christ, now present, might present our petitions to the Father in heaven.[55] In the fifth *ordo*, we praise the Father, Son and Spirit, that our petitions might be fulfilled,[56] and in the sixth *ordo*, we honor and glorify the Father through Christ.[57] Finally, in the seventh *ordo*, we pray for the peace of God.[58]

The movement of the liturgy as understood by Richard is very simple. Our gifts are transformed into the body and blood of Christ, who now being present, provides us with both the spiritual assistance we need, and with an opportunity for petitioning God the Father. The entire movement depends upon and centers around the real presence.

There is no doubt about Richard's belief in the real presence. In discussing the reasons why Christ is present under the species of bread and wine, he explains that the glory of Christ unveiled would be beyond the strength of humans to bear. He illustrates his point with a remarkable story from a contemporary Augustinian house in Viviers. One of the canons, in extreme devotion during Mass, saw the glory of Christ revealed above the altar, and was struck blind.[59] The story exemplifies in a graphic way the combination of individual piety and the strong belief in the real presence which Richard presents.

Despite Richard's emphasis on the real presence, the presence itself has spiritual value in terms of the moral regeneration of the individual. As different as Richard's theology might be from Isaac of Étoile's, the purpose of the eucharistic action remains the same: not simply the mere presence of Christ on the altar, but the possibilities which that presence presents for the moral regeneration of the individual.

Speculum de mysteriis ecclesiae

An anonymous work from the same period, entitled *Speculum de mysteriis ecclesiae*, comes from the hand of a person familiar with the liberal arts, and with the school of St. Victor in Paris.[60] The *Speculum* appears to have been a well-read book in the twelfth century and forms one of the important sources for Simon of Tournai's theological summa, *Institutiones in sacram paginam*.[61] Although it is difficult to date this work with accuracy, it appears to have been written c. 1160–1175.[62]

The *Speculum* describes the offering of the gifts as twofold. The offering of the people in the form of money (*munera*) corresponds to the offerings made by the Jewish people at the dedication of the temple of Solomon and more importantly stands as a symbol of their offering of themselves to God.[63] The Gospel, Creed and Offertory follow one another because hearing the Gospel precedes belief, and belief makes possible an acceptable sacrifice.[64] The author of the *Speculum* stresses the inner state of believers as essential in offering themselves and their gift to God. The offering of the priest is the bread and wine, prefigured by the offering of Melchisedech and the offering of Christ at the Last Supper.[65] The introduction of this offering leads the author into a long discussion of theological issues concerning the Eucharist, to which I shall return after following the author's general allegory on the Mass.

In each of the prayers said over the gifts, the *Speculum* explains the type of the sacrifice in the Holy of Holies of the Old Testament which pertains to the prayer, the corresponding action of Christ in the redemptive act, and the appropriate action in the present liturgy. For instance, the commentary on the first of these prayers reads:

> The high priest formerly entered the holy of holies once a year with blood, and Christ through his own blood once for all entered the sanctuary, having won an eternal redemption for us (Hebrews 9:12). Thus the minister of the church enters the holy of holies with blood, as often as he bears in mind the victory of the blood of Christ.[66]

This section of the liturgy is the most sacred, for it contains the words of consecration and the sign of the cross by means of which the body and blood of the Lord are made present, although how this comes about surpasses the understanding of men and angels.[67] Food for the body becomes food for the soul in order that the person who receives worthily might receive eternal life.[68] The prayers over the gifts, too, have a meaning especially for the inner person. The priest shares in holy sacrifice when he "bears in mind" the sacrifice of Christ. The presence of the body and blood brought about by the prayers of consecration only become food for the soul of the person who receives worthily.

The commentary on the Communion simply reads: "The communion, which is sung after this, signifies all of the faithful in communion with the body of Christ, which the minister receives sacramentally on behalf of all, that both he and they might receive spiritually."[69] The author certainly understands the reception of the body and blood to be important only in the personal spiritual realm.

By returning to the theology of the Eucharist discussed earlier by the author, this emphasis throughout the commentary on the personal spiritual state can be explained. Following the teaching of Hugh of St. Victor, the *Speculum* argues that a sacramental reception of the

Eucharist alone accomplishes nothing, only a spiritual reception gives the grace of salvation.[70] The spiritual reception consists, however, in uniting, consecrating and conforming ourselves to Christ in faith and love.[71] He goes so far as to argue that spiritual reception alone suffices for salvation when not in contempt of the ritual.[72] In short, the author describes the entire liturgical action and even the real presence as a commemorative aid, and not an absolutely necessary aid, for the spiritual life of a person dedicating his or her life to Christ. The individual and his or her attitude and response to the liturgy determine its efficacy, despite the author's strong belief in a real presence.

The author of the *Speculum* also provides a classification of the human faculties. The senses (*sensus*) correspond to the first level of awareness, the imagination (*imaginatio*) to the second level, reason (*ratio*) to the third level and faith (*fides*) to the fourth level. Dialectic belongs to the third level, and the mystery of the body and blood of Christ can only be grasped on the level of faith.[73] Thus the author attacks those who treat the Eucharist through dialectic, i.e., on the wrong level. This classification offers two important insights into the theology presented here. First, he does not see faith as an entirely separate realm, apart from the natural attributes of man. Faith forms the highest region within the psychological realm of man, not a separate realm above man's grasp. Indeed intellect surpasses faith in those cases where the saints are allowed to grasp the secrets of heaven.[74] Secondly, the author rejects any discussion of a "metaphysical" presence in the Eucharist. The presence exists on the level of faith and is grasped by faith. This emphasis on psychology rather than metaphysics is extremely important in understanding the approach taken to the eucharistic liturgy in the second half of the twelfth century.

Robert Paululus

A fifth commentary, probably written c. 1175–1180, is that of a secular priest of Amiens, Robert Paululus.[75] Paululus' work treats of all of the church, and includes a complete commentary on the Mass.

The commentary on the Offertory expresses the joy of the believer as he sees the mystery of his salvation being prepared before him when the deacon, subdeacon and priest prepare the bread and wine.[76]

Robert's commentary on the Canon copies almost verbatim the commentary of Isaac of Étoile which he conscientiously intersperses with material from other commentaries.[77] In fact, he provides nearly two complete commentaries on the Canon.[78]

Fortunately, Robert provides summaries of the movement he envisions in the liturgy. At one point, he describes the order of the liturgical action:

> Notice the order: first God creates the bread and wine according to nature. He sanctifies these same offerings according to grace, through the words of the first action. Thus they have been sanctified before sanctification and set apart from common uses. Then God gives life to these gifts, which have been sanctified by setting them apart, through the sacred words of the second action, when he transubstantiates them into the body and blood of Christ, and blesses them when he gives them the effect of that highest blessing, which is the unity of head and members, which the third action commemorates.[79]

Despite the fact that Robert copies most of Isaac's commentary, he lacks Isaac's subtle mysticism. For Robert, the presence of Christ is the central action necessary to bring about the union of God and man. Robert makes a similar relationship here between nature and faith as that found in the *Speculum*. The natural gifts of God are raised to the status of gifts of faith. Indeed Robert insists that this most holy sacrifice can only be perceived by faith, only profits in faith, and is accepted only by the merit of faith.[80]

Robert offers another summary, however, which shows his interest in the devotional stance of the believer. In the first action, we ought to conform ourselves to Christ's passion. We ought to conform ourselves to his resurrection in the second action by offering the mystery of faith with the gift of devotion, and conform ourselves to his ascension in the third action by contemplating Christ crowned in glory and honor on the right hand of the Father.[81]

Robert refers several times to the devotion which the believer must offer to God, and in which the believer must daily grow. Our hearts must be celestial to receive celestial food.[82] The priest extending his hands in the Canon shows externally that he has crucified himself with Christ in his heart.[83] The fire of the Spirit calls forth the tears first of remorse, and then of devotion.[84] The more we tend toward devotion to God, the more we know we are unable to comprehend him.[85] It is with the eyes of the heart that the priest sees the angels who are standing around the altar.[86] That the sacrifice is taken up by the hand of the angel means nothing else than that the angel has joined us in our devotion.[87] The priest raises the gifts and makes the cross over them in order that he might show how the glory of the Trinity can be acquired by the minds of the faithful through Christ.[88] Finally, Robert offers a commentary on the Lord's Prayer that we might be excited to devotion.[89] Again and again, he expresses his concern for the heart of the believer, the mind of the believer, the faith of the believer, the devotion of the believer.

Robert offers little original material, but for that very reason, he may be seen as a trustworthy witness to the general mood of this time. The mood he expresses is one of personal devotion to Christ as present in the Eucharist, but present in faith. If he would not deny the real presence, he would, as the commentators before him, see the presence as important only insofar as it relates to the psychological state of the believer.

Stephen of Autun

Stephen, the second bishop of that name to hold the see of Autun in the twelfth century, probably wrote the *Tractatus de sacramento altaris* during his episcopacy, 1170–1189.[90] The *Tractatus* offers a commentary on the offices of the church, the sacred vestments, and the Mass.

Stephen's commentary on the Offertory (like most of his predecessors') admonishes the believer to offer not only the gifts, but a humble and contrite heart.[91] For Stephen, this commonplace becomes a central theme. No prayer, no meditation, no work will be acceptable to God, unless it is offered in a spirit of humility.[92] The person who renders himself or herself acceptable by good works, rightly gives thanks to God.[93] To pray without charity is unfruitful.[94] Stephen compares our offering with the offering of the saints. We offer with things, they with faith and devotion; we offer by completing sacraments, they offer by doing God's will; we offer wine and they offer a holy and devout mind. [95]

In two lengthy passages, Stephen compares our sacrifice with sacrifices of the Old Testament. First, he speaks of the sacrifice of Cain and Abel. Like Abel, we must offer a contrite and pure heart with our sacrifice. If our sacrifice contains our heart with it, it will lead to our salvation; if not, it will lead to our damnation. [96] Speaking of the sacrifices of Abel, Abraham, and Melchisedech, he argues that if we wish to imitate the patriarchs, we must offer our hearts to God, that we might be found pleasing to Him by sober, pious and just living. [97] For Stephen there are only two possibilities: to offer a true sacrifice of one's whole self to God, and thus gain salvation, or to offer an external sacrifice alone, and merit damnation. Probably for this reason, he rejects the possibility of purgatory. [98]

Stephen's interpretation of the movement of the liturgy differs little from Richard or Robert Paululus. We pray to God to change the bread and wine into the body and blood of Christ in order that he might intercede for us before the divine throne. [99] Here he adds that we remember the passion of Christ, not that the memory might be lost from our hearts, but that we might crucify ourselves with our vices and thus rise renewed with Christ. [100]

In his discussion of the real presence, Stephen speaks of the presence as understood—known in the realm of faith, above the senses, above the intellect, and beyond dialectic. [101] As one might expect, he speaks of the reception of the Eucharist as either unto redemption or damnation, depending on the faith and love of the believer. [102] There is no need to belabor the point that Stephen exhibits the same interest in the believer's individual devotion that is so apparent in these commentaries. At times, he breaks into emotional exclamations of devotion that leave no doubt of the reverential piety which he wishes to instill: "Who can despise, like a wretched servant unmindful of his benefits, while holding the Lord in his hands who was crucified and died for him, that testament enacted by His death?" [103] Stephen, like Robert Paululus, is important, not for his originality, but for his expression of the common current of thought that he transmits.

Sicard of Cremona

Sicard, the bishop of Cremona, famous for his teaching in canon law, produced an extensive treatment of the offices of the church in his *Mitrale*, written c. 1185–1195.[104] The third book of this work contains a complete commentary on the Mass.

Sicard's commentary on the Offertory contains an interesting discussion arising out of the question of the use of leavened bread by the Greeks. Following the opinion of Rupert of Deutz, Sicard claims that only two things are necessary for transubstantiation, the repetition of the words and faith. Whoever says the words and does not believe is like an ass lifting up his ears to the lyre, but not understanding the melody of the song. Whoever visibly eats the body of Christ, but invisibly rejects it through unbelief, kills Christ. The life present to us is spiritual life, not animal life.[105] This passage is interesting for two reasons. First, because Sicard insists on the necessity of faith, both in the act of consecration and in the act of communion. Secondly, he quotes precisely those passages of Rupert which William of St. Thierry had criticized earlier in the century for not insisting strongly enough on the change of substance which takes place in the Eucharist.[106] Probably, Sicard had not known of William's criticism, but the point remains that Sicard chose those passages of Rupert's which insist most strongly on a spiritual understanding of the presence of Christ in the Eucharist. Like the other commentators of this period, Sicard insists that this change must be understood by faith, and he offers the same analysis of human understanding as the *Speculum* to explain it.[107]

In several passages, Sicard refers to the devotion which different actions and signs in the liturgy ought to inspire. Some Mass books contain a representation of the crucifixion at the beginning of the text of the Canon in order to place the passion before the eyes of our heart.[108] The same impression is made by the letter *T* of the *Te igitur*, the first words of the Canon.[109] We offer gifts (*dona*) when we offer ourselves to God. We offer tribute (*munera*) when we are mindful of our benefits from God. We offer a spotless sacrifice (*sacrificia illibata*) when we devote our humility and praise to God.[110] Morally, we offer a pure, holy and immaculate offering when we offer our sacrifice with a pure heart, a good conscience and a true faith.[111] Like Stephen of Autun, Sicard also offers a long allegory on the gifts of the patriarchs. He concludes by urging the believer to imitate the patriarchs by offering the sacrifices of innocence, obedience and justice.[112]

An overall understanding of the movement of the liturgy appears only vaguely in Sicard's work. He sees the purpose of the liturgy as the union of Christ with the members of the Church, which makes it possible for earthly persons to rise to heaven.[113] He describes the liturgy as centering around the act of transubstantiation, whereby Christ is made present to mediate our petitions to the Father.[114]

Despite the eclectic nature of Sicard's work, the same general interest appears in the relationship in faith between the believer and Christ achieved in the liturgy.

Innocent III

The longest commentary on the Mass from this period is the *De missarum mysteriis* of Innocent III, written c. 1190–1197, when he was cardinal archdeacon of SS. Sergius and Bacchus.[115] The commentary, which describes the ceremony of a papal high Mass, covers six books and includes extensive allegorical and theological material. An entire book is dedicated to discussing the words of consecration, a discussion which comprises a compendium of the scholastic debates concerning the Eucharist in the twelfth century. The work was extremely popular, and was used by most of the later commentators.[116] As with the other commentators, our concern here will be with the general approach to the movement of the eucharistic liturgy which Innocent presents, and less with his formal theological discussions.

Innocent offers less moral allegory than his predecessors in relation to the size of his work. Several passages, however, reveal that he was not immune to his contemporaries' interest in the heart and mind of the believer. In his commentary on the Offertory, Innocent relates the Creed, the Offertory Antiphon, and the offering itself as expressions first of the faith of the heart, second of the praise of the mouth, and third of the fruit of the works.[117] At the beginning of the Canon, Innocent urges the priest to enter into the chamber of his heart (*in cubiculum cordis*) and there to close himself away from any distraction, that the Holy Spirit might nourish his mind.[118] The repetition of the words used to describe the offering (*haec dona, haec munera, haec sacrificia*) is the expression of pious devotion and praise of this sacrament.[119] In a lengthy allegory on the three sacrifices of the Church, Innocent describes the spiritual state which each of the sacrifices represents. In the sacrifice of penance, we offer the wine of sorrow and remorse, the water of grief and lamentation, and the bread of toil and adversity. In the sacrifice of justice, we offer the bread of fortitude and constancy, the wine of rectitude and prudence, and the water of gentleness and temperance. In the sacrifice of the Eucharist, we offer the bread of unity, the wine of charity and the water of fidelity.[120] In speaking of the Mass as a commemoration of the death of Christ, Innocent offers an example to explain why Christ left us this memorial. It is like a man, who, planning to travel abroad, leaves a token with a good friend of his. If the man who receives the gift really is a true friend, he will never be able to look at the gift without remembering their friendship with great lamenting and longing. So when Christ left this world, he left the Mass as a memorial for us. [121] In fact, Innocent gives as one of the reasons why Christ instituted this sacrament the desire of Christ to be with us not only through the indwelling of grace, but also through his corporeal presence.[122] Innocent gives vivid expression here to that attitude which the commentators express so often regarding the believer's sympathetic relationship with Christ, of rapport in mind and heart with the suffering of Christ. The same interest and sympathy prompts Innocent's description of the sufferings of Christ as not only physical, but mental and emotional.[123]

Like Sicard, Innocent gives only hints at a comprehensive understanding of the movement of the liturgy. Certainly, he considers the consecration the focal point of the Mass. [124] He appears to adopt the approach, not uncommon among the commentators, that the presence of Christ, once achieved, provides the merits of grace and intercession and the purpose of the Mass is to achieve this presence.[125] Despite the compendium of theological information which Innocent provides, he is very firm in asserting that the sacrament of the Eucharist and the real presence are matters for faith, and not for reason. [126] Like the author of the *Speculum*, he argues that if a man does not receive the Eucharist spiritually, that is in faith (*in fide cordis*), he receives unto his damnation. [127]

Innocent's work offers no change from his predecessors. Although perhaps more insistent on the real presence as an end in itself, he also insists on the importance of the liturgy for the spiritual progress of the believer, both in offering the sacrifice of the Mass, and in the reception of communion.[128] Certainly, he shows the same interest in the relationship established in devotion between the believer and Christ and remains firm in asserting the role of faith over reason in the understanding of the Eucharist.

ANALYSIS OF THE COMMENTARIES

Why were the allegorical commentaries written? In many cases, the authors were seeking to instill in their readers a deeper awareness of the moral demands which the liturgy places on the Christian. The means by which this was accomplished no longer appeals. We have lost much of the art of eliciting truth through symbols. Our own mistrust of this method of fathoming the psychological and spiritual depths of both the liturgy and scripture has severely limited our appreciation of medieval allegory.[129] This, I would suggest, witnesses more to our own loss of symbolic sensitivity than to any theological difference between the allegorists and present views on the Eucharist. The means of expression may be strange to us, but the message of the allegorists is clear. The Eucharist makes moral demands upon a participant, and to take part in the rite while ignoring those demands is the worst sort of blasphemy.

Nor were the medieval commentators merely mouthing pious platitudes when they urged conscientious participation in the eucharistic celebration. Church law and practice encouraged and enforced such participation. Reception of the Eucharist in the twelfth and thirteenth centuries was generally limited to thrice yearly, or after the council of Lateran IV in 1215, to annual reception.[130] At least in the thirteenth century, special permission was required to receive the sacrament apart from the Easter duty.[131] The reason for this reluctance to receive was not indifference, but reverence and in some cases, fear of damnation through unworthily approaching the Lord's table. Prospective recipients were expected to fast and abstain from conjugal relations during the days preceding receptions, and confession (at least in theory) was considered essential for worthy reception.[132] Beginning in the twelfth century, confessors and popular writers like the allegorists began to demand not just a formal cleansing from sin but a true longing for union with Christ demonstrated by acts of penance and charity. Some theologians actively discourage frequent reception on the grounds that this kind of familiarity with the sacrament would breed indifference.[133] Sicard expressed the view of many of his contemporaries when he exclaimed: ". . . it has been instituted that (the people) communicate three times a year, Christmas, Easter and Pentecost, but if only they would communicate once worthily!"[134] This viewpoint may at least partially underlie the legislation of Lateran IV which limited reception to an annual event.

The medievals adopted a definite ecclesiastical stance to the moral demands which they saw as implicit in the Eucharist. Every effort was made to insure that reception was made only under the most favorable conditions, and those known publicly to eschew the teaching or practice of the Church faced the social ostracization of excommunication. Excommunication in the Middle Ages entailed many social and legal consequences, but in essence remained excommunication, the inability to participate in the sacrament of the Eucharist.[135] Despite the difficulty involved in preparation, great social pressure was brought to bear on the individual to receive on the high feast days. Not to receive was a public admission of serious sin and public refusal of communion could easily arouse suspicion, even of heresy.[136] Odo of Ourscamp, a theologian at Paris and contemporary of Peter Lombard, argued that a priest ought not publicly to deny the sacrament except to those who were declared excommunicants, because he might thereby cause false accusations. Stephen Langton, himself a well-respected Parisian theologian before becoming the archbishop of Canterbury, famous for supporting the Magna Carta, similarly stated that a priest should not publicly refuse anyone the sacrament, even if he knew him privately to be in serious sin: "not only because of scandal, but especially that his crime not be made public."[137]

The medieval church, both laity and clergy, so closely linked the sign of participation in the life of Christ and the living out of that life, that not to participate in the sign was proof of not living the life of a Christian. Participation in the Eucharist was an extremely important moral and social act, establishing oneself publicly as a member in good standing in the Christian community. It was an act not undertaken lightly, and one which was seen as committing the participant to a life of Christian morality.

CONCLUSION

In conclusion, then, the commentaries on the eucharistic liturgy in the second half of the twelfth century offer a special kind of eucharistic piety: a devotion to Christ in the species, but not an adoration of the species; a great compassion and sympathy for Christ in the passion that went beyond ritual actions to make demands in the believer's moral life; and a fresh and alarmingly personal veneration that challenges the standard histories of liturgy and devotion in the Middle Ages.

Of course, what the treatises offer is an ideal. They explain what their authors felt the liturgy ought to be at its very best, not what it too often was. In reality, the lives of peasants and priests, nobles and bishops, popes and kings, all fell short of the devotion described in the commentaries, and sometime those lives even flatly contradicted those ideals. And yet to study the ideals of a people, and to study them in the form in which they themselves delighted to express them, takes one deep into the medieval mind. In this, I submit, lies the importance of these neglected little treatises.

Notes

1. The best overview of the history of liturgical commentaries is that of Roger Reynold, "Treatises on Liturgy," *DMA* 7, 624–633. The following abbreviations will be used throughout: *DACL* = *Dictionnaire d'archéologie chrétienne et de liturgie,* ed. Fernand Cabrol (Paris, 1907–1953); *DHGE* = *Dictionnaire d'histoire et de géographie ecclésiastique,* ed. Albert Baudrillart (Paris, 1912–1988); *DMA* = *Dictionary of the Middle Ages,* ed. Joseph R. Strayer (New York, 1982–1989); *DSAM* = *Dictionnaire de spiritualité ascétique et mystique,* eds. Marcel Viller, F. Cavallera, J. de Guibert (Paris, 1932–); *DCT* = *Dictionnaire de théologie catholique,* eds. A. Vacant, E. Mangenot and E. Amann (Paris, 1930–1950); *LThK* = *Lexicon für Theologie und Kirche,* ed. Michael Buchberger (Freiburg, 1957–1965); *NCE* = *New*

Catholic Encyclopedia (New York, 1967–1989); and *PL* = *Patrologiae cursus completus . . . Series latina,* ed. Jacques Paul Migne (Paris, 1878–1890).

2. On the rise of eucharistic devotion in the twelfth century, see Gary Macy, *Theologies of the Eucharist in the Early Scholastic Period* (Oxford: Oxford University Press, 1984), 86–93; Miri Rubin, *Corpus Christi: The Eucharist in the Late Medieval Culture* (Cambridge: Cambridge University Press, 1991), 83–163; Cheslyn Jones, Geoffrey Wainwright, Edward Yarnold and Paul Bradshaw (eds.), *The Study of Liturgy* (Oxford: Oxford University Press, rev. ed. 1992), 281–282 and David N. Power, *The Eucharistic Mystery* (New York: Cambridge, 1993), 185–195. On the first use of the term "transubstantiation" see Joseph Goering, "The Invention of Transubstantiation" *Traditio* 46 (1991), 147–170.

3. *Toward an Understanding of Eucharistic Acclamation: An Examination of the Sanctus, Great Amen and Agnus Dei Especially as Treated in Select Expositiones Missae* (Ph.D. Dissertation, Pontifical Liturgical Institute, Athenaeum of Sant'Anselmo, Rome, 1973).

4. *A Medieval Commentary on the Mass: Particulae 2–3 and 5–6 of the De missarum mysteriis (c. 1195) of Cardinal Lother of Segni. (Pope Innocent III)* (Ph.D. Dissertation, University of Notre Dame, 1977).

5. *The Sententia Ivonis Carnotensis Episcopi de Divinis Officiis: Text and Study* (Ph.D. Dissertation, Toronto, 1982).

6. *Twelfth-Century Latin Commentaries on the Mass* (Ph.D. Dissertation, University of Notre Dame, 1983).

7. *Allegorical Liturgical Interpretations in the West from 800 AD to 1200 AD* (Ph.D. Dissertation, Toronto, 1985).

8. Adolf Franz, *Die Messe im deutschen Mittelalter: Beiträge zur Geschichte der Liturgie und des religiösen Volksleben* (Freiburg, 1902; reprinted Darmstadt, 1963), ix. On the allegorical commentaries, see especially pp. 407–458.

9. "L'intérêt de ces petites sommes n'est pas dans leur exégèse, où l'imagination donne libre cours aux interprétations les plus fantaisistes, symbolisme naif qui séduisait les contemporains, mais qui déconcerte aujourd'hui l'esprit le mieux préparé a goûter ces pieuses allégories." La 'Summa de officiis ecclesiasticis' de Guillaume d'Auxerre," *Études d'histoire littéraire et doctrinale du XIIIe siècle,* 2ème serie, 2 (1932), 25. A discussion of other modern authors who speak of the commentaries may be found in Wright, *A Medieval Commentary on the Mass*, 5–43.

10. (Simon and Schuster: New York, 1950), 50, 59.

11. To mention just a few modern authors who describe the effect of commentaries as detrimental to a true understanding of the Eucharist: J. Bauer, *Liturgical Handbook for Holy Mass* (London, 1961), 10; Theodor Klauser, *A*

Short History of the Western Liturgy (London, 1969), 94; Joseph Powers, *Eucharistic Theology* (London, 1968), 22; Louis Bouyer, *Eucharist* (Notre Dame, IN, 1968), 366; and David Power, *The Eucharistic Mystery,* 195.

12. A list of some thirty manuscripts appears in Gary Macy, "A Bibliographical Note on Richardus Praemonstratensis," *Analecta Praemonstratensia* 52 (1976), 64–69. since this article was written I have discovered references to some thirty further manuscripts.

13. Heribert Douteil, in his edition of Beleth's work, *Iohannis Beleth Summa de ecclesiasticis officiis*, Corpus christianorum, continuatio mediaevalis, 41 (Turnhout, 1976), vol. 1, pp. 75–271, lists 149 manuscripts of this work, while Wright, *A Medieval Commentary*, p. 50, mentions that there are 194 known manuscripts of Innocent's commentary.

14. Odo describes the intention of his work in the preface (*PL* 160, 1053D–1054D). Fulgentius was abbot of Affligem from 1088–1122, see U. Berliere, "Affligem," *DHGE*, vol. 1, pp. 672–674.

15. The letter can be dated from the appeal Isaac makes to the bishop for assistance against the attacks of a kinsman of the bishop, Hugh of Chauvigny (*PL* 194, 1896A–B). A ruling was made on this dispute by the bishop in 1167 (cf. G. Raciti, "Isaac de l'Étoile," *Cîteaux* 13 (1962), p. 209, n. 268), this providing a *terminus ante quem*. Raciti, in his article in *DSAM* (cf. no. 28), gives 1165 as a *terminus post quem*, but offers no explanation for this date. John Bellesmains became bishop of Poitiers in 1162 (cf. Ph. Pouzet, *L'Anglais Jean dit Bellesmains* (Lyons, 1927), 20), and so I have used this date as a *terminus post quem*.

16. See the introductory letters to Honorius' *Gemma animae* (*PL* 172, 541–544) and the prologus to Gerhoh's *Expositio super canonem,* edited by Damien and Odulf van den Eynde and Angelinus Rijmersdael, *Gerhohi praepositi Reichersbergensis Opera inedita,* vol. 1 (Rome, 1955), 3.

17. Ivo, in *Sermo I* of his *Sermones de ecclesiasticis sacramentis et officiis,* appears to be addressing clergy: "Quoniam populus ad fidem vocatus, visibilibus sacramentis instruendus est, ut per exhibitionem visibilem, pertingere possit ad intellectum invisibilium, nosse oportet, Domini, sacerdotes, qui haec sacramenta contrectant, modum et ordinem sacramentorum, et veritatem rerum significatarum . . . " (*PL* 162, 505C). It would seem reasonable to assume that this series of sermons was addressed to his own clergy at Chartres. This is the opinion of E. Amann and L. Guizard, *DTC* 15, 3633–3634. On the sermon of Richard at Clairvaux, see Macy, "A Bibliographical Note."

18. On the life of Beleth, his work, the manuscript tradition, and influence of the *Summa de ecclesiasticis officiis,* see Heribert Douteil, *Iohannis Beleth Summa de ecclesiasticis officiis,* praefatio cum appendice.

19. Beleth explains his purpose in his preface: "Quid autem in temporibus nostris est agendum, ubi nullus vel rarus qui invenitur legens vel audiens qui intelligat, videns vel agens qui animaduertat? . . . Sed, *ne claudantur ora canentium: Ad te, Domine, Deus meus,* Deo auxiliante contra hoc dampnum triplicis lectionis adhibeamus remedium . . . " Ibid., vol. 41a, p. 2.

20. In a passage on the Canon of the Mass, Beleth deliberately leaves out those sections which he feels should be discussed only by priests, indicating that he was addressing an audience which included those other than priests: "Secuntur postea multa ut de nominibus apostolorum, martirum, pontificum, militum, medicorum, uiginum, qui omnes per Christo nostro sacrificio morti se exposuerunt, et quedam alia, que nobis non licet exponere nisi forte solis sacerdotibus et ideo de isto tacebimus." Douteil, ibid., p. 82. Jean-François Maurel, "Jean Beleth et la 'Summa de ecclesiasticis officiis," *Positions de thèses de l'École des Chartres* (1953), p. 77, notes: "Du texte de la *Summa,* on peut conclue que Beleth n'était pas moine, mais probablement prêtre, qu'il écrivait surtout pour des clercs, mais non spécialement pour les prêtres."

21. According to Maurel, p. 79, Beleth used the scholastic method of argument: "'*formules nota quod . . . , queritur . . .* ' appel à plusieurs autorités entre lesquelles l'auteur se réserve de choisir." His pupils continued to add marginal notes, which later became incorporated into the text. According to Maurel, p. 80: "ces notes sont, d'ailleurs, trés vite apparues, puisqu'on les trouve déjà presque toutes trente ans après le rédaction." It would be extremely interesting if Beleth actually lectured on the liturgy, or if his book was used in the university. It is worth noting that, although Beleth presumably taught theology at Paris, the only work of his that survives, or that medieval authors quote (cf. Maurel, p. 78), is the *Summa de ecclesiasticis officiis.*

22. Franz, p. 444; Joseph Jungmann, *The Mass of the Roman Rite: Its Origin and Development (Missarum Sollemnia),* translated by Francis Brunner (New York: Benziger Brothers, 1951), vol. 1, p. 109.

23. Cf. Douteil, pp. 361–364 where the dependency of Beleth on Honorius is amply displayed in tabular form.

24. The closest Beleth comes to an outline of this kind is in his description of the Mass as a battle against the devil, c. 32–33 (Douteil, pp. 61–64).

25. Douteil, pp. 75–76.

26. Ibid., p. 77.

27. Ibid., p. 64.

28. For this text, cf. n. 20 above.

29. "Secreta dicitus, quia secreto pronunciatur, cum olim tamen alta uoce diceretur, unde et ab hominibus laicis sciebatur. Contingit ergo ut quadam die

pastores super lapidem quendam ponerent panem, qui ad horum uerborum prolationem in carnem conversus est, forsan transubstantiatur est panis in corpus Christi, in quos diuinitus facta est acerrima uindicta. Nam percussi sunt diuino iudicio celetus misso." Douteil, p. 78. This story appears in many of the commentators of this period. According to Franz, p. 627, the first commentator to use this story was Albinus (wrongly identified by Franz as Remigius of Auxerre) (*PL* 101, 1256), although the story itself is older (cf. Franz, pp. 627–628). Of the commentators discussed here, the story is repeated by John Beleth, the *Speculum de mysteriis ecclesiae* (*PL* 177, 368), Sicard of Cremona (*PL* 213, 125A), and Innocent III (*PL* 217, 840C–D).

30. Douteil, p. 82.

31. Douteil, p. 85. On the substitution of these practices for reception, see Macy, *Theologies of the Eucharist,* pp. 93–95 and Rubin, *Corpus Christi,* pp. 73–77.

32. A great deal of research has been done on Isaac of Étoile in recent years. The most valuable account of his life is contained in Gaetano Raciti, "Isaac de l'Étoile et son siècle," *Cîteaux* 12 (1961), 281–306; 13 (1962), 18–34, 133–145 and 205–216. This work has been corrected and criticized by Anselm Hoste, in the introduction to *Isaac de l'Étoile, Sermons, vol. 1 (Sources chrétiennes,* vol. 130, Paris, 1967), 7–25, and by Raciti himself in his article, "Isaac de l'Étoile," *DSAM* 7 (1971), 2011–2038. This last-mentioned article also contains a useful bibliography. Bernard McGinn summarizes this scholarship in *The Golden Chain, A Study of the Theological Anthropology of Isaac of Stella,* Cistercian Studies Series, no. 15 (Washington, DC, 1972).

33. See note 15 above.

34. Although the list is not complete, twenty-three manuscripts of Isaac's letter have been found, at least seven of which date from the twelfth century. They are listed by Raymond Milcamps, "Bibliographie d'Isaac de l'Étoile," *Collectanea ordinis cisterciensium reformatorum* 20 (1958), 180–182. Additions to this list have been made in a note by A. Hoste, *Cîteaux in de Nederlanden* 9 (1958), 302, and by G. Raciti, "Isaac de l'Étoile," *Cîteaux* 13 (1962), 216. Isaac's work was used by Robert Paululus and Innocent III in their commentaries on the Mass. For the dependence of Robert Paululus on Isaac, see Franz, *Die Messe,* pp. 441–442. Innocent seems to have borrowed from Isaac in discussing the different aspects of sacrifice necessary to offer worthily. Compare the text given in Wright, *A Medieval Commentary,* pp. 192–193 with the text from Isaac given in n. 33 below. According to Raciti, "Isaac de l'Étoile," *DSAM* 7: 2020, both the edition by Tissier (printed in *PL* 194, 1889–1896) and that of Luc d'Archery (*Spicilegium,* 3rd ed., Paris, 1723), vol. 1, pp. 449–451 are faulty. I have referred to the text in the *PL* simply because it is the most widely available, but there is clearly a need for a new edition of this work.

35. *PL* 194, 1889D–1890B.

36. Ibid., 1890D.

37. Ibid.

38. Ibid., 1891D–1892A.

39. Ibid., 1892A–B.

40. Ibid.

41. Ibid., 1893A–B.

42. Ibid., 1894B.

43. Ibid., 1894A–B.

44. Ibid., 1894C.

45. Ib:d., 1894D–1895A.

46. See n. 39 above.

47. See n. 45 above.

48. This work has long been misattributed; on the few facts known about this work and its author, see Gary Macy, "A Bibliographical Note."

49. See note 12 above.

50. *PL* 177, 455D. Once again for the sake of simplicity, I have used the text of this work edited by the canons of St. Victor in 1648 and reprinted in *PL* 177, 455–470.

51. Ibid., 457A.

52. Ibid., 458A–B.

53. Ibid., 461D.

54. Ibid., 462B–C.

55. Ibid., 463A.

56. Ibid., 465A.

57. Ibid.

58. Ibid., 467A.

59. "Unde miraculum istud contigit in Vivariensi ecclesia Praemonstratensis ordinis. Cum celebraretur missa in praefata ecclesia, quidam frater respiciens de choro ad altare uidit super illud circulum claritatis immense; et columbam miri candoris super calicem in eadem claritate. Coepit igitur admirari, et admirando intueri: et subito stupefactus et territus amisso uisu cecidit in chroro prostratus. Quem fratres ad manus deducentes, et euentus veritatem perquirentes; tandiu precibus institerunt donec ei Deus uisum restitueret." Ibid., 461B–C. The church at Viviers was one of the oldest Augustinian houses, the canons having replaced the secular clergy in 1124–1126 (cf. Norbert Backmund, *Monasticon Praemonstratense,* vol. II (Straubing, 1952), 537).

60. For a discussion of the original mistaken attribution of this work to Hugh of St. Victor, cf. Barthélemy Hauréau, *Les oeuvres de Hugues de Saint-Victor. Essai critique* (Paris, 1886), 199–203. Heinrich Weisweiler, "Zur

Einflussphäre der 'Vorlesungen' Hugos von St. Victor," *Mélanges Joseph de Ghellinck, S.J.* (Gembloux, 1951), 523–570, offers the best discussion of the work, demonstrating its dependence on the lectures of Hugh of St. Victor as preserved in the *reportatio* of Laurentius (Oxford, Bodleian Library MS. Laud. 344), on the *De Sacramentis,* and on the *Summa Sententiarum,* thus placing it clearly within the influence of the Victorine school. The author of the *Speculum* describes himself as more familiar with logic than theology: "Cum autem libentius, quia facilius et audentius, logicas quam theologas, jure consuetudinis, revolvam sententias: dubitare coepi, an contradicere, an potius scribere mallem" (*PL* 177, 335A).

61. The influence of the *Speculum* on Simon of Tournai has been traced by Damien van den Eynde, "Deux sources de la Somme théologique de Simon de Tournai," *Antonianum* 24 (1949), 19–42. The *Speculum* was also used by another commentary on the Mass, the *Tractatus de sacramento altaris* of Stephen of Autun (cf. n. 90 below). B. Hauréau, *Les ouvres,* pp. 201–202, lists fifteen manuscripts of this work. For references to research on this work, including a list of English manuscripts unknown to Hauréau, see Macy, *Theologies of the Eucharist,* p. 65 and note 120 of chapter three.

62. Damien van den Eynde, "Deux sources de la Somme théologique de Simon de Tournai," p. 41, and "Le Tractatus de sacramento altaris faussement attribué à Etienne de Baugé," *Recherches de Théologie ancienne et médievale* 19 (1952), 241, dates this work c. 1160. He takes as his *terminus post quem* the publication of the sentences of Peter Lombard (1153–1158) which the *Speculum* uses. Since the *Speculum* does not use John Beleth, nor any of the other later commentators, and since Beleth was such a popular work, van den Eynde argues that the *Speculum* was written before the appearance of Beleth's work (1160–1164). It would be safer, however, to date this work between the publication of Peter Lombard's work and that of Simon of Tournai, roughly 1160–1175. Again for simplicity, I have used the text printed in Migne, *PL* 177, 335–380.

63. *PL* 177, 361C.

64. Ibid.

65. Ibid., 361C–D.

66. "Pontifex olim intrabat in sancta sanctorum cum sanguinem semel in anno; et *Christus, per proprium sangiunem introiuit semel in sancta, aeterna redemptione inuenta.* Sic minister ecclesiae intrat cum sanguine in sancta sanctorum, quoties in mente memoriam sanguinis Christi gerens . . . " Ibid., 369B.

67. Ibid., 370A–C.

68. Ibid., 370C–371A.

69. "Communio, quae post cantatur, innuit omnes fideles corpori Christi communicare, quod pro omnibus minister assumit sacramentaliter, ut sibi et omnibus sumatur spiritualiter." Ibid., 373C.

70. "Sacramentalis autem communio est communis bonis et malis, quae sine spirituali non prodest." Ibid., 366A–B. Cf. Hugh of St. Victor, *De sacramentis christianae fidei,* 1.II, pars 8, c. 5 and c. 7 (*PL* 176, 465B–C, 467C–D). On spiritual communion in the twelfth century, see Macy, *Theologies of the Eucharist,* pp. 73–105.

71. *PL* 177, 365D.

72. "Spiritualis autem sumptio, quae vera fide percipitur, sine sacramentali, ubi non est contemptus religionis, sufficit." Ibid., 366B.

73. Ibid., 362A–B.

74. Ibid., 362B.

75. Although printed among the works of Hugh of St. Victor (*PL* 177, 381–456), this work has long been identified as a work of Master Robert Paululus, a priest at Amiens. The identification was made by Jean Mabillon and Luc d'Archéry, *Acta sanctorum ordinis S. Benedicti,* saeculum III, pars prima (Paris, 1672), lv. They refer to a manuscript of Corbie (now Paris, Bibliothèque Nationale Latin 11579), which attributes this work to Robert Paululus. They also refer to three charters of Corbie bearing the signature *Magister Robertus Paululus, minister Episcopi Ambianensi,* and dated 1174, 1179, and 1184. Robert refers to his own profession as that of a secular priest (1.I, c. 32, *PL* 177, 399C–D). The only manuscript of this work to which I have seen reference is Bibliothèque Nationale Latin 11579, and I know of no other author who borrows from Robert. E. Amann, "Robert Paululus," *DTC* 13, 2753, contains references to the few modern scholars who mention Paululus. To this list should be added Barthélemy Hauréau, *Les oeuvres de Hughes de Saint-Victor,* pp. 203–204. I have used the text printed in Migne, *PL* 177.

76. *PL* 177, 424D.

77. Franz, *Die Messe,* pp. 441–442, was the first to notice the dependence of Robert on Isaac.

78. *PL* 177, 425D–430A and 430A–435C.

79. "Vide ordinem: primo Deus panem et vinum creat per naturam. Eadem in altari oblata sanctificat per gratiam, per verba Actionis primae. Jam tunc enim ante sanctificationem sanctificata sunt et a communibus usibus separata. Deinde per sacra verba secundae Actionis sanctificata promovendo vivificat, dum ea in corpus et sanguinem Christi transubstantiat, et benedicit, dum eis summae benedictionis effectum tribuit, quae est in unitate capitis et membrorum, de qua tertia Actio meminit." Ibid., 433D–434A.

80. Ibid., 429A.

81. Ibid., 432A.

82. Ibid., 425B.

83. Ibid., 426C.

84. Ibid., 429B.

85. Ibid., 429D.

86. Ibid.

87. Ibid., 433A.

88. Ibid., 435A.

89. Ibid., 435B.

90. This work has received close textual study from Damien van den Eynde, "On the attribution of the *Tractatus de sacramento altaris* to Stephen of Baugé," *Franciscan Studies* 10 (1950), 33–45, and "Le Tractatus de sacramento altaris faussement attribué à Etienne de Baugé,: Recherches de Théologie ancienne et médiévale 19 (1952), 225–243. Van den Eynde dates this work from internal evidence c. 1180. I have found no references to known manuscripts of this work and have used the text printed in Migne (*PL* 172, 1274–1308).

91. *PL* 172, 1284C–D. As van den Eynde has pointed out ("Le *Tractatus de sacramento altaris,*" pp. 225–237), the author of the *Tractatus* depends heavily on the Speculum for his allegorical and doctrinal material.

92. *PL* 172, 1285C–D.

93. Ibid., 1286C.

94. Ibid., 1288A.

95. Ibid., 1288D.

96. Ibid., 1292B–C. Stephen's source here is Odo of Cambrai, *Expositi in canonem missae* (*PL* 160, 1060D–1061B).

97. *PL* 172, 1298C. For the entire passage on the offerings of the patriarchs, cf. ibid., 1298B–C.

98. Non est medium inter infernum ubi est damnatio, et coelum ubi est beatitudo et salus. Qui enim non damnantur, omnes salvari non dubitantur." Ibid., 1291A.

99. Ibid. 1287C–D and 1291C.

100. Ibid., 1297B–C.

101. Ibid., 1293A; cf. also 1294D.

102. Ibid., 1296D.

103. " . . . quis tenens in manibus Dominum suam pro se crucifixum et mortuum, quasi servus nequam et imemor beneficiorum contemnat quod morte sua conscripsit testamentum?" Ibid., 1295B.

104. The best study of the life and work of Sicard, bishop of Cremona, 1185–1215, is that of Ercole Brocchieri, "Sicard di Cremona e la sua opera letteraria," *Annali della bibliotheca governativa e libreria vivica di Cremona,* 11 (1958), fasc 1. He dates the work within the first ten years of Sicard's

episcopate. The *Mitrale* was certainly written after Sicard's *Summa Decretum,* written between 1179 and 1181 (cf. Charles Lefebvre, "Sicard de Cremone," *Dictionnaire de droit canonique* 7 (1965), 1009). Brocchieri, p. 72, argues that the *Mitrale* was written before the introduction by Sicard of the cult of St. Himerius (1196) and of St. Omnebonus (canonized in 1199), as the *Mitrale* makes no mention of these saints during Sicard's treatment of the feastdays of the church year. Charles Lefebvre, ibid., and Leonard Boyle, "Sicard of Cremona," *NCE* 13 (1967), 190, give the date of the composition of the Mitrale as 1200 but offer no support for this dating. Although no list of manuscripts exists for this work, Brocchieri, p. 73, mentions four manuscripts to which he has seen references. The only text available to me was that printed in *PL* 213, 14–434.

105. Cf. *PL* 213, 118B with Rupert of Deutz, *De divinis officiis,* edited by Rhaban Haacke, *Ruperti Tjuitiensis Liber de divinis officiis,* Corpus christianorum, Continuatio medievalis, 7 (Turnhout, 1967), 1.II, c. 22 (p. 54); 1, II, c. 9 (pp. 41–42 and 44).

106. William wrote a short letter to Rupert criticizing the eucharistic theology of the *De diuinis officiis* (printed in *PL* 180, 341–344). The two passages he takes issue with are both from 1.II, c. 9 and are quoted in part by Sicard. William insists that only the substance of the body and blood remain after the consecration and rejects Rupert's distinction between *uita spiritualis* and *uita animalis* as applied to the real presence. For an overview of this conflict, see Macy, *Theologies of the Eucharist,* pp. 66–67. A more complete discussion occurs in John van Engen, *Rupert of Deutz* (Berkeley: University of California Press, 1983).

107. *PL* 213, 129B–C. For the text in the *Speculum*, cf. ns. 73 and 74 above.

108. Ibid., 124C.

109. Ibid., 125B.

110. Ibid., 127B.

111. Ibid., 131A.

112. Ibid., 131C–D. Sicard's source here is probably Odo of Cambrai, not Stephen of Autun, cf. n. 92.

113. Ibid., 130C. Sicard copies Rupert of Deutz, 1.II (Haacke, pp. 45–46).

114. Ibid., 131B.

115. The best discussions of the work are Giuseppe Barbéro, *La dottrina eucharistica negli scritti di a papa Innocenzo III* (Rome, 1953), Michele Maccarone, "Innocenzo III teologo dell' Eucharistia," *Studi su Innocenzo III.* Italia sacra: Studi e documenti di storia ecclesiastica, vol. 17 (Padua, 1972), 340–431 and Wright, *A Medieval Commentary.* The title printed in Migne, *De sacro altaris mysterio,* is incorrect. Both Barbéro (p. 16, n. 26) and Maccarone

(pp. 334 and 371) describe the text as printed in *PL* 217, 765–916, as inadequate and Wright did not edit the section commenting on the Mass. I have provided references to this text, however, as the only printed edition currently available.

116. See n. 13 above.

117. *PL* 217, 831A.

118. Ibid., 839D–840C.

119. Ibid., 842A.

120. Ibid., 842D–843A. Innocent appears to have copied Isaac of Étoile (*PL* 194, 1892A–B), but changes *sacrificia intelligentiae* to *sacrificia eucharistiae*. Cf. n. 39 above.

121. Ibid., 883C–D.

122. Ibid., 885C.

123. Ibid., 894D.

124. Ibid., 851D.

125. Ibid., 893D–894A and 885A–B.

126. Ibid., 861C–D. On Innocent's basic approach to this issue, cf. Maccarone, pp. 366–370.

127. Ibid., 866C; 867C and 883A.

128. Ibid., 889C. This conclusion follows a long allegory explaining the sacrifices of Abel, Abraham, and Melchisedech as symbols of the offering of our lives to God. Innocent's source here is Sicard of Cremona, cf. n. 112 above.

129. Henri de Lubac in his monumental work, *Exégèse médiévale: Les quatre sens de l'ecriture* (Paris, 1959–1964) and his later work, *The Sources of Revelation,* translated by Luke O'Neill (New York, 1968) has urged the importance of spiritual exegesis in the Christian tradition: "Finally—and here again we have an important point—the spiritual meaning, understood as figurative or mystical meaning, is the meaning which, objectively, leads us to the realities of the spiritual life, and which, subjectively, can only be the fruit of a spiritual life" (*The Sources of Revelation,* p. 20). Pere de Lubac's insights have yet gone largely unheeded.

130. On the whole questions of the frequency of lay reception in the Middle Ages, see Peter Browe, *Die häufige Kommunion in Mittelalter* (Münster, 1938), 19–32; idem, *Die Pflichtkommunion in Mittelalter* (Münster und Regensberg, 1940), 34–40; Walter Durig, "Die Scholastiker und *due communio sub una specie,*" *Kyriakon. Festschrift Johannes Quasten,* ed. Patrick Granfield and Josef A. Jungmann (Münster, 1970), vol. 2, pp. 867–868 and Rubin, *Corpus Christi,* pp. 145–155.

131. For references to primary and secondary literature dealing with the general attitude discouraging frequent reception, see Macy, *Theologies of the Eucharist,* pp. 118–121 and Rubin, *Corpus Christi,* pp. 63–66.

132.   Macy, *Theologies of the Eucharist,* p. 120.

133.   Ibid., pp. 188–189, n. 149.

134.   ". . . institutem est ut ter in anno communicent: Natali, Pascha, Pentecoste, et utinam semel digne communicent!" *Mitrale,* 1, 3, c.. 8 (*PL* 213, 144B).

135.   On the question of excommunication in the Middle Ages, see F. Donald Logan, *Excommunication and the Secular Arm in Medieval England* (Toronto, 1968) and Elizabeth Vodola, *Excommunication in the Middle Ages* (Berkeley, 1986).

136.   See Browe, *Pflichtkommunion,* p. 14. See, for instance, c. 13 of the Council of Toulouse, 1229: "Nam si quis a communione, nisi de consilio proprii sacerdotis, abstinuerit, suspectus de haeresi habeatur." G.D. Mansi (ed), *Sacrorum onciliorum nova, et amplissima collectio* vol. 23, col. 197C.

137.   The text is given, and the issue discussed in Macy, *Theologies of the Eucharist,* pp. 120–121.

APPENDIX
A Tentative List of Commentaries on the
Mass Written 1060–1225

The following list of commentaries is certainly not exhaustive and excludes commentaries on the liturgy from this period which do not discuss the Mass. Since at present no similar guide exists, the following list is offered merely as a general aid for further research.

1. John of Avranches, *Liber de officiis ecclesiasticis,* written 1060–1068. Printed *PL* 147, 27–62; critical edition by R. Delamare, L*e De officiis ecclesiasticis de Jean d'Avranches* (Paris, 1923) with an introduction by P. Battifol. See J. Rjjousee, *Catholisme* 6 (1967), 527, and Guy Oury, *DSAM* 8 (1974), 283.

2. Bernold of Constance, *Micrologus de ecclesiasticis observationibus,* written c. 1073–1085. Printed *PL* 151, 979–995. See Fernand Cabrol, *DACL* 2 (1912), 817–820, Johanne Autenrieth, "Die Domschule von Konstanz zur Zeit des Investtiturstreits," *Forschungen zur Dirchen-und Geistesgeschichte,* n.f., 3 (Stuttgart, 1956). S. Robinson, "Zur Arbeitwsweise Bernolds von Constance und seines Kreises," *Deutsches Archiv* 34 (1978), and idem, *DMA* 2 (1983), 197.

3. Bonizo of Sutri, *Libellus de sacramentis,* written c. 1084–1099. Printed *PL* 150, 857–866. L. Jadin, *DHGE* 9 (1937), 994–998, and T. Schieffer, *LThK* 2 (1958), 597.

4. Ivo of Chartres, *Sermo de convenientia veteris et novi sacrificii,* written c. 1090–1115. Printed *PL* 162, 55351–562. See E. Amann and L. Guizard, *DTC* 15 (1950), 3633–3634, R. Sprandel, *Ivo von Chartres und seine Stellung in der Kirchengeschichte* (Stuttgart, 1962), and Roger E. Reynolds, Ívonian *Opuscula on the Ecclesiastical Officers,"* *Studia Gratiana, Mèlanges Gèrard Fransen II,* 20 (1976).

5. *De sacrificio missae,* wrongly attributed to Alger of Liège. Edited Ronald J. Zawilla, *The Sentenia Ivonis Carnontensis Episcopi de Divinis Officiis: Text and Study* (dissertation, Toronto, 1982). Older editions exist in *PL* 180, 853–56 and H. Hurter, *Sanctorum, patrum opuscula selecta,* vol. 23

(Innsbruck, 1872), 371–77. See *DTC* 1, 828, *DHGE* 2, 423f., *DMA* 7 (1986), 631.

6. Odo of Cambrai, *Expositio in canonen missae,* written c. 1095–1113. Printed *PL* 160, 1053D–1054D. See E. Amman, *DTC* 11 (1931), 932–9251.d and Tullio Gregory, *Platismo medievale: Studi e richerche,* Istituto storico italiano per il medio evo, Studi storici, 26–27 (Rome, 1958), 31–51.

7. Rupert of Deutz, *De divinis officiis,* written in 1111. Critically edited by Rhaban Haacke, *Ruperti Tjuitiensis Liber de divinis officiis,* Corpus christianorum, Continuatio medievalis, 7 (Turnhout, 1967). See Wolfgang Beinert, *Die Kirche-Gottes Heil in der Welt: Die Lehre von der Kirche nach den Schriften des Rupert von Deutz, Honorius Augustodunensis und Gerhoh von Reichersberg. Ein Beitrag zur Eklesiologie des 12. Jahrhunderts,* Beiträge zur Geschichte der Philosophie und Theologie des Mittelalter, Texte und Untersuchungen, 13 (Münster, 1973), John van Engen, *Rupert of Deutz* (Berkeley, 1983), and Michael McCormick, *DMA* 10 (1988), 570–1.

8. Hildebert of Lavardin, *De mysterio misse,* written c. 1110–1130. Critical edition and discussion of Hildebert's work occurs in A.B. Scott, *A Critical Edition of the Poems of Hildebert of Lavardin* (Oxford, Bodleian Library, MS.D.Phil. d. 2403). See W.T.H. Jackson, *DMA* 6 (1985), 225–7.

9. Petrus Pictor, *De sacra eucharistia,* written c. 1102–1130. Printed *PL* 171, 1198–1212 and *PL* 207, 1135–1154. See E. Amann, *DTC* 12 (1935), 2036–2037, and B.J. Comasky, *NCE* 11, 226–227.

10. Honorius Augustodunensis, *Gemma anima,* written c. 1102–1133. Printed *PL* 172, 541–738. Idem, *Sacramentarius*, written c. 1102–1133. Printed *PL* 172, 737–806. See Gary Macy, *The Theologies of the Eucharist in the Early Scholastic Period: A Study of the Salvific Function of the Sacrament According to the Theologians c. 1080–c. 1220* (Cambridge, 1984), 65, 223–24, and Janice L. Schulte, *DMA* 6 (1985), 285–6.

11. Gerhoh of Reichersberg, *Expositio super canonem,* written c. 1135–1140. Critical edition by Damien and Odulf van den Eynde and Angelino Rijmerdael, *Gerhohij praepositi Reichersbergensis Opera inedita,* vol. 1,

Tractatus et libelli, Spicilegium pontificii athenaei antoniani, 8 (Rome, 1955), 3–61. See Peter Classen, *Gerhoh von Reichersberg. Eine Biographie mit einem Anhang über die Quellen, ihre handschriftliche Überlieferung und ihre Chronologie* (Wiesbaden, 1960) and Josef Szövérfly, *DMA* 5 (1985), 424–5.

12. William of Malmesbury, *Abbrevatio* of Amalarius' *De ecclesiasticis officiis,* written before 1143. Unpublished. Mentioned in Dom Hugh Farmer, "William of Malmesbury's Life and Works," *Journal of Ecclesiastical History* 13 (1962), 50–51. On William, see Mary Lynn Rampolla, *DMA* 12 (1989), 639–40.

13. Hervé de Bourg-dieu, *Expositio missae,* written before 1153. Unpublished. Mentioned by B. Hauréau, *Histoire littéraire du Maine,* vol. 6 (Paris, 1873), 106–116. See Guy Oury, *DSAM* (1969), 373–375.

14. Gilbert of La Porrée, *Instructiones circa divinum officium,* written before 1154. Unpublished. Mentioned by H.C. Van Elswijk, *Gilbert Porreta. Sa Vie, son oeuvre, sa pensée* (Leuven, 1966), 44. On Gilbert, see Joseph R. Stayer, *DMA* 5 (1985), 528.

15. Richard the Premonstratensian, *Sermo in canone misse,* written c. 1150–1175. Printed *PL* 177, 455–470. See Gary Macy, "A Bibliographical Note on Richardus Premonstratensia," *Analecta premonstratensia* 52 (1976), 64–69.

16. John Beleth, *Summa de ecclesiasticis officiis,* written c. 1160–1165. Critically edited and discussed by Heribert Douteil, *Iohannis Beleth Summa de ecclesiasticis officiis,* Corpus christianorum, Continuatio mediaevalis, 41 (Turnholt, 1976).

17. Isaac of Stella, *De Officio missae,* c. 1162–1167. Printed *PL* 194, 1889–1896. Gaetano Raciti, "Isaaac de l'Étoile et son siècle," *Cîteaux* 12 (1961), 281–306, 13 (1962), 18–34, 133–145 and 205–216; Anselm Hoste, *Isaac de l'Etoile, Sermons,* vol. 1 (Sources Chrétiennes, vol. 130) (Paris, 1967), 7–25, Raciti, "Isaac de l'Étoile," *DSAM* 7 (1971), 2011–2038, and Bernard McGinn, *The Golden Chain, A Study of the Theological Anthropology of Isaac of Stella* (Cistercian Studies Series, n15) (Washington, DC, 1972). The *De officio missae* has been translated by C.W. Boyle, *De Officio Missae. The Epistle of Isaac of Stella to John*

Bishop of Poitiers. Translation and Commentary (Washington, DC, 1963).

18. *Speculum ecclesiae,* written c. 1160–1175. Printed *PL* 177, 335–380. For references to research on this work including a list of known English manuscripts, see Macy, *Theologies of the Eucharist,* p. 65 and note 120 of chapter three.

19. Stephen II of Autun, *Tractatus de sacramento altaris,* written c. 1170–1189. Printed *PL* 172, 1274–1308. Damien van den Eynde, "On the attribution of the *Tractatus de sacramento altaris* to Stephen of Baugé," *Franciscan Studies* 10 (1950), 33–45, and idem, "Le *Tractatus de sacramento altaris* faussement attribué à Étienne de Baugé," *Recherches de Théologie ancienne et médiévale* 19 (1952), 225–243.

20. Robert Paululus, *De officiis ecclesiasticis,* written c. 1175–1180. Printed *PL* 177, 381–456. See E. Amann, *DTC* 13 L (1937), 753, and B. Hauréau, *Les oeuvres de Hughes de Saint-Victor. Essai critique,* 2nd edition (Paris, 1886), 203–204.

21. Sicard of Cremona, *Mitrale,* written c. 1185–1195. Edited *PL* 213, 14–434. Ercole Brocchieri, "Sicard di Cremona e la sua opera letteraria," *Annali della bibliotheca governativa e libreria vivica di Cremona,* vol. 11 (1958), fasc. 1, Charles Lefebvre, "Sicard de Cremone," *Dictionnaire de droit canonique* 7 (1965), 1009, and Leonard Boyle, "Sicard of Cremona," *NCE* 13 (1967), 190.

22. Innocent III (Lothar of Segni), *De missarum mysteriis,* written c. 1195. Critical edition of the majority of this work plus a critical discussion in David Frank Wright, *A Medieval Commentary on the Mass: Particulae 2–3 and 5–6 of the De missarum mysteriis (c. 1195) of Cardinal Lother of Segni (Pope Innocent III)* (Ph.D. thesis, University of Notre Dame, August 1977). On Innocent, see S.C. Ferruolo, *DMA* 6 (1985), 464–5.

23. Peter of Roissy, *Manuale de mysteriis ecclesia,* written c. 1208–1213. Unpublished. See V.L. Kennedy, "The Handbook of Master Peter Chancellor of Chartres," *Mediaeval Studies* 5 (1943), 1–38.

24. William of Auxerre, *De officiis ecclesiasticis,* written c. 1215–1225. Unpublished. See R.M. Martineau, "La 'Summa de officiis

ecclesiasticis' de Guillaume d'Auxerre," *Études d'histoire littéraire et doctrinale du XIIe siècle,* 2ème serie 2 (1932), 25–58.

READING THE WORD IN A EUCHARISTIC CONTEXT: THE SHAPE AND METHODS OF EARLY MEDIEVAL EXEGESIS

Marie Anne Mayeski

The liturgy was the primary context within which medieval Christians heard, read and understood the Bible. It is not surprising, then, that the liturgical context shaped significantly the process, methods and style of biblical interpretation throughout the Middle Ages. The structure of both the Eucharist and the Liturgy of the Hours impelled the exegete to read the biblical text with certain important presuppositions. The existence of a real worshipping community, often enough known to the interpreter, provided a concrete audience for his exegesis. The literary genre of the "homily," created by the traditional dynamics of the eucharistic action, imposed its own constraints and requirements, even as it provided an important and unique format for composing the fruits of one's exegetical efforts. It is clear at the outset that these liturgical elements and their formative influence on biblical interpretation were not new to, nor created by, the practitioners of the Middle Ages. In this, as in so much else, medieval exegetes were the grateful inheritors of Christian antiquity. But their dependence on inherited structures and traditional wisdom must not blind us to the importance of reconsidering these constitutive elements of earlier exegesis in their medieval context. For too long, unexamined generalizations about medieval exegesis as merely derivative and as dominated by allegorical extravagance have permitted a most interesting body of exegetical work to remain in obscurity. This in spite of the good foundational work done by Beryll Smalley, Robert E. McNally, Jean LeClercq, and Henri de Lubac.[1] Happily, the situation is changing. Works previously available only in the Migne edition are appearing in new, critical editions (the *Corpus*

Christianorum series is invaluable) and in good English translations.[2] Finally, interpretive and analytical works are now bringing to scholarly attention the important contributions of medieval exegetes.[3]

However, as yet, little attention has been paid to the formative influence of the liturgy on medieval exegesis, an oversight which I hope to begin to remedy here. In this essay, I shall limit myself to exploring the influence of the eucharistic liturgy, principally that part of the eucharistic liturgy now called the "Liturgy of the Word," upon biblical interpretation in the Middle Ages.[4] That liturgy, common to monastic and lay communities, contributed significantly in its structure and in its setting to the most common methods of interpreting the sacred text. In the structure of the Eucharist, medieval exegetes found the important principle of typology, foundational to all applied exegesis, embedded in the lectionary system of readings. They also found the method of concordant allusion, the process by which scripture is used to interpret itself, in the entire structure of the Liturgy of the Word, not only in the selection of primary readings, but, most importantly, in the use of the *graduale* psalms. In the homily, central to the liturgy of the word from the time of Justin Martyr, the medieval exegete discovered not only an appropriate genre for expressing exegetical conclusions but also a mandate for applying the liturgical readings to the present situation of the worshipping community. Finally, as the Liturgy of the Word moved inexorably to its enactment in the sacramental rite of thanksgiving offered and accepted, the medieval interpreter found a model for moving from word to action, from the privilege of hearing the word to the necessity of doing it.

The lectionary system, with its selection of matching texts, was, perhaps, the most important formative element in medieval exegesis. The history of the development of the lectionary system is the subject of many fine studies,[5] and I shall not concern myself with that history here. Whatever subtle twists and turns mark that history, however important regional differences may be to its understanding and whatever the criteria by which choices were made over a long period of time,[6] the existence of the lectionary system was a hermeneutical given by the late classical period and, certainly, by the Middle Ages. This meant, first, that they were drawn toward a typological interpretation suggested by the companion readings and, second, that they often shaped their interpretation to the seasonal context. Undoubtedly, the typological interpretation of scripture remains the most significant exegetical consequence of the lectionary system.

Much attention has been paid to the allegorical interpretation of scripture so beloved of medieval interpreters. Bearing the authority of Paul, Origen and, especially, Gregory the Great, allegory did, of course, play a central role in the way in which medieval writers read the biblical text. But what modern exegetes generally describe as "allegory" is often a more complex reality than is always recognized; the classical authorities beloved of the medievals bequeathed a multi-faceted legacy.[7] Augustine's insistence on the superiority of the spiritual sense over the literal was honored, but the commentaries of Jerome were much read, and they frequently exposed the historical reality of the places and situations within the biblical texts. In his *Historia Ecclesiastica*, the Venerable Bede introduces us to the work of one Adamnan, an Irish abbot and scholar, who wrote a book which Bede much valued on the places of the Holy Land. Not only does he include excerpts from Adamnan in his own history; he takes pains to witness to their authenticity, based as they are on the descriptions of Arculf, a bishop of Gaul who had traveled to the Holy Land, and he indicates their usefulness for "those who live at a great distance from the places where the patriarchs and Apostles lived, and whose only source of information about them lies in books."[8] Bede clearly values this book for more than its entertainment value; for him, it is the work of a man "grounded in the knowledge of the scriptures."[9] Bede's comments suggest that Jerome's own respect for the Holy Land and the resultant historical meaning of the scriptures continued into Bede's generation and beyond. Gregory the Great had made the search for four levels of meaning in the scriptural text a commonplace of the medieval method, but typology was the foundation of all allegory and pervaded the interpretations of the best medieval exegetes. Typology was both the basis for some of the more important and most ancient choices of readings in the lectionary system and a result of understanding those readings within the context of the lectionary.

Typology is a method by which Old Testament events are seen as types or figures of the work of Christ; more than that, it reflects a theological understanding of salvation as enacted and revealed in history.[10] The typological imagination sees in the events and persons in the history of Israel patterns which anticipate the fullness of salvation brought by Christ and worked out within the life of the early faith communities. This is the kind of interpretation which allowed the church to understand the preparatory work of God in history and to set up, for example, the concatenation of Old Testament readings for the Easter Vigil, all of which are seen to be most fully realized in both the resurrection of Christ, celebrated at the Vigil, and in Christian baptism, therein accomplished.

In its liturgical context, typology has three terms: 1) prefigurement; 2) fulfillment; and 3) actualization in the worshipping community. The salvation that was prefigured in Old Testament event and fully *expressed* in the New was made actual in the readings and rituals of the particular believing community assembled for liturgical worship. Jean Danielou, S.J. points out the essential connection between these three terms.

> But these eschatological times [in which O.T. figures are fulfilled] are not only those of the life of Jesus, but of the Church as well. Consequently the eschatological typology of the Old Testament is accomplished not only in the person of Christ, but also in the Church. Besides Christological typology, therefore, there exists a sacramental typology . . . this means furthermore that the sacraments carry on in our midst the *mirabilia*, the great works of God in the Old Testament and the New. . . . [11]

A typological understanding of liturgical texts and action gathers the later Christian community, when assembled for sacred action, into the full flow of salvation history since liturgy is concerned with the immediate appropriation of the sacred realities attested to by the texts. Inasmuch as liturgical action is prepared for and completed by Christian life outside the assembly, it was an easy step to view all of life itself as part of the panoramic flow of salvation history. Historical typology, particularly as experienced in a liturgical context, collapses to some degree the hermeneutical distance between the reader and the world of the biblical text; the world of past salvific events becomes, not just a moral ideal to be striven for but a present reality to be embraced. Thus typology, especially as nuanced by liturgical reading of the texts, helps to form the theological basis for understanding the biblical text within the specific context of one's own life and history. Liturgical or sacramental typology requires that one take human history very seriously indeed and the understanding of salvation as history is not limited to its past expressions for it is the continual ground for both human existence and divine activity. Though this understanding was particularly important within the monastic tradition where liturgical reading and personal reading were intimately intertwined, it was also a critical element in all of the exegesis of the early medieval period. The scripture was, on the one hand, the expression of the full mystery of salvation (understood within the ecclesial community); on the other hand, the reading of scripture, whether in liturgical assembly or privately, was the occasion of the deep encounter with that mystery in personal experience, the condition of its understanding.

Historical typology, understood in its liturgical context, is the warp of medieval biblical exegesis. Examples of it are everywhere. Lawrence T. Martin has, for instance, documented the centrality of typological exegesis in Bede; he notes that Bede made full use of typological patterns already standardized in his day (such as that of the Hebrew temple as a type of the church). On the other hand, Martin considers "Bede's practice of reading New Testament events as types or figures of events in the history of the church"[12] a more original strategy, one designed "to bridge the gap between the world of the gospel story and the world of his listeners."[13] A good example of this is to be found in Bede's analysis of the story of the Syro-Phoenician woman,[14] an interpretation which he finds in Jerome's *Commentary on St. Matthew* but to which he gives his own twist. Following Jerome, Bede says that the woman is a "type" of the church, but in the light of his own historical situation he nuances her typological significance in a way that brings it close to his own concrete circumstances. She is the church gathered from the nations ("ecclesiam designat de gentibus collectam," 1368–69),[15] and therefore a type, specifically, of his own particular church, that gathered from the *gentis anglorum.* Bede underlines the importance of the woman's move beyond her own borders. This makes her not only "ecclesia" but also "evangelista" who leaves her own land in order to save her people. One thinks immediately of the closing book of his *Historia ecclesiastica gentis anglorum* in which Bede demonstrates the maturity of the English church by their sending of missionaries to the people of Saxony to whom they were related. Perhaps he is even thinking specifically about such women as Bertha, Queen of Kent, who left Christian Gaul to marry Ethelbert and whose prayerful Christian presence anticipated and prepared the ground for the missionary activity of Augustine of Canterbury. Original or not, this reading of the New Testament text in terms of later historical experience gives new depth to the "historical meaning" of the text and demonstrates the way in which typology founded Bede's exegesis.

A similar use of typology, which brings New Testament events and figures to the interpretation of the Old and the experiences of the worshipping community to the illumination of both, can be found abundantly in the twelfth-century homilies of the Cistercian fathers. An example from Aelred of Rievaulx, countryman of Bede, can demonstrate this. In a homily for the feast of the Assumption,[16] Aelred sets up a traditional typological connection between Abraham and Mary. Both have left land and family to follow God into the story of salvation. Abraham is the man of faith and obedience whose story is the beginning of salvation, and Mary is the woman who, by a similar if more exalted faith and obedience initiates the full story of salvation, the inheritance of the promise given to Abraham. What is important for Aelred the Abbot is that the dynamics of grace that are expressed in the stories of Abraham and Mary are also to be found in the monastic community. Like Abraham, they leave all things to follow the will of God and like Jesus, son of Mary, this initial leaving brings them to the fullness of self-sacrifice. Monks who, as Aelred says, have read the whole story withhold nothing from God, sacrificing all self-will even as Abraham was willing to sacrifice his son and Christ, the best son of a truly faithful mother, was indeed sacrificed, in her presence and with her full acceptance.[17] Abraham is the first in a long line of those who believe and who follow; Mary takes her place in this line, followed by all who have come after in the story of salvation, including Aelred and his monks. For Aelred, as for Bede, typology not only serves to interpret the Old Testament texts but to open up the meaning of the lectionary readings to the contemporaneous situation of the worshipping community.

With Aelred and his Cistercian brothers, we are at the full expression of what Jean LeClercq calls the "phenomenon of reminiscence whereby the verbal echoes so excite the memory that a mere allusion will spontaneously evoke whole quotations and, in turn, a scriptural phrase will suggest quite naturally allusions elsewhere in the sacred books."[18] Quite clearly, this phenomenon is an almost inevitable outcome of the lectionary system itself, in which the connection between two quite separate texts has been consciously organized. Yet it was reinforced by other elements, inside the liturgical tradition and outside of it, that were also important legacies of Christian antiquity to the medieval exegesis. From within the liturgy of the word, the practice of the *graduale* psalm played an important role in creating an exegetical method of echo and allusion.

Although brief references to the practice of using a psalm as a transition between two readings in the liturgy of the word can be found earlier, the prominent use of psalms in the eucharistic liturgy begins, according to Josef Jungmann, in the third century, just as the popularity of privately composed hymns declines.[19] The earliest description which we have of the liturgy of the word, that of Justin Martyr in the *First Apology*,[20] makes no mention of a psalm. According to Jungmann, Hippolytus of Rome (d. 236) mentions a psalm at the beginning of the *agape* to which the people shall repeatedly respond "alleluia," and in *De fuga* c. 24, Athanasius describes a deacon reciting a psalm to which the people respond in responsorial style. By the fourth century, according to the testimony of the *Apostolic Constitutions*, Augustine and Chrysostom, the psalm has a more or less consistent place within the liturgy of the word and was usually sung in responsorial style with a cantor singing all the verses and the people responding with a repeated refrain.[21] Augustine's practice makes clear that the Psalm could be treated as an independent text and made the subject of the homily; he himself sometimes chose the psalm. But the trajectory of psalm selection seems to have been toward using the psalm to echo the narrative or prophetic readings. Among the few early references mentioned above, the comment by Athanasius (c. 296–373) is suggestive. Since, in fact, we do not yet seem to know through exactly what influences the psalm, as *transitional* text, enters into the liturgy of the word, a small text of Athanasius (which Jungmann does not mention and which is not often commented upon), seems to supply a possible theological rationale for such usage. In the "Letter to Marcellinus,"[22] Athanasius writes to someone, possibly a deacon, in the church at Alexandria, who is specifically looking for the practical theology to be found in the psalms. Athanasius proposes the psalms as a kind of hermeneutic key by which the essential teaching of various Old Testament books could be best understood and through which the meaning of other, specifically Old Testament, texts could be appropriated by those who heard them. Though he occasionally raises allegorical possibilities for interpreting the psalms in this text, Athanasius is here most concerned to show how the Psalter relates to the rest of the scripture and under what concrete circumstances a particular psalm can most appropriately be prayed or sung. He develops in some detail the way in which the psalms speak of Christ, but he makes two other points as well which seem to illuminate the use of the psalms in the Liturgy of the Word. He develops the idea, first of all, that the psalms are essentially a *summary* of all of the Old Testament books in song. While "each sacred book supplies and announces its own promise," Athanasius says, enumerating the deeds of the patriarchs, the possession of the land, the construction of the temple and so forth, "the Book of Psalms is like a garden containing things of all these kinds, and it sets them to music. . . " (101–102). He thus posits the Book of Psalms as a kind of melodic recapitulation of the entire story of salvation, a culminating refrain by which one may repeat biblical themes and praise the God who acts in the narratives. This makes the psalms a hermeneutic key for interpreting the Bible as a whole, not simply in its Christological (allegorical) meaning but also in its historical sense. Put another way, the psalms illuminate and clarify what happened in the history of salvation, not only the way in which that history points to Christ.

Secondly, Athanasius describes the particular power that the Book of Psalms has for the spiritual life of the Christian, in his/her own concrete circumstances. Thus, for Athanasius, the use of the psalms in the Liturgy of the Word not only supplements the typological interpretation of all of the selected readings but is important for the personal application of the text to the life-experience of the one who sang them. His own words say it best and merit a somewhat lengthy citation:

> There is also this astonishing thing in the psalms. In the other books,
> those who read what the holy ones say, and what they might say
> concerning certain people, are relating the things that were written
> about those earlier people. And likewise, those who listen consider
> themselves to be other than those about whom the passage speaks, so
> that they only come to the imitation of the deeds that are told to the
> extent that they marvel at them and desire to emulate them. By

contrast, however, he who takes up this book—the Psalter—goes through the prophecies about the Savior, as is customary in the other scriptures, with admiration and adoration, but the other psalms he recognizes as being his own words. And the one who hears is deeply moved, as though he himself were speaking, and is affected by the words of the songs, as if they were his own songs. (109)

Athanasius speaks of what he considers a particular contemporaneity of the psalms, their ability to reflect the particular circumstances and emotions of whoever sings them. They thus provide a powerful link between the historical narrative of salvation and the individual life of later Christians; they allow the Christian to understand her own life in terms of the larger story and to envision its possibilities in biblical terms. Whether or not, this particular text of Athanasius was influential in promoting the use of the psalms as a meditative response upon lectionary readings taken from the Old Testament, there is little doubt that later exegetes used the assigned psalm in this way. Further, the thought of Athanasius certainly reinforces the use of scripture to interpret scripture through linguistic echo and allusion.

Augustine played a role in this development (as in virtually all other exegetical work) as well. In a short chapter from the *De doctrina christiana*, a book which became the educational charter of the Middle Ages, Augustine describes a simple method for studying the scriptures appropriate to the growing number among his readers for whom Latin was a second language and who would have had to struggle with the language of the biblical text before they confronted its theology. The text to which I refer is contained in Book II, Chapter 9 of the *DDC*.[23] It is a short passage and a dense one. As Augustine describes it, the first step of the beginner's study is to know all of the books contained in the Catholic canon, both Old and New Testaments. Augustine intends for his students to memorize the complete biblical text as far as possible. "Although we may not yet understand them, nevertheless, by reading them we can either memorize them or become somewhat acquainted with them."[24] It is only by knowing the text from memory that the student can do what Augustine recommends throughout this chapter of the *DDC*, to move, in their own minds, from passage to passage with great ease, hearing the verbal echoes of one text in another and thereby able to have almost a concordance of texts in their memory. Concerned about their inability to read the language of the bible, even in available Latin translations, Augustine recommends, in Chapter 14 of Book II, that students keep a running list of unknown words in their minds so that when they meet the word again, in another place, the new context might give them its meaning.

For Augustine, one learned the language of the bible by studying the usage of words in all of its various contexts; one learned the *meaning* of the text in the same way. The student begins with those texts which are more easily understood, those which contain "rules, governing either life or belief"[25]; presumably these are either more obvious in the text itself and/or are understood because they are central to Christian life and have been explained by the church. These rules, which include both credal formulae and moral codes, must be "studied more intelligently and more attentively" because such study leads to "discernment."[26] When discernment is gained, the student can turn to the more obscure passages of scripture. Now a "certain intimacy with the language of the Holy scriptures" will enable her to understand obscure passages more easily and the wisdom achieved from studying and practicing the rules of faith and life will "remove the uncertainty from doubtful passages."[27] Again Augustine notes that in this total process of appropriating the scriptures, the memory is crucial. The method of letting one piece of scriptural text explain the meaning of another will not work at all well if the texts themselves have not been committed to memory.[28] That Augustine worked this way himself is clear. His own expositions on the psalms, to cite only one example, often read as if he were working from a modern concordance; an important word in one text is explained by its context in other passages. Obviously intended for private study, these recommendations of Augustine were incorporated into all the methods of biblical interpretation: the *lectio divina* of the monastic tradition as well as the more scholarly exegesis which comes down to us in the commentary and homily traditions. Pick up any text of medieval exegesis and you find the "phenomenon of reminiscence and allusion."

We have already noted above that liturgical typology was essentially sensitive to the situation and the needs of its audience, the worshipping community. For classical and medieval exegetes alike, the biblical texts were not completely understood unless their fulfillment in the Christian community was part and parcel of the exegesis. The position of the homily in the Liturgy of the Word, present (at least in theory) from the time of Justin Martyr, reinforced this principle and expressed it. It was a genre created by the liturgical context and directed specifically to the pastoral needs of the liturgical community; the prominence of homilies among the writings of Christian antiquity testifies to the importance of this literary genre in the development of biblical interpretation. The *corpus* of Gregory the Great, great transmitter of patristic thought, indicates that the homily did not lose importance during the transition to the Middle Ages[29] and Bede's collection of fifty *Homilies on the Gospels* was, along with his commentaries, the basis of his significant reputation in his own day and for centuries afterward. Henri Barre has documented the resurgence of the homily during the Carolingian period.[30] Charlemagne himself requested that Paul the Deacon compile for him a collection of readings, taken from the *Patrum dicta*, to accompany the lectionary readings for each day of the liturgical cycle and thus initiated a new and lively interest in the traditional form. Barre notes the abundant homiliary material which dates from this period; "hundreds" of homiliaries are to be found in the libraries, he says, and he describes those collections he considers most important. According to Barre, Carolingian homiliaries are distinguished in at least two important ways. They were principally designed for the *spiritual reading* of those who commissioned them; rarely did they reflect an actual preaching situation. They were also largely derivative. Gathered from whatever patristic material was available to the collector, they generally demonstrate his originality only in the ways in which the collection is organized, in which epistle and gospel are considered (separately or in connection with one another) or in which deletions or editorial comments are made. At the same time, like the exegetical work modestly accomplished in Carolingian commentaries, they are marked by their concern for the pastoral needs of the recipient; the pastoral point to which the earlier homily impelled biblical interpretation endures in the Carolingian variation. As John J. Contreni says of all Carolingian exegesis, "It was the desire to teach, to introduce the Bible to the educated layman or laywoman, to the busy ecclesiastical administrator, and to the beginning student that mattered most."[31]

Though Carolingian homilies may be distinguished from their antecedents in Christian antiquity, little or no distinction exists between

the *kind of exegesis* one finds in both homily and commentary in the
Middle Ages (or indeed in many of the earlier exegetes). The same
methods are used in both; the same practical and pastoral intention is
evident, whatever the literary form. In the homily, to be sure, there is
most likely some attention to both the major readings of the lectionary,
while in commentaries the major trajectory of interpretation follows
sequentially the text of a single book. But, even here, with the method
of concordant allusion so predominant in all writers, a wide variety of
other texts are integrated into the interpretation of a single book. One
need only search the footnotes of a critical edition or good translation
of Bernard of Clairvaux's *Commentary on the Song of Songs*, for
instance, to identify the wide variety of other texts with which Bernard
explains the meaning of that book of wisdom.[32] An earlier author,
Alcuin of York, exemplifies the same tendency (if less prolifically) in
his commentary on the Epistle to Titus. In commenting on the
requirements for a bishop in Titus, Alcuin quotes Lev 10:8 and Num 6:
2–5 (on abstention from wine and strong drink) to support the
recommendation that the bishop not be a drunkard; he cites 1 Tim 6:8
and 1 Cor 9:13 to gloss the injunction that he not be greedy for gain.[33]
So that, although a *commentary* (as distinct from a homily) in some
way followed the text of a single biblical book, all medieval exegesis
followed similar patterns of intertextuality and all was structured to the
needs and situation of a particular audience, present or envisioned. The
liturgical context was foundational to all biblical exegesis and
contributed to its universal practical and pastoral character.[34]

Even in those Carolingian homilies composed or collected
primarily for *reading*, the audience is often envisioned as a liturgical
community gathered in the act of worship. A particular homily of Paul
the Deacon is instructive here. In a homily for the feast of the
Assumption found in his collection for the sanctoral cycle and dating
from about 770[35], Paul gives a lengthy treatment of Mary's many
privileges, her position in the economy of salvation and her special role
as mediator for the Christian community. Then he moves to an
exhortation where he describes the kind of Christian response which the
mystery of the Assumption requires of the faithful. Already in the
paragraphs on Mary's mediation, Paul was careful to affirm that she
cannot be an intermediary if the faithful do not deplore and detest their
sins; this is repeated in the exhortation, where he describes a very

traditional conversion of life as the sign of true devotion to Mary. At the same time, this conversion of life is described in terms particular to the *liturgical celebration* of the feast. Thus while the feast of the Assumption becomes the occasion for conversion of life, the various aspects of festal celebration become a metaphor for understanding what that conversion specifically entails. As Mary is raised up to be Queen of Heaven, the first obligation of those devoted to her is to rejoice and to celebrate. Paul has a deeply liturgical sense of Christian life: to fully grasp and respond to the story of salvation and its present reality in one's life means, first of all, to rejoice, to celebrate, to praise. The vocation of Baptism is primarily the call to stand in the assembly of the faithful, to anticipate participation in the celestial liturgy described in the Book of Revelation and already a reality for Mary, whose assumption into that liturgy is the occasion for the present celebration. Moral and practical responses, true conversion of life, follow from, and are dependent upon, the initial obligation of worship and praise. Paul describes the activities of moral conversion as the ways of preparing for the feast, ways of cleansing and dressing oneself, as it were, in a manner that fits the occasion. He paints a word picture of a very important matron, the hostess of a significant banquet, indignant when she is dishonored by a servant inappropriately attired and daring to serve with dirty hands.[36] Undoubtedly behind these descriptions of festal preparations, necessary for both liturgical and secular celebrations and here used as metaphors for conversion, lie the rituals of hospitality familiar to the aristocratic and royal persons for whom Paul is writing. The only way to celebrate the liturgical festival, he says, is to love justice and hate iniquity because "unseemly is praise upon a sinner's lips" (Sir 15:9) and "special foods, no matter how deliciously prepared, cannot be pleasing if they are offered on dirty dishes."[37] The practicalities of daily living and the moral obligations of the Christian are thus clearly connected to the liturgical life and, in particular, to this feast honoring the queen of heaven.

A similar liturgical context is acknowledged by Bede in his commentary on the Syro-Phoenician woman, referred to above. In his concluding thought on that pericope, Bede interprets the woman's intercession for her daughter in an explicitly liturgical context, seeing a justification for infant baptism in the fact that the woman's faith brought about the exorcism of the daughter. So too, he says, can the confession of faith on the part of the parents in baptism free small children from the devil.[38]

In the structure of the eucharistic liturgy, the liturgy of the readings is fulfilled and completed by the liturgy of the bread and wine. Word flowers into liturgical action, and the homily was meant to effect the transition from one to the other, from reading into action. The understanding that the sacred scriptures were only understood when they were performed was central to medieval exegesis. First of all, reading itself was considered "action." The words were pronounced aloud, heard as well as seen and, as Jean LeClercq reminds us, the result was "a muscular memory of the words pronounced and an aural memory of the words heard."[39] The parallel between the scriptural text and the bread and wine, set up by the liturgical structure, was consistently reinforced by exegetical references to the "eating" or "chewing" of the Word of God; the wisdom of the "Bread of Life" was to be "tasted" and "savored." Again quoting LeClercq, "the vocabulary is borrowed from eating, from digestion, and from the particular form of digestion belonging to ruminants. For this reason, reading and meditation are sometimes described by the very expressive word *ruminatio.*"[40]

If reading was essentially an action, then enacting the scriptures was an essential condition of understanding.[41] A ninth-century text is particularly illuminating in demonstrating widespread adherence to this principle. The *Liber Manualis*[42] is a handbook of spiritual and worldly wisdom written by Dhuoda of Septimania, wife of a Carolingian magnate, for the formation of her sons. In this text, she never tires of repeating to William that he must read, internalize, and enact the words that he finds in scripture, in classical writings and in her own text. For Dhuoda, reading is incomplete without action; learning is a matter of intellectual understanding that arises from personal experience and the practice of what one reads and, subsequently, flows into right action.[43] In Book I, for instance, when she begins to expose the mystery of God, she writes to William, "I admonish you continually to mull over the words of the holy gospels and the writings of the fathers concerning these [things]. . . . By thinking, speaking and acting rightly, you may believe in the everlasting God, who remains one in trinity and triune in unity."[44] Here Dhuoda makes explicit her understanding of what true meditation is: it is an extended process in which thinking flows into speaking that, in turn, becomes action. This three-step process leads to authentic faith which is not merely an understanding of God, but union with and possession of the divine reality. In Book II, 2, on the theological virtues, she bids William to seek and to find all the goods appropriate to him, earthly goods certainly, but heavenly goods as well, of which the chief good is God. "God is the one from whom you hope to receive all good things: desire God by thinking, ask in word, and move toward God in your actions. By acting in this three-fold manner, you will arrive at the height of perfection which is called charity."[45] The goal of reading is a virtuous understanding; the text is not just words about God but the power of God for salvation. Its full meaning is not to be had by study alone (though Dhuoda insists repeatedly that study is the irreplaceable first step) but by the habitual practice of what is read. Dhuoda expresses in this text the classical understanding of the relationship between scripture, life and salvation. It is the medieval variant of the "hermeneutical circle"[46] which became a permanent legacy of the Western church through the monastic practice of *lectio divina* and was intrinsic to the hermeneutic tradition from the late classical period to scholasticism. It has its roots, however, in the reading of scripture within the context of the eucharistic liturgy.

In one of the earliest references we have to the mutual informing of Word and Eucharist, Luke tells the story of the two disciples on the road to Emmaus, exposing the slow process by which the disciples come to recognize the presence of the Lord. First they have the interior and Christological interpretation of the ancient scriptures opened up for them by the Lord, as yet unrecognized. At the meal which they press him to share with them, he enacts the ritual of the "breaking of the bread." In that act, all becomes clear; they recognize Jesus and, retrospectively, they understand that they had already, though not fully, experienced his meaningful presence in the word explained. "Were not our hearts burning within us," they wonder aloud, "while he was talking to us on the road, while he was opening the scriptures to us" (Lk 24:32)? When they put the message of the word/sacrament into action, by returning to the community and the mission which they seem to have been in the process of abandoning, the interpretive circle is complete. Now they have fully understood their experience; now they can tell what had happened to them on the road. Their experience and their understanding, narrated to "the eleven and their companions," pass into the apostolic witness and, eventually, into the written gospel. Were I a medieval exegete, I would easily identify this story as the paradigm within which to understand the dynamics of medieval exegesis. Medieval interpreters of the bible will hear the scriptural text read in the eucharistic context; even when reading it for private study and prayer, they most often "hear" the text liturgically. Having heard the texts in dialogue with one another and reflected in the song-poems of the psalms, they will use a variety of simple methods (typology and reminiscence, *inter alia*) which allow different texts to illuminate each other. Though they will use every scholarly tool available to them— Jerome's *Onomasticon*, for instance, or, as in Bede, Adamnan's *De Locis Sanctis*—their purpose remains primarily homiletic: to open up the moral meaning of the scriptures as the basis for a life of discipleship. Just as the Emmaus disciples discovered the full (christological) meaning of the scriptures only in the eucharistic action, so the medieval exegete would find the full interpretation of the scriptures in the drama of salvation continued in his own life and the lives of those he knew and labored for. That drama continued in the sacramental action, but it also was played out in the practicalities of daily life. Over and over, the concrete possibilities contained in the lives of the community are the touchstone by which the meaning of the biblical text is negotiated. Finally, as the disciples of Emmaus returned to the community, so the medieval exegetes returned repeatedly to the community's treasury of interpretation, taking what was useful and contributing what they had understood. Unlike the story of Luke's two travelers, however, the work of medieval exegetes has not, as yet, passed fully into the common inheritance. Perhaps reflection upon the liturgical character of biblical exegesis can inspire and assist the task of reclaiming the large body of work they left behind.

Notes

1. Smalley's *The Study of the Bible in the Middle Ages,* 2nd Ed. (Notre Dame, IN: University of Notre Dame Press, 1964) is well known and often cited. De Lubac's four-volume work, *Exegese Medieval: le quatre sens de l'ecriture* (Lyons: Aubier, 1959–1962) is exhaustive and necessary while

McNally's *The Bible in the Early Middle Ages* (Westminster, MD: The Newman Press, 1959) is small but remains very helpful. LeClercq's *The Love of Learning and the Desire for God,* trans. by Catharine Misrahi (New York: Fordham University Press, 1961) is important for understanding the monastic context of so much of medieval exegesis.

2. Cistercian Publications and Liverpool University Press are playing a significant role in making available early medieval works—those from Bede through the twelfth-century Cistercian authors.

3. I note, in particular, the work of E. Ann Matter, thinking not only of *The Voice of My Beloved: The Song of Songs in Western Medieval Christianity* (Philadelphia: University of Pennsylvania Press, 1990), but of such earlier pieces as "The Lamentations Commentaries of Hrabanus Maurus and Paschasius Radbertus," *Traditio* 38 (1982), 137–163. See also my own book on the exegetical work of Dhuoda of Septimania in the *Liber Manualis* (c. 842), published by University of Scranton Press under the title *Dhuoda: Ninth Century Mother and Biblical Theologian.*

4. An immediate *caveat* is necessary. The "medieval period" covers almost a thousand years of liturgical and exegetical history and significant changes occur throughout those centuries. Though much of what I theorize about liturgical influences on biblical interpretation will remain true, in greater or lesser degree, until the Reformation, my analyses, and the examples which support them, will focus primarily on texts from Bede to the early twelfth century.

5. See the bibliography by Peter G. Cobb in "The Liturgy of the Word in the Early Church," *The Study of Liturgy.* Edited by Cheslyn Jones, Geoffrey Wainwright, Edward Yarnold, S.J. and Paul Bradshaw (London and New York: SPCK, Oxford University Press, 1992), 219. See also John F. Baldovin, S.J., *The Urban Character of Christian Worship* Orientalia Christiana Analecta 228 (Rome, Pontifical Institute for Oriental Studies, 1987) and Joseph A. Jungmann, S.J., *The Mass of the Roman Rite,* Vol. I, translated by Francis A. Brunner (Westminster, MD: Christian Classics, Inc, 1986), 393–403.

6. Cobb notes the following: "by their appropriateness for some ceremony in the catechumenate, by some catch-word suitable to the season, by the situation of the Roman stational church or the history of their martyrs or by the proximity of the feast of some great saint. . . ," 227.

7. De Lubac's work acknowledges and exposes the subtle differences between kinds of allegory.

8. Bede, *A History of the English Church and People,* trans. by Leo Sherley-Price (New York: Penguin Books, 1955),300.

9. Bede, 299.

10. As G.W.H. Lampe says so well, "Yet this proleptic honour enjoyed by the events of the Old Testament in no way deprived them of straightforward historical reality; indeed it is their historicity that bestows upon them an evidential value denied to imaginative speculations," *Essays on Typology*, Studies in Biblical Theology 22 (London: SCM Press Ltd., 1957), 13.

11. *The Bible and the Liturgy* (Notre Dame, IN: University of Notre Dame Press, 1956), 5. See also Jean Danielou, "La Typologie biblique traditionnelle dans la liturgie du Moyen Age," *Biblia* 4, 141–161.

12. "The Two Worlds in Bede's Homilies: The Biblical Event and the Listeners' Experience," *De Ore Domini: Preacher and Word in the Middle Ages*, edited by Thomas L. Amos, Eugene A. Green and Beverly Mayne Kienzle (Kalamazoo: Medieval Institute Publications, 1989), 29.

13. Ibid., 30.

14. His interpretation of this pericope is to be found in two places. The first is *In Marci Evangelium Exposito*, ed. D. Hurst, *Corpus Christianorum* CXX (Turnholt: Brepols, 1960), 523–525. See also his Homily 1.22: *In Lent, Homilies on the Gospels*, translated by Lawrence T. Martin and David Hurst OSB (Kalamazoo, MI: Cistercian Publications, 1991), 215–221. My analysis follows the line of thought in the commentary.

15. In the homily, Bede repeats this phrase. There, however, he also describes this woman as having the virtues described by revelation, though not the revelation itself (because she is a Gentile), p. 215 of the English translation. It is a provocative suggestion about the possibility of moral righteousness in those outside the faith.

16. Found in C.H. Talbot (ed), *Sermones ineditie B. Aelredi Abbatis Rievallensis* (Rome: Cisterciensis, 1952), 161–175.

17. Ibid., 171.

18. LeClercq, *The Love of Learning and the Desire for God*, p. 91.

19. *The Mass of the Roman Rite*, II, pp 346 and 422. Jungmann cites Hippolytus of Rome in the *Apostolic Traditions*, Tertullian, *De ore* and Athanasius, *De fuga*.

20. Dated around 150, the *First Apology* describes the Sunday gathering for worship in Chapter 67; Justin itemizes the reading of "the memoirs of the apostles" and "the writings of the prophets." He further describes the homily which follows all the readings and in which the one who presides gives moral exhortation.

21. Jungmann notes that the *Apostolic Constitutions* (II, 57, 6) prescribes a psalm of David to be read by one reader after another has finished two readings. See also Cobb, 227.

22. Translated by Robert C. Gregg in *Athanasius* (New York: Paulist Press, 1980). The date of this letter is uncertain.

23. I follow here the translation by John J. Gavigan in *Writings of Saint Augustine*, C 4 (New York: Cima Publishing, 1947). Citations are by page numbers.

24. Ibid., 71.

25. Ibid.

26. Ibid., 71–72.

27. Ibid., 72.

28. At the same time, reliance on memory often means that texts are paraphrased rather than quoted directly. This often engages modern readers in the difficult task of tracing biblical *echoes* rather than explicit citations in medieval texts.

29. Several series of his sermons delivered to the people of Rome survive: those on the Gospel lessons for Sundays and feast days, one of the opening and closing chapters of the Book of Ezekiel and two on the Song of Solomon. The sermons on the gospels are in Migne, *PL* 76 and are translated by Dom David Hurst, *Forty Gospel Homilies*, Cistercian Studies 123 (Kalamazoo, MI: Cistercian Publications, 1990). The critical edition of the homilies on Ezekiel was done by M. Adriaen, *CCSL* 143, 143A, 143B (1979–1985) and of the Song of Solomon by P. Verbraken, *CCSL* 144 (1963).

30. Barre, Henri. *Les Homéliares Carolingiens de L'école d'Auxerre*, Studi E Testi 225 (Vatican City: Biblioteca Apostolica Vaticana, 1962).

31. Contreni, John J., "Carolingian Biblical Studies," *Carolingian Essays*, edited by Uta-Renate Blumenthal (Washington, DC: The Catholic University of America Press, 1983), 79–80.

32. LeClercq analyzes Bernard's process at somewhat greater length than I do here, demonstrating the "psychological development, determined by the plan of associations" and digressions which take off from second verse of the Canticle. He concludes thus: "Now, this series of digressions has taken up six complete sermons," *Love of Learning*, 93.

33. Alcuin of York, *Commentary on the Epistle to Titus*, trans. by George E. McCracken and Allen Cabaniss in *Early Medieval Theology, Library of Christian Classics* IX (Philadelphia: The Westminster Press, 1957), 202.

34. See the article by David C. Steinmetz, "The Superiority of Pre-Critical Exegesis," *Theology Today* 37 (1980), 27–38; Steinmetz considers what he calls "pre-critical exegesis" superior precisely because of this pastoral character.

35. Migne, *PL* 95, 1490–1497. This is, by the way, not a homily taken from an earlier author but composed for the feast; it takes its starting point, not from the lectionary readings per se but from the mystery of the feast, taken as a whole.

36. "Ipsi, fratres, judicate: Si servus nudus, aut turpiter conscissis vestibus indutus, et sordidas habens manus, coram pudica et severa aliqua matrona ministrare praesumpserit, nonne abominabilis est illi? Nimirum avertet oculos cum indignatione, ac dehonestari se arbitrabitur illius ministerio magis quam honorari" (1497B).

37. "Quomodo ergo coram tremenda illa totius mundi domina, quam tota coelestis curia cum omni reverentia honorat, iniquitatibus pleni apparere, festivitatibus ejus interesse, et laudes ejus pronuntiare audemus, de qua certum est quod diligit justitiam, et odit iniquitatem? Non est speciosa laus in ore peccatoris. Placere non possunt epulae quantumvis pretiosae, in sordido vase oblatae" (1497C).

38. "Propter humilem matris fidelemque sermonem filiam deseruit daemonium. Ubi datur exemplum cathecizandi et baptizandi infantes quia uidelicet per fidem et confessionem parentum in baptismo liberantur a diabolo paruuli qui necdum per se sapere uel aliquid agere boni possunt aut mali" (1419–1423).

39. *Love of Learning*, 90.

40. Ibid.

41. Paul Ricoeur has investigated, from a contemporary perspective, the importance of action in the hermeneutic process. See "The Model of the Text: Meaningful Action Considered as a Text," in *Hermeneutics and the Human Sciences*, ed., trans., intro. J. Thompson (Cambridge: Cambridge University Press, 1981).

42. Dhuoda, *Manuel pour mon fils*, ed. by Pierre Riché, *Sources Chretiennes* 225 (Paris: Editions du Cerf, 1975). A good English translation of this text has been done by Carol Neel with the title *Handbook for William: A Carolingian Woman's Counsel for Her Son* (Lincoln and London: University of Nebraska Press, 1991).

43. As Burton-Christie notes (with reference to both Gadamer and Tracy), "The recognition that the risk of interpretation can bring about transformation suggests the importance of praxis or *applicatio*. It has been noted that *applicatio* is intrinsic, not extrinsic to interpretation. This means that interpretation, if it is to be complete, must be understood as always involving praxis and leading to some form of transformation." Douglas Burton-Christie, *The Word in the Desert* (New York & Oxford: Oxford University Press, 1993), 23.

44. "Hoc te admoneo ut et in uirtutes, et in elementa, et in corporis sensus, dicta sanctorum euangeliorum, cum aliorum documenta Patrum in tua semper reuoluas mente, ut unum in trinitate et trinum in unitate, bene cogitando, bene loquendo, bene operando, sine fine posse credas manentem ipsum qui dicitur Deus," I, 5, 42–47.

45. "A quo bona cuncta speras accipere, quare cogitando, pete loquendo, pulsa operando. Haec tria agendo ad summam et perfectam uevies, quae dicitur karitas" (II, ii, 29–31).

46. See Richard J. Bernstein, *Beyond Objectivism and Relativism: Science, Hermeneutics and Praxis* (Philadelphia: University of Pennsylvania Press, 1983), especially Parts Two and Three, for a general discussion of the relationship between *praxis* and interpretation in the contemporary debate. See also Burton-Christie's development of this idea in relation to the desert fathers, p. 23.

Bibliography

Primary Sources

1. Aelred of Rievaulx. *Sermones inediti B. Aelredi Abbatis Rievallensis*, ed. by C.H. Talbot. Rome: Cisterciensis, 1952.

2. Alcuin of York, *Commentary on the Epistle to Titus* (Selections), *Early Medieval Theology,* trans. by George E. McCracken and Allen Cabaniss. Library of Christian Classics IX. Philadelphia: The Westminster Press, 1957.

3. Athanasius. "Letter to Marcellinus," *Athanasius*, trans. by Robert C. Gregg. New York: Paulist Press, 1980.

4. Augustine. *De Doctrina Christiana*, trans. by John J. Gavigan. New York: Cima Publishing, 1947.

5. Bede. *A History of the English Church and People*, trans. by Leo Sherley-Price. New York: Penguin Books, 1955.

6. ———. *In Marci Evangelium Exposito*, ed. by D. Hurst. Corpus Christianorum CXX. Turnholt: Brepols, 1960.

7. ———. *Homilies on the Gospels*, trans. by Lawrence T. Martin and David Hurst, OSB. Kalamazoo, MI: Cistercian Publications, 1991.

8. Dhuoda. *Manuel pour mon fils*, ed. by Pierre Riché. *SC* 225. Paris: Editions du Cerf, 1975.

9. ———. *Handbook for William: A Carolingian Woman's Counsel for Her Son*, trans. by Carol Neel. Lincoln and London: University of Nebraska Press, 1991.

10. Paul the Deacon. "Homilia XLV: In Assumptione Sanctae Mariae," *Patrologia Latine* 95, 1490–1497.

Secondary Sources

11. Baldovin, John F., S.J. *The Urban Character of Christian Worship*. Orientalia Christiana Analecta 228. Rome: Pontifical Institute for Oriental Studies, 1987.

12. Barre, Henri. *Les Homéliares Carolingiens de L'école d'Auxerre*, Studi E Testi 225. Vatican City: Biblioteca Apostolica Vaticana, 962.

13. Bernstein, Richard J. *Beyond Objectivism and Relativism: Science, Hermeneutics and Praxis*. Philadelphia: University of Pennsylvania Press, 1987.

14. Bradshaw, Paul F. "The Use of the Bible in Liturgy: Some Historical Perspectives," *Studia Liturgica* 22 (1992), 35–52.

15. Burton-Christie, Douglas. *The Word in the Desert: Scripture and the Quest for Holiness in Early Christian Monasticism*. New York and Oxford: Oxford University Press, 1993.

16. Cobb, Peter G. "The Liturgy of the Word in the Early Church," *The Study of the Liturgy*, ed. by Cheslyn Jones, Geoffrey Wainwright, Edward Yarnold, S.J. and Paul Bradshaw. London and New York: SPCK, Oxford University Press, 1992.

17. Contreni, John J. "Carolingian Biblical Studies," *Carolingian Essays*, ed. by Uta-Renate Blumenthal. Washington, DC: The Catholic University of America Press, 1983, 71–98.

18. Danielou, Jean. *The Bible and the Liturgy*. Notre Dame, IN: University of Notre Dame Press, 1956.

19. ———. "La Typologie biblique traditionnelle dans la liturgie du Moyen Âge," *Biblia* 4, 141–161.

20. de Lubac, Henri. *Exégèse médiévale: les quatre sens de l'écriture*. Lyons: Aubier, 1959–1962.

21. Grégoire, Reginald. *Les Homéliaires du moyen âge*, Rerum Ecclesiasticarum Documenta, Series Maior, Fontes VI. Rome: Herder, 1966.

22. Jungmann, Josef. *The Mass of the Roman Rite: Its Origins and Development*, 2 volumes. New York: Benziger Bros., 1951.

23. Kannengiesser, Charles. *Le Bible de tous les temps*. 4 Vols. Paris: Beauchesne, 1984–1985.

24. Lampe, G.W.H. *Essays on Typology*. Studies in Biblical Theology 22. London: SCM Press Ltd., 1957.

25. Leclerq, Jean. "Le IIIè livre de Homélies de Bede le Vénérable," *RecTh* 14 (1947), 211–218.

26. ———. *The Love of Learning and the Desire for God: A Study of Monastic Culture*. Translated by Catharine Misrashi. New York: Fordham University Press, 1961.

27. Martin, Lawrence T. "The Two Worlds in Bede's Homilies: The Biblical Event and the Listeners' Experience," *Preacher and Word in the Middle Ages*. Edited by Thomas L. Amos, Eugene A. Green and Beverly Mayne Kienzle. Kalamazoo, MI: Medieval Institute Publications, 1989, 27–39.

28. Matter, E. Ann. "The Lamentations Commentaries of Hrabanus Maurus and Paschasius Radbertus," *Traditio* 38 (1982), 137–163.

29. *The Voice of My Beloved: The Song of Songs in Western Medieval Christianity*. Philadelphia: University of Pennsylvania Press, 1990.

30. Murphy, Roland E. "Patristic and Medieval Exegesis—Help or Hindrance," *The Catholic Biblical Quarterly* 43 (Oct. 1981), 505–516.

31. McNally, Robert E. *The Bible in the Early Middle Ages*. Westminster, MD: The Newman Press, 1959.

32. Riché, Pierre (ed). "Instruments de travail et méthodes de l'exégete a l'époque carolingienne," *Le moyen âge et la Bible*. Volume IV of *Bible de tous les temps*. Edited by Charles Kannengiesser. Paris: Beauchesne, 1984.

33. Ricoeur, Paul. "The Model of the Text: Meaningful Action Considered as a Text," *Hermeneutics and the Human Sciences*, ed. and trans. by J. Thompson. Cambridge: Cambridge University Press, 1981.

34. Smalley, Beryl. *The Study of the Bible in the Middle Ages*. Second Edition. Notre Dame, IN: University of Notre Dame Press, 1964.

35. Smetana, Cyril L. "Aelfric and the Early Medieval Homiliary," *Traditio* 15 (1959), 163–204.

36. Steinmetz, David C. "The Superiority of Pre-Critical Exegesis," *Theology Today* 37 (1980), 27–38.

37. Vogel, Cyrille. *Introduction aux sources de l'histoire de culte chrétien au moyen âge*. Spoleto: Centro italiano di studi sull'alto medioevo, 1964. (trans. and revised by William Storey and Niels Rasmussen. Washington, DC: The Pastoral Press, 1986).

38. Walsh, Katherine, and Diana Wood (Eds). *The Bible in the Medieval World*. Oxford: Basil Blackwell, 1985.

OTHER RITES

A SKEIN OF SACRED SEVENS: HUGH OF AMIENS ON ORDERS AND ORDINATION[1]

Jan Michael Joncas

Hugh of Amiens' *Three Books on the Church and Its Ministers* [hereafter *TBCM*] (entitled by its first editors *Against the Heretics of His Time*)[2] not only offers a glimpse of how a reforming prelate structured the roles and functions of the clergy of mid-twelfth century Normandy but also provides a case-study of how one medieval thinker generated a theology of orders and ordination.

After providing a sketch of Hugh's life and writings, this article discusses the dating of *TBCM* and provides a brief outline of its contents. The heart of the study is a detailed reading of Book II of *TBCM*, examining what Hugh affirmed about the roles and functions of the clerical orders and how Hugh constructed his theology of orders and ordination as a "skein of sacred sevens."

HUGH OF AMIENS' LIFE AND WRITINGS[3]

Hugh seems to have been born around 1085, a member of the house of Boves, descending from the counts of Amiens by alliance if not in direct blood-line. Along with his relative Matthew (later to become prior of St. Martin des Champs, bishop of Albano, and legate of the Holy See), Hugh was educated at the celebrated school of Anselm and Ralph at Laon.[4] Both Matthew and Hugh later became Benedictine monks at Cluny (possibly at the turn of the century) and Peter the Venerable became an intimate friend of Hugh while both were monks there. In 1113 Hugh was named prior of Saint Martial at Limoges, to replace Adalbert of Userque who had become abbot of St. Martial at the death of its former abbot, Peter. After only a short time there, Hugh was made prior of Saint Pancras at Lewes in England under the direction of its abbot Lanzon at the express wish of Henry Beauclerc (more commonly known as King Henry I of England). When Henry (with Abbot Pontius of Cluny) founded Reading Abbey in the diocese of Salisbury in 1125, Hugh became the first abbot of that community; among Hugh's innovations at Reading was the introduction of the Feast of the Immaculate Conception. Journeying to Rouen at the end of 1129 for a pastoral visitation, Hugh so impressed the clergy of that city that they elected him to fill the episcopal vacancy created by the death of their archbishop, Geoffrey the Breton, on 28 November 1128. With the consent of the bishop of Salisbury, the king of England, and the Holy See,[5] Hugh was solemnly consecrated archbishop of Rouen by Richard of Bayeux at the church of Saint-Ouen on 14 September 1130, the Feast of the Exaltation of the Cross; Henry I and numerous bishops of Normandy were in attendance.

The early years of Hugh's episcopate at Rouen were marked by his interactions with Henry I. Pope Innocent II visited Hugh at Rouen in May, 1131, having gained French support for his claims to the papacy against Anacletus. At the Council of Rheims held in October 1131, Hugh brought letters from Henry I recognizing Innocent as the legitimate Pope. Innocent demonstrated his gratitude for Hugh's support by ordering the abbeys of his province to swear an oath of fealty to the archbishop. Concern for their long-standing independence from episcopal control made many of the abbeys resist Hugh's extension of metropolitan authority. Henry I interceded on the abbeys' behalf, regarding an oath of fealty to Hugh as moving beyond spiritual jurisdiction to political suzerainity and thus a threat to his own royal prerogatives. Hugh refrained from pressing his claims as long as Henry I remained in power. In 1135 Hugh attended the Council of Pisa, remaining in Italy after the council's conclusion to carry out various legatine commissions for the Pope, activities that caused annoyance both to the clergy of Rouen and the king of England. Henry I was even more greatly displeased when Hugh refused to ordain the king's candidate for the episcopal see of Bayeux (Richard, son of the duke of Gloucester) due to the impediment of illegitimacy. The confrontation between Hugh and Henry was resolved when the Pope granted Richard a dispensation from this impediment and the consecration took place without further difficulties. Hugh attended Henry I in the king's final illness and was present when he died on 1 December 1135.

The middle years of Hugh's episcopate were marked by his relationship to Stephen of Blois, duke of Normandy from 1135–1144 and king of England from 1135–1154. Upon Henry I's death, Stephen had contended with his aunt Mathilde, wife of Geoffrey Plantagenet, the duke of Anjou, and daughter of Henry I, for control of Henry's lands. Hugh supported Stephen in this altercation and, when Stephen proved victorious, Hugh felt free to press his claims of spiritual and temporal sovereignty over the abbeys of his province with Stephen's support. In response to Hugh's initiative, Theobald, abbot of Bec and later archbishop of Canterbury, was forced to pledge obedience to Hugh in a spoken oath. Hugh again took Stephen's side when a dispute between the king and some English bishops broke out at a council presided over by the king's half-brother, Henry, bishop of Winchester, in 1139. In 1144 Hugh was invited by Abbot Suger to be present at the dedication of the completed basilica of St. Denis and to consecrate the altar dedicated to the Blessed Virgin in that structure. In 1147 Hugh took part in a council held in Paris that condemned the theological errors of Gilbert of Poitiers, asserting that one ought not to refer to the persons of the Trinity as "three singular things" *(tria singularia)* but as "a singular unity" *(unum singulars)*, a phrase taken from *TBCM* Book III, Chapter 8. The following year Hugh also attended a council held at Rheims. In addition to these political and ecclesiastical affairs, Hugh continued the rounds of his archepiscopal duties: confirming the foundations of various religious houses, consecrating bishops of dioceses within his province, blessing abbots, and making pastoral visitations of the dioceses of his province (Évreux, Séez, Avranches, Coutances, Bayeux, and Lisieux).

The final period of Hugh's episcopate was marked by the accession of Mathilde's son, Henry fitzEmpress, as duke of Normandy in 1150; Hugh was in attendance in Westminster when Henry fitzEmpress was crowned as King Henry II of England in 1154. During this period Hugh attended councils at Beaugency in 1152 (where the legitimacy of the divorce between Louis VII of France and Eleanor of Aquitaine was considered) and Nuefmarché in 1160 (where the legitimate papacy of Alexander III against Victor the anti-pope was recognized by the bishops of Henry II's realm). Hugh died on 11 November 1164, "full of faith and good works," in the stereotyped words of Lambert, archdeacon of Rouen, written to Louis VII of France, informing him of the archbishop's death.

In addition to Hugh's pastoral responsibilities, he also produced a significant number of literary works. The first of his theological treatises, the *Dialogues* or *Seven Books on Theological Questions*[6] dedicated to his relative Matthew, was composed in two periods between 1125 and 1133. Hugh wrote the first six books while abbot of Reading, adding some material to the end of the sixth book (defending his understanding of the effect of deposition or excommunication upon the sacramental activity of those ordained) and an additional concluding book soon after becoming archbishop of Rouen.[7]

André Wilmart ascribes an anonymous tract defending Benedictine monasticism on the basis of ancient monastic usages against the criticisms of St. Bernard of Clairvaux to Hugh of Amiens; he believes that it was written between 1127 and 1128 while Hugh was abbot of Reading.[8]

Sometime after 29 April 1132 (when the narrative records the subject's death), Hugh wrote a *Life of St. Adjutor*[9], about a man who had taken part in the First Crusade, was imprisoned by the enemy but delivered through the invocation of Sts. Madeleine and Bernard of Tiron, and became a monk of Tiron notable for his holiness and wonder-working abilities. This is less a theological tract than a hagiographical romance.

Between 1141 and 1146 (most probably in 1142)[10] Hugh produced a *Commentary on the Six Days of Creation*[11] dedicated to Arnoulf of Lisieux, purporting to be a literal and historical explication of the sacred text, rather than an allegorical or tropological exposition. The commentary has come down to us only in incomplete forms.

A variety of shorter works completes this listing of Hugh's literary output. *Concerning the Catholic Faith and the Lord's Prayer,*[12] dedicated to Hugh's archdeacon Gilles (later bishop of Evreux), is a pastoral commentary on the Apostles' Creed and the Our Father. It was probably written between 1155 and 1159.[13] *Three Books in Praise of Memory*[14] is dedicated to an otherwise-unknown Philip; some scholars identify the recipient of this tract as Philip of Harcourt, bishop of Bayeux (1142–1163). It discusses God, Trinity, Incarnation, the origin and results of sin, and the remedies for sin provided to humanity by

Christ's mercy. This is probably the last of Hugh's major works to be written, composed between 1160 and 1164.[15] Numerous letters from Hugh (to Louis VII of France, Suger, Innocent II, Eugene III, and various bishops and abbots) give a glimpse of his political and ecclesiastical activity.[16]

Hugh of Boves/Amiens/Rouen is also the author of various poetic works attributed to Hugh of Ribémont/Amiens.[17] His life and work produced contrasting assessments. Hugh's friend Arnoulf of Lisieux composed the following epitaph that, in spite of its stereotyped expressions, indicates how highly one of his contemporaries esteemed Hugh's years of ministry:

> Worthy of particular honor among bishops,
> Here Hugh lays down the burden of our flesh.
> His members, consigned to the grave, are confined for a brief time,
> But neither grave nor heavens confine the acts of this man.
> Whatever grace dispenses and shares with everyone,
> It gathered and exceeded in this man.
> Therefore by an abundance of virtues this man
> Bore fertile fruit, beyond and praised beyond other men.
> Finally after the happy times of an honored life,
> The hour that brings tears came upon this tired old man.
> Martin, one equal to you has been assigned by lot
> As your future partner in commemorating [both on] the same day.[18]

In contrast a contemporary historian, Gunar Freibergs, evaluates Hugh's activities less benignly:

> Hugh of Amiens . . . was a conservative cleric. . . . He appears to have been . . . not the kind of person who would be interested in academic pursuits, but rather an ambitious member of the clergy climbing the ladder of success within the ecclesiastical hierarchy. His monastic conservatism, authoritarian manner, reputation as a strict disciplinarian, support of Bernard of Clairvaux's opposition to rational inquiry into the meaning of scripture, and the polemical nature of his writings have caused Hugh to be regarded as a rigorist theologian and one of the most redoubtable twelfth-century champions of Church tradition.[19]

DATE AND CONTENTS OF *TBCM* [20]

The dating of *TBCM* has been a matter of some dispute. Since no names, places, or dates for the heresies and the heretics it discusses are contained in the body of the text, scholars date the document on the basis of the dedicatory letter prefixed to it:

> To the son of the holy Roman church, Alberic, bishop of Ostia, so often legate of the apostolic See, the sinner Hugh, however [also] bishop of Rouen [writes]: Reverend Father, I have for some time delayed to obey your commands, without, however, forgetting them; therefore grant pardon to one who seeks it from you, to him to whom you are accustomed to give your favor. A reminiscence worthy of being recalled stays in my memory: how we had the honor to assist you when you were in the lands of the Gallican people, at the Sea of the Bretons, in the city of Nantes. There you presented (with a great crowd of the faithful in attendance) the bodies of the holy martyred brothers, Donation and Rogatian, that you had received. You repositioned [the relics] that had been presented with proper honor and thanksgiving. There with you we saw a comet falling headfirst in the direction of the West, signifying (according to your assessment) the ruin of the heresy that had then appeared in Armorica. There indeed the heretical populace was not able to stand against your orthodox preaching. Their leader in heresy feared greatly and did not presume to appear. Thus it was pleasing to you [to suggest] that we write some things on the heresies that are arising and we accepted that task on the authority of your command, but [have done so] with a succinct work of brief character. [21]

In a recent article Gilles Bounoure argues that Hugh and Alberic viewed the return of Halley's comet in Brittany in late May/early June 1145,[22] indicating that *TBCM* must have been written after that date. Damien van den Eynde notes that *TBCM* must have appeared before 1148 when its addressee died; he thinks that the work was most probably presented to Alberic at the Easter celebrations of 1147 when both Hugh and Alberic were present at the Council of Paris. [23]

The first of *TBCM*'s three books is divided into fourteen chapters. The topics treated include the mysteries of the Trinity and of the Incarnation; the unity, holiness and authority of the church; the necessity of baptism for all human beings; the excellence of the

Eucharist; and the obligation of all faithful adults to participate in the Eucharist. The second book discusses ecclesiastical orders in ten chapters and will be treated in detail below. In the nine chapters of the third book Hugh tackles other theological positions taken by his opponents in Brittany: explaining and defending the custom of clerical tonsure; justifying physicalist understanding of the resurrection of the dead against ridicule; maintaining the holiness of conjugal bond and its sacramental character; supporting (on the authority of St. Paul) the vows of continence taken by those in holy orders and monastic life; and declaring that the purpose of the church is to gather all the faithful and instruct them, to communicate to its members the graces of the Holy Spirit through the sacraments, to nourish them on the Eucharist and to encourage them to obey God's commandments so as to enjoy eternal happiness after this earthly life. It should be clear that Hugh's treatment of the ecclesiastical orders is contextualized by his systematic exploration of the nature of the church and its sacramental character.

ROLES AND FUNCTIONS OF THE ORDAINED ACCORDING TO *TBCM*

TBCM Book II provides much information about Hugh's understanding of the roles and functions of the ordained. In contrast to theologies that present orders from doorkeeper through acolyte as "stepping stones" on the path to major orders, Hugh clearly presents them as ministries in their own right. A difficulty in interpretation, however, lies in determining if Hugh's account of the roles and functions of the ordained in the church of Rouen in the mid-twelfth century reflects general consensus based on actual practice, Hugh's attempt to reform practice, or a pious copying of earlier texts on these topics, texts no longer reflecting actual practice.

Bishops

For Hugh the role of the bishop is essential if the church is to exist at all. Although Hugh finds precedents in the Old Testament for the bestowal of the Holy Spirit by designated mediators in the relation of

Moses to the seventy elders,[24] to Joshua,[25] and to Aaron and his sons,[26] as well as in the relation of Elijah and Elisha,[27] he sees the foundation of the office of bishop in the direct action of Jesus:

> For as our high pontiff and universal bishop, Jesus Christ, chose twelve from all his disciples, whom he named apostles, setting them above the rest, and whom as pure men he made sharers in his own office and possessors of the divine magnificence, so he made their successors in episcopal grace directors or pontiffs to be preeminent in singular excellence. . . . [28]

Hugh cites Jesus' commission to Peter not to justify offices of metropolitan, patriarch, or pope but to ground the office of bishop in the will of Christ:

> Moreover "when the fullness of time came" in which "God sent his Son" as pontiff and bishop according to the order of Melchizedech unto eternity, the superabounding and copiously flowing sevenfold grace of the Holy Spirit was poured forth from the seat of majesty; from him [i.e., God's Son] pontifical authority and episcopal dignity grow more fully [Galatians 4:4]. He said to Peter: "You are Peter and upon this rock I will build my church" [Matthew 16:13]. For Peter is in it and it [is] in Peter: the bishop in the church and the church in the bishop. *The bishop is the foundation of the church because through the bishop the Church has the Holy Spirit.* . . . From this rock, upon which mother church is founded, struck twice by the pastoral staff (i.e., stirred up for the love of God and of neighbor), the generous waters, the health-giving waters, the living waters flow. . . . [29]

Hugh emphasizes that the bishop is pre-eminent among clerical orders because only the bishop can confer the Holy Spirit from the plenitude of the episcopal office:

> Those who are considered [to be] of a lower rank (such as presbyters, deacons, and the rest promoted to canonical grade in the church) indeed possess the Holy Spirit by whom they live well and diligently serve day by day in their office in God's church. But they cannot give the Holy Spirit by the imposition of hands to those others whom they receive. Only bishops have received this power by special prerogative from the Lord, that by this most excellent work they give the Holy

Spirit whom they possess (who gives by giving himself) to others on whom they piously lay hands out of their pontifical office, after prayers have been poured forth to the Lord.[30]

In *TBCM* Book II the primary task of the bishop is to "administer with Christ's power and above all build God's house."[31] However when Hugh lists the episcopal functions that specify this task of administration/edification, they are almost entirely liturgical:

By apostolic custom they give the Holy Spirit to those on whom they impose hands with due religious ceremonies . . . [32]

It is the bishop's [task] to confect the sacred chrism, the holy oil [and] the oil of the sick; to consecrate God's churches and altars, the chalice and corporals, the officials and their vestments, and all the church's implements; to confirm the baptized; [and] to anoint emperors and kings. [33]

Nonetheless Hugh seems to connect the bishop's liturgical activity with his role as a teacher of the truths he has received by receiving the fullness of the Holy Spirit:

"Whoever drinks," it says, "the water that I will give, it will become in him a fountain of water springing up to eternal life" [John 4:13]. And another time: "Whoever believes in me, streams of living water will flow from his side: for he said this concerning the Spirit which those believing in him were to receive" [John 7:38–39]. It says: "When the Spirit of truth comes, he will teach you all truth" [John 16:13]. And so that which a man by himself could not know through his own understanding, a man full of the Holy Spirit can: according to what he says: "Everything that I heard from my Father, I have made known to you" [John 15:15]—known in the Spirit of truth, known in the fullness of charity. To such people "it is given to know the mystery of the reign of God" [Mark 4:11]. However lest anyone should presume not to listen to them or to make null their precepts, he says: "Whoever hears you, hears me; and whoever scorns you, scorns me. And whoever scorns me, scorns him who sent me" [Luke 10:16]. And again he says: "It is not you who are speaking, but the Spirit of your Father, who speaks in you" [Matthew 10:20].[34]

Thus in *TBCM* Book II the controlling image of the bishop is as a conduit of the Holy Spirit. The episcopal task is to build up the church, primarily through liturgical activity and doctrinal orthodoxy. Hugh does not advert to the bishop's role in ecclesial and political government or in evangelization: the first had grown in importance in the West ever since the collapse of the Roman Empire while the second had declined with the rise of monastic missionaries.

Presbyters

For Hugh the role of the presbyter is to be a representative of Jesus as the unique mediator between God and humanity:

> The excelling power of this office and the surpassing dignity of this power has been given not to the angels nor to any majesty of the heavenly citizens. The God-man has given it to man, not by human desire but by celestial, not for the acquisition of merit but by the choice of piety, graciously received from the gift of the Holy Spirit, by which the consecrated one is made worthy for this work in Christ. . . . And so *the consecrated priest stands as mediator between God and human beings by the power of Christ before the most high Father*. . . . [35]

This mediatorial role is primarily expressed in the liturgical functions of celebrating the Eucharist and reconciling penitent sinners:

> [T]he consecrated one is made worthy for this work in Christ, so that he might directly effect on the altar the very thing that Christ did with his own hands during the paschal meal. Therefore these hands, hands consecrated for this task, by which one holds the body and blood of Christ that has been confected on the holy altar, these indeed are the hands of Christ, by which the Son who takes away the sins of the world is offered to the Father and makes the faithful departed, freed from punishments, participants in eternal blessedness. And so the consecrated priest stands as mediator between God and human beings . . . when he bears the ineffable sacraments above to the open heavens and elevates [them] from the altar, by which he makes the sons of the Church participants by communion, while in the Holy Spirit which he

receives he both dismisses sins from penitents and reconciles those he
absolves with God.[36]

There is no hint in *TBCM* Book II of the patristic notion that
presbyters form a "college of elders" entrusted with advising the
bishop. Presbyters' tasks of preaching or evangelization, of parochial
governance, of baptizing, of witnessing marriages or of anointing the
sick are not delineated. On the other hand, the power of the presbyter to
offer the eucharistic sacrifice for the needs of the living as well as for
the dead and his authority both to forgive sins as well as to reconcile
the penitent to the church and God is strongly highlighted.

Deacons

For Hugh the role of the deacon is to be assistant to the bishop and the
presbyters:

> They are the eyes of the bishop and the presbyters, so that, insofar as
> they are able, they make them to have quiet and peace.[37]

When Hugh lists the deacon's functions, his responsibility to
evangelize and catechize the populace receives the most attention. One
wonders if Hugh's emphasis on the deacon's role in establishing quiet
for preaching is an oblique reference to a liturgical role of calling for
silence before the proclamation of the gospel or if it refers to keeping
civil order when orthodox preachers confront their opponents:

> They endeavor to teach the people and to pray more quietly. . . . By
> [the Spirit of understanding] they understand the sacraments that they
> dispense. . . . By [the same Spirit] they establish, as far as they can,
> peace and quiet for the preachers of the Word of God, by removing
> the disruptive and noisy. . . . Through their diaconal assemblies [?]
> they establish a path of teaching for the bishops, and, concerning each
> of the things that they learn from the bishop, they come to know these
> things more certainly. And the bishops also establish them to be
> evangelists. . . .[38]

Hugh also notes the liturgical functions of deacons, as assistants at the
altar, distributors of communion, and as proclaimers of the gospel:

[Deacons are consecrated] so that they might be present in God's church at the altar when the sacraments of the Lord's body and blood are confected on it. . . . They receive from the one consecrating [the task of] distributing the real body and blood of Jesus Christ. For from the hand of the bishop or of the presbyter they receive that by which they refresh themselves and others in munificent generosity by life-giving food. . . . They keep watch over the performance of the sacraments. . . . Indeed in the celebration of the Lord's Mass when they proclaim the holy gospel to the gathered church, "Glory to you, Lord" is answered to them by the harmonious voice of the faithful.[39]

Finally Hugh lists the care of the church's material possessions among the deacon's functions:

They dispose the goods of the Church under the will of the bishop. . . . By [the Spirit of knowledge] they piously take care of the things committed to them.[40]

Thus in *TCBM* Book II the deacon's role is to make the bishop's and presbyter's roles and functions easier. Their primary tasks lie in evangelizing and catechizing, liturgical service at eucharist, and care for the church's goods. Hugh does not mention baptizing, visiting the sick with communion, or witnessing marriages among the tasks of a deacon.

Subdeacons

According to Hugh, just as deacons are to be assistants to the bishop and the presbyters, so subdeacons are to be obedient to deacons and presbyters:

Subdeacons are brought forward . . . so that they might be obedient to the Levites and to the presbyters.[41]

While Hugh emphasizes subdeacons' commitment to celibacy, the functions he lists for this order are entirely connected to liturgical service at Eucharist:

> Subdeacons are brought forward . . . so that . . . they might prepare
> the sacred vessels in which the body and blood of Christ is confected.
> According to custom they prepare the bread and wine and water and
> the vessels appropriate for this things: the curtains of the altar and the
> torches, with prompt solicitude and diligence. . . . Having received
> the Spirit [of counsel], the subdeacon commits himself . . . to present
> cleansed vessels for the sacraments.[42]

Apparently for Hugh, subdeacons had no particular responsibilities in
evangelizing, catechizing or administration, tasks that are reserved to
those in higher orders.

Acolytes

Although he does not define their role, acolytes have a dual function
according to Hugh, liturgical service and modeling right behavior for
the rest of the faithful:

> Acolytes follow . . . so that they might carry in God's church the
> cruets and washbasins and hand-towels fit for this office, so that
> before the presence of the gospel they might diligently carry lit
> candles given to the candle-bearers. The justice of the kingdom of
> God declared through the gospel should thus appear in them by the
> light of true faith, by the splendor of most certain hope, and by the
> ardor of charity. They should seek it and should urge others to seek it
> by the example of their light. Indeed as they conduct themselves so
> should they conduct others to receive the sacraments by hungering for
> them earnestly.[43]

Exorcists

Hugh specifies that the role of exorcists is to cast out Satan and
wickedness from the possessed and demoniacs:

> The bishop's blessing makes [exorcists] rulers, not of earthly benefit
> or of carnal power, but from the power of God, by which they expel
> Satan and all wickedness from the possessed and from demoniacs by

the invocation of the name of Jesus and praying the prayer mentioned previously by exsufflation [These things are done] so that they might be made worthy to attain the grace of holy baptism and to participate in the sacraments. [44]

Although he notes that the exorcisms performed should prepare the subjects for baptism and other sacraments, he does not call the subjects of this ceremony "catechumens," thus leading one to wonder if exorcists in mid-twelfth century Normandy served at infant baptisms.

Readers

Clearly for Hugh the role of a reader is public proclamation in a liturgical setting. What is of interest is his categorization of the texts to be proclaimed: sacred scripture, patristic writings, and "those texts to be heard with veneration" (perhaps an oblique reference to saints' lives or episcopal decrees?):

They read the words of both the Old and of the New Testament. They read by established custom at a specified time and appropriate place, announcing in public the holy pages of the old and new document [Testament?], as well as the holy writings of the Fathers, harmonized and fulfilled in our one Lord Jesus Christ. And [they also read] those things always owed a hearing with veneration and those to be preserved through time. [45]

Doorkeepers

We have already noted above that Hugh lists two functions for doorkeepers: guarding the entryways of the church building and ringing the church bells. In addition Hugh charges doorkeepers with enforcing decrees of excommunication, an emphasis that probably stems from Hugh's offensive against his doctrinal opponents. Correlated with the diaconal function of establishing peace for preaching examined above, these prescriptions suggest that civil disorder could attend liturgical functions:

By their office the doorkeepers let in those whom they know to be Catholics and they exclude non-believers, whom they know to be mockers or disturbers of the peace. They also properly reject them whom they know for certain to be deprived of the bishop's communion.[46]

THE CONSTRUCTION OF A THEOLOGY OF ORDERS AND ORDINATION IN *TBCM*

It was not enough for Hugh to define and describe the offices and functions of the various clerical orders operating in his day. He also ventured a theoretical explanation for their differentiation and activities, a genuine theology of orders and ordination. We will now consider how Hugh wove this theology as a "skein of sacred sevens," grounded in scripture and tradition.

The Structure of TBCM Book II

An important key to understanding the structure of the treatise on orders and ordination in *TBCM* Book II appears in chapter nine, where Hugh addresses the reader directly:

> Pay attention you who are reading. . . . Pay attention to the seven steps, these seven columns, distinguished in order, strengthened by blessing and adorned by sacraments by the mouth of God's wisdom through the bishop's hands. The bishop raises up these seven by seven petitions of prayer. He strengthens them by the seven gifts of the Holy Spirit. He fills them with the honor of seven beatitudes. . . . The Lord Jesus Christ established that such columns be ordained through the bishops and designated seven by ranks. Occupying these ranks himself, he also proposed that they are to be occupied by his authority.[47]

This passage outlines the structure created by Hugh for *TBCM* Book II. First Hugh discusses the role of the bishop rather extensively. He then treats in "descending" order the seven clerical grades springing from the bishop's ministry in somewhat less detail; each order is yoked with a distinctive petition of the Lord's Prayer, a gift of the Holy Spirit, and one of the virtues cited in the Matthean form of the beatitudes. Then Hugh constructs an "Ordinal of Christ," dominical warrants for each of the seven clerical grades in "ascending" order. He finally extends these warrants to the figure of the bishop in greater detail than he treats any of the other grades.

The Use of the Number Seven in TBCM Book II

Many scholars have noted the significance of particular numbers to medieval thinkers; seven seems to have been especially important.[48] Hugh is no exception to this tendency. Indeed one wonders if discrepancies in his numbering of clerical orders in *TBCM*[49] stem from his desire to guarantee that there would be seven.

As was noted above, Hugh's controlling image for the seven clerical orders springing from the bishop is that of the seven columns sustaining the house of wisdom (cf. Proverbs 9:1), identified as "Christ's house" and "God's church:"

> After the apostles there followed apostolic men, pontiffs and bishops, who by heavenly power always built Christ's house which they sustained by *seven columns*. . . . If these should presume to act without the command of the bishop or against the bishop, they cut them off from the number seven; they spring back from the *seven columns* enumerated above; they vanish, having fallen from wisdom's house. . . . Let us say something briefly about the *seven columns* of God's church. . . . [50]

> [Mother Church,] your servants are bishops, hard-working providers and most strong teachers. From you they produce for you strong and honest sons. From those whom they regard as good, they choose and lift up [some for clerical life]. From these they create seven grades of honor, *seven columns* of strength, whom they consecrate with seven dominical petitions, whom they illuminate with the seven gifts of the Holy Spirit, whom they glorify with seven beatitudes. These *seven columns* both sustain God's church and shine with eternal splendor.[51]

Hugh's theological program appears in his yoking of each clerical order with a petition of the Lord's Prayer, a gift of the Holy Spirit, and one of the beatitudes:

Jesus Christ thoroughly taught those complete and perfect petitions enumerated earlier. By his own generosity he gave seven wonderful gifts of the Holy Spirit. He bestowed seven beatitudes on his faithful unto eternity. Beyond this, the seven gifts of the Holy Spirit are sought by these seven petitions; the seven beatitudes are acquired by the seven gifts. Faith in the petitions, hope in the gifts, charity in the beatitudes are equally allotted. Zeal in the petitions, reward in the gifts, joy in the beatitudes—if you piously seek, you will find [these] in abundance. . . . Behold through the seven petitions, through the seven gifts, through the seven beatitudes you are truly blessed, Mother Church, most fully abounding with divine sacraments. In you sins are forgiven, mercy is exhibited, and grace is bestowed.[52]

A dense series of interrelations appear in this program. According to Hugh, the seven petitions of the Matthean version of Lord's Prayer generate both faith and zeal in asking for the gifts of the Holy Spirit. Receiving the gifts of the Holy Spirit in turn generate both hope and reward as they are crowned by the qualities of life enunciated in the Matthean version of the beatitudes. The beatitudinal virtues manifest both charity and joy, states of soul thoroughly congruent with the destiny of the faithful in eternity. Hugh describes the dynamic of petitions-answered-with-gifts-generating-beatitudinal-virtues as a blessing bestowed on the church as a whole. One wonders if Hugh further sees forgiveness of sins correlated with the petitions of the Lord's Prayer, the exhibition of mercy correlated with the gifts of the Holy Spirit and the bestowal of grace correlated with the life-qualities associated with the beatitudes.[53]

Having established a general foundation for petitions, gifts, and beatitudes in the life of the church, Hugh specifies the relation of particular petitions, gifts and beatitudes to individual clerical orders. By associating seven gifts of the spirit with seven clerical orders, Hugh concurred with a widely held opinion that was to be made especially popular in a document generated about the same time as *TBCM*, Peter Lombard's *Sententiae*. In chapter 2 of Book IV, Distinction 24, the Master of the Sentences writes:

There are seven [clerical orders] on account of the sevenfold grace of the Holy Spirit. Those who do not share in this grace come to the ecclesiastical orders unworthily. But those in whose minds the sevenfold grace of the Holy Spirit is diffused are believed to receive more abundant grace in advancing to spiritual rank when they come to ecclesiastical orders.[54]

Hugh's theological program is to map the standard enumeration of the gifts of the Holy Spirit[55] onto the "descending" pattern of the seven clerical orders springing from the bishop. Hugh also maps the seven petitions of the Matthean version of the Lord's Prayer (Matthew 6:9–13) onto the "descending" pattern of these clerical orders (although one may strain to find the mapping in some of the texts). In contrast Hugh maps the seven Matthean beatitudes (Matthew 5:3–9) in the order given by the Vulgate where "the meek" appear before "those mourning") onto the "ascending" pattern of these same seven clerical orders.

Presbyters

Hugh yokes the presbyteral order with the Spirit of wisdom (Isaiah 11:2), the first petition of the Lord's Prayer ("Hallowed be your name": Matthew 6:9) and the seventh beatitude on the peacemakers (Matthew 5:9) in the following passage:

> In this activity the Spirit of wisdom by which the name of Father is hallowed (just as whoever is [a member of the] faithful prays in the Lord's Prayer) shines forth in them [i.e., presbyters]. They are made peacemakers and therefore are considered blessed "for they will be called sons of God." These men in the present life make peace with God on humanity's behalf, by means of sacraments celebrated properly by their own order, by their own merits and by their hands full of heavenly remedy. Thus this is to be known and preached with all veneration that the Spirit of wisdom sanctifies them as sons for God our Father, not everyone, but the peacemakers, and therefore the blessed, both in the present age and in the future.[56]

Given Hugh's emphasis on the presbyter as a mediating representative of the solitary Mediator between God and humanity, it is appropriate that "hallowing God's name" would be associated with this order. Since Hugh does not stress the presbyter's functions of preaching, instructing or catechizing, the reference to the "Spirit of wisdom" might be surprising. However if Hugh sees presbyters as a first line of defense against the "heretics of Brittany" he might be yoking the presbyter's championing of orthodoxy (inspired by the Spirit of wisdom) with a peacemaking role in communities stirred up by his opponents' teaching.

Deacons

Hugh connects the diaconal order with the Spirit of understanding (Isaiah 11:2), the second petition of the Lord's Prayer ("Your kingdom come": Matthew 6:10), and the sixth beatitude on the pure of heart (Matthew 5:8) in the following passage:

> In this activity of Levites or deacons the Spirit of understanding shines forth. By this spirit they understand the sacraments that they dispense. By this spirit they piously take care of the things entrusted to them. By this spirit they establish peace and quiet for the preachers of God's word by removing the disruptive and noisy insofar as they can. These men, adorned by chastity and blessed with a pure heart, seek the kingdom of God, while through their diaconal assemblies [?] they create a path of teaching for the bishops and, concerning each of the doctrines that they learn from the bishop, they come to know them with more certainty. The bishops also establish them to be evangelists, and they have enough to do in their order by diligently following the commands of their bishops. [57]

Since Hugh had laid such stress on the deacon's tasks of evangelizing and catechizing, it is not surprising that he yokes the "Spirit of understanding" with this order. Similarly the deacon's commitment to celibacy might find some resonance with the beatitude on the pure of heart (although given Hugh's emphasis on the subdeacon's acceptance of celibacy, one might have thought this beatitude more appropriate for that order). It is difficult to see how the petition "your kingdom come" specifies diaconal ministry, unless it might be an oblique reference to the deacon's role of distributing the church's goods to the poor, seeing in this charitable ministry an image of the kingdom to come.

Subdeacons

Hugh links the subdiaconal order with the Spirit of counsel (Isaiah 11:2), the third petition of the Lord's Prayer ("Your will be done on earth as in heaven": Matthew 6:10), and the fifth beatitude on the merciful (Matthew 5:7) in the following passage:

> In this activity the Spirit of counsel whom the subdeacon specially receives appears when he is consecrated by the prayer of the bishop. Having received the spirit, the subdeacon commits himself to serve pure and chaste, to prepare himself for the mysteries and to present cleansed vessels for the sacraments. These do not in the least way presume [to do these things] from their own power, but submit their will to the Lord's will and humbly say: "Your will be done on earth just as in heaven"—just as in our spiritual fathers so also in us their sons insofar as we are on the earth, to that extent we are to be on guard against desires of the flesh. They become merciful from this action, more faithfully entreating mercy from God.[58]

None of the scriptural warrants Hugh provides for subdeacons seem especially appropriate to this order. Perhaps the "Spirit of counsel" sustains the subdeacon's task of being obedient to the deacons and presbyters. If subdeacons were directly involved in the charitable ministry of deacons (although *TBCM* only notes the subdeacons' liturgical functions), then the beatitude on the merciful and the petition that God's will be done on earth as in heaven might mirror their tasks.

Acolytes

Hugh joins the order of acolytes with the Spirit of fortitude (Isaiah 11:2), the fourth petition of the Lord's Prayer ("Give us this day our daily bread": Matthew 6:11), and the fourth beatitude on those hungering and thirsting for justice/righteousness (Matthew 5:6) in the following passage:

> The justice of the kingdom of God declared through the gospel should thus appear in them [i.e., acolytes] by the light of true faith, by the splendor of most certain hope, and by the ardor of charity. They should seek it and should urge others to seek it by the example of

their light. Indeed as they conduct themselves so should they conduct others to receive the sacraments by hungering for them earnestly. In this activity the Spirit of fortitude appears, by which they already live among the storms of the power of the air and the tempests of the age by the light of faith, they already advance by hope, and they already persevere by charity. For these are blessed in this: that they hunger and thirst after justice, that they piously eat our daily bread, on the Lord's altar ever-living and ever-whole.[59]

None of the scriptural warrants Hugh provides for acolytes seem especially fitting for this order. One might argue that the petition for daily bread could correlate with the acolyte's liturgical service at the Eucharist (which may be the ritual reminder of acolytes' earlier responsibilities in distributing the Eucharist), but *TBCM* notes the acolyte's task of carrying cruets, washbasins, hand-towels, and candles, not the transportation of patens with bread to be consecrated. In spite of Hugh's yoking the Spirit of fortitude and the beatitude on those hungering and thirsting for righteousness with the three theological virtues, particular connections with the office of acolyte remain obscure.

Exorcists

Hugh couples the order of exorcists with the Spirit of knowledge (Isaiah 11:2), the fifth petition of the Lord's Prayer ("Forgive us our debts as we have forgiven our debtors": Matthew 6:12), and the third beatitude on those who mourn (Matthew 5:5 [Vulgate]) in the following passage:

The Spirit of knowledge appears in this work, lest they should attribute it to themselves or become proud because of it, but so that they might know what they were by nature and what they merited through sin and what they could be consecrated by the bishop to do through grace. They are the blessed who mourn for the things that were theirs before they had fallen from the good and lapsed into evil, but they are consoled in the Lord Jesus Christ, who saved them from evils and made them rulers over Satan for powerfully casting out his wickedness. Therefore it is well for these to humble themselves under the powerful hand of God, first for their own redemption by supernal mercy and then for those whom they have taken from the wickedness of the demons by the power given to them by God, saying with suppliant voice: "Forgive us our debts as we also forgive our debtors." In this by the Spirit of knowledge there is present to them what it is proper for rulers to do by their office, nevertheless they know themselves to be sinners by their weakness. [60]

Yoking the "Spirit of knowledge" with the order of exorcists is quite understandable: not only are exorcists presented with a book of exorcisms at their ordination (the ritual transfer of "professional" knowledge), but a long-standing *topos* traces the exorcist's office back to Solomon, noted for his knowledge. [61] Despite Hugh's attempts, determining how the petition for forgiveness of sins and the beatitude on those mourning apply to exorcists is problematic, although it may echo a theological yoking of sinfulness and possession.

Readers

Hugh associates the order of readers with the Spirit of piety (Isaiah 11:2 [LXX]), the sixth petition of the Lord's Prayer ("Do not bring us to the trial" "Lead us not into temptation": Matthew 6:13), and the second beatitude on the meek (Matthew 5:4 [Vulgate]) in the following passage:

> The Spirit of piety appears in this work, when they presume to read and dare to explain not with the image of pride, nor with the self-exaltation of bragging, nor with evil cunning, nor with heretical contempt, but with pious contemplation and Catholic direction they do not reduce the Scriptures to their own power of perceiving but apply their power of perceiving to the Scriptures. "Blessed are" these "meek, for they will possess the earth" [Matthew 5:4]: gathered from the waters and from the streams of the sea in the beginning, this is the firm truth shut away from errors and the streams of errors. So that they might escape such things and be made free from them they should offer this humble prayer to the Lord: "And lead us not into temptation" [Matthew 6:13]. And so having the Spirit of piety they are made meek in proclaiming the truth, in avoiding the snares of temptation and making progress in the Scriptures. [62]

While none of the scriptural warrants adduced by Hugh for the order of readers is particularly germane, associating the "Spirit of piety" and the beatitude on the meek with the public proclamation allows him to denounce his opponents. The "heretics of Brittany" criticize orthodox sacramental practices and hierarchical organization by appealing to the scriptures, but by presenting an idealized portrait of an ordained reader, Hugh covertly criticizes his opponents for their presumption and misinterpretation of the scriptures. Perhaps the petition against being led into temptation could be viewed as a warning to readers of the scriptures against joining Hugh's opponents.

Doorkeepers

Finally Hugh correlates the order of doorkeepers with the Spirit of fear of the Lord (Isaiah 11:3), the seventh petition of the Lord's prayer ("Deliver us from [the] evil [one]": Matthew 6:13), and the first beatitude on the poor in spirit (Matthew 5:3) in the following passage:

> In this activity the Spirit of the fear of the Lord appears, who makes the poor in spirit blessed, and by whose reception the doorkeepers segregate the evil from the good for the kingdom of God, which is the church of Christ. Praying that this be done already in the present and be fulfilled internally in the future, they petition the Lord and say: "Deliver us from evil." This Spirit of the fear of the Lord makes [the doorkeeper] chaste and humble and introduces [him] to wisdom. "The beginning of wisdom," [the Spirit] says, "[is] fear of the Lord" [Psalm 91: 10]. This fear of the Lord is not slavish, is not of sin, but is of charity, which serves freedom. The doorkeeper receives this [Spirit] so that he might be freed from evil and might receive the kingdom of God [prepared] for the poor in spirit.[63]

Since Hugh has emphasized the functions of the doorkeeper in excluding from the liturgical assembly both those who disturb the peace and those deprived of eucharistic communion, the petition to be delivered from evil is quite appropriate for this order. The suitability of the "Spirit of the fear of the Lord" and the beatitude on the poor in spirit seem less pertinent to doorkeepers, unless Hugh wishes to

emphasize their humble position as the first grade of the ecclesiastical
hierarchy.

In the light of the foregoing analysis, Hugh's program of coupling
the gifts of the Spirit, the petitions of the Lord's Prayer, and the
beatitudes with seven orders seems less than completely successful.
Although some grades of the hierarchy (presbyter, deacon, exorcist,
doorkeeper) seem well served by Hugh's theological program, others
(subdeacon, acolyte, reader) are associated with warrants less from
thematic connections and more from where they are positioned in the
seven-factored series.[64]

CONCLUSION

Although contemporary readers may find Hugh's attempt to associate
the seven-fold structure of the clerical orders of his day with other
scriptural "sacred sevens" less than convincing, this text gives us
insight into his thought world. Since the church's order (manifest in
"holy orders") stems ultimately from the creative act of God and since
the Bible authentically reveals God's creative activity, one should
expect to find resonances between the structures of written revelation
and ecclesiastical office. Hugh's theological task is simply to search for
such resonances and to articulate the fruits of his search. By so doing he
reinforces the "sacred canopy" under which he and his contemporaries
live, but he also assigns divine authorization to contingent social
constructs. Contemporary theological reflection on the structures of the
church's ministry may gain from studying *TBCM* a similar "blessed
rage for order"; it will also need a self-critical skepticism about
assigning heavenly warrants for earthly organizations.

Notes

1. I wish to thank Avril Henry, Thomas Amos, William T. Flynn,
Patrick W. Connor, and Charles D. Wright, members of the MEDTEXTL
discussion list (medtextl@uiucvmd.bitnet), for their assistance with bibliography for this study. The participants in the medieval liturgy study group of

the 1994 North American Academy of Liturgy meeting likewise provided helpful critiques.

2. The first printed edition of *Contra haereticos sui temporis sive de ecclesia et ejus ministris libri tres* appears in *Venerabilis Guiberti abbatis B. Mariae de Novigento Opera Omnia*, ed. d'Achery (Paris, 1651), 691–714 and is reprinted in *PL* 192, 1255–1298. In the absence of a contemporary critical edition, references will be made to the *PL* reprinting.

3. In the absence of a modern biography, this sketch is synthesized from *Gallia Christiana nova* XI, 43ff and *Histoire littéraire de la France* XII, 647ff as reprinted in *PL* 192, 1111D–1130D; *Lexicon für Theologie und Kirche* V, 517; *Catholicisme* V, 1038–1039; *Dictionnaire de théologie catholique* VII, 205–215; P. Hebert, "Un archevêque de Rouen au XIIe siècle: Hughes III d'Amiens (1130–1164)," *Revue des questions historiques*, new series 20 (1898), 325–371; Jamieson B. Hurry, *The Octocentenary of Reading Abbey* A.D. *1121–*A.D. *1921* (London: Elliot Stock, 1921), 19–23; Franz Bliemetzrieder, "L'oeuvre d'Anselme de Laon et la littérature théologique contemporaire. 11: Hughes de Rouen, "*Recherches de théologie ancienne et medievale* 6 (1934), 261–283; 7 (1935), 28–51 [especially 41–43]; Odon Lottin, "Les théories du péché originel au XIIe siècle: Tradition Augustiniene, " *Recherches de théologie ancienne et médiévale* 12 (1940), 236–274 [esp. 238–239]; Damien van den Eynde, "Nouvelles précisions chronologiques sur quelques oeuvres théologiques du XIIe siècle," *Franciscan Studies* 13 (1953), 71–118.

I have not been able to consult Jean François Pommeraye, *Histoire des archevêques de Rouen* (Rouen: chez Laurens Maurry, 1667) on this topic.

4. For a balanced account of contemporary scholarship on the school of Laon, see Marcia L. Colish, "Another Look at the School of Laon," *Archives d'histoire doctrinale et littéraire du moyen-âge* 53 (1986), 7–22.

5. Although the response from the Holy See is no longer extant, the request made by the clergy of Rouen to Pope Honorius reads as follows: "Domino papae universali Honorio, Rothomagensis Ecclesia omnem in Christo obedientiam. Elegimus electione communi filium nostrum Hugonem abbatem Radingensem nobis in pontificem. Super hoc quaesivimus assensum domini nostri Henrici regis Anglorum, et obtinuimus. Ab episcopo quidem Salesberiensi, sub cujus manu abbatis officio fungebatur, nobis eum reddi liberum et absolutum quaesivimus, et cum libertate suscepimus. Sed quia, ipso revelante, percepimus, quod sine auctoritatis vestrae assensu eum habere non poteramus, cum et hoc in litteris vestris praedicto regi Anglorum directis ita scriptum legimus: *Ipsum itaque sub primo jure absque dominio nostro tanquam specialem beati Petri et sanctae Romanae Ecclesiae clericum retinemus;* eapropter donari eum nobis a sublimitate vestra requirimus; quam tanto chariorem habebimus, quanto a vestra gratia quaerimus, ut sub nullius umquam

jure vel potestate, nisi sub vestra tantummodo pia protectione eum persistere gaudeamus, charissime pater et domine." *PL* 192, 1113B–D.

6. *PL* 192, 1141–1248

7. Van den Eynde, "Nouvelle précisions," 74–77.

8. "[L]e personage le plus capable d'avoir conçu cette audacieuse riposte, et done la carrière, de surcroît, offrirait le cadre le mieux adapté, serait Hugues d'Amiens, parent, croit on, du cardinal Mathieu d'Albano, successivement prieur de Saint-Martial de Limoges en 1113, plus, peu après, de Lewes, le grand prieuré clunisien d'Angleterre, et de là, en 1125, abbé de Reading, maison affiliée a l'Ordre, jusqu'au moment où ses mérites divers le firent asseoir sur le siege de Rouen (1129–1130). C'est à Reading, exactement, que je l'imaginerais, vers les années 1127–1128, s'ecrimant contre l'illustre Cistercian." André Wilmart, "Une riposte de l'ancien monachisme au manifeste de Saint Bernard," *Revue Bénédictine* 46 (1934), 296–344 [here 307].

9. *PL* 192, 1345–1352.

10. Van den Eynde, "Nouvelles précisions," 77.

11. F. Lecomte provides a critical edition of the work in *Archives d'historie doctrinals et litteraire du moyen-âge* 33 (1958), 227–274; a fragmentary version is printed in *PL* 192, 1247–1256.

12. *PL* 192, 1323–1345.

13. Van den Enyde, "Nouvelles précisions," 80–82.

14. *PL* 192, 1299–1324.

15. Van den Eynde, "Nouvelles précisions," 82–83.

16. *PL* 192, 1131–1138.

17. A letter of Hugh of Ribémont (a town in the diocese of Laon) to Gravion, certainly written prior to 1127 and probably dating between 1099 and 1113 according to van den Eynde ["Nouvelles précisions," 71–72], appears in *PL* 166, 833–836. J. Huemer has edited this letter along with certain poetic works found in the same manuscript source as *Hugonis Ambianensis sive Ribomontensis opuscula* (Vienna: A. Holder/K.K. Hof-und Universitäts-Buch-handlung, 1880).

18. "Inter pontifices speciali dignus honore
     Hic nostrae crnis Hugo resignet onus.
Consignata brevi clauduntur membra sepulcro,
     Non tamen acta viri claudit uterque polus.
Quidquid dispensat et compartitur in omnes,
     Gratia contulerat, praestiteratque viro.
Fecundos igitur virtutum copia fructus
     Fecit et ultra hominem et magnificatus homo.
Tandem post celebris felicia tempora vitae,
     Sustulit emeritum flebilis hora senem.

Par, Martine, tibi consorsque futurus eamdem
Sortitus tecum est commoriendo diem." *PL* 192, 1118C–D.

19. Gunar Freibergs, "Hugh of Amiens: An Abelardian Against
Abelard," in *Aspectus et Affectus: Essays and Editions in Grossteste and
Medieval Intellectual Life in Honor of Richard C. Dales*, ed. Gunar Freibergs
(New York, AMS Press, 1993), 81.

20. Raoul Manselli studies TBCM for the information that it gives
concerning the "heretics of Brittany" in "Ugo arcivescovo di Rouen e gli eretici
di Nantes," in *Il secolo XII: religione popolare ed eresia* (Roma: Jouvence,
1983), 287–294.

21. "Sanctae Romanae Ecclesiae filio ALBERICO Ostiense episcopo,
quamsaepe sedis apostolicae legato, peccator HUGO Rothomagensis utcunque
sacerdos. Reverende Pater, tuis obedire mandatis pro tempore distuli, non
tamen illud omisi, sed praesta petenti veniam, cui soles praestare gratiam.
Digna sedet mihi memoria reminisci, qualiter in finibus Galliarum prope mare
Brittanicum, civitate Nannetensi meruimus assistere tibi. Ibi sanctorum corpora
martyrum Donatiani et Rogatiani fratrum, multo coetu praesente fidelium,
suscepta praesentasti, praesentata relocasti cum digno honore et gratiarum
actione. Ibi tecum aspeximus cometam praecipiti lapsu in occiduo ruentem,
ruinam haeresis, quae in Armorico tunc scatebat, te protestans signantem. Ibi
quidem coram orthodoxa praedicatione tua plebs haeretica stare non poterat.
Eorum haeresiarches pertimuit, nec apparere praesumpsit. Proinde placuit tibi
super haeresibus insurgentibus non aliqua scribere, quod et suscepimus tuae
jussionis auctoritate; sed succincto opere, sed brevi charactere." *PL* 192,
1255B–1256B.

22. "Les estimations actuelles, mêlant calculs et critique des documents
anciens, permettent de décrire cette apparition comme moins 'brillante', pour
parlet commairement, que le précédent passage [de la comète de Halley], si
fameux, de 1066, mais au moins aussi spectaculaire: une queue nettement plus
longue, une période de visibilité exceptionnelle, et une luminosité suffisante
pour qu'on l'ait vue 'même quand la lune fut pleine (les 8 mai, 6 juin et 7
juillet)'. Si Hugues et Albéric l'observèrent évidemment après le passage au
périhélie, et dans le ciel du soir 'glissant tête la première vers l'ouest', ce ne put
être qu'en mai ou au début de juin, puisque le légat se trouvait avec saint
Bernard dès le 2 juillet à Bordeaux. Une date plus précise est peut-être à tirer de
l'ostension de reliques mentionnée par Hugues d'Amiens: bien que ce fût loin
d'être une règle, on aimait à level les reliques le jour de la fête du saint. N'y a-t-
il pas à parier qu'Albéric et Hugues, se trouvant à Nantes en mai–juin 1145, ont
profité pour se rendre en l'église Saint Donatien de ce que la fête des saints
Donatien et Rogatien, martyrs nantais, tombait justement le jeudi 24 mai.
C'était peu après la nouvelle lune, quand la comète brillait au plus fort de la

nuit. . . . " Gilles Bounoure, "L'archevêque, l'hérétique et la comète (Première partie)," *Medievales: Langes, textes, histoire* 14 (1988), 119–120.

23. "Albéric, créé cardinal en 1138, fut successivement légat en Angleterre (1138), en Syrie et en Palestine (1139–1140). En 1144 il est envoyé par Lucius II en France, où pendent l'année 1145 il s'efforce d'extirper l'hérésie henricienne. Il y a retourne au début de 1147, dans la suite d'Eugène III. Pendant les fêtes de Pâques (20 avril—8 juin), il assiste au concile de Paris, le premier qui s'occupa des erreurs de Gilbert de la Porrée. Après le 22 novembre de la même année, son nom diparaît des actes pontificaux. Il mourut à Verdun au début de l'année suivante, avant le concile de Reims.

Les événements de Nantes, que Hugues rappelle dans sa préface, se sont passés au mois de mai 1145, durant la légation d'Albéric en France. Le *Contra haereticos* se situe dès lord entre fin 1145 et fin 1147. Il se rapproche toutefois davantage de la dernière date, car Hugues s'excuse d'en avoir retardé notablement la composition après l'entrevue de Nantes. D'un autre côté, l'ouvrage ne contient pas encore d'allusions ni aux erreurs de Gilbert de la Porrée ni au concile de Paris, ou pourtant Hugues se rencontra de nouveau avec Albéric et où il prit une part active aux débats.

Je pense donc que Hugues acheva son écrit antihérétique en vue de sa rencontre avec Albéric à Paris vers Pâques 1147 et qu'il le lui offrit à cette occasion." Van den Eynde, "Nouvelles précisions," 78–79.

24. "Mirandum quippe miraculum omni veneratione dignum, non tamen novum, non quidem est insolitum, sic nempe olim Dominum egisse legimus de Moysi Spiritu in libro Numeri: *Et dixit Dominus ad Moysen: Congrega mihi septuaginta viros de senibus Israel, et duces eos ad ostium tabernaculi foederis, faciesque ibi stare tecum, ut descendam, et loquar tibi, et auferam de spiritu tuo, tradamque eis ut sustentent tecum onus populi, et non tu solus gravens (Num.* XI, 16, 17). *Venit igitur Moyses, et narravit populo verba Domini, congregans septuaginta viros desenioribus Israel, quos stare fecit circa tabernaculum; descenditque Dominus per nubem, et locutus est ad eum auferens de spiritu qui erat in Moyse; et dans septuaginta viris. Cumque requievisset Spiritus in eis, prophetaverunt, nec ultra cessaverunt (*ibid., 24, 25). Solus quippe Moyses sanctum acceperat Spiritum, quo regere poterat commissum sibi a Domino populum. Ipsum itaque Moysi Spiritum, non humanum esse sentias, sed divinum; Deus enim erat Spiritus quem a Domino Moyses habuit, quem a Moyse sumptum mentibus aliorum Dominus infudit: erat quidem in Moyse Spiritus Domini, qui et datus est aliis, quos more divino replevit; totus in Moyse, totus in illis. Moyses ipse hunc Spiritum fatetur esse divinum, ubi mox respondit, dicens: *Quis tribuat ut omnis populus prophetet, et det eis Dominus Spiritum suum (Num.* XI, 29)." PL 192, 1274A–C.

25. "Ipse etiam Moyses pontifex et sacerdos Domini, super Josue ministrum suum manus imposuit, eique Spiritum sanctum dedit. In Deuteronomio legis: *Josue vero filius Nun, repletus est Spiritu sapientiae, quia Moyses posuit super eum manus suas: et obedierunt ei filii Israel, feceruntque sicut praecepit Domiinus Moysi (Deut.* XXXIV, 9)." *PL* 192, 1274C.

26. "Iste est Moyses qui Aaron primum sub lege pontificem, et filios ejus consecravit, eisque Spiritum sanctum ad agenda divina mysteria pontifex ipse et sacerdos mirifice dedit. De ejus sacerdotio Psaimista sic ait: *Moyses et Aaron in sacerdotibus ejus; et Samuel inter eos qui invocant nomen ejus (Psal.* XCVIII, 6)." *PL* 192, 1274C–D.

27. "Elias quoque, si bene recolo, non solummodo Spiritum sanctum habuit, sed etiam Eliseo dedit: *Oro,* inquit Eliseus Eliae, *oro ut spiritus tuns duplex fiat in me (V Reg.* 11, 9). At ille: *Si videris, inquit, quando tollar a te, erit quod petisti (V Reg.* 11, 10). Ad hoc Eliseus perstitit, vidit et accepit. Proinde filii prophetarum ita dixerunt: *Requievit spiritus Eliae super Eliseum* (ibid., 15). Unde et Eliseo sicut prius Eliae subditi permanserunt." *PL* 192, 1274D–1275A.

28. "Sicut enim summus pontifex et universalis episcopus noster Jesus Christus, ex omnibus discipulis suis elegit duodecim, quos caeteris praeferens apostolos nominavit, quos etsi puros homines, sui tamen officii fecit esse consortes, et divinae magnificentiae compotes: ita quoque ipsorum in episcopali gratia successores praesules sive pontifices excellentia singulari praeminere fecit. . . . *PL* 192, 1273C–D.

29. *"Ubi* autem *venit plenitudo temporis,* in qua *misit Deus Filium suum* pontificem, et episcopum secundum ordinem Melchisedech in aeternum, effusa est a sede majestatis superabundans, et largiflua septiformis gratia Spiritus sancti; ex quo pontificalis auctoritas, et episcopalis dignitas plenius excrevit *(Gal.* IV, 4). Hinc Petro ait: *Tu es Petrus, et super hanc Petram aedificabo Ecclesiam meam (Matth.* XVI, 13). Est enim et Petrus in ea, et ipsa in Petro, episcopus in Ecclesia, et Ecclesia in episcopo. *Est episcopus Ecclesiae fundamentum, quia per episcopum habet Ecclesia Spiritum sanctum. . . .* De petra ista, super quam fundata est mater Ecclesia, sub pastorali virga bis percussa, ad amorem Dei et proximi excitata, fluunt aquae largissime, aquae salutares, aquae vivae. . . ." *PL* 192, 1275A–B [emphasis added].

30. "Qui autem ordine censentur inferiori, ut presbyteri, diacones, et caeteri gradu canonico in Ecclesia promoti, habent utique Spiritum sanctum, quo bene vivunt, et in Ecclesia Dei pro officio die deserviunt; sed aliis quem acceperunt sanctum dare Spiritum manus impositione non possunt. Soli hoc episcopi a Domino speciali praerogativa susceperunt, quod praeceflenti opere, ipsum quem habent Spiritum sanctum, ipso donante qui dedit, donant et aliis,

quibus ex officio pontificali, fusis precibus ad Dominum, pie manus imponunt."
PL 192, 1273D–1274A.

31. "Episcopi ... funguntur vice Christi, et principaliter aedificant domum Dei." *PL* 192, 1273C.

32. "[M]ore apostolico sanctum donent Spiritum his, quibus rite manus imponunt." *PL* 192, 1273D.

33. "Est episcopi conficere chrisma sacrum, oleum sanctum, oleum infirmorum; consecrare basilicas Dei et altaria, calicem et corporalia, officiales et eorum vestes et omnia Ecclesiae instrumenta. Baptizatos confirmare, caesares et reges sacrare." *PL* 192, 1275B.

34. *"Qui biberit,* inquit, *aquam, quam ego dabo, fiet in eo fons aquae salientis in vitam aeternam (Joan.* IV, 13). Et alibi: *Qui in me credit, flumina de ventre ejus fluent aquae vivae: hoc autem dicit de Spiritu quem accepturi erant credentes in eum (Joan.* VII, 38, 39). *Cum,* inquit, *venerit Spiritus veritatis, docebit vos omnem veritatem (Joan.* XVI, 13). Quod itaque non potest solus homo scire sensu suo, potest homo plenus Spiritu sancto: secundum hoc ait: *Omnia quaecunque audivi a Patre meo, nota feci vobis (Joan.* XV, 15). Nota in Spiritu veritatis, nota in plenitudine charitatis. Talibus *datum est nosse mysterium regni Dei (Marc.* IV, 11). Ne quis autem praesumat eos non audire, vel eorim praecepta cassare, dixit: *Qui vos audit, me audit; et qui vos spernit, me spernit: qui autem me spernit, spernit eum qui misit me (Luc.* X, 16). Et alibi: *Non,* inquit, *vos estis qui loquimini, sed Spiritus Patris vestri, qui loquitur in vobis (Matth.* X, 20)." *PL* 192, 1275B–C.

35. "Hujus officii praecellens potestas, et potestatis praecelsa dignitas, non angelis, non cuilibet supernorum civium majestati collate est. Deus homo eam homini dedit, non ope humana, sed caelesti; non acquisitione meriti, sed electione pietatis, ex dono Spiritus sancti gratanter accepti, quo consecratus ad hoc opus in Christ's meruit. . . . *Consecratus itaque sacerdos stat, vice Christi coram Patre summo Dei et hominum mediator. . . ."* *PL* 192, 1276A–B [emphasis added].

36. "[C]onsecratus ad hoc opus in Christo meruit, ut prorsus idem ipsum efficiat in altari quod Christus fecerit manibus suis in coena paschali. Quapropter manus illae, manus ad hoc sacratae, quibus Christ corpus et sanguis in altari sacro habet confici, manus utique sunt Christi, quibus, offertur Patri Filius, qui tollit peccata mundi, et defunctos fideles liberata poenis, et aeternae beatitudinis participes facit. Consecratus itaque sacerdos stat, vice Christi coram Patre summo Dei et hominum mediator, dum sacraments ineffabilia desuper apertis coelis profert et elevat ab altari, quibus Ecclesiae filios participes communione facit, dum in Spiritu sancto quam accepit, et poenitentibus peccata dimittit, et Deo reconciliat quos absolvit." *PL* 192, 1276B–C.

37. "Sunt oculi pontificum et presbyterorum, ut in quantum possunt quietam et pacem eos habere faciant." *PL* 192, 1276D–1277A.

38. "[Q]ui docere populos, et orare quietius elaborant. . . . Spiritus intellectus, quo et sacramenta quae dispensat intelligunt. . . . quo praedicatoribus Verbi Dei pacem et quietam, removendo perturbatores et inquietos, pro posse fuo faciunt. . . . [P]er diaconias suas episcopis viam doctrinae faciunt, et de singulis episcopo quae norunt, certius innotescunt. Et hos etiam evangelistas esse pontifices statuunt. . . ." *PL* 192, 1277A.

39. "[C]onsecrantur Levitae seu diaconi . . . ut in Ecclesia Dei praesto sint altari, dum in eo fiunt sacramenta corporis et sanguinis Domini. . . . [S]uscipiunt a consecratore dispensationem veri corporis et sanguinis Jesu Christi. De manu . . . pontificis, seu presbyteri, suscipiunt quo se et alios munifica largitione alimento vitali reficiunt. . . . [Q]ui peragendis sacramentis invigilant. . . . Hi quoque in celebratione Dominicae missae dum sanctum Evangelium pronuntiant praesenti Ecclesiae, respondetur eis, *Gloria tibi, Domine,* consona fidelium voce." *PL* 192, 1276C–1277B.

40. "[B]ona Ecclesiae sub episcopi voluntate disponunt. . . . [Spiritus intellectus] quo res sibi commissas pie disponunt. . . . " *PL* 192, 1276D–1277A.

41. "[S]ubdiaconi promoventur . . . ut obedientes pareant Levitis, atque presbyteris." *PL* 192, 1277B.

42. "[S]ubdiaconi promoventur . . . ut . . . praeparent sacrata vasa in quibus conficitur corpus et sanguis Christi. Praeparent pro more panem, et vinum, et aquam, et vasa his convenientia: pallas quoque altaris, et prandea [al. brandea], prompta sollicitudine et diligentia. . . . [Q]uo [Spiritu consilii] suscepto . . . intendit . . . mundata praesentare vasa sacramentis." *PL* 192, 1277B–C.

43. "[S]equuntur acolythi . . . ut in Ecclesia Dei ferant urceola, aquamanilia, manutergia officio convenientia, ut ante faciem Evangelii praeferant ipsi luminaria accensa, cerogerulis diligenter imposita; ita ut in ipsis appareat quod verae fidei lumine, quod spei certissimae splendore, quod charitatis ardore justitiam regni Dei, per Evangelium declaratam, et ipsi quaerant, et alios ad quaerendum sui luminis exemplo commoneant; et exinde tam seipsos, quam et alios ad percipienda sacramenta fortiter esuriendo perducant." *PL* 192, 1277D–1278A.

44. "Exorcistas benedictio pontificalis imperatores facit, non emolumenti terreni, non potentiae carnalis, sed ex virtute Dei, qua Satanam, et omnem nequitiam ab energumenis et quibusque daemoniacis, invocato nomine Jesu, praemissa oratione facta ex sufflatione, propellunt; ut ad baptismi sacri gratiam, et ad percipienda sacramenta pervinire valeant." *PL* 192, 1278B.

45. "[L]egant verba Veteris ac Novi Testament, legant more solito, tempora statuto, et loco congruo, protestantes sacras novi ac veteris instrumenti

paginas, et Patrum agiographa, in unum Dominum nostrum Jesum Christum consona et completa; et ea debita veneratione semper audienda, pro tempore servanda." *PL* 192, 1278D.

46. "Hi pro officio suo eos intromittunt quos Catholicos esse cognoscunt, non credentes excludunt, quods irrisores vel esse perturbatores sentiunt. Illos etiam valde rejiciunt, quos ab episcopi communione privatos esse pro certo noverunt." *PL* 192, 1979A–B.

47. "Attende qui legis, ... attende hos septem gradus, has septem columnas, ore sapientiae Dei, per manus episcopi ordine distinctas, benedictione firmatas, sacramentis ornatas. Has septem episcopus septem orationis precibus elevat, septem donis sancti Spiritus affirmat, septem beatitudinum honore cumulat. Columnas tales per episcopos ordinari Dominus Jesus Christuis instituit, et septem gradibus designavit. Ipse etiam in seipso tenens gradus istos proposuit auctoritate sua tenendos." *PL* 192, 1279C–1280A.

48. See Heinz Meyer, *Die Zahlenallegorese im Mittelalter: Methode und Gebrauch* (Munich, 1977) and Heinz Meyer and Rudolf Suntrup, "Zum Lexikon der Zahlenbedeutungen im Mittelalter. Einführung in die Methode unde Probeartikel: Die Zahl 7," *Frühmittelalterliche Studien* 11 (1977), 1–73. For an application of medieval number theory to holy orders, see Roger E. Reynolds, "'At Sixes and Sevens'—And Eights and Nines: The Sacred Mathematics of Sacred Orders in the Early Middle Ages," *Speculum* 54/4 (1979), 669–684.

49. In *TBCM* 11, I Hugh lists the members of the church: "'All' are clearly the bishops, deacons, subdeacons, acolytes, exorcists, readers, doorkeepers, and the rest under the clerical crown [of tonsure]; princes and power of this earthly government; and the rest signed by the name Christian" ("omnes videlicet episcopi, diaconi, subdiaconi, acolythi, exorcistae, lectores, ostiarii, et caeteri sub corona clericali; principes quoque et potestates hujus terreni moderaminis, et reliqui nomine Christiano signati" *PL* 192, 1273C). Note that the named clerical orders number seven by omitting presbyters.

Yet later in the same chapter Hugh writes: "There are seven very useful and necessary grades, adorned by sevenfold grace at the hand of the pontiff, for sustaining and preserving God's house. These are the men of the second order (that is to say, presbyters), and after them Levites or deacons; then subdeacons, acolytes, exorcists, readers, doorkeepers, for the offices delegated to them by the bishop." ("Septem enim sunt gradus illi perutiles et necessarii, ad sustentandam et conservandam domum Dei manu pontificis perornati gratia septiformi. Hi sunt secundi ordinis viri, scilicet presbyteri, et post eos Levitae seu diaconi; exinde subdiaconi, acolythi, exorcistae, lectores, ostiarii, pro officiis ab episcopo sibi delegatis." *PL* 192, 1275D). Now the clerical grades number seven by the omission of the bishop.

50. "Post apostolos enim secuti sunt viri apostolici, pontifices et episcopi, qui virtute coelesti semper aedificant domum Christi quam sustentant septem columnis.... Isti si absque nutu episcopi, vel contra episcopum agere praesumunt, a septenario numero decidunt, a septem columnis praetaxatis resiliunt, a domo sapientiae prolapsi pereunt.... de septem columnis Ecclesiae Dei aliqua sub brevitate dicamus." *PL* 192, 1275D–1276A [emphasis added].

51. "Ministri tui sunt episcopi provisores strenui, tutores fortissimi. Ex te tibi generant filios fortes et ingenuos; ex his quos approbant, eligunt et exaltant; ex his creant septem gradus honoris, septem columnas fortitudinis, quas septem precibus Dominicis consecrant, septem donis sancti Spiritus illustrant, septem beatitudinibus glorificant. Hae septem columnae et Ecclesiam Dei sustentant, et perpetuo splendore clarificant." *PL* 192, 1280A [emphasis added].

52. "Praetaxatas septem preces illas Jesus Christus edocuit plenas et perfectas, deditque pro sua magnificentia septem sancti Spiritus dona mirifica, et septem beatitudines suis fidelibus in aeternum largitur et ultra, septem istis precibus septem dona sancti Spiritus impetrantur; septem donis illis septem beatitudines acquiruntur. Fides in precibus, spes in donis, charitas in beatitudinibus pariter assignantur; in precibus studium, in donis praemium, in beatitudinis gaudium, si pie quaeris citius invenis.... Ecce pro septem precibus, pro septem donis, pro septem beatitudinibus vere beata es mater Ecclesia, sacramentis plenissime divinis uberrima in te solvuntur peccata, praestatur venia, donatur gratia." *PL* 192, 1279C–D.

53. In this tripartite structure is there a possible echo of the purification/illumination/perfection program that marks the liturgical theology of Pseudo-Dionysius the Areopagite in *The Ecclesiastical Hierarchy*?

54. "Septem [ordinem] autem sunt propter septiformem gratiam Spiritus Sancti: cuius qui non sunt participes, ad gradus ecclesiasticos indigne accedunt; illi vero in quorum mentibus diffusa est septiformis gratia Spiritus Sancti, cum ad ecclesiasticos ordines accedunt, in ipsa spiritualis gradus promotione ampliorem gratiam percipere creduntur." *Magistri Petri Lombardi Parisiensis Episcopi Sententiae in IV Libris Distinctae. Tomus 11: Liber Ill et IV.* Spicilegium Bonaventurianum, 5 (Grottaferrata [Romae]: Collegii S. Bonaventurae ad Claras Aquas, 1981), 394.

55. The list of the seven gifts of the Holy Spirit ultimately stems from Isaiah 11:2–3. In the Hebrew original there are only six gifts listed, "fear of the Lord" being listed twice. The LXX however translated the list in this passage "pneuma sophias kai suneseôs, pneuma boulês kai ischous, pneuma gnôseôs *kai eusebeias* emplêsei auton, pneuma phobou theou" [emphasis added]. The Vulgate in turn translated this version of the text into Latin, thus producing the standard medieval list. See Reynolds, "At Sixes," 669, n. 3.

56. "Praefulget in hoc opere Spiritus sapientiae quo in eis sanctificatur nomen Patris, sicut in oratione Dominica precatur quisque fidelis. . . . fiuntque pacifici, ideoque beati censentur, *quoniam filii Dei vocabuntur*. . . . Pacificant isti in vita praesenti Deum homini, pro ordine suo sacramentis rite celebratis, suisque meritis, et manibus suis coelesti medicamine plenis. Sciendum est itaque, et omni preadicandum veneratione, quia Spiritus sapientiae sanctificat eos Patri nostro Deo in filios, non quoscunque, sed pacificos, ideoque beatos, et in praesenti saeculo, et in futuro." *PL* 192, 1276C–D.

57. "Praefulget in hoc opere Levitarum seu diaconorum, Spiritus intellectus, quo et sacramente quae dispensant intelligunt; quo res sibi commissas pie disponunt; quo praedicatoribus Verbi Dei pacem et quietam, removendo perturbatores et inquietos, pro posse suo faciunt. Hi perornati castitate, et beati mundo corde, quaerunt regnum Dei, dum per diaconias suas episcopis viam doctrinae faciunt, et de singulis episcopo quae norunt, certius innotescunt. Et hos etiam evangelistas esse pontifices statuunt, et hic vices pontificum diligenter exsequi pro ordine suo satagunt." *PL* 192, 1277A.

58. "Apparet in hoc opere Spiritus consilii quem specialiter accipit, dum consecratur oratione pontificis, quo suscepto servare seipsum mundum et castum intendit, et praepare se mysteriis, et mundata praesentare vasa sacramentis. Isti quidem de seipsis minime praesumunt, sed voluntatem suam voluntati Domini supponunt, et humiliter dicunt: *Fiat voluntas tua sicut in coelo et in terra* . . .: sicut in spiritualibus Patribus nostris, sic et in nobis eorum filiis adhuc terrenis, adhuc decertantibus contra concupiscentias carnis. Fiunt isti misericordes ex hoc fiducialius misericordiam a Deo postulantes." *PL* 192, 1277C–D.

59. "[I]ta ut in ipsis appareat quod verae fidei lumine, quod spei certissimae splendore, quod charitatis ardore justitiam regni Dei, per Evangelium declaratam, et ipsi quaerant, et alios ad quaerendum sui luminis exemplo commoneant; et exinde tam seipsos, quam et alios ad percipienda sacramenta fortiter esuriendo perducant.

Apparet in hoc opere Spiritus fortitudinis, quo inter procellas aereae potestatis, et tempestates saeculi, jam fidei lumine vivunt, jam spe proficiunt, jam charitate persistunt. Hi quoque in hoc beati sunt, quia esuriunt et sitiunt justitiam. . . . quia panem nostrum quotidianum semper vivum, semper integrum in altari Dominico pie degustant." *PL* 192, 1277D–1278A.

60. "Apparet in hoc opere Spiritus scientiae, ne hoc sibi attribuant, ne inde superbiant, sed sciant quid fuerint per naturam, quid meruerint per culpam, et quid ipsi ab episcopo consecrati possint facere per gratiam. Sunt beati qui lugent suos in quibus ante fuerant a bono defectus. . . . ad mala prolapsos, sed consolantur in Domino Jesu Christo, qui eos a malis eruit, et imperatores super Satanam, ad propellandam ejus nequitiam potenter effecit.

Bene igitur bene isti primum pro seipsis misericordia superna redemptis, deinde pro illis, quos potestate sibi a Deo collata eruunt a daemonum nequitiis, humiliantur sub potenti manu Dei, dicentes voce supplici: *Dimitte nobis debita nostra, sicut et nos dimittimus debitoribus nostris. . . .* In hoc Spiritu scientiae eis praesto est quod, licet pro officio sint imperatores, sciunt tamen pro fragilitate sua esse peccatores." *PL* 192, 1278B–C.

61. See Bede's *Super acta apostolorum expositio* 19: "Josephus mentions that King Solomon contrived to teach his people the types of exorcism, i.e., of adjuring, by which unclean spirits expelled from a person never return again later on" ("Refert Josephus regem Salomonem excogitasse, suamque gentem docuisse modos exorcismi, id est, adjurationis, quibus immundi spiritus expulsi ab homine ulterius reverti non sint ausi") *PL* 92, 983A.

62. "Apparet in hoc opere Spiritus pietatis, dum non typo superbiae, non elatione jactantiae, non astu maligno, non fastu haeretico praesumunt legere, audent exponere, sed pio intruitu, Catholico ductu Scripturas non suo sensui, imo sensum suum applicant Scripturas. *Beati mites,* isti *quoniam possidebunt terram (Matth.* V, 4), ab aquis et fluctibus maris, ab initio segregatam hoc est solidam veritatem ab erroribus et efforum fluctibus sequestratam. Haec ut evadant et liberi fiant hanc ad Dominum humilem effundunt precem: *Et ne nos inducas in tentationem (Matth.* VI, 13).

Habentes itaque Spiritum pietatis fiunt mites in pronuntiatione veritatis, evitantes laqueos tentationis et proficiunt in Scripturis." *PL* 192, 1278D–1279A.

63. "Apparet in hoc opere Spiritus timoris Domini, qui beatos pauperes spiritu facit *(Matth* V, 3), quo suscepto, ostiarii a regno Dei, quod est Ecclesia Christ, secludunt malos a bonis. Hoc fieri jam in praesenti, et compleri penitus in futuro orantes, petunt a Domino, et dicunt: *Libera nos a malo (Matth.* VI, 13). Spiritus iste timoris Domini castum et humilem facit et sapientiam introducit. *Initium,* inquit, *sapientiae timor Domini (Psl* CX, 10).Timor iste Domini non est servilis, non est peccati, sed charitatis, quae libera servit. Hoc ostiarius accipit, ut liberetur a malo, et pro paupertate spiritus recipiat regnum Dei." *PL* 192, 1279B.

64. It should be noted that Hugh enriches his theology of sacred orders by concluding *TBCM* Book 11 with an "Ordinal of Christ," a collection of brief texts by which each office-holder in the ecclesiastical hierarchy is pictured as an imitator of Christ through (a) particular event(s) in Christ's life.

In his magisterial study of this late antique and medieval literary genre, Roger E. Reynolds signals the distinctive character of the Hugh's Ordinal: "The sanctions which Hugh uses in his Ordinal of Christ are extraordinary for several reasons. First, Hugh uses a number of Old Testament sanctions which were to his time unknown in the Western Church. Many

authors of early medieval tracts on the ecclesiastical orders had found
precedents and parallels for the grades in the Old Testament Temple hierarchy,
and there were Old Testament theophanies, cited in such Ordinals as the Latin
intermediate forms . . . and the English pontificals. . . . But Hugh goes back
even further, to creation itself, and through a variety of Old Testament passages
argues that the ecclesiastical hierarchy was established by and patterned after
the actions of the eternal Christ in the form of God or the Logos. Secondly, the
traditional dominical sanctions which Hugh uses are extraordinary for their
phraseology and for the way Hugh mixes several dominical sanctions under a
single grade which in earlier Ordinals of Christ would have been attached to
distinct grades. . . . The tendency to combine diverse sanctions under one grade
may stem from Hugh's earlier training by the great sentence collectors, Anselm
and Ralph of Laon. It is also possible that Hugh's defense of the ecclesiastical
hierarchy caused him to multiply dominical sanctions related in any way to an
individual grade." (Roger E. Reynolds, *The Ordinals of Christ from their
Origins to the Twelfth Century*, Beiträge zur Geschichte und Quellenkunde des
Mittelalters, 7 [Berlin-New York: Walter de Gruyter, 1978], 131–132).

PENANCE IN TRANSITION: POPULAR PIETY AND PRACTICE

Michael S. Driscoll

INTRODUCTION

It may be said that Penance was to the Middle Ages what Baptism was to the Patristic period.[1] Yet in the time of Alcuin of York (ca. 735–804) the penitential practices were in a state of transition as the older form of canonical penance[2] gave way to the monastic practice of tariffed penance. Tariffed penance gets its name from the biblical trilogy of praying, fasting and almsgiving. The Celtic and Anglo-Saxon monks organized their penitential practices so that every possible sin corresponded to a specific tariff in conjunction with the biblical trilogy. In the course of time, these tariffs were catalogued and codified in books called penitentials. Much has already been written about the Irish and Anglo-Saxon monastic contribution to the penitential metamorphosis towards private penance, but there is still something to be said about the monastic spirituality which produced the various penitential practices. This chapter will revisit the question of the penitential books which governed the practice of penance in the early Middle Ages, attempting to contextualize them in their spiritual milieu. Other documents will be examined in order to evaluate the penitential practices which were in a state of transition.

Among Celtic and Anglo-Saxon monks, the abbot of each monastery assumed the role of spiritual director or spiritual doctor of all monks in his charge. In old Irish, he was called the *amnchara* or "soul friend". According to an Irish proverb, "a person without a confessor is like a body without a head."[3] This spiritual practice gave rise to two kinds of historical document which attest to the importance of penance at this period, namely the penitential books (*libri paenitentiales*) and the prayer booklets (*precum libelli*). Both groups of documents have

their origins within Celtic monasticism and subsequently were circulated first in England and later on the Continent, exercising an
important influence upon the spirituality of the early Middle Ages. The
penitential books indicate with graphic detail the punishments levied
for the various sins. The punishment was conceived of as a kind of
tariff or a medicine which corresponded to the specific illness. These
tariffs included the recitation of the psalms, corporal punishments, such
as fasting on bread and water, and other kinds of corporal works. The
prayer booklets contained such things as the psalms and litanies to be
used for the accomplishment of penances prescribed by the
penitentials.[4] For this reason these two kinds of documents need to be
studied together as complementary manuals.[5] To these two genres of
documents a third should be added, namely that of the *specula* or
spiritual mirrors. These treatises on moral virtue were manuals destined
for lay use in the search for Christian perfection. At times, the
distinction between a *speculum* and a *precum libellus* blurs as we find
large sections of prayers, usually associated with the prayer books, in
the mirrors.

These three types of documents (*libri paenitentiales, libelli precum*
and *specula*) are the monuments *par excellence* of Carolingian popular
penitential piety. In order to gauge the importance and proper usage of
the *libri paenitentiales* the writings of Alcuin of York in relation to
these three categories will be studied. Among the above mentioned
genres two examples have long been attributed to Alcuin, namely
several prayer books and a mirror. In addition to these, Alcuin
composed a letter entitled *Ad Pueros Sancti Martini* which was in
reality his treatise on penance. This study, therefore, will attempt to
obtain a fresh examination of the *libri paenitentiales* in the light of
other penitential writings. In the past, the penitential books have
received harsh criticism as aberrant texts reflecting twisted views about
God's mercy and the value of human penance. An examination of an
ensemble of textual genres will help to contextualize properly the
penitential books and to show their mutual influence. It must be said
from the outset that when speaking of lay popular spirituality, one is
limited to the practices of a certain group of lay persons, those educated
in the monastic schools. Much of their spiritual piety was in imitation
of the monastic practices that they experienced while at school and
which they needed to adapt for a spiritual life in the world.

Lest we exaggerate the importance of confession for the expiation of sins, the Penitential of Cummean (ca. 650) spells out twelve ways in which sins are forgiven:

Here begins the Prologue of the health-giving medicine of souls. As we are about to tell of the remedies of wounds according to the determinations of the earlier fathers, of sacred utterance to thee, my most faithful brother, first we shall indicate the treatments by the method of abridgment.

The first remission then is that by which we are baptized in water, according to this [passage]: "Unless a man be born again of water and of the Holy Spirit, he cannot see the Kingdom of God" (Jn 3:5). The second is the emotion of charity, as this [text] has it: "Many sins are remitted unto her for she hath loved much" (Lk 7:47). The third is the fruit of alms, according to this: "As water quencheth fire so doth alms extinguish sin" (Ecclus 3: 33). The fourth is the shedding of tears, as saith the Lord: "Since Ahab wept in my sight and walked sad in my presence I will not bring evil things in his days" (I King 21:29). The fifth is the confession of offenses, as the Psalmist testifies: "I said, I will confess my injustices to the Lord, and thou hast forgiven the iniquity of my sin" (Ps 31:5). The sixth is affliction of heart and body, as the Apostle comforts us: "I have given such a man to Satan unto the destruction of the flesh, that his spirit may be saved in the day of our Lord, Jesus Christ" (I Cor. 5:5). The seventh is the amendment of morals, that is, the renunciation of vices, as the Gospel testifies: "Now thou art whole, sin no more, lest some worse thing happen to thee" (Jn 5:14).The eighth is the intercession of the saints, as this text states: If any be sick, "let him bring the priests of the church and let them pray for him, lay their hands upon him, and anoint him with oil in the name of the Lord, and the prayer of faith shall save the sick man and the Lord shall raise him up, and if he be in sins they shall be forgiving him," and so forth; and "the continual prayer of a just man availeth much before the Lord" (Jas 5:14–16). The ninth is the merit of mercy and faith, as this says: "Blessed are the merciful for they shall obtain mercy" (Mt 5:7). The tenth is the conversion and salvation of others, as James assures us: "He who causeth a sinner to be converted from the error of his way shall save his soul from death and shall cover a multitude of sins" (Jas 5:20); but it is better for thee if thou art sick, to lead a solitary life than to perish with many. The eleventh is our pardon and remission, as He that is the Truth has promised, saying: "Forgive and ye shall be forgiven" (Lk 6:37). The twelfth is the passion of martyrdom, as the one hope of our salvation pardoned even the cruel robber, God replying to him: "Amen I say to thee this day thou shalt be with me in paradise" (Lk 23:43). Therefore, since these things are cited on the authority of the canon, it is fit that thou shouldst search out, also, the determinations of the fathers who were chosen by the mouth of the Lord, according to this passage: "Ask thy father and he will declare unto thee, thy elders and they will tell thee" (Deut 32:7); moreover, let the matter be referred to them. And so they determine that the eight principal vices contrary to human salvation shall be healed by the eight contrary remedies. For it is an old proverb: Contraries are cured by contraries; for he who freely commits what is forbidden ought freely to restrain himself from what is otherwise permissible.[6]

LIBRI PAENITENTIALES

The principal genre of penitential writing which contributes to the understanding of the Carolingian period is the Penitential Book. In the main, these books date from the seventh to the ninth centuries, although a few odd copies were compiled as late as the fifteenth and sixteenth centuries. They are a compilation of tariffs codified around lists of sins. Many are so detailed that warnings were issued to monks bearing the books not to let them fall into the hands of the faithful lest they be given new ideas about sins heretofore unknown to them. The penitential books are of Irish and Anglo-Saxon monastic origin and were for the use of confessors in assigning penances. In the past, many scholars have been hypercritical of their use often casting aspersions upon any positive value.[7] Today one recognizes their use in the social, political and cultural areas of medieval life. More recent studies recognize their relation with national churches and the different cultures,[8] and they have been studied in relation to other religions,[9] missiology,[10] monasticism,[11] canon and civil law,[12] literature,[13] liturgical studies and moral theology,[14] manuscript traditions[15] and linguistics[16] and finally to civilization in general. But to the degree that there are exhaustive lists of sexual sins and bizarre delineations of penances assigned as compensation, they have attracted attention as aberrant texts. Nonetheless, these books fit into the overall picture of the penitential spirituality which marked the age. Understood in the proper spiritual and sacramental context, they provide a valuable witness of the popular penitential piety.

Although the impression has been given that the admission of one's sins was a novelty in the medieval period, that was really not the case. Confession of sins to a priest already existed as attested by many sources.[17] The sheer number of penitential codes whose possession was reserved to confessors, indicates the necessity to confess to a priest. It is therefore not confession *per se*, but the manner in which it was practiced which constitutes the newness. Beginning with the eight principal vices regarded as contrary to human salvation, the confessor sought to heal the penitent by applying the eight contrary remedies. According to an old proverb: "contraries are cured by their contraries."[18] The new technique introduced by the Irish and Anglo-Saxon monks, required a detailed account of one's sins in order that a proper penance could be assigned, thus giving the name of tariffed penance to the new regime. The tariffs corresponded to the biblical trilogy[19] of fasting, praying and giving alms assigned by a confessor with great discretion.

The penitential books are extremely important because they indicate the penitential spirit of the early medieval period. First they are presented as remedies for the wounds caused by sin. They also have a juridical aspect[20] as well as a pedagogical intention.[21] Penance which characterized the Celtic church was conceived of as a remedy to apply to vices at their roots rather than a satisfaction offered to God and to the church. The moral and ascetical dimension predominated over the juridical aspect.[22] What is of interest concerning the *libri paenitentiales* is their possible sacramental usage. The detailed admission of sins was the condition *sine qua non* which allowed the confessor to impose the precise tariffs corresponding to the fault.[23]

The earlier insular penitentials, which had an influence on the eighth century, are divided into two groups: the first group goes back to the sixth and seventh centuries, and it subdivides into three groupings as follows:

1. British-Welsh
2. Irish (Canons of St. Patrick and the Penitential of Vinnian)

   3. Colomban (Penitential de St. Colomban, d. 615, associated
      with Luxeuil and Bobbio).

The second group marks the flowering of the penitentials from the
seventh century until about 813/850. These form three families, as
follows:

   1. the cycles of Cummean and of Theodore (insular origin);
   2. the so called cycles of Bede (d. 735),
              of Egbert of York (732–766),
              of pseudo-Bede and pseudo-Egbert (eighth century,
              insular origin)
   3. the cycles of continental origin but following insular models.

Concerning the insular penitentials, some scholars think that they
are of Egyptian[24] or Byzantine[25] origin of monastic determination.
Others look to ancient Gaul.[26] Given the deplorable state of the current
editions, it would be too precocious to attempt any definitive
determinations. In general, the penitential books used on the Continent
in the eighth century are of insular origin[27] with some continental
modifications. The Celtic characteristics are obvious: first, according to
the monastic rule, the Celtic monks told each other their faults; and
secondly, as a form of asceticism, they mutually prescribed the tariffs.
One finds this precedent in the Anglo-Saxon and Germanic cultures
under the form of *wehrgeld*,[28] a kind of financial compensation for any
infractions of the law. In the penitentials this juridic idea was
transposed onto the religious plane. One should not depend too much
however upon this influence as direct from the Irish, because the idea of
the *wehrgeld* was foreign to them. Rather it was introduced into the
Irish penitentials as a corruption, a result of contact with continental
currents. The Frankish and Germanic penitentials therefore are good
witnesses to the missionary activity of the Irish and Anglo-Saxon
monks. In the Frankish region in the North of Europe, for example,
these manuals seem to have been distributed through the monasteries
founded by these monks and had a wide influence in the surrounding
areas, such as at Fulda, Lorsch, Mainz, Corbie, Cologne, Würzburg,
Reichenau.[29]

CRITIQUE OF THE PENITENTIALS

The *libri paenitentales* give witness to a certain penitential practice in the Carolingian period. But in terms of their foundation in the Gospel ideal of *paenitentia*, some have criticized them as aberrant documents. Cyrille Vogel[30] for example, finds them to be a deprivation or decadence in the moral sense, constituting a negative witness to the true sense of penitence for the following reasons:

1. The penitentials hardly attest to the spirit of Gospel *metanoia*, and the biblical passages quoted therein are either of a blasphemous irony or limit themselves to eating interdictions.

2. They represent a legal conception transposed to the moral order, constituting a gross *do ut dos*. The legalism constitutes a type of early casuistry.

3. In several mss. there is an instruction in the preface (*Quo-tiescumque christiani*) which contains an allusion to Jewish hypocrisy (Matt 23:4: "they tie heavy burdens . . . then they themselves refuse to lift a finger"), yet in general, these penitentials fall into this kind of hypocrisy by contradicting themselves in the application of penances.[31]

Despite the severity of this critique, and admitting to its partial correctness, there may be another dimension to consider. Since these books were a human method to mete out justice in the Church and to reconcile Christians with God, the penitentials were not infallible as such and lent themselves to human abuse. This weakness was already recognized during the period in which they were employed, and the bishops as well as the various councils and synods placed the priests on guard against the improper use of these books. In Alcuin's writings, for example, one finds a definition of penance which foresees all the possible abuses: "True penance, he writes, is not counted in a number of years, but rather in the bitterness of the soul. . . . For God, sincerity of this regret is far more important than the duration of the penance."[32] This attitude of the heart is underlined in Alcuin's *vita* when he is reputed to have wanted to make a *sincere* confession and do a *worthy* penance. A simple mechanical application of the penitential books would not assure the interior conversion about which he writes in his pastoral letters. On the other hand their use was not excluded. It was simply a question of achieving a harmony between the needs of the Church and the interior disposition of the penitent. In order to avoid the mechanical aspect of the penitentials, penitents were called to overcome their smallness and to undergo a deeper conversion of the heart (*metanoia*). History supplies us with the proof of the contrary; we read about the system of commutations and redemptions which favored the rich in their perpetration of penance. According to this system, the penitential redemption (in the penitential this is designated by the terms *redimere* or *se redimere*) or the commutation modified, in attenuating the penitential tariff, through fasting most ostensibly or through other works of mercy. Thus in the redemptions, where the fast is replaced by prayers or a series of genuflections, etc., it was also possible to reduce the fast by having a number of Masses said. Whatever the modality, the redemptions lent themselves to the abuse by the rich, because they had the financial means to give alms or to pay someone else to satisfy their penance.

However it is worth noting that the higher an individual was in the social order, the more obliged he/she was to do more severe penance. The prayer booklets *(libelli precum)* and the moral writings *(specula)* attest to this fact. In judging by the many different genres of penitential writing from the Carolingian period, one can conclude that the *libri paenitentiales* did figure into the overall shape of penance of the Carolingian period as well as into the penitential spirituality. In order to appreciate the full importance of the penitential books, we should situate them in their proper historical and cultural context, giving fuller consideration to the liturgical and devotional aspects. Thus we may understand better the popular piety of the age[33], and in so doing, we may glean a more positive appreciation of the penitential books within Christian society.

RITUALS OF RECONCILIATION

Although the *libri paenitentiales* played an important role in the execution of penances, there is little indication about the ritualization of this process. The eighth-century penitential books in the main are silent on the question as to their ritual use, if any at all, with only a few notable exceptions, namely the Penitential of Bobbio (ca. 700–725), the Fleury Penitential (ca. 775–800), and Tripartite St. Gall Penitential (ca. 800). Of these three penitential *ordines*, Bobbio and St. Gall seem to be describing the earlier form of canonical penance, in which the ritual focuses upon the confession of sins and the imposition of hands. We have reference to this gesture as late as the sixth century in *Statuta ecclesiae antiqua*,[34] and the eighth-century Gelasian sacramentary suggests this usage in regards to the reconciliation of penitents on Holy Thursday. The lack of any formula of absolution is noteworthy.[35]

The Bobbio Penitential (ca. 700–725) [Paris B.N. Lat. 13246], showing strong Irish influence both in script and in contents, contains two prayers to be prayed by the priest over the penitent.[36] The first prayer asks that pardon may be granted to the penitent making reference to baptism, while the second prayer refers to the Eucharist. The St. Gall Penitential (ca. 800) also reflects the canonical form of penance showing affinity with *ordo Romanus antiquus*.[37] The role of the priest as spiritual companion is again important as revealed in the instruction: "When, therefore, anyone comes to a priest to confess his sins, the priest ought first to pray by himself in the secret of his own heart."[38] Three prayers are indicated which again comment on the role of the priest as spiritual friend, the value of penance as a medicine and the importance of doing penance, but there is no indication of any formula of absolution.[39]

The most explicit reference to any ritual of tariffed penance is found in the Fleury Penitential (ca. 775–800), which opens with an order for reconciliation:

> ... And when the man has given his entire confession, the priest himself shall prostrate himself before the altar with him, confessing they shall repeat the psalms with groaning and if possible with weeping, and both, alike prostrate, shall say the passages: "Turn me, O Lord" (Ps 6:5), and "Our help is in the name of the Lord" (Ps 123:8). And afterward he shall begin, "O Lord, not in thy wrath," I and II (Pss 6:1 and 37:1) and, "Have mercy upon me, O God," as far as "blot out my iniquity" (Ps 50:3), and "Bless the Lord, O my soul, " I, as far as "thy youth shall be renewed like the eagle" (Ps 102: 1–5), and the passage, "Remember not our iniquities" (Ps 78:8). And afterward let them together rise up and [let him be questioned] once more whether he believes that through his confession itself he obtains

pardon; if he will do penance; and if he is willing to promise words that in this matter he will observe as far as he is able whatever is meanwhile determined; or how he ought afterwards to abstain; if he is weak or not; and if he has given an answer on all matters.

If later he offends criminally, either a presbyter or a deacon shall say the collects over his head, and afterward, prostrate on the ground, he shall be commended to the Lord God of heaven, and they shall say the passage, "Confirm this, O God" (Ps 67:29). And so thereafter he shall be treated according to his guilt and his devotion; or it shall be as far as possible indicated to him what definite time [of penance] he has to ought to observe; and the passage: "The Lord keep thee from all evil" (Ps 120: 7), shall be said to him—and thou shalt leave him.[40]

Again the role played by the confessor as spiritual companion is underlined, but one is struck by the extensive use of psalmody in the ritual enactment. The priest helps incite the person to true penitence by prayer and outwards signs of contrition, such as groaning and crying. It is also noteworthy that there is no mention of any formula of absolution. It is through the confession of sins itself that one receives pardon.

Psalmody is an important method for expiation of one's sins. When the penitentials were written, the Psalter was the chief liturgy of penitents. Psalmody is a very frequent element in the satisfaction that the penitentials enjoin. Individual psalms or portions were common-place requirements in these handbooks. The *Beati* (Ps 118) was a favorite assignment, probably on account of its extraordinary length. So common was this exercise of psalmody in penance that it may go far to explain the *laus perennis*, or perpetual praise, which was a notable feature of some continental Irish monasteries.[41] One is immediately struck by the similarity of the Fleury penitential ritual and the prayer books of the same period. An examination of this genre of spiritual writing, otherwise known as the *libelli precum*, will indicate its probable use in the satisfaction of penances as prescribed by the penitential books. Because the number and types of *libelli* are so abundant, our examination will limit itself to the *œuvre* of Alcuin of York.

Rather than thinking of the context for penance in a strictly sacramental sense, it is more helpful to conceive of the use of this penitential ritual in the context of non-sacramental spiritual direction. Even the distinction sacramental/non-sacramental would probably be anachronistic for this period, yet the context is clearly monastic. For example, in the *Custom of Tallaght* (ca. 831–840) we read:

> §23. Concerning the matter of spiritual direction, some think it sufficient if they have merely made their confession, though they do no penance afterwards. He [Maeldithruib, abbot of Tallaght, a monastery near Dublin] does not approve of this. He thinks it well, however, that one should show them what is profitable to them, even though he does not ask for confessions. This is what Helair did in the matter: at first he had received many, but he ended by sending them all away, because he saw that their penance was not zealously performed, and also that they concealed their sins when making confession. After that he finally refused to receive anyone at all to spiritual direction. However, he would sometimes allow holy persons to consult him. [42]

ALCUIN OF YORK

In studying the works of Alcuin of York[43] (ca. 735–804), one is struck by the strong penitential character of his writings. One could falsely presume that this age was populated by greater sinners than the world has known before or since. Another assumption might be that Alcuin was deeply troubled by the sense of sin, almost to the point of scrupulosity. It seems fairer to say that the penitential practice, governed by the penitential books, combined with the monastic goal of Christian perfection, lent itself to this kind of manifestation of popular piety. Thanks to the monastic orders, Western civilization and Christian culture survived the barbarian invasions and gave a rich patrimony to the West.[44]

Alcuin himself was not a monk. We know that he was an ordained deacon. However he had been heavily influenced by the monastic traditions, first at York where he was educated at the monastic school and later on the Continent when he was named abbot of several monasteries. He exercised a decisive role on the liturgical and spiritual development of the Carolingian period. Summoned by Charlemagne to renew the educational system in the Frankish court, Alcuin first had to renew the monastic orders because the monks would be the primary teachers in the schools and there was need for a unified monastic system to insure the success of the educational reform. The third element of the Carolingian *renovatio* was the liturgical reform which fits into the broader scope of reform envisaged by Charlemagne as a way of bringing disparate and often divisive liturgical practices into a unified whole within the realms of the emperor's influence. Alcuin's writings furnish an interesting commentary about the proper use of the Penitentials and present the reader with a fairly comprehensive understanding of the importance of penance in the early Middle Ages.

Three types of writings will be examined as a gauge of his thought on the subject of penance, namely, the prayer books (*libelli precum*), a mirror (*speculum*), and a letter-treatise. Alcuin, not being a confessor, never composed any penitential books nor had any need for their direct use, yet he would have been conversant with them concerning their use in the confession of sins. A case might be made that his attitudes about penance were partially shaped by the penitential practices of his time, including the penitential books. He, in turn, exercised a role for the subsequent shape and use of penitential books in the early ninth century. His writings on penance were widely circulated as attested by the manuscript transmission throughout Europe.

I. LIBELLI PRECUM

The *libelli precum* or the small booklets of prayer are revelatory of what seems to be a spirituality marked by a strong sense of penance.[45] Prayers of Irish and Anglo-Saxon origin, called confessions, punctuate these prayer books along with many other penitential prayers. These *precum libelli*, destined for spiritual exercises, offer a great interest for the history of Christian prayer in general, but especially for the Carolingian period. These booklets were compiled principally in the Celtic and Anglo-Saxon lands and are patterned after the monastic Psalter. Most of the prayers which are of a devotional nature seem to have been for private use, so typical of Irish spirituality at this time.[46] These prayers were inspired by liturgical orations and responded to the spiritual needs of England and the Continent, explaining their wide circulation. The structure of the "hours" attests to a pre-Benedictine usage,[47] much like the *Concordia Regularum* of Benedict of Aniane. One can posit their use in the fulfillment of penance as prescribed by the penitential books.

Regarding penitential literature, several noteworthy characteristics appear: the specification of the seven penitential psalms, each one followed by a special prayer, and a number of prayers called confessions, one of which is attributed to Alcuin (*Deus inaestimabiles misericordiae*),[48] which was composed for Charlemagne as an act of contrition or an examination of conscience, similar to those used by the monks. These confessional prayers are addressed directly to God asking for pardon in general, much like an act of contrition. They do not mention specific faults of the sinner but have as their end a means to reflect upon one's life. There is the implicit idea that God forgets the sins which we remember with remorse.[49] Since the time of Caesarius of Arles (ca. 470–543), it was believed that confession of minor sins to God was satisfactory for forgiveness. With Alcuin, however, the accent falls upon the accomplishment of a penance, probably due to the Irish influence at York. On the other hand, one notes strong Roman characteristics in these booklets, especially in the inclusion of Roman collect prayers, which would indicate Alcuin's fundamental orientation towards Rome.[50] Several allusions are made to confession and to the role of the priest as the one who pardons.[51] Alcuin, however, emphasizes the role of the priest-confessor much less than that of the penitent. He rarely speaks about the sacramental system, seemingly to underline that penance is way of life, a kind of conversion. Having been neither a monk nor a priest, he offers a very specific point of view regarding confession and penance. This perspective is extremely valuable in researching the penitential devotional practices of this era. Although several prayers mention the intercessory role of the priest, it is the penitent who is the speaker in these prayers.

Even the form of these booklets suggests their ultimate use. Referred to as a *liber manualis* this kind of book was intended for daily use in the prayer life of any lay person. The small format suggests that these were pocket books, easily transportable for quick reference. Sometimes these are attached to the back of beautiful Carolingian manuscripts of the Psalter. This gave rise to the Books of Hours, a posterior development in prayer books of this genre.

One question which must be asked is whether these prayer books had a liturgical use. The distinction between liturgical and devotional prayer is anachronistic during this historical period because we find examples of liturgical prayers in the devotional books and elements of popular piety which were incorporated into the liturgy. It seems plausible that the prayer books may have been used for the completion of penitential tariffs. This can be corroborated through a study of the prayer forms. Pierre Salmon in his detailed study of nine such *libelli* concludes that a good number of prayers seem to have been composed for strictly private use.[52] For example, many are addressed from the first person singular and express a rather sentimental and personal piety, suggesting private usage. But it is not absolutely excluded that such prayers could not have had a communal use. For example, in the mouth of a presider, the prayer could have expressed the feelings of all the participants. Salmon also discovered other prayers which are clearly more communal in form, such as the orations which follow each of the seven psalms of penance, the *pater* and the *capitula* which were borrowed from Roman *collectes*[53] and seem to indicate a more strict liturgical use. Also the inclusion of litanies and hymns represents a use which goes beyond private prayer. The overall structure for each day is as follows: invitatory prayer or introductory invocation, psalmody, and a concluding prayer. The strong liturgical style reflects an office which goes beyond the bounds of strictly private prayer. Due to varying compositions and forms of the many manuscripts of *libelli,* it is impossible to conclude with certitude their exact use. In fact, the form of certain manuscripts would most assuredly indicate a monastic origin. The distinction between monastic and popular liturgy, nevertheless, would be anachronistic. Only in 817 was monastic liturgy fixed in conformity with the Benedictine *cursus,*[54] clearly distinguishing itself from a more secularized liturgy. One of the most significant differences lies in the Psalter where the psalmody was integrally practiced in some monasteries. It is difficult to speak in great generalities about liturgical prayer since the *libelli* are not a homogeneous group, and the local liturgies of this period are very diverse even within some geographical regions. These liturgical differences can be explained by the fact that the Roman liturgy, in particular the *cursus* of the canonical hours, had barely penetrated into the kingdoms of the Franks and of the Anglo-Saxons, as well as into the Germanic tribes. In spite of the efforts of St. Boniface, Amalarius of Metz, Chrodegang, Pipin the Short, and even Charlemagne, the new office was not adopted without difficulty. In the absence of an uniform *cursus,* the differences were widespread.[55] One must wait until the ninth century for a clear distinction between assembly prayer and private devotional prayer. The *precum libelli* could have served both for devotional and general communal prayer. These booklets therefore are nothing more than collections of prayers not yet fully differentiated.

These *libelli* are an eloquent witness to the penitential spirituality of the early Middle Ages and serve page by page to delimit the boundaries of the penitential and confessional discipline of this age. The fact that in these prayer books the penitential spirituality is described not from the point of view of a priest-confessor, but from the perspective of the penitent, makes these booklets extremely valuable. The authorship of these books is thorny and the originality of these texts not noteworthy. The choice of texts and the compilation, however, is very revelatory of the spirituality of this age, and especially of Alcuin as the abbot of Tours at the end of his life. Four prayer books were edited by Dom Wilmart[56] in which the booklets are described by Alcuin himself in cover letters which accompanied them or indicate Alcuinian influences attributed to the scriptorium of Tours. These booklets studied together with Alcuin's other writings indicate incontestably the influence that he had on the penitential spirituality of his time, especially at the end of his life. A more detailed study of the prayer forms reveals the provenance of the prayers and the influences from Celtic and Anglo-Saxon prayer forms as well as classical Roman prayer forms.

Prayer Forms

Far from being original, the *libelli* are more of a replica of prayer collections fairly well circulated. Instead of considering Alcuin as an author, it would be preferable to give him the title "compiler," because he has assembled several prayer genres, of which very few are directly of his hand.[57] In general, one notes two principal currents which run through the booklets, indicating Roman and Irish origins. Together these strains exercised a formative influence upon the composition of prayers.

First, the Roman style[58] is characterized by its simplicity and soberness. Possibly influenced by the succinct and precise nature of the Latin language, the tone of these prayers is almost juridical. Normally the prayers of Roman origin are short and extremely well refined, eliminating excess verbiage. The prayers are addressed to the Father through the Son and the Holy Spirit. In the case of these *libelli,* compiled by Alcuin and others, one notes the ample use of Roman collect prayers, which follow the psalms in the praying of the divine office and which are characterized by their brevity and conciseness. Contained within the prayer booklets are the seven Psalms of Penitence[59] which played an important role in the penitential spirituality and the satisfaction of penance. Each of these seven psalms was followed by a collect, the majority of which are of Roman origin. Here is an example of the collect following Psalm 129 (*De profundis*):

> Lord, we beseech,
> that the ears of your mercy
> be attentive to prayers of supplication,
> because with you is forgiveness of sins,
> so that you may not notice our iniquities,
> but grant to us your mercies,
> through our Lord. . . . [60]

One is struck by the conciseness and soberness of this collect. Not a word is wasted. The prayer summarizes and echoes the psalm which has just been prayed and collects the mind of the person praying to focus on redemption through God's loving mercy. The prayer has the function to transmit, to illustrate and to apply the mystery of Christ fully realized in the prayer itself. In a few brief lines, a complete theology of redemption and reconciliation is sketched and delimited. The form of the prayer is telegraphic in order to celebrate in a few words the mysteries of faith.

Although the prayer opens and closes with the word "Lord," a stylistic characteristic of Roman *collectae* is their consistent address to the Father. Prayers are addressed to Father and conclude by praying to the Father through the Son and the Holy Spirit. Customarily the closing formula "through our Lord . . . " was known by heart, so it was sufficient to give only the opening words. There was a tendency, nonetheless, to read the psalms in a Christian context through a Christocentric lens. Certainly here the word "Lord" is sufficiently ambiguous allowing a reference to either/both the Father and the Son.

The collect prayer which follows Psalm 142 is an interesting exception to the general rule concerning Roman collects. Unlike the collects of the strict Roman style, this prayer blends Frankish elements into the general Roman structure, giving rise to something new. Judging by the more elaborate style and the theological content, the following prayer suggests Gallican influences of the ninth century:

> God, who made the morning of your holy resurrection into
>   resounding delight;
> when returning from hell, you filled with joy the earth that you left in
>   darkness.
> We ask the ineffable majesty of your power that as you made the
>   company of apostles rejoice most piously,
> so now you would deign to light up with radiant heavenly splendor
> this your Church which entreats you with outstretched hands,
> you who live and reign with the Father and the Holy Spirit now and
>   forever. Amen.[61]

Although this collect is addressed to God without any further qualification, it becomes clear in the course of the prayer that we are addressing Jesus. This becomes apparent when we speak about the morning of his resurrection and in the closing doxology when we pray to Jesus "with the Father and the Holy Spirit," a most uncharacteristic feature of Roman collects. One explanation for this modification with such a strong Christocentric emphasis is the fact that the Carolingian age was embroiled in Christological controversy, notably in Spain with the Adoptionist heresy.[62] The oblique reference to Jesus as God would have the effect of overcoming the heretical view of the adoptionists.

By contrast, the Irish forms are much more prolix. They witness eloquently to penance especially from a psychological perspective. One feature of the Celtic prayers is the confession of sins *(confessio peccatum)*. The sinner enumerates all the parts of the body as though each one has been guilty of perpetrating sin. By way of this anatomical

catalog, every possible sin imaginable is mentioned as committed by
eyes, ears, nostrils, mouth, hands, feet, tongue, throat, neck, breast, and
the heart. Then the invisible parts of the body are enumerated, such as
bones, marrow, kidneys. Even teeth, hair, fingernails, tears and spittle
are accused of having sinned. The penitents speak as though they are
guilty of all these sins. Even if they were the greatest of sinners, it
would be virtually impossible to sin to this degree. In reality, the form
is less of a confession of real sins than an examination of conscience.
As a prayer, it was intended to be recited slowly so as to consider the
implications of sin in act, in word and in thought. Given that the
monasteries founded by the Irish both in the British Isles and on the
Continent were the great penitential centers for monks and laity alike,
one can understand better the form of this kind of prayer. In these
monasteries the penitents sought out a confessor or a director of
conscience, corresponding to the *amnchara,* or soul friend, indicating
the importance of this person in the spiritual development of the one
being directed. In this context, penance was more a way of life than a
confession of sins properly speaking. In the light of the penitentials, yet
to be studied in conjunction with the *precum libelli,* one understands
the very detailed and exhaustive nature of the Celtic prayers. [63]

Another typical form of Irish prayer, strikingly parallel to the
confessions, is the *lorica* or the "breastplate" prayer in which one prays
to God to protect all the part of the body. Again the anatomical catalog
is enumerated as one exhausts all the possibilities of danger.[64]
Contrasted to the brevity and the soberness of the Roman style of
prayer, one is struck by the affective exuberance, so characteristic of
Irish devotion. In one of the invocations addressed to the Holy Spirit
one finds a tenderness and a delicacy accompanied by a most
flamboyant sort of language.

The *confessio peccatum,* attributed to the pen of Alcuin, [65] is of an
equivalent length to the Irish examples and contains the typical
anatomical list, but in reverse order beginning with the feet and
terminating with the head. Composed for Charlemagne, this prayer
underlines the Celtic influence on the deacon from York. Here the feet
are slow to obey the commandments of the Lord, the knees bend more
in fornicating than in prayer, the stomach swells with gluttony and
drunkenness, etc. The way in which one speaks of the sins is very

dynamic, i.e., the feet run, the nostrils flare, the stomach swells, the head bows, etc.

The prayer uses medical metaphors while sin is referred to as wounds. In this case the confessor is seen as the doctor of the soul. These images are typical of Alcuin's language when speaking of penance as found in his many letters on the subject. He draws from his insular heritage, adapting it to his own theology of penance and literary style. Noteworthy is Alcuin's avoidance of the Celtic excesses and exuberance, rendering this prayer truer to real life.

Alcuin's genius does not lie in his originality in prayer composition. Rather, his originality lies in the choice and arrangement of existent texts. [66] The predominant element is his interest in penance, a trait which seems typically Celtic, as witnessed to by the *Book of Cerne*. These prayers put into high relief the interior aspect of the person. One would err in thinking that Alcuin was one of the greatest sinners judging by the list of sins in his confession. Rather this prayer reflects a highly sensitized person and a form of spirituality of this historical period which favored an extremely thorough examination of the conscience. The numerical and detailed character noted also in the penitential books of this epoch marks the attention given to the interiority of the person at prayer. The lists of the most minute sins reveals a concern for the interior state of the penitent.

II. SPECULA

A second genre of penitential writing is the *speculum* or mirror. This booklet served as a complement to the *libelli*, and was used by the laity in their spiritual development. [67] The destination and the purpose of both the *specula* and the *libelli precum* are similar. They seem to have been compiled for a cultivated social class, a kind of lay élite, [68] who were instructed in the monastic schools, having acquired there certain spiritual practices and monastic sensibilities. Alcuin composed a *speculum* entitled *De virtutibus et vitiis*, [69] where he treats questions about confession and penance. The *speculum*, being a kind of moral manual *(manualis libellus)*, was utilized in Frankish Gaul as a tool for spiritual growth. Normally composed by clerics, these *libelli exhortatorii* gave the laity the directives adapted to their state of life. [70]

In a letter addressed to Count Wido, a marquis of the March of Brittany,[71] Alcuin treats the question of how a lay person must keep the Gospel. This letter accompanied his *speculum* and serves as a preface for the work. He describes it as a small rule of life for the laity. The work is constructed in four parts, each one written in a different style. It is subdivided into thirty-five chapters, each one distinct as to its content. One of them is consecrated to confession. After the thirty-fifth chapter, there is an addition which is in the form of a peroration. In the first twenty-six chapters, the following subjects are presented (Note the number of penitential themes in these chapter headings): wisdom, faith, charity, hope, the reading of Holy Scripture, peace, mercy, pardon, patience, humility, remorse, confession, repentance, return to God, fear of God, fasting, alms, chastity, a cautionary note about fraud, the judgments, false witnessing, envy, pride, anger, deception and perseverance in good works. In chapters twenty-seven through thirty-four, the eight capital sins are catalogued[72]; chapter thirty-five, by comparison, describes the four cardinal virtues. One notes the absence of homogeneity in style. When it deals with virtues, the style is homiletic, while for vices, it is descriptive.

The book is presented as a *breviarium*,[73] composed of brief sermons. By its brevity, each chapter allows someone engaged in the world to meditate on an aspect of the true Christian life. Alcuin realized the demands made upon the laity and adapted this breviary for them. His purpose can be deduced from the subjects treated as well as by the preface letter and the peroration. One should mistrust Alcuin's claim that he would have written at the request of Wido, since this kind of claim served as a kind of rhetorical device known by Alcuin.[74] Nonetheless, the fact that he may have composed this *speculum* is consonant with his concern for the spiritual development of the laity.

The philosophy of the treatise is simple: life is presented as a struggle between the eight vices and the four virtues. The vices can be overcome by the practice of the virtues. For each vice there is a corresponding antidote: pride is conquered by humility, fornication by chastity, anger by patience, etc. Life is the place of confrontation of opposites, and the virtues finally triumph.

In the middle of the first section there are two short chapters, one on confession and the other on penance. The two subjects are inextricably linked to each other. Once again the accent is placed on the necessity of confessing one's sins to a priest. The language of confession, presented as a remedy and a judgment, is typical of Alcuin. One notes the frequent use of scriptural quotes that are found in Alcuin's other writings. Judging by his interest in the psychological and spiritual state of the penitent, Alcuin seems more concerned about the interior attitude of penitence than in the form of confession and penance. For this reason, confession and penance are dissimulated among other themes such as compunction of the heart and conversion. These two interior aspects are the conditions imposed upon the soul which ultimately leads to penitence.[75] Confession and penance without the interior dispositions of compunction and conversion are without value and efficacy and are empty.

Alcuin establishes a link between penance and fear of the Lord. Sinners, fearing the consequences of their misdeeds, are called to convert.[76] The distinction between filial fear and servile fear is made; one fears one's own father out of love, whereas one fears one's master due to chastisement. In the first case, fear is the consequence of love, while in the second, it is a consequence of an evil. Elsewhere this filial fear is connected to contrition, whether perfect or imperfect. Being born from the virtue of humility, compunction is manifested through tears. It is the condition *sine qua non* of true penitence.

It is clear that penance plays an important role in the development of virtue in the life of the individual. The *specula* give confession and penance an important role, but these must be tempered by an attitude of penitence. Throughout Alcuin's writings, and especially in his mirror, he seems to be distinguishing between penance and penitence. Penance indicates the outward actions, such as confession and making satisfaction for sins. Penitence, on the other hand, is more of an attitude, a precondition for doing acts of penance. In biblical terms, this might be called *metanoia* or conversion. Tears, therefore, would be the outward sign of an interior state of penitence.

III. EPISTOLA

Since Alcuin's small treatise on penance is cast in the form of a letter, it is worthwhile to examine briefly the epistolary genre in the Carolingian period. Letters represent an important genre since antiquity.[77] St. Paul, for example, used letters to develop his theological ideas, especially in his letter to the Romans. Alcuin's letters have for their primary purpose to sustain friendship,[78] but they often were used for many purposes,[79] often cast in the form of an exhortation to promulgate his theology and reform policies.

As a literary form, the letter was neither too prolix nor too brief. Comparing them to books, one might say that letters were to the Carolingian period what scholarly "articles" are to the present age. This was possibly necessitated by the high cost of parchment at the time. The letter usually followed a set literary form: a salutation, an introductory section announcing the subject of the letter, the body and a conclusion.

One leading characteristic of medieval letters was their public reading. Almost all the letters were meant to be circulated among a certain number of people, and often were recopied in the various *scriptoria*. The surviving collections of correspondence witness to this fact. Especially letters from famous people were widely circulated due to their great public interest. Concerning the letter collections of Alcuin,[80] four distinct groups emerge based upon four persons to whom he addressed his works: Dodo, Arn, Adalhard and Angilbert.

The theological interest of a letter was based upon the doctrinal importance given to it, but usually the letters were occasioned by a specific need which was usually pastoral. It is sufficient only to examine the dedicatory letters that accompanied his letter-treatises to determine why such and such a theological treatise was composed. For this reason, "the greater part of the writings of the Middle Ages were requested by a certain occasion and they maintain the character of circumstantial writings."[81] The reader was not anonymous and the letter had neither an abstract nor an impersonal character. The preface epistle announces the purpose of the document which is to follow, and the proposed solutions to a concrete pastoral problem are usually very concrete.

Alcuin had engaged himself in several doctrinal controversies, such as adoptionism and iconoclasm, usually in the form of an exchange of letters. There is therefore a great deal of his teachings found in these letter collections. It was along these lines that he composed his small treatise in the form of the letter *Ad pueros*. It has both theological and spiritual value for the understanding of the importance of confession and penance for his period. A letter from Alcuin therefore was a carefully composed piece of work intended to be read by a larger audience than simply the school boys at St. Martin of Tours. For this reason he did not hesitate to send it to his friend Arn in response to a request for a treatise on penance and the necessity of confession.

Letter to the Children of St. Martin of Tours [82]

To the sons most dear in Christ and the adolescents upon whom I build my great hopes, who consecrate themselves to Jesus-God in the Church of the supreme pontiff and the great protector, the blessed Martin, and who are instructed by the masters of the church in the house of God. Wishing you well, namely the prosperity of your eternal salvation, I, Alcuin, greet you in God, the Christ. I have therefore taken the trouble to address you some admonitions because of paternal affection in a discourse full of gentleness, in order that you may earn prosperity in the present life and blessedness in the life to come through God's mercy, and having been educated in the service of God, you may bring the fragile years of your age to the completed day of your old age. To you as well, holy fathers, lights of this fraternal congregation, doctors and guides of the youth in that which is good, I ask you to invite them (I would like to call them your disciples) that they may apply themselves to learn that which pleases God, and that which touches the salvation of their souls. To the degree that they progress and succeed will assure for you your eternal reward from God. Exhort them to serve God in soberness, chastity, modesty, humility and obedience, through their good actions, a holy way of life, religious chastity, and above all by the *confession of their sins*. In fact, youth are exposed to numerous traps of diabolic trickery, of carnal desires and of other adolescent vices. But through God's grace, the devil in his wickedness can never succeed if the young people desire a *sincere confession* and do worthy fruits of *penance* (Lk 3:8), which means that they do not add new wounds to the old ones and that they do not open again the healed wounds. For it is the salutary *remedy of penance* not to commit again the deeds for which you would have to do penance. For it is written, "God gives a part of justice to those who are penitent" (Sir 17:20). Therefore, penitent, act. *Confess your sins*. List them in a *secret confession* of your iniquity. That which you have done in secret is known to God. If the tongue does not avow them, your conscience will not be able to keep them. You believe in vain that your sins are hidden behind the walls. Even if you could hide your sins from the eyes of people, there is nothing however which would remain hidden from God. *Tell your sins in confession* before you feel the anger of God's judgement. Believe me, every sin that you have committed will be forgiven, if you *do not blush to confess* them and if you take care *to purify yourself through penance*. Thus says the psalmist: "I confessed my sins to the Lord and you took away the guilt of my sin" (Ps 32:5).The Lord awaits from us the sacrifice of confession in order to give us the sweet grace of forgiveness, because he wants that everyone be saved (1 Tim 2:4) and that no one perish. In fact it says in another passage of Scripture: "Whatever the day that sinners may be converted, they will live and will not die" (Ez 33:12 &15). Oh exceptional favor of the most merciful judge! Oh magnificent treasure of divine mercy! If He wants only to receive from sinners the *gift of confession*, it is in order that He will never have to punish them. Let us not be ungrateful before such an indulgence on the part of our Redeemer who would rather ignore than punish, rather save than lose. That which is not punished in the servant enriches the Lord; and much is given by the Author, if the condemned are forgiven of their faults through His grace. He does not wish to seek revenge Himself, He who is ready to show mercy. Concerning [God] Himself, He says through the prophet: "I do not want the death of the sinner but I want that he may be converted and that he live" (Ez 33:11). Here is the true Author of life, He who does not want the death of the sinner, but the life of those who are converted. For this reason, in the Gospel of Truth it says: "There will be more joy in heaven with your Father and His angels for one sinner who does *penance*" (Lk 15:7). Elsewhere with the prophet: "First tell your injustices in order that you may be justified" (Is 43:26?). How He is vigilant, He who gives pardon, He who accords the joy of eternity instead of temporal affliction. Again it says: "Happy are they who cry now, for they will be consoled" (Mt 5:5). Elsewhere we read: "Come to me, you who suffer and labor under the yoke, and I will comfort you" (Mt 11:28). In fact it says, and I repeat: "First tell your sins in order to be justified" (Is 43:26?) and not condemned; in order that the reward of penance might dwell within you and not the vindication of sins.

Is not it true that God, as if He were ignorant, exhorts us *to confess our sins,* He who knows them even before they are committed? Everything hidden will be made known by His providence. In fact you will be able to obtain the perfect favor of a remedy, if you do not hide the wounds of your conscience from the doctor. I believe that if the doctor is not called, the sick person is not cured. Your *confession is the remedy* for your wounds and the most certain help for your salvation. An ill person asks for a remedy from the doctor who often takes great care to treat the illness by an uncertain practice. But God heals without effort, giving the remedy of pardon without delay, if the *sincere penance,* written in *tears*, is divulged into the ears of His compassion. Oh man, no one can heal you better that He who made you. No one else will save you, if it is not He who feels and cares. For He alone knows the fragility of your work, He who waits only one thing, your *confession*. There will be no delay in healing. For it is said through the prophet Ezekiel: "When you will be converted and cry out, you will be saved" (Ez 33:12).

The most watchful judge gives us an occasion *to accuse ourselves of our sins before a priest of God,* in order that the devil may not accuse us in another circumstance before Christ the judge. He desires that these may be forgiven in this world so that they will not be driven out of the world to come. Thus the merciful Father, when He sees that we are condemning our sins through penance rejoices in being merciful and wishes to exercise his grace of mercy in favor of the penitents. As the prophet Isaiah witnesses: "I am He who takes away your sins" (Is 43:25). And elsewhere: "Turn to the Lord your God, for He is merciful and good, patient and his mercy is abundant" (Joel 2:13). Knowing this, the blessed David said: "I made known my sins to you, and I have not hidden my iniquities" (Ps 32:5). Conversely if the sin that a man has committed is denied, the punishment for the fault accumulates, because the obstinacy to deny the sin is punished. But perhaps you will say that the greatness of my sins terrifies me. By contrast, it is all the more necessary to attach yourself to the *remedy of confession.* Oh sinner, otherwise you will rot in the gangrene of your wounds, if you blush to uncover to the doctor the multiple aches of your ulcers. In no case will the number of your sins pass beyond the abundance of the mercy of God. "Do not delay from day to day, says the Scriptures. Turn back, for you do not know what will happen the day later" (Sir 5:8). In fact, you will be judged such as you are found on the last day. God does not want that you may know this day in advance in order that you might be ready. Prepare yourself for what you desire to be when you appear before God. While you have the time to act, be a pious merchant. Purchase for yourself the kingdom of God through the profits of *penance* and remember what the Lord said: "Do penance, and the kingdom of God is near to you" (Mt 3:2).

Thus for you, oh youth, God made himself man in order to ransom you and to deliver you from death in order to save you in this life. Why do you lie in the death of your sins? Arise and say; "Father, I have sinned against the heavens" (Lk 15:18 & 21). Draw to yourself the faithful witness of your penance. You want to have clean clothes. Why do you not look also to have a clean soul? You do not want to appear dirty in the eyes of people. Why are you not afraid to appear soiled by your sins before God? Wash yourself in the fountain of *tears. That* nothing in you may offend the eyes of His majesty. I ask, who in falling does not try to get up? Who in being sick does not wish to be healed? Who in a dangerous situation does not wish to escape from it? You will regret by your delay, if you do not think about that which will be useful for your soul in view of salvation.

Arise, sons, arise, that your penance will appease the Father whom you have offended through your fault. *Confess your sins* in order that you may be treated by the doctor. Worry about your salvation. If you do not take care of yourself, who might be helpful for your salvation? Who will be faithful to you if you show that you are unfaithful towards yourself? It is a great infidelity not to take care of your salvation, to not be raised up by penance when you die by your sins. The farther you have gone from God through the greatness of your sins, the more you must make an effort to approach Him through penance. The loving Father is ready to receive you if you do not wait to come to Him. To abandon your carnal desires may seem to you to be a rude conversion. But you are giving yourself over to something even worse, to burn in the eternal flames for the luxury of a little time when you will be delivered to eternal torment. How many of the condemned to the torments of hell would like to turn back, if the time for repentance were given to them! In truth all the sufferings of this time appear light and even pleasant in comparison with the torments of hell. You have served the devil in excess; serve Christ in chastity. Look where the two lead. For excess sends people into the flames; chastity linked with charity leads us to the kingdom of God. Return to the path which you have abandoned that the body may be affected by fast, and that the beauty of the soul may be restored. That the worship of the body may be counted for nothing; but the body itself is the first decoration of sanctity. The perseverance to remain vigilant in prayers and in the praise of God is an imitation of the angelic life. A frugal meal is the food of the soul. If you have, you can lend a hand to the poor, because the hand of the poor is a treasure where one gives to Christ. You would not be able to justify yourself if you disrobe yourself from the work of mercy, when a glass of cold water will be paid for a perpetual reward. To visit the sick, to console the unfortunate, to go after the visitors, to comfort those who suffer from hunger or thirst, is to possess the kingdom of God in the heavens, like one reads in the Gospel (Mt 25:35ff). In the doing of such works, oh son, the forgiveness of sins is obtained which procures above all the entrance into perpetual beatitude.

Refuse to have a degenerate soul. You have been consecrated a son of God through baptism. Nonetheless this great nobility can be maintained only by the great dignity of actions. The heavenly Father, greater yet, the Lord of all, refuses to have a son subjected to sins. Cast off from your neck the yoke of diabolical captivity. Take recourse in the bounty of paternal love. Return to God, [my] son, return; from death return to the living and that you who was lost, may be restored. The Good Shepherd seeks the lost sheep and witnesses much more to the joy of having found [it] again than the ones never lost (Lk 15:6). He will carry him back on his shoulders into the company of the angels. Notice the very lenient sentence of the Lord's mercy who says: "Amen, I have not come to call the just, but to call sinners to penance" (Lk 5:32). The Lord therefore calls the sinners to penance because he loves more to save than to condemn, and he rejoices rather to see us in the state of joy with the saints than to punish us with the devil. He himself calls us; He calls us through the Holy Scriptures; He calls us even through the catholic doctors in order that we may return to Him who is ready to receive us, if we do not hesitate to go to Him. Let us listen to the blessed Evangelist John who exhorts us to penance. He says, in fact in his Epistle: "If we say that we have no sin, we separate our very selves and the truth is not in us. But if *we confess our sins*, God is faithful and just, to the point of forgiving us our sins and purifying us of all iniquity" (I Jn 1:8). If no one is without sin, who is that who would not need penance? Without *confession*, this person is hardly able to be fruitful. Let us consider the commandment of the blessed apostle James who said: *"Confess your sins one to another"* (Jas 5:16). Let us recall that our Savior preferred the publican who recognized his sinfulness to the Pharisee who praised himself for his justice (Lk 18:10). For our Creator knows the fragility of our nature, and in forgiveness he gives our wounds the remedy of penitence. Let us say with the prophet: "Heal me, Lord, and I will be healed" (Jer 17:14). Elsewhere: "Lord, heal my soul because I have sinned toward you" (Ps 41:5).

For this reason, my dear sons, hasten to the *remedy of confession*. Expose the wounds in confession so that the medicines of salvation may take force to be effective in you. The days of this life pass and the hour in which the dust returns to the dust and the spirit returns to God who gave it, to be judged according to its works (cf. Mt 16:27), is uncertain for each one of us (Sir 12:7). The soul then will feel everything that was hidden here below, when it was linked to the flesh. If it blushes to confess its sins and to make amends by penance, the diabolical accuser will raise us against the soul, he who beforehand had counselled the person to sin. In fact, no sins that we humbly confess can be charged against us by the devil in this fearful judgement of our life. Act well, young adolescents and children. Free yourselves from diabolical slavery. Run together through penance to the very sweet mercy of the All Powerful God. Do not lose the heavenly joys through your carnal desires, and the blessedness of the eternal kingdom among the company of the angels; but ready yourselves and fight courageously against your adversary, in order that you may be worthy to be crowned for your happiness with the saints of God and to possess the eternal glory with them.

To you, most holy masters and fathers of this family, teach your sons to live sincerely, soberly, and chastely in the presence of God and (cf. Ti 2:12) *to make a transparent confession of their sins to the priests of Christ. Teach* them also *to wash by the tears of penance* the stain of carnal excess and not to repeat it because the sins committed later are worse than those which have preceded (cf. 2 Pt 2:20).You know that yourselves will be rewarded eternally by God for the salvation of your sons, since by these to whom you minister on the earth, you will participate in the heavens in the perpetual reward of their prosperity.

SUMMARY

The subject of penance and confession is a central one in the Carolingian period as witnessed by the writings of Alcuin. He is but one voice, however, among many who were concerned about the question of penance, the proper usage of the penitential books, and the general spiritual state of those in his care. In order to understand the fuller penitential tone of the period, several types of documents (*libri paenitentiales, libelli precum, specula* and *epistolae*) have been examined as gauges of the popular penitential piety and practice. In addition to these, there are other examples of penitential writings: i.e., liturgical writings, devotional works, occasional letters, and small treatises. It is interesting to note that the genius of Alcuin as well as the principal focus of his work at the court of Charlemagne lie in pedagogical concerns. Within the school reform, however, we find traces of theological thought,[83] most notably his ideas regarding penance.

Alcuin died in 804 but traces of his thought and work survived long after his death. The inclusion of his Votive Masses in the Gregorian Sacramentary as well as the wide circulation of his letters in letter collections, give eloquent testimony to this fact. As an educator and a reformer in the service of Charlemagne, he was concerned about the moral and spiritual development of monk and lay person alike. Clearly he saw the practice of confession and penance within this context, and thus contributed to the penitential theology of his time. It would be misleading, however, to think that all of Alcuin's efforts made in the area of penitential reform and spirituality bore fruit. The very fact that he drafted the long letter to the children and adolescents of St. Martin of Tours attests to the fact that they were unaccustomed to confessing their sins to a priest. The apologetic tone of the letter aims at convincing them not to blush with embarrassment and to seek the medicine of penance. On another occasion, Alcuin wrote a long letter to the monks of Septimania[84] where he encourages them to go to confession and to abandon any ideas that confession was not necessary for their spiritual well-being.

In addition to the penitential books of Anglo-Saxon origin, Alcuin would have known the penitential manuals of Frankish origin used in the eighth and ninth centuries for private penance. Moreover, the penitential system was sometimes used by the state and the penitential prescriptions had the value of civil law. Thus the Frankish church and the state were collaborators, forming the two swords of the emperor— one representing temporal power and the other spiritual power. At times the penitential books lent themselves for the control of subjugated peoples. For example, the most serious abuse of the penitential books can be seen in the capitulary of Paderborn,[85] promulgated in 785, to control the Saxons. If the vanquished Saxons refused to have their children baptized as Christians or if they did not observe the Lenten fast, they could be put to death.

Rightfully, the bishops were concerned about the proper usage of the penitential books. The great number of inconsistencies in the tariffs as well as the confusion in the organization of the content created some most inequitable situations. The preponderant judgement of the priest in the imposition of penances favored abuses. The confusion was due to the fact that the continental penitential books were of mixed origin, sometimes having several sources in the same book. Very often there were great inequalities from one group of penitential books to another in assigning penances. Five reforming councils were held in the year 813 with the view of correcting some of the abuses in the practice of penance. The principal agreement of these councils held that public sins demanded canonical penance while private sins could continue to be expiated through the tariffed penitential system.[86] Once again the very fact that such legislation was enacted indicates that there were problems with the discipline of penance at this time.

The influence of Alcuin can be measured not only through his writings but also through his students. One such student was Rabanus Maurus to whom we attribute two penitential books.[87] Compiled around 840, they reflect the spirit of his teacher and the statutes of the reforming councils. He maintains the distinction between public penance for crimes committed publicly and private penance for sins committed secretly. On the other hand, the penitential discipline is again in transition because the majority of the text is dedicated to canonical penance and hardly refers to the older penitential books.[88] Although the form of penance was again in flux the underlying attitude maintained that penance was an affair of the heart requiring penitence and conversion. To this end Rabanus was faithful to his master Alcuin. If the penitential practice was destined to change, the theology and spirituality of penitence which stood behind them should remain constant. Herein lies Alcuin's importance for the history of penitence.

Notes

1. The Patristic period placed great emphasis on how one became a Christian. Tertullian, the third century lawyer and theologian, wrote, "Christians are not born but made" (*De testimonio animae*, I: "fieri non nasci solet christiana"). He understood that one was called to become a Christian and this required a process which endured one's entire life. The process was a three-fold formation: intellectual, spiritual and moral. The process would initially take several years, including four phases: a period of inquiry, a period of catechumenate, a period of purification and enlightenment, and a period of mystagogia. The first three phases can last several years and are brought to their culmination in the events of Lent and Easter when the catechumens are presented to the community, prayed over and finally initiated at the Easter vigil. The last phase initially lasts the fifty days of Easter, up to Pentecost, but in reality consists of the rest of the Christian's life. This is the shape of initiation through the fifth century, the golden age being the fourth and fifth centuries. Afterwards the initiatory practices experienced a subsequent decline.

2. Canonical penance was a form corresponding with the early Church canons. A person could be admitted to the order of penitents for only the most serious of sins, the notable three being murder, apostasy and adultery. After a lengthy period the person was readmitted to the Church by a process resembling the early catechumenate. Just as baptism was only possible one time in one's life, so too the canonical form of penance was administered one time.

3. Cf. P. Riché, "Spirituality in Celtic and Germanic Society," in *Christian Spirituality: Origins to the Twelfth Century* (World Spirituality, 16) (New York, 1985), 167. Irish proverb: "body without head is man without confessor" (colann cen chenn duine cen anamcharait). The etimology of *anamchara*: from *animae carus* who was the *pater confessionis* or the *pater confessarius*.

4. Two other prayer elements were used for the completion of penances prescribed by the Penitential Books, namely the recitation of the psalms and the saying of votive masses; therefore a study of the various Psalters and the psalmodic form of prayer would help uncover some spiritual practices and votive masses containing penitential themes were extremely important. See J. Pierce, "New Research Directions in Medieval Liturgy: The Liturgical Books of Sigebert of Minden (1022–1036)," in *Fountain of Life* (Washington, DC, 1991), 31–67; Pierce notes the strong link between the *libelli precum* and the development of the medieval Mass.

5. Many studies exist regarding the penitential books. Some of the most notable are the following: P. Fournier, "Etudes sur les pénitentiels," in *Rev. d'histoire et de la litt. rel. 6* (1901), 289–317; 7 (1902), 59–70, 121–127; 8

(1903), 528–553; 9 (1904), 97–103; L. Bieler, "The Irish Penitentials: Their Religious and Social Background," in *Studia Patristica* 8 (1966), 329–339; T. Oakley, "The Penitentials as Sources for Medieval History," in *Speculum* 15 (1940), 210–223; J. McNeil, "The Celtic Penitentials and Their Influence on Continental Christianity," in *Revue Celtique* 39 (1922), 257–300; 40 (1923), 51–103, 320–341; Schmitz, *Die Bussbücher und das kanonische Bussverfahren* (Düsseldorf, 1898; reprinted in Graz, 1958); C. Vogel, *Les Libri Paenitentiales* (Typologie des sources du moyen âge occidental, 27) (Turnhout, 1978); R. Pierce, "The Frankish Penitentials," in *Studies in Church History,* 11 (Oxford, 1975), 31–39.

6. J.T. McNeill, op. cit., pp. 99–101.

7. H. Lea, *A History of Auricular Confession and Indulgences* vol. II (New York, 1896, reprinted 1968), 106: "Crude and contradictory as were the Penitentials in many things, taken as a whole their influence cannot but have been salutary. They inculcated on the still barbarous populations lessons of charity and loving-kindness, of forgiveness of injuries and of helpfulness to the poor and the stranger as part of the discipline whereby the sinner could redeem his sins"; S. Kuttner, "Pierre de Roisy and Robert of Flamborough," in *Traditio* 2 (1944), 493–494: He describes the penitentials in unflattering terms as being "gross tariffs and clumsy casuistry," and "a crude schedule of misdeeds and penances."

8. Cf. P. Fournier, "Etudes sur les pénitentiels," in *Rev. d'histoire et de la litt.* rel. 6 (1901), 289–317; 7(1902), 59–70, 121–127; 8 (1903), 528–553; 9 (1904), 97–103; L. Bieler, "The Irish Penitentials: Their Religious and Social Background," in *Studia Patristica* 8 (1966), 329–339; H. Mayr-Harting, The Coming of Christianity to Anglo-Saxon England (London, 1972); T. Oakley, "The Penitentials as Sources for Medieval History," in *Speculum* 15 (1940), 210–223.

9. Cf. R. Pettazzoni, "Confession of Sins in the Classics," in *Harvard Theological Review* 30 (1937), 1–14.

10. Cf. J. McNeill, "The Celtic Penitentials and Their Influence on Continental Christianity," in *Revue Celtique* 39 (1922), 257–300; 40 (1923), 51–103, 320–341.

11. Cf. M. Bateson, "Rules for Monks and Secular Canons after the Revival under King Edgar," in *EHR* 9 (1895), 690–708; J. Ryan, *Irish Monasticism: Origins and Early Development* (Dublin, 1931; reprinted, New York, 1972).

12. Cf. C. de Clercq, *La législation religieuse franque de Clovis à Charlemagne: études sur les actes des conciles et les capitulaires, les statuts diocésains et les régles monastiques,* 2 vols. (Paris, 1936; Antwerp, 1958); D.

Binchey, ed., *Corpus Iuris Hibernici*, 6 vols. (Dublin, 1978); F. Attenborough, ed. and tr., *The Laws of the Earliest English Kings* (Cambridge, 1922).

13. Cf. A. Frantzen, *The Literature of Penance in Anglo-Saxon England* (New Brunswick, New Jersey, 1983); E. Arnould, *Le manuel des péchés: étude de littérature anglo-normande* (Paris, 1940); J. Carney, *Studies in Irish Literature and History* (Dublin, 1955).

14. Cf. M. Bloomfield, *The Seven Deadly Sins* (East Lansing, Mich., 1952); R. Fowler, ed., "A Late Old English Handbook for the Use of a Confessor," in *Anglia* 83 (1965), 1–34; H. Schmitz, *Die Bussbücher und das kanonische Bussverfahren* (Düsseldorf, 1898; reprinted, Graz, 1958).

15. Cf. B. Bischoff, *Lorsch im Spiegel seiner Handschriften* (Munich, 1974).

16. Cf. D. Binchey, "The Linguistic and Historical Value of the Irish Law Tracts," in *Proceedings of the British Academy* 29 (1943), 195–227.

17. Vogel, "La discipline pénitentielle en Gaulle des origines au IXe s.: Le dossier hagiographique," in *Revue des sciences religieuses* 30 (1956), 1–26, 157–186. Vogel cites several hagiographical examples to show that the confession made to a priest existed already on the Continent before the apparition of the Irish and Anglo-Saxon monks. In the *vita Bavonis*, for example, after the death of his spouse, Bavo goes to the bishop to confess all his sins both *maximis et minimis*: "Ad viam conversionis Amandum sanctissimum pontificem expetiit (post mortem uxoris) cum lacrimis veniam postulans, pedibus quoque beati pontificis provolvitur cum compunctione sua confessus facinora . . . pro peccatis *maximis* et *minimis* paenitentiam acturus," *M.G.H., Scr. rer. merov.*, IV, p. 536.

18. Penitential of Cummean, "contraria contrariis sanantur," J.T. McNeill and H.M. Gamer, *Medieval Handbooks of Penance: A Translation of the Principal Libri Poenitentiales* (New York: Columbia, 1938, 1990), 100.

19. Cf. Matt 6:1–8; Tob 12:8.

20. T. Oakley, *English Penitential Discipline and Anglo-Saxon Law in Their Joint Influence* (New York, 1923, reprinted, 1969), a study of the juridical importance of the penitential books in the execution of civil laws.

21. In the Penitential of Cummean the pedagogical intention is well defined: Bieler, ed., *Irish Penitentials*, p. 134: "Quid est autem repropitiare delictum, nisi, cum adsumpseris peccatorem (ad poenitentiam), admonendo, hortando, docendo, instruendo adduxeris eum ad poenitentiam, ab errore correxeris, a vitiis emendaveris et efficeris eum talem ut ei converso propitius fiat Deus, pro delicto repropitiare diceris?"

22. Cf. M. Rubelin, "Vision de la société chrétienne à travers la confession et la pénitence au IXe siècle," in *Pratiques de la Confession* (Des pères du désert à Vatican II: quinze études d'histoire) (Paris, 1983), 53–70. The

author supposes that the penitentials were used by clerics to manipulate people whereby the priest-confessor was more of a judge than a spiritual doctor.

23. C. Vogel, *Les Libri Paenitentiales* (Turnhout, 1978), 55.

24. Beginning with the idea of penance as a spiritual remedy and as an expiation or satisfaction for sin, an idea found in the Irish penitentials, T. Oakley, in "The Origins of Irish Penitential Discipline," in *The Catholic Historical Review* 19 (1933), 320–332, sees their roots in Southern Gaul at the time of Cassian, Hillary of Poitier and Caesarius of Arles.

25. Idem, "The Penitentials as Sources," op. cit., p. 214, Oakley thinks that the roots are of patristic origin from Egyptian monasteries. Given that Cassian had drawn from Egyptian sources for his rule, one can possibly distinguish Egyptian as well as Gallican roots.

26. Fournier, in "De quelques infiltrations byzantines," op. cit.; departing from some comparisons between Greek and Anglo-Saxon juridical texts, the author proposes that Theodore, due to his Byzantine background, could have influenced the development of the penitentials.

27. Against the idea of insular origins of the penitentials, Schmitz, op. cit., formulates the hypothesis of Roman origin. This idea is rejected by the majority of scholars who agree with Wasserschleben, op. cit., and Fournier, op. cit., on the fact of the insular origins of the Frankish Penitentials. In the more recent study of the sources for the penitentials of Halitgar of Cambrai and of Rabanus Maurus, executed by Kottje, *Die Bussbücher Halitgars von Cambrai und das Hrabanus Maurus. Ihre Überlieferung und ihre Quellen* (Berlin, 1980), the hypothesis in favor of insular origin is all the more verified.

28. Cf. Chélini, op. cit., p. 163.

29. Cf. Frantzen, op. cit.

30. In a letter written by Cyrille Vogel to Pierre Riché, dated January 31, 1982, he vehemently criticizes the overall use of the penitential books. The salient features of this letter is cited with the permission of Dr. Riché.

31. Ibid., p. 3.

32. Alcuin, *Liber de virtutibus et vitiis, P.L.* 101, 622: "Poenentia vera non annorum numero consetur, sed amaritudine animi.... Non enim longitudinem temporis tantum requirit Deus, quantum affectum sinceritatis (poenitentis) pensat."

33. Cf. J. Leclercq, *La Spiritualité du moyen âge* (Paris, 1961), p. 86.

34. "Is qui poenitentiam in infirmitate petit, si casu, dum ad eum sacerdos invitatus venit, oppressus infirmitate obmutuerit ... dent testimonium qui eum audierunt et accipiat poenitentiam. Et si continuo creditur moriturus, reconcilietur *per manus impositionem* et infundatur eius ori Eucharistia," *PL* 56, 882C.

35. J.T. McNeill, op. cit., pp. 16–17: "The sacramental element in penance is suggested by the rite of the imposition of hands in reconciliation. The implications of this rite are not always clear, as it was employed in services not connected with penance, and at various aspects of penance J.A. Jungmann strikingly remarks that the words of absolution of the later period [late medieval] expressed "what the earlier imposition of hands aimed to say." [*Die lateinischen Bussriten in ihrer geschichtlichen Entwicklung* (1932), p. 253.] To employ the word "absolution," however, in connection with the reconciliation of penitents at this period would be misleading if it involved a recognition of the medieval application of the term. Absolution was granted not at the beginning of the penance but at its close, and it is not to be distinguished from reconciliation or admission to communion. No formularies of absolution of the period are preserved, and all information on the point indicates the use of a prayer, not of a declarative form." (cf. M.J. O'Donnell, *Penance in the Early Church*, rev. ed., p. 119. Cf. the prayers given in the *Gelasian Sacramentary*, ed. by H.A. Wilson, pp. 64 ff.).

36. J.T. McNeill, op. cit., pp. 279:

A Prayer over a Penitent:

Dearly beloved brethren,

let us beseech the almighty and merciful God,

Who desires not the death of sinners,

but that they be converted and live;

may this Thy servant, making amends unto true pardon,

be accorded the pardon of mercy; if there

are any wounds which he has received from all his offenses

after the wave of the sacred bath,

in this public confession of his misdeeds may

they be so healed that no signs of the scars remain.

Through our Lord Jesus Christ.

Another Prayer:

Our Savior and Redeemer

Who, gracious and pitiful,

dost grant pardon not only to penitents

but even to all those who do not previously desire to come,

as suppliants we seek that the pardon

bestowed of the communion of thy body and blood

may win for this Thy servant the celestial benediction.

Through [our Lord Jesus Christ].

37. As it appears in Codex Vallicell. D 5.

38. J.T. McNeill, op. cit., p. 284–85.

39. *A Prayer*
> Lord God almighty,
>> be Thou propitious unto me a sinner,
>> to make me, on behalf of sinners and those who
>> confess their sins,
>> a worthy mediator between Thee and them.
> And Thou who desirest not the death of sinners,
>> but that they should be converted and live (Ez 18:23–32; 33,11),
>> accept the prayer for Thy servant which I pour forth before the
>>> face of Thy glory,
>> for Thy menservants and maidservants who desire to do
>>> penance;
>> that Thou mayest both release them from their sins for the future
>>> and keep them unharmed from every offense.

But when he has come to thee, say over him this prayer:

> O God, who purifiest the hearts of all who make confession to Thee
>> and dost set free from the chain of the iniquity of all men
>> those who accuse their own conscience,
> give grace to the captives and grant healing (medicinam)to the
>> wounded,
>> that, the domination of sin have been overthrown,
>> they may serve Thee with free minds
>> through [Our Lord Jesus Christ].

Another prayer:

> Grant us, O Lord,
> that as Thou wast moved to favor by the prayers and confession of
>> the Publican
> so also, O Lord, thou mayest be favorable to this Thy servant,
> that, abiding in faithful confession and continuous expiation
>> he may quickly win Thy mercy
>> and that Thou mayest restore him to the holy altars and
>>> sacraments,
> [and that] he be made a partaker in the celestial glory above.

40. J.T. McNeill, op. cit., p. 280–82.

41. Cf. ibid., p. 30–31.

42. Ibid., p. 422–423.

43. See S. Allott, tr, *Alcuin of York: His Life and Letters* (York: William Sessions LTD, 1974); E.S. Duckett, *Alcuin, Friend of Charlemagne.* (New York: Macmillan, 1951); G. Ellard, *Master Alcuin Liturgist* (Chicago: Loyola University Press, 1956); P. Godman, *Alcuin: The Bishops, Kings and Saints of York* (Oxford: Oxford University Press, 1983); L. Wallach, *Alcuin and*

Charlemagne: Studies in Carolingian History and Literature (Ithaca: Cornell University Press, 1959).

44. See J. Leclercq, *La Spiritualité du moyen âge* (Paris, 1961), p. 68. Also see T. Cahill, *How the Irish Saved Civilization* (New York: Doubleday, 1995).

45. M. Driscoll, *The Precum Libelli and Carolingian Spirituality* (Proceedings of the North American Academy of Liturgy, 1990), 68–76; see P.-M. Gy, "The Different Forms of Liturgical Libelli," in *Fountain of Life* (Washington, DC, 1991), 23–34.

46. Cf. J. Leclercq, *La Spiritualité du moyen âge* (Paris, 1961), p. 86.

47. P.-M. Gy, "Bulletin de liturgie," in *Revue des Sciences Philosophiques et Théologiques* 67(1983), 315.

48. A. Wilmart, *Precum libelli quattuor aevi karolini* (prior pars) (Rome, 1940), 21, 56 et 73. Cited nearly in its entirety in note #65 below.

49. Expositio in Psal, XXXI, *Patrologia Latina* 100, 577: "Idem est cogitum facere et non operire, hoc est, confiteri. Quia si homo peccatum non agnoscit, Deus non ignoscit"; Theodulf of Orleans, I Capitulary, *MGH, Capitula episcoporum* (Hannover, 1984), 127, ch. 30: "Confessio vero, quam deo soli facimus, in hoc iuvat, quia quanto nos memores sumus peccatorum nostrorum, tanto horum obliviscitur."

50. J. Wallace-Hadrill, *The Frankish Church* (Oxford, 1983), 207: "Perhaps the stress on penance owed most to Irish influence at York; and indeed his approach to the liturgy in general shows no disposition to scrap Irish usage. Much stronger, however, was his determination to preserve whatever he thought was genuine Roman usage; and of this, too, York had been a guardian. Alcuin's influence on liturgical and biblical reform in Francia was Rome-oriented."

51. A. Wilmart, op. cit., from the *Libellus Turonensis*, p. 63: "Confiteor domino et tibi domine *sacerdos* omnia peccata et scelera mea quecumque feci et memorare possum inprimis quod in baptismo diabolo abrenunciavi"; ibid., p. 65, this confession bears the title *Confessio Sancti Fulgentii Eppiscopi ad penitentiam dandam*: "Ego confiteor tibi domine pater caeli et terrae coram hoc *sacerdote* tuo omnia peccata mea et omnia quecumque dei pietas michi ad memoriam reducit"; ibid., p. 67: "Supplico te dei *sacerdos*, ut de his omnibus sis mihi testis in die iudicii, ne gaudeat de me inimicus meus. Et dignare pro me deo misericordiam deprecari, ut donet mihi veniam indulgentiae, et omnium peccatorum meorum remissionem."

52. P. Salmon, *Libelli Precum du VIIIe siècle* (Analecta Liturgica, 273) (Vatican, 1974). Also cf. R. Constantinescu, "Alcuin et les *Libelli Precum* de l'époque carolingienne," in *Revue d'histoire de la spiritualité* 50 (1974), 17–56. The latter author believed to have uncovered another collection of *libelli* of

Alcuin found in the Stadtbibliothek, *ms. Misc. Patr. 17* in Bamberg, Germany, yet from examination of internal and external evidence, I believe his hypothesis of Alcuinian authorship to be untenable.

53. Cf. L. Brou and A. Wilmart, *The Psalter Collects* (London, 1949).

54. The *cursus* is the fixed manner in which the liturgy would be prayed, especially the liturgy of the hours which punctuated the day and night of monastic life. Prior to the monastic reform brought about partially due to Alcuin's efforts in conjunction with the work of Benedict of Aniane, there was great diversity in liturgical practices from monastery to monastery. The Rule of Benedict of Nursia was brought from Monte Cassino and copied in the scriptoria of the monasteries to be imposed upon the monks for a unified monastic practice in the Frankish kingdom.

55. Cf. N. Rasmussen, "Unité et diversité des pontificaux latins aux VIIIe, IXe et Xe siècles," in *Liturgie de l'eglise particulière et Liturgie de l'eglise universelle* (Rome, 1976), 393–410.

56. Ibid., pp. 5–6. Dom Wilmart takes great pain to study the manuscripts from a codicilogical and paleographical perspective in order to show Alcuin's familiarity with these four *libelli*.

57. A strong resemblance exists between the *libelli* of Alcuin and those of Nunnaminster, edited by W. de Gray Birch (Winchester, 1889) and *The Book of Cerne*, edited by A.B. Kuypers (Cambridge, 1902).

58. See K. Hughes, "Types of Prayer in the Liturgy," in *The New Dictionary of Sacramental Worship* (Collegeville: Liturgical Press, 1990), 959–967.

59. The seven penitential psalms are Pss. 6, 31, 37, 50, 101, 129 and 142. Cf. Cassidore, *Exposition Psalmorum I–LXX* (Corpus Christianorum, XCVII) (Brepolis, 1958), commentary on Psalm 50, p. 469: "Hinc est quod dum in hoc libro septem psalmi paenitentium esse doceantur, Ecclesiarum usu receptum est; ut quoties peccatorum venia petitur, per istum magis Domino supplicetur, non immerito. Primum quoniam in nullo psalmorum quae paenitentibus maxime necessaria est, tanta virtutis humilitas invenitur, ut rex potens et in prophetali culmine constitutus, tamquam extremus hominum sua festinaverit peccata deflere. Deinde quia post absolutionis promissionem tanta se constrinxit necessitate lacrimarum, quasi ei minime fuisset ignorum. . . . " Also see U. Hahner, *Cassiodors Psalmenkommentar: Sprachliche Untersuchungen* (Munich, 1973).

60. "Intendant quaesumus domine pietatis tuae aures supplicum preces,
                        quia apud te est propitiatio peccatorum,
                   ut non observes iniquitates nostras,
                        sed inpercias nobis misericordias tuas,

per dominum."
Precum Libelli, op. cit., pp. 30, 53 and 78.

61. "Deus qui matutinam sacrae resurrectionis tuae auditam fecisti iocunditatem cum ex inferno rediens replesti terram gaudiis quam reliqueras in obscuris, rogamus potentiae tuae ineffabilem maiestatem, ut sicut tunc catervam apostolorum gaudere fecisti piissimus, ita hanc ecclesiam tuam misericordiae tuae expansis manibus flagitantem splendore caelesti iubaris inlustrare digneris, qui cum patre et spiritu sancto vivis et regnas in saecula saeculorum. Amen." *Precum Libelli*, op. cit., pp. 30, 53 and 79.

62. J. Cavadini, *The Last Christology of the West: Adoptionism in Spain and Gaul, 785–820*. Philadelphia: University of Pennsylvania Press, 1993.

63. Cf. L. Bieler, "The Irish Penitentials: Their Religious and Social Background," in *Studia Patristica* 8 (Berlin, 1966), 335–339.

64. "Watch over my mouth lest it speak in vain and tell profane stories . . .

Watch over my eyes lest they look at a woman with carnal desire . . .

Watch over my ears lest they hear with disparagement or idle words of liars . . .

Watch over my feet lest they frequent brothels . . .

Watch over my hands lest they often tend to give gifts . . . ."
Kypers, op. cit., #10.

65. "Deus inaestimabilis misericordiae, deus inmensae pietatis, deus conditor et reparator humani generis, qui confitentium tibi corda purificas et accusantes se ante conspectum divinae clementiae tuae ab omni vinculo iniquitatis absolvis, virtutem tuam totis exoro gemitibus, ut secundum multitudinem miserationum tuarum de omnibus peccatis meis de quibus mea me accusat conscientia puram mihi coram te concedas *agere confessionem* veramque ex his omnibus et condignam mihi tribuas *penitentiam* quaecumque peccavi in cogitationibus pessimis, in meditationibus pravis, in consensu malo, in consilio iniquo, in concupiscentia atque delectatione inmunda, in verbis otiosis, in factis malitiosis, in visu, auditu, gustu, odoratu et tactu. Tu enim misericors deus ad operandam mihi animae meae salutem membra singula humanis usibus apta dedisti; sed ego miserrimus omnium et peccator te aeternae salutis auctorem contempsi, et aeterna mihi inimico incendia praeparanti suadente consensi, lapus sum in peccatis, corrui in delictis, cecidi in tantis et tantis criminibus, sceleribus, facinoribus, In membris singulis naturae modum excessi, et impiissime pravis et perversis laboribus obnoxium me feci. *Pedes* mei ad currendum in malum sequendo libidiiinem supra modum veloces fuerunt, et in oboedientia mandatorum inbiciles. Crura mea ad me sustinendum in malum fortes. *Genua* mea ad fornicationem potius quam ad orationem libenter flexi. In *femoribus* et *genitalibus* meis supra modum in ommnibus me

inmundiciis contaminare non metui, et reum me omni hora peregi. *Venter* meus et *viscera* omni crapula sunt iugiter et ebrietate distenta. In *renibus* et *lumbis* inlusione diabolica ac flamma libidinis, turpissimo ardeo desiderio. *Latera* enim mea luxoriam malitiae non formidant perpetrare. *Dorsum* meum ad iniqua roboravi opera, et *collum* in carnali erexi superbia. *Umera* mea ad portanda nequitiae onera subdidi, et *brachia* inlecebrosis iugiter amplexibus praebui. *Manus* meae plenae sunt sanguine, omnibusque sordibus sunt pollutae, prumtae ad omne opus pravum, pigre ad aliquid operandum bonum. *Os* meum nefario pollutum est osculo, et iniqua est concupiscentia maculatum. Verbisque luxoriosis ac fabulis otiosis superhabunter me mendacio coinquinavi. *Gutter* meum insatiabili semper ardet ingluviae. *Aures* meae dolosae sunt obtunsae loquelis, prumptae ad omne malum, surdae ad omne bonum. In *naribus* namque saepius iniquis delectatus sum odoribus, in quibus etiam putredinem delictorum minime horrui. Quid igitur dicam de *oculis*, qui omnibus me hominibus fecerunt obnoxium, omnemque sensum cordis mei averterunt quibus in omni consensi libinine? . . . " *Precum libelli*, op. cit., pp. 21–23, emphasis mine.

66. F. Cabrol, "Le Book of Cerne, les liturgies celtiques et gallicanes et la liturgie romaine," in *Revue des Questions Historiques* 76 (1904), 210–222.

67. See P. Hadot, "Fürstenspiegel," in *Reallexikon für Antike und Christentum*, vol. VIII (Stuttgart, 1972), coll. 555–632; H. Anton, "Fürstenspiegel und Herrscherethos in der Karolingerseit," in *Bonner historische Forschungen* 32 (1968); L. Born, "The Specula Principis of the Carolingian Renaissance," in *Revue Belge de philosophie et d'histoire* 12 (1933), 589–592; R. Bradley, "Backgrounds of the Title *speculum* in Medieval Literature," in *Speculum* 29 (1953), 100–103; O. Eberhardt, Via Regia, *Der Fürsten-spiegel Smalagda von St. Mihiel und seine literarische Gattung* (Munich, 1977); F.-J. Jakobi, "Früh- und hochmittelalterliche Sozialstrukturen im Spiegel liturgischen Quellen," in *Geschichte im Wissenschaft und Unterricht* 31 (1980), 1–20.

68. See A. Frantzen, *The Literature of Anglo-Saxon England* (New Brunswick, 1983), 115.

69. *PL* 101: 613–618: Liber de virtutibus et vitiis; See H.M. Rochais, "Liber de virtutibus et vitiis d'Alcuin," in *Revue Mabillon* 41(1951), 77–86; R. Terkar, *Eine altenglische übersetzung von Alcuins De virtutibus et vitiis*, Kap. 21 (Munich, 1977).

70. Alcuin in his letter n. 116, *MGH Ep*. IV, p. 171, defined his notion of a mirror thus: "*Speculum* est enim pontificalis vitae et medicina contra singula diabolicae fraudis vulnera." According to this definition the *specula* resemble the penitential books. Elsewhere one notes an identical conception in the *speculum* composed by a friend of Alcuin, Paulinus of Aquileia for Eric of Friuli. See P. Riché, *Dhuoda: Manuel pour mon fils* (Paris, 1957), p. 13; idem.,

La vie quotidienne dans l'Empire carolingien (Paris, 1973), 99–100; idem., *Les Ecoles et l'enseignement dans l'Occident chrétien de la fin du V siècle* (Paris, 1979), p. 288; G. Mathon, "Les fondements de la morale chrétienne selon le Manuel de Dhuoda," in *Sapientia Doctrina*, 1980.

71. *MGH Ep*. IV, n.305, pp. 464–465: "Haec tibi, dulcissime fili Wido, brevi sermone, sicut petisti, dictavi; ut habeas cotidie quasi manualem in conspectu tuo libellum, in quo possis te ipsum considerare, quid cavere, vel quid agere debeas: atque per singulas vitae huius prosperitates vel adversitates exortari, quomodo ad culmen perfectionis ascendere debeas. Nec te laici habitus vel conversationis secularis terreat qualitas; quasi in eo habitu vitae caelestis ianuas intrare non valeas. Igitur sicut in omnibus aequaliter regni Dei predicata est beatitudo, ita omni sexui, aetati et personae aequaliter secundum meritorum dignitatem regni Dei patet introitus. Ubi non est distinctio, quis esset in seculo laicus vel clericus, dives vel pauper, iunior vel senior, servus aut dominus, sed unusquisque secundum meritum boni operis perpetua coronabitur gloria. Amen"; see Gal 3:28; Col 3:11).

72. The fundamental sources of the catalogue of the eight capital sins are Cassian (*Collatio* V, I and V, 16, 5; op. cit.) and St. Gregory (*Moralia* in the book of Job XXXI, 45; *PL* 76, 620–622).

73. The terms *libellus* and *manualis* indicate that these books had a format which facilitated easy transport. Like a breviary, they were destined for people engaged in the *vita activa*.

74. L. Wallach, "Alcuin on Virtues and Vices: A Manual for a Carolingian Soldier," in *Harvard Theological Review* 48 (1955), 175–195.

75. *PL* 101, 623: "Noli desperare de venia peccatorum, nec de vita longiori confidere. Convertere ergo, et poenitentiam age. Cras, inquies, convertam." Alcuin was greatly influenced by the writings of Caesarius of Arles for his notion of conversion. A comparison of chapter fourteen of Alcuin with Sermon 18, 2–6 of Caesarius (ed. G. Morin, *CCL* 103, 83–86) shows clearly the relationship between the two texts.

76. Ibid., col. 624: "Qui timet Dominum, recedit ab itinere pravo, et ad virtutis semitam vias suas dirigit. Timor Domini repellit peccata, et adjicit virtutes. Timor cautum facit hominem et sollicitum, ne peccet . . . Timor Dei timorem gehennae expellit. Sic ergo timeamus Deum, ut diligamus eum." See A. Frantzen, op. cit., p. 179: the author argues that fear is the true motive for doing penance. If penitents do not believe in the death, resurrection and redemption, they would not have any reason to fear the consequences of their misdeeds. On the other hand, it seems that one can interpret the text in the light of conversion, because just prior to the chapters on confession and penance, Alcuin deals with compunction of the heart, which is for him the true condition of penance. It is from compunction that one goes on to confess one's sins which

leads to penance. Compunction comprises the fear of judgement as well as humility and the memory of having sinned.

77. T F.-J. Schmale, "Briefe, Briefliteratur, Briefsammlungen: lateinisches Mittelalter," in *Lexicon des Mittelalters*, vol. II (Munich and Zurich, 1981), col. 649.

78. The idea of friendship holds a key position in the thought of Alcuin, judging simply by the multiple references to it in his letters and poetry (cf. Epp. 18, 28, 76, 141, and Carm. LXII, verse 59 and 120, among other examples). Cf. J. Leclercq, "L'Amitié dans les lettres au moyen âge," in *Revue du Moyen Age Latin* 1(1945), 391–410; A. Fiske, "Alcuin and Mystical Friendship," in *Studi Medievali*, 3 ser., v. 2.ii, pp. 551–575. Spoleto, 1961.

79. Idem, *L'Amour des lettres et le désir de Dieu* (Paris, 1957, 1963), 173. The author lists the following genres of letters composed in the Middle Ages:

    1) Letters of vocation,
    2) Letters of exhortation, of consolation, of "spiritual direction,"
    3) Doctrinal consultations, exchanges of responses,
    4) Business letters,
    5) Letters of recommendation,
    6) Letters of exhortation to die well,
    7) Funeral announcements and
    8) Letters of friendship.

This last genre abounded among the monastic communities. These letters were meant to please the recipient and often coincide with other letter genres listed above. Often, however, they had no other intention than a simple friendly exchange.

80. On the subject of epistolary genre, in general, cf. G. Constable, *Letters and Letter Collections* (Typologie des Sources du Moyen Age Occidental, 17) (Brepols, 1976). For Alcuin's letters specifically, cf. E. Dümmler, ibid. and Th. Sickel, ibid.

81. J. Leclercq, "Le Genre epistolaire au moyen âge," in *Revue du Moyen Age Latin* 2 (1946), 63–70: "Quand un auteur déclare avoir été sollicité de livrer un livre au public, ce n'est pas une excuse factice pour son besoin de célébrité; on sait qui l'a prié, et l'on peut souvent lire en tête du traité la lettre de demande. Un ouvrage est presque toujours la solution d'une problème réelement posé par la vie, et ceci donne à cette littérature un caractère concret et animé. Un prologue n'est pas simplement une introduction, c'est une adresse."

82. *MGH Ep*, IV, n.131, pp. 193–198. Italics are mine to emphasize some specific penitential themes.

83. Concerning Alcuin as a theologian, E. Gilson writes: "On ne se tromperait pas moins en attribuant à maître Alcuin un génie dont ses œuvres ne

portent pas la trace. Exégète et théologien de deuxième ordre, poète médiocre, il ne nous a laissé que de bien modestes contributions à l'étude des libéraux. . . .," *Philosophie au moyen âge des origines patristiques à la fin du XIVe siècle* (Paris, 1944), 191. In spite of these faint words of praise, Gilson dedicates his volume on medieval philosophy to the Anglo-Saxon master. To call Alcuin a theologian is to do him an injustice, since his formation was other than theology, trained most especially in elementary education. He simply was responding to the ecclesial needs of his time in delving into theological matters, thus bequeathing a certain number of fundamental manuals to the Frankish clergy. Elsewhere, Gilson states: "La vraie grandeur d'Alcuin tient à sa personne et à son œuvre civilisatrice plutôt qu'à ses livres. Elle se révèle partout dans ses lettres et dans les quelques passages de ses traités où s'expriment son admiration profonds pour la culture antique et sa volonté de la maintenir," ibid., 191–192.

84. *MGH Ep.* IV, ep. 138; *PL* 100, c. 337–341.

85. *MGH Leges* I, sect. II, pp. 68–70 (Capitulary of Paderborn).

86. *MGH Leges III, Conc.*, t. 2, (Council of Arles, May, 813), p. 253, c. 26: "Ut qui publico crimine convicti sunt rei publice iudicentur et publicam paenitentiam agant secundum canones."

87. *PL* 110, col. 191 and coll. 467–494.

88. Cf. Vogel, *Le Pécheur et la pénitence au moyen âge* (Paris: Cerf, 1969), 200.

RITES OF MARRIAGE IN THE WESTERN MIDDLE AGES

John K. Leonard

> And may a bridegroom bring her to a house
> Where all's accustomed, ceremonious.
> For arrogance and hatred are the wares
> Peddled in the thoroughfares.
> How but in custom and ceremony
> Are innocence and beauty born?
> Ceremony's a name for the rich horn
> And custom for the spreading laurel tree.
>> W.B. Yeats, from "A Prayer for My Daughter"

One of the most interesting things about studying the history of Christian marriage rites is that weddings (like funerals and other services marking human passage) have never been fully under the control of church authorities. Marriage practices have always been heavily influenced by local customs and law. Christians continued to give and take one another in marriage in their accustomed ways for centuries with few modifications before ecclesiastical authorities felt obligated to involve themselves when two of the faithful decided to get married. Moreover, it was only very slowly and rather late that marriage rites began to appear in liturgical books and to become a matter for church legislation. But in every age, the need to mark this significant moment in human life with "custom and ceremony" produced a variety of local traditions for marrying "in Christ."

All the rites of Christian marriage recognize that marriage pre-existed the Christian dispensation. Marriage existed "from the beginning," from the very time of creation. It is thus an anthropological phenomenon before it is a Christian institution and it may be helpful to review briefly what anthropologists have long known about the ritualization of this human reality.

ANTHROPOLOGY OF MARRIAGE

What is marriage? What is involved in "getting married"? Given the enormous variety of customs, laws, practices, it is impossible to give a simple answer that will be true for every people and in every age. But there are some basic ("deep") structures that can be identified. The three stages which Arnold van Gennep identified when investigating initiation rites in primitive societies are also identifiable in marriage: (a) rites of separation; (b) a period of marginality or liminality; (c) rites of incorporation or aggregation.[1] Van Gennep saw all marriage rites and customs as negotiating a transition or series of transitions:

> Marriage constitutes the most important of the transitions from one social category to another, because for at least one of the spouses it involves a change of family, clan, village, or tribe, and oftentimes the newly married couple even establish residence in a new house.[2]

Separation: Betrothal is the rite whereby the promise of future marriage is made and the initial separation from the former state begins. In most cultures, this is not left up to the individuals but is arranged by parents or families and marked by an exchange of some gifts, coins or some type of contract.

Liminality: Once engaged, the fiancés are in a class by themselves (betrothed or engaged). No longer permitted to date and carry on like their unattached friends, neither are they supposed to live like married people (children born during this period are considered in several societies to be unredeemably illegitimate). It is a period of liminality, on the threshold between being single and being married, marked by an engagement ring or a veil or some other outward sign that one is "spoken for."

Incorporation/Aggregation: The marriage or wedding includes all those rites and customs whereby the couple are fully incorporated into the ranks of married folk. In almost all societies the rites include the bride being led or carried to the groom's house or into the wedding chamber, a meal wherein the sharing of food (wedding cake) and drink seals the common life they begin, and other symbols finalizing the union: joining hands; being roped, veiled or crowned together; sitting together, eating or drinking from the same cup or dish.

As early as the twelfth century, the ritualization of all three of these stages began to be celebrated on the same day with the betrothal/consent celebrated at the church doors, the marriage prayers and Eucharist at the altar, and the blessing of the bed chamber at home. Since that time, most western liturgical rites have been further abbreviated, leaving the betrothal, engagement, and entry into the bed chamber entirely beyond the purview of the ecclesial authorities.

The process of marrying may be very short or very extensive depending on the social structures and cultural customs of the society. The process may begin as early as infancy or at puberty (for women, the mark of marriage ability) and may continue long after cohabitation has begun. For some, it may become "indissoluble" only after children are born or when the "bride-price" is paid in full—or it may never achieve that status and end in divorce.

Throughout the Middle Ages the particulars of Christian marriage rites varied considerably from one region to the next even though the "deep" structures remain to this day. But the understanding of marriage and many of its customs in the Christian West have antecedents in the Graeco-Roman and Germanic worlds.

ROMAN MARRIAGE LAWS AND CUSTOMS

In the Roman empire, the various populations retained their own marriage customs and there was no attempt to impose ritual uniformity. Nevertheless, Roman law held primacy of place. In every culture at the time, the formation of the marriage bond was done in stages involving the families as well as the couple. Rome was no different, but Roman law reduced "getting married" to a simple, perfunctory contract. The basic principle for Roman marriage was *Consensus non concubitus facit matrimonium* (Consent, not cohabitation, makes a marriage). From this principle it followed that

- marriage could be contracted *in absentia*
- a husband who died before consummation left his wife a widow with right of her dowry
- no legal formula was required, *in absentia*, a letter would suffice.
- the object of the consent was the will to form a *iustum matrimonium*, i.e., the husband acknowledged this woman as his

"lawful wife" and intended to show her the affection and respect
due to a wife (*affectio maritalis*) and the wife would share her
husband's status.

- it was impossible to contract legal marriage between persons of
  social inequality; senatorial families could not marry ex-slaves
  or women of the theater.
- slaves could not marry because they had no "legal will of their
  own"
- lack of legal consent and failure on the part of either to render
  the *affectio maritalis* meant that the union was not a lawful
  marriage and laws relating to legitimacy, inheritance, use of
  dowry, husband's authority, etc. were inapplicable.

Therefore only *the intent of the spouses* differentiated between marriage
with all its legal and social ramifications, and simple concubinage.

Concubinage could be stable, permanent, loving, even respectable;
but it was not marriage. It could be transformed into marriage by the
intent of the couple. Such a change required no formal or public act and
therefore would be difficult to prove.

The procreation of children was taken for granted to assure the
continuation of the father's line; the local magistrate was informed of
the marriage primarily so that if children were not born, divorce could
be readily achieved.

The principle of Roman Law that the bond of marriage was
effected by the exchange of consent was known by the Latin Fathers,
(Ambrose, Augustine, Jerome) and Popes (esp. Siricius, Innocent, Leo
and Gelasius) and consequently had an enormous influence on the
history and theology of marriage in the West. So too, the Roman
customs and ceremonies which accompanied betrothal and marriage
played a significant role in the evolution of the medieval rites of
marriage.

Betrothal was normally celebrated several years before the marriage
(sometimes even in infancy). The agents involved were those with
"legal wills," the *patres familiarum*, while the children, as long as they
were under the authority of their *paterfamiliae*, could not refuse to
marry. Of course the children would, it was hoped, give their own

consent as individuals to the arrangement but such was not required by law. The consent required was the consent of the ones in authority.

The betrothal was accompanied by familial, social, and religious ceremonies, none of which were required by law. If the betrothal was celebrated, it usually took place in the home of the future bride in front of witnesses. In the beginning of the Christian era it included the exchange of the agreements (*sponsalia*) and gifts. Among the gifts, the fiancé gave a ring to his future bride [Pliny says it was of iron, Tertullian refers to it as gold].[3] The betrothal was not legally binding until very late. If the boy's family reneged, they forfeited all claims on future gifts; if the girl's family wanted out, they had to send back the gifts and the ring.

NUPTIALS[4]

In general, there were three forms of marriage or "ways to get married" that were recognized by Roman custom—*Usus*, *Coemptio*, and *Confarreatio*:

Usus: Because consent makes the marriage, there were some who simply lived together for a period of a year, similar to what would later be known as a common-law marriage. As long as the woman had not absented herself from her husband's company for three nights in a row, she came "under her husband's hand" legally. *Usus* was the most common form of nuptials among the plebeians, and little is known with certainty about the ritualization with which this cohabitation may have begun.

Coemptio: Coemptio consisted of the fictitious sale of the woman to the husband made in the presence of 5 witnesses: First, a single coin was laid in the scales; then their right hands were joined and consent was exchanged; the final element was the procession or *domumductio* during which the bride was led to the house of the groom. Prayer and/or sacrifices to the gods/goddesses either preceded or followed the *domumductio*.

Confarreatio: The most ancient and solemn form of nuptials consisted of the *traditio puellae*, the *domumductio*, and the *confarreatio*. Even when it became clear that the religious ceremony was not legally required and that the consent of the partners was sufficient to constitute a marriage, most in the upper class continued the traditional ceremonies. The reader will note the great emphasis placed on the bride throughout the entire process.

The choice of day was significant: some days were propitious, others were not (among the Greeks, the full moon in autumn was considered ideal; in the Late Empire, nuptials were celebrated during the time of the orange blossoms).

(1) On the evening before the nuptials, the bride dedicated some of her hair, her garments and childhood toys to the Lares (the household goddesses).

(2) On the morning of the ceremony, the bride was dressed by her mother in a *tunica recta* (a white dress woven in one piece) which was tied at the waist by a woolen cord with a "knot of Hercules" that could only be untied by her husband. Over this she wore a saffron-colored cloak or *palla* with matching sandals, and round her neck a metal collar. Her hair was protected by six pads of artificial hair separated by narrow bands of cloth such as those worn by the Vestal virgins during their period of service; over it was placed the *flammeum*, a veil of flaming orange, which modestly covered the upper part of her face. On top of the veil was placed a wreath of myrtle and orange blossoms that she was to have picked and woven herself. Duly dressed, she was introduced by the *pronuba* (an older, well-respected woman married only once = matron of honor) to the waiting assembly of family and friends on both sides.

(3) Everyone adjourned to a neighboring temple or to the atrium of the house to offer a sacrifice to the gods. Then the auspex examined the entrails in order to guarantee that the auspices were favorable.

(4) In the third and fourth centuries CE, a marriage contract (*tabula nuptialis*) was then signed by ten witnesses, five from among the family and friends of each. The contract which had originated in the east,[5] recorded the purpose of marriage (*for the sake of having children*) and the dowry brought by the bride. The contract became the property of the groom or of his *paterfamilias*.

(5) In marriages of the senatorial class, an additional sacrifice of fruit and a wheat cake (*panis farreus*) was made by the *pontifex maximus* [president of the 15 pontiffs] or by the *Flamen Dialis* (priest of Jupiter) while the couple sat on two seats which had been bound together and covered with a sheepskin.[6]

(6) In some cases each would be asked, *An vellet sibi mater/ pater esse?* (Do you wish to be a mother/father?). But the most common form of public consent was the exchange: *Ubi/Quando tu Gaius, ego Gaia* (Where/When you are Gaius, I am Gaia).

(7) The *pronuba* placed the right hand of the bride into the right hand of the groom (*iunctio dextrarum*). This effected the marriage and the guests burst into congratulations and good wishes: *Feliciter!* May happiness wait upon you!

(8) The festivities—banquet, music, dancing, drinking, etc.—began and lasted until evening.

(9) The *Domumductio* began when the groom snatched the bride from her mother's arms. The bride was led by the hand by two boys; a third led the way with a torch. Flute players and singers accompanied the procession which, according to both those who approved and disapproved, was noisy and licentious! Such was not simple debauchery but had arisen from the need to frighten evil spirits away from the bride who was no longer under the protection of her family's household gods and not yet under the protection of those of her new husband.

(10) Upon arrival at the groom's house, the bride smeared the doorposts with oil and decorated the door with garlands. Next she was lifted over the threshold so her foot did not touch it. Only a few invited guests entered with them, including three bridesmaids: the *pronuba,* a second carrying the distaff, the third carrying her spindle.

(11) The groom sprinkled her with lustral water, gave her a flaming torch, and led her to the hearth where she lit the fire. Next they fed each other a piece of wheat cake, sealing the beginning of their common board. The *pronuba* led the bride to the wedding

chamber. The groom removed her cloak and woolen girdle and the guests withdrew. . . .

(12) The next morning, bride made an offering to the *Lares* and *Penates* (household gods of home and hearth) and the *Manes* (family ancestors) and the groom offered her a morning gift. The rest of the day a banquet was held for the immediate families on both sides at the groom's expense.

CHRISTIAN MARRIAGE IN THE ROMAN EMPIRE

Marriage in facie ecclesiae[7]

[Christians] marry, like everyone else, and they have children, but they do not expose their offspring to the elements. They share their board with each other, but not their marriage bed. It is true that they are "in the flesh" but they are not "of the flesh."[8]

Christians in the Roman Empire did marry and they did so according to local custom and law. As was the case with their non-Christian contemporaries, marriage was a domestic affair. It is most likely that the parents of bride and groom presided at the various ceremonies in their respective homes, probably leading the prayer to God through Christ in the place of the pagan sacrifices. It is probable that the bishop and other Christians were among the guests for it is hard to imagine them not being part of the "family," at least for a marriage between two Christians. It is also possible that as *paterfamilias* of the Christian assembly, the bishop may have led the prayer.[9] Of course some Christians advocated more involvement of the Church in all decisions that affected the life of the community.[10] At the time of Augustine (d. 434), the bishop would be invited to the home when marriage was to be celebrated, he would sign the *tabula nuptialis* along with the other witnesses and give his blessing to the newlyweds. But this was only at the invitation of the families concerned. Augustine never got involved in arranging marriages and would not accept invitations until all plans were agreed upon. In this he consciously followed the pastoral practice of Ambrose of Milan.[11]

Christians probably conducted their marriages quietly, especially in times of persecution, but they could hardly avoid inviting pagan friends and family or accepting invitations from pagans.[12] Christians generally avoided the noisy and lascivious aspects of Roman marriage—at least in the pre-Constantinian period[13]—but they were known to celebrate with singing, dancing and banquets that resembled those of their contemporaries in every other way.[14]

Christians followed the prescriptions of civil law on marriage except that they recognized marriages between slaves and free persons as legitimate. Hippolytus of Rome (c. 225), who regarded himself a traditionalist, noted that secret marriages between patricians and slaves (those which would have to avoid publicity in pagan society) required the consent of the bishop and that any from the ranks of the clergy required permission of bishop to marry.[15] In his well-known *Apostolic Tradition,* Hippolytus indicates that marital status of catechumens was examined and that concubinage was to give way to marriage:

> If any man has a wife, or a woman a husband, they shall be taught to be contented, the man with his wife and the woman with her husband. But if any man is not living with a wife, he shall be instructed not to fornicate, but to take a wife lawfully or remain as he is (ch. 15). . . . A man's concubine, if she is his slave and has reared her children and remained faithful to him alone, may be a hearer; otherwise, let her be rejected. Let any man who has a concubine cease, and take a wife lawfully; but if he is unwilling, let him be rejected (ch. 16).

Nuptial Blessing

Although Christians in the Western part of the empire were influenced by the marriage customs of Rome, the prayers which replaced the pagan nuptial sacrifices were biblical in imagery and inspiration and, like other early Christian prayers that have survived, structured after Jewish patterns.[16] One of the earliest wedding blessings is found in the Book of Tobit which dates from the second century BCE. In describing the wedding of Tobias and Sarah the text records a blessing pronounced by Sarah's father, Raguel: "From now on you belong to her and she to you; she is yours forever from this day. May the God of Abraham, the God of Isaac, and the God of Jacob be with you, and may he himself join you together, and fill you with his blessing" (Tobit 7:12 Vulgate). Before they sleep together the first night, Tobias prays with Sarah as follows:

> Blessed are you, O God of our ancestors, praised be your name forever and ever. Let the heavens and all your creation praise you forever. You made Adam and Eve, his wife, to be his help and support; and those two were the parents of the human race. You said: 'It is not good for the man to be alone; let us make him a partner like himself.' Now, Lord, you know that I take this my beloved wife, not out of lust but for a noble purpose. Call down your mercy on me and on her and allow us to live together to a happy old age (8: 5–7).

The next morning, Raguel pronounces yet another blessing: "May blessing be said over your wife and over your parents; and may you see your children's children to the third and fourth generation; and may your seed be blessed by the God of Israel who reigns for ever and ever" (Tobit 8:10–12, Vulgate). These three texts from Tobit are used in a variety of ways and contexts throughout the Middle Ages. The themes of praise for creation, the recounting of the divine institution of marriage, the invocation of God's blessing on the marriage at hand through procreation and a long life together are constants in all the rites. But at Rome, the emphasis on the bride—her veiling, the role of the *pronuba*, the *domumductio*, etc.—had its own influence on the texts. With the eventual spread of the Roman liturgy throughout the West,[17] this bridal focus in the prayer texts would make its way into every medieval marriage rite.

The Nuptial Blessing at Rome[18]

The earliest Roman evidence for a ritual of Christian marriage is a set of six Mass prayers included in a collection known as the *Veronensis* (Verona, Biblioteca Capitolare *codex* 85, sixth century)[19] under the heading, *Incipit velatio nuptialis* (Here begins the Nuptial Veiling). Included are an opening prayer, a prayer over the gifts, a special prayer within the Canon that mentions the *pronuba* (who made the offering[20]) and the bride (on whose behalf the offering is made), a prayer after communion, a prayer introducing the nuptial blessing and the nuptial blessing itself. This final prayer is a series of blessings which includes themes of creation, creation of man and woman as subordinate and weaker, procreation, children for this woman, prayer for a good marriage. The second section sketches the ideal of the married woman: loving, wise, long-lived and loyal, honest, faithful, loyal to one bed, serious, modest, above reproach, instructed in wisdom of heaven, fruitful with children. This ideal has to be understood against the background not only of the woman's subordination to man but also as a reaction to the license and immorality of late antiquity. Thus the prayer reflects both cultural presuppositions and a counter-cultural exaltation of marriage as a form of the Christian life.

In spite of the heading, none of the prayer texts mention the veiling, and there is no indication that the veiling covered both bride and groom as in northern Italy and other rites.[21] Some have proposed that the brilliant Roman *flammeum* drew attention to this part of the domestic ritual and gave its name to the Mass that followed the bride's introduction by the *pronuba*. Others have noted that the veiling of virgins became a public rite at the same time that the nuptial blessing made its appearance and that, while the consecration of virgins adapted the "veiling" from popular marriage custom, it, in turn, transformed the marriage veil and led to the use of white rather than flaming orange.[22]

The Roman blessing's exclusive emphasis on the bride has been explained in a variety of ways In his *Commentary on Corinthians*, Ambrosiaster (fl. 366–384) reasoned:

> The nuptial blessing of Christians is in continuity with God's blessing on the first married couple (Gn 1:28). The blessing used in the synagogue was likewise given in the Church. . . . The groom is not to be blessed because he was made in the image of God while the bride was only an image of man and only through man the image of God. It is unthinkable that anyone should bless God so it was out of the question that anyone should bless the groom (cf. I Cor 11:3, 7–10).[23]

On the other hand, the bridal focus may be explained by the ancient Roman customs of marriage—including the reading of the auspices and offering of the sacrifice and the *pompa* of the *domumductio,* motivated at least in part by the need to pray for and protect the bride during this major transition.

Many of the Mass texts which appear in the *Veronensis* made their way to the medieval marriage rites by way of what is known as the Gregorian Sacramentary tradition.[24] Unlike the *Veronensis*, the Gregorian tradition indicates clearly that the nuptial blessing with its introductory prayer is said before the Kiss of Peace and before Communion. Although the Gregorian uses several of the Verona texts, it provides an original Preface to the Canon and a re-worked nuptial blessing. The two Roman books do share a common understanding of marriage: the same view of the weakness of woman which makes the bride the obvious and exclusive focus of the Church's prayer; the same emphasis on marriage as a divinely instituted state into which people enter; the accent on the moral virtues expected of the Christian wife; marriage as a companionship lived ideally in peace and harmony. But the Gregorian adds a reference to Ephesians 5 ("You have consecrated the bond of marriage with such an excellent mystery as to prefigure in the covenant of marriage the sacrament of Christ and his Church") and to the belief that even original sin and the flood at the time of Noah did not obliterate the God-given holiness of marriage. Even more interesting is the recalling of both the past dimension of marriage rooted in the dawn of creation and its future culmination in the eschatological marriage of the Lamb and his Bride, Christ and the Church. As Searle/Stevenson point out, the "bridal pair assumed a larger, archetypal identity, in which both past and future meet."[25]

By the time the Gregorian was compiled, marriage customs seem to have shifted slightly: the *pronuba's* offering on behalf of the bride— mentioned in the prayer within the canon—seems to have been replaced by an offering from the families. Some manuscripts of the Gregorian (non-Roman in provenance) also introduce plural forms into the nuptial blessing in an attempt to broaden the focus to include both partners. Again, it is worth noting that while procreation still features as the chief reason for marriage, the *Veronensis'* references to the social importance of marriage as a way of bonding families and ensuring the family line have been "baptized" into assertions that marriage provides the Church with new members. Finally, the end of the blessing has been re-worked to incorporate the petition based on Tobit 9:11 that she "may see her children's children to the third and fourth generation" and which will recur in almost all later Western rites.[26]

THE GALLICAN AND GERMANIC HERITAGE

The Roman nuptial blessing and its accompanying Mass did not immediately replace any of the other domestic rites or customs which surrounded the marriage of Christians at Rome. It would be several centuries before these Roman prayers became the norm and the intervening history of marriage in the West is not easy to trace. Soon after Christianity became the religion of the empire under Theodosius, the Vandals overran N. Africa, destroyed Hippo and wiped out the Christian population within a generation after Augustine's death (434). Italy was terrorized by the Ostrogoths (early fifth century) Huns (mid fifth), Byzantine Greeks (sixth), and Lombards (seventh). Spain was overrun first by the Vandals and then by the Visigoths; Roman Gaul by the Burgundians and Franks (fifth and sixth). Each successive wave of migration brought its own languages, legal systems, and/or customs which were more or less merged with the system of Roman law. Roman law's minimal requirement of an expression of consent to constitute a legal marriage made it all the more amenable to merge with the diverse marriage laws and customs of the various conquering tribes. The outcome was a pluriformity which survived until well into modern times.

I. Rome and Italy

A. *Roman Population in Italy*

1. *Betrothal* had become very important with the introduction from the East of arrhabon/ring-betrothal into Roman law. Christian morality and the strictness with which the Church regarded promises may have contributed to the seriousness of this first phase in the marriage process.[27] The Kiss of Betrothal became common in Italy, probably from the time of Constantine, as did the writ of dowry probably drawn up at the time of betrothal.[28]

2. *Marriage.* While classical Roman law retained marriage by consent and without form (at least among social equals), Justinian's code (565) effectively superseded it and declared that a ceremony was necessary. Nevertheless, the idea that the ceremonies were not essential remained very much alive in Italy.[29]

Many of the marriage customs of pagan Rome remained substantially in use into the Christian era and beyond. Ambrose testifies to the wearing of the *flammeum* as distinct from the *velamen* of the marriage rite,[30] but the *domumductio* was definitely abandoned in marriages of the clergy.[31]

B. Lombards in Italy

In 568, the Arian Lombards controlled all of Italy apart from the duchy of Rome, the Exarchate of Ravenna and a few places in the south. By 680 they were all Catholic. Lombardic law (*Lex Langobardii*) was the most complete system of all the Teutonic legal systems[32] with two kinds of marriage: *Friedelehe* and *True Marriage.*

Friedelehe: (*Friede* from *frilla* = *Liebchen*, sweetheart) even before emancipation from male tutelage there was a form of marriage which i) was for a limited time; ii) did not involve transfer of guardianship; iii) did not involve the husband giving the wife a betrothal gift but instead a "morning gift."

1. *Betrothal* = *Verlobung*: had all the characteristics of a contract of exchange between the prospective groom and the clan or *Vormund* (guardian) of the girl, so that she was effectively sold in marriage. It was a legal transaction carried out as follows:

  a. The man pledged, with a deposit of money and guarantees (=*Wadia* or *Wette*), to take the woman in marriage and to endow her with part of his property (*Wittum*). If he subsequently withdrew, he would forfeit the deposit.

  b. The maiden's *Vormund* (guardian) betrothed her by handing over various symbols of power: *per ensem et watonem, per gladium et clamidum.* The woman is thereby given over to the authority of her future husband who, in returning the symbols, returns her to her guardian until the appointed day.

  c. The Lombards added the giving of an engagement ring, a practice borrowed from the Romans.

2. *Marriage* = *Trauung*. The legal act of marriage began with drawing up the document in which the groom stipulated the *wittum* or endowment of property which would belong to his wife, and the *Malschatz*, the price for transfer of the *mundium* (authority).

Her *Vormund* then put the woman's right hand into the right hand of her husband, thus placing her under his authority. Then the *Vormund* himself received a gift (*Launegild*) from the groom.[33]

True Marriage: At the actual time of the marriage, the groom received from the bride's father, tutor, or family, the *mundium*, i.e., the right to protect and speak for his wife. This transaction, originally a single act, took place in two stages: *Desponsatio* (betrothal) and *traditio puellae* (the 'giving away' or 'handing over' of the bride).

II. Marriage in Romano-Merovingian Gaul

A. Law and Custom in Roman and Frankish Gaul

The Romanized population of Italy continued to live by Roman law long after the 'barbarians' had effectively ended Roman dominion. However, Roman law as recognized by Germanic rulers north of the Alps differed in some respects from that codified by Justinian; for example, the *Lex Romana Burgundianum*, promulgated by Gondaband (501–515) recognized as valid only those marriages contracted with the *nuptialis donatio*.

> Marriage is legally contracted if it is celebrated with the coming together of the parents of free men and by the morning gift according to the law. If the two parties are of equal rank, consent establishes the marriage, but only if the marriage donation is solemnly carried out. Otherwise the children born of such a union shall not be considered legitimate.[34]

The solemn carrying out of the nuptial donation was done in writing, as had been the case since the time of Constantine.

In late antiquity, *betrothals* were celebrated with great pomp among the nobility of Roman Gaul, and were accomplished with the giving of the arrhas. In addition, the man gave his fiancée an engagement ring and they exchanged the betrothal kiss. There followed an exchange of gifts such as shoes or sandals for the fiancée. Marriage among the rich was an occasion for displaying wealth; the house where the wedding took place and the bridal chamber were highly decorated. The bride wore the *flammeum* and a jeweled coronet.[35]

Frankish law, on the other hand, required the observance of tribal customs to constitute a valid marriage. Like other Germans, the Franks distinguished betrothal from the marriage itself. The right of a tribal member to choose a wife was limited by the authority of the woman's father and the need for the consent of the clan (*Geschlechts-vormundschaft* = guardianship of the generation of the tribe) but from time to time, Merovingian kings issued decrees forbidding their freemen to marry slaves/serfs or overruled a father's authority by royal command.[36] The betrothal money given by the intended to his fiancée's family consisted of a *solidus* and a *denarius* which had to be handed over publicly before witnesses. Sometime before the wedding took place, the husband-to-be drew up a written pledge of the *wittum* (endowment he would transfer to his wife). The *wedding* took place at a banquet celebrated in the house of the bride. After the banquet, the bride was handed over to her husband. This was followed by the *Brautlauf,* or *cursus nuptialis*—the procession of bride and groom to their new home. That evening, they celebrated the *Beilager,* a symbolic ceremony to mark the union of the spouses. The Germanic tribes considered this 'lying together' a juridical act which established the marital bond.[37]

The *Friedelehe,* also recognized in Frankish law, lacked either dowry or public celebration—a cause for grave concern on the part of the Church. It was not so much a question of regulating marriage ceremonies, but of teaching the meaning of marriage, preventing incest, and prohibiting the abduction of women. The church also opposed the right of the king to betrothe young women, especially those who previously had been betrothed to a third party. For the first time in the eighth century, a church synod decreed that marriages, whether of nobles or lay commoners, were to be contracted publicly. Also in an effort to end *Friedelehe,* synods forbade the marriage of young people without the consent of their parents and of serfs without the consent of their overlords.[38]

B. Liturgical Celebrations in Roman and Merovingian Gaul

Blessing of Betrothals. By the time of the Frankish invasions, the native (Roman) population of Gaul was familiar with the custom of blessing and exchanging *arrhas* at the time of betrothal. The Franks, on the other hand had an exchange of the *wadia* but apparently without a blessing.

Blessing of the Bedchamber. The *Benedictio in thalamo* was the oldest of the Gallican marriage blessings. Several witnesses, including Innocent I's Letter to Victrix of Rouen (15 Feb. 404), support the practice. The blessing of the bedchamber may predate a sixth-century bestseller, the Gallic version of the apocryphal *Acts of Thomas*. The *benedictio thalamum* recorded in the *Acts* is found soon after in manuscripts from England, France, Germany, Spain, and Scandinavia:

> . . . [The Apostle, Thomas] entered the wedding chamber with the king and placed his hand on both their heads and said, 'God of Abraham, God of Isaac, God of Jacob, bless both these young people . . . that what they learn to their advantage they might also desire to perform through Jesus Christ, the restorer of humankind, who lives and reigns with you and the Holy Spirit for ever and ever. [39]

Perhaps the popularity of blessing the couple at this point in the celebration was itself suggested by the Acts of Thomas. The long-standing custom is attested by Stephen the African and Avitus of Vienne (sixth century) who compare the blessing of the bride in the bridal chamber to the blessing received by a virgin on her dedication at the altar. It was obviously not a liturgy "for getting married" but a blessing for the inception of marriage which took place in the home of the newlyweds. The practice of blessing the wedding chamber remained common throughout the Middle Ages and lasted until the French revolution and even later in some places. [40]

The Nuptial Mass. In his attempt to follow Roman and Italian practice, Caesarius of Arles (d. 542)[41] regularly ordered that those who intended to marry should present themselves in the basilica "three days before their wedding out of reverence for the blessing" but it is unclear whether he meant a nuptial Mass by this. There are no liturgical manuscripts from before the eleventh century that combine the Roman Nuptial Mass and the Gallican *benedictio thalamum* although the presence of the Roman sacramentaries and the fact that so many of them were copied in Francia would lead one to believe that the nuptial

Mass was celebrated at least for those who wished it. Roman discipline reserved the nuptial Mass and blessing for those who entered marriage *incorrupti*. Extramarital liaisons were so numerous in sixth-century Gaul that bishops could no longer enforce excommunication of offenders. Caesarius exhorted the men in Arles to preserve their virginity as they expected their brides to preserve theirs—their failure to do so would mean forfeiting the nuptial blessing.[42]

The Gallican *Bobbio Missal* (Northern Italy, sixth century),[43] the Anglo-Saxon *Pontifical of Egbert* (England, tenth century),[44] the Anglo-Norman *Canterbury Benedictional* (Canterbury, eleventh century),[45] and a Romano-Gallican *North-Italian Sacramentary* (eleventh century)[46] each include blessings and prayers to be used on the occasion of betrothals, for the blessing of rings and/or the blessing of the bedchamber, but there is no mention of a nuptial Mass.

Even though the Gregorian sacramentary was well known in England and Normandy at least from the ninth century,[47] the first example of combining in one source the Roman Nuptial Mass with domestic wedding prayers of the Gallican tradition appears in the *Benedictional of Robert of Jumiéges* (Rouen, eleventh century).[48] The Mass prayers are precisely those found in the Gregorian sacramentary but with an additional (optional?) nuptial-blessing series in Gallican (over both bride and groom) rather than Roman style (over the bride alone). After Mass, the domestic prayers include two for blessing the ring, separated by Ps 68:28–30 and, for the first time in the manuscripts, an actual rite for giving the ring. This is followed by the singing of Ps 127, probably to accompany the procession to bridal chamber where three prayers from the Anglo-Saxon Egbert collection are prayed over the couple.[49]

The similarities found in these Italo-Gallican texts on the one hand and the Anglo-Saxon ones on the other indicate that the Gallican domestic customs continued to mark betrothals and weddings long after the Carolingian reforms of the ninth century attempted to spread the Roman rite throughout the West.

C. Other Marriage Customs

The *Nights of Tobit*, refraining from sex on the first night (or first three nights) after the wedding, is unknown outside of Christianity. The custom arose in imitation of Tobias who, according to the Vulgate, refrained from sex for three nights before 'consummating' his marriage to Sarah. Caesarius' admonition to come for the nuptial blessing three days before the wedding may have been inspired by this, though the first definite reference to the practice is provided by Jonah of Orleans (d. 843) and the Penitentiary of Pseudo-Egbert (late ninth century).[50]

The mistrust of sex and the growing reverence for the Sacred Mysteries may have contributed to another custom—*Abstaining from Church for 30 Days*. Caesarius mentions that women absent themselves from church for 30 days after the wedding and that their husbands should do the same. Canon 24 from the Council of Orleans (541) and the Canons of Theodore of Canterbury account for the penitential and purificatory texts provided for Mass on the 30th day after the wedding.

The *Joining of Right Hands* by the priest was not practiced in Merovingian Gaul except when ecclesiastics had right of guardianship, feudal lordship, or both.[51]

III. The Iberian/Visigothic Tradition

A. Marriage in the Roman Period (218 BCE–414 CE)

The people of the Iberian peninsula had been engaged in trade with the Eastern Mediterranean (Mycenians, Phoenicians, etc.) from earliest times. Roman occupation began in 218 BCE but was only completed by Caesar Augustus (19 BCE). In the subsequent 400 years of peace, Christianity, mostly in the form of small communities, was established throughout much of Hispania. Synods of Elvira (306 and later) represent the metropolization of Christian communities around Tarragona (fourth century), Seville (fifth century), and Toledo (since 531), and reflect the mixed society of Christians, pagans and Jews.

Around the year 400, Vandals moved through Hispania on their way to North Africa. Not long afterward (414–419), the Suevi and the Visigoths settled in to rule Iberia. The Visigoths had been converted to Arianism while in the Balkans, and remained so long after Arianism was forbidden in the empire by Theodosius. The Catholic Romans/Iberians and Arian Visigoths lived side by side for more than a century until all Visigoths embraced Catholicism during the reign of Reccared (586–600) who converted before his wedding in 589.[52]

Eastern influence, always strong in pre-Roman times, may explain the pre-Roman use of the *arrhas* (betrothal coins) and a priestly blessing as part of the betrothal. In 336, Constantine sent a rescript to Tiberianus, the Vicar *Hispaniae*, concerning the betrothal gifts and kiss given by a man to his fiancée.[53] Apparently, the *arrhas* included the betrothal ring in Roman and Visigothic usage. The solemnity surrounding the betrothal pointed to its binding nature and commended itself to the Church in the Christian period. The betrothal practice of the non-Christian Iberians corresponded to that of pagan Rome since they continued to live under Roman law even under the Visigoths.[54]

B. Marriage in the Visigothic period (414–711)

As mentioned above, pre-Visigothic Spanish Christians were Catholic and continued to enjoy freedom of religion under the *Lex Visigothorum*: (506). After Recarred's conversion (589), Catholicism became the religion of the kingdom and a process of religious and political unification began wherein a single system of law was formed from Canon (ecclesiastical), Roman, and Visigothic law. According to the new *Lex Romanum Visigothorum*, for example, baptism was required for full citizenship in the state.[55]

Laws and Customs. As was the case among other *Germani*, Visigothic marriages were arranged by families or clans. A young woman who did not want to be cut off from her kin had to accept the right of her father, widowed mother, or brothers to betrothe her. Young men were subject to the same rule as long as their parents were alive. Marriages contracted without the consent of parents were valid, but the woman remained under the *mundium* (authority) of her family, not of her husband. A free woman who attempted marriage or had sex with a slave was severely punished.[56]

Lawful betrothal was marked when the intended husband gave his fiancée an *arrha,* which eventually replaced the Germanic *Wadia* and *Malschatz*. Originally, this gift bound only the woman but by the seventh century the *arrha* committed both.[57] This physical gift and the verbal exchange of promises were sometimes accompanied by a written contract of engagement. The wedding celebration (banquet, *traditio puellae*, etc.) included the assignment of the *Dos* which originally replaced the bride price (*Wittum*) and later, the "morning gift" for the bride herself.[58]

C. Rites of Marriage in the Visigothic Liturgy (sixth–eleventh centuries)

The liturgy in use in Spain, especially in the area dominated by the Visigoths from 419, is properly called "Mozarabic" from 711–1492 when Spain was controlled by the Moors. At the core of this rite are native elements and a unique structure that is quite distinct from the better known Roman Liturgy. Nevertheless, the Visigothic/Mozarabic rite was highly influenced by Roman liturgical books and practices and also has much in common with the Gallican rites. Although the earliest manuscripts date only from the tenth and eleventh centuries, the vast majority of texts reached their 'fixed' form during the seventh century thanks to the efforts of three successive bishops of Toledo who were masters of orthodox euchology. The Mozarabic rite was gradually edged out by Roman liturgy until it was prohibited in 1080 by Gregory VII.[59]

The giving of a nuptial blessing and the veiling of the bride is attested in the fourth-century letter of Pope Siricius to Himerius of Tarragona,[60] but the first full description of the marriage rite is provided in the *De ecclesiasticis Officiis* of Isidore of Seville (b. 570; bishop 600–636).[61] He offers allegorical explanations of the necessity and indissolubility of the priestly blessing, the veiling of the bride, the binding of the couple with the *Vitta* (a garland braided of white and purple), the placement of the wedding ring on the fourth finger of the bride, and the signing of the *dotales tabulae*.

Sometime after Isidore, the rite developed into the more extended form which Ritzer described as "particularly rich."[62] It can be reconstructed from several documents including the *Liber Ordinum* (a pontifical/rituale),[63] *Liber Antiphonarius* (chant texts for Mass and liturgy of the hours),[64] the *Sacramentario de Vich* (a missal with some elements from the rituale),[65] and the Pontifical of Roda (bishop's book adapted for the use of presbyters).[66] Although none of the documents include all of the following elements, and some arrange the various services differently, the ordering below is based on that of the *Liber Ordinum* supplemented by the *Liber Antiphonarius* as an example of what this rich celebration may have looked like.

Structure and Content of the Visigothic/Mozarabic Marriage Liturgy

1. *Ordo ad Thalamum Benedicendum* (Service for Blessing the
   Wedding Chamber)
   —Saturday, 9:00 A.M.; house/room sprinkled with salt
   (exorcism?)
   —priest enters with versicle from Ps 89: 16–17
   —Prayer
   —Lord's Prayer
   —Blessing

2. *Ordo Nubentium: Ad Vesperum* (Cathedral Vespers on
   Saturday evening?)
   —Lucernarium
   Deacon carries in the Vesper Candle; then lights all lamps
   in the church.
   Refrain: "Offer your evening sacrifice, children of
   humans, and hope in the Lord" with verses of Ps 4
   Altar and entire church are honored with incense
   Sono = Intricate/melismatic Hymn (only on Sundays and
   Feasts)
   —Psalmody
   Antiphon w/ psalm ("Exaltate Deo" = Psalm 99:5 or 9 ff)
   Alleluiaticum w/ *cento* of scripture/psalm verses (Ps 69:33
   or 105:4 ff)
   [Hymn on ordinary days]
   —Prayers
   Completuria = collect/introduction to L.P. (only the last
   part of this prayer survives)
   Lord's Prayer
   Blessing (3-fold)

3. *Ordo Nubentium: Ad Matutinum* (Cathedral Morning Prayer
   on Sunday after sunrise?)
   —Psalmody
   Antiphon w/ Psalm (98: 2ff)
   Antiphon w/ Psalm (81: 4)
   Alleluiaticum w/ Psalm (113:20 =115:12)
   ?   [Hymn on ordinary days]
   —Reading

—Responsory [= Response, Verse, repeat second half of
    Response, Doxology(?), Response]
—Prayers
    Completuria = collect/intro to L.P.
    Lord's Prayer
    Blessing (3-fold)

4. *Ordo Arrarum* (Order of the Arrhas)
(Originally this may have been all there was to the betrothal rite,
which was celebrated separately from the wedding: in the
eleventh century it was performed immediately before the
wedding Mass.)
    —presentation of rings [sic] to priest [= earliest evidence of
        two rings]
    —Prayer
    —[Lord's Prayer? if a separate service]
    —Blessing (3-fold)
    —Exchange of rings (one ms.: *"After the blessing, they take*
their rings. Then the man gives his ring to the girl placing it on
the finger next to her right thumb; similarly, the girl places hers
on last finger of his right hand, and gives him the kiss of peace,
which is [sign of] a true covenant.")`

5. *Ordo ad Benedicendum eos qui Noviter Nubunt* (= Order for
        Blessing of Newlyweds)
    [Sunday(?)] Mass celebrated as usual but with special chants
      and readings
    —Jeremiah 29:5–7 ('Take wives, have sons and daughters . . .')
    —Psallendum / Versus = Responsory and verse (Ps 128)
    —I Cor 7:1–14 ('Let each man have his own wife and each
        woman her husband . . . ')
    —Jn 2:1–11 (Wedding feast at Cana) or Mt 19:3–6 (Wedding
        banquet)
    —Laudes = Alleluia Gospel Acclamation (chanted after, not
        before Gospel as in Roman rite)
    —Sacrificium = Chant for the Offertory (Gn 2:7 and Gn 24:1)
      [no special texts for the variable prayers of the
        Mass/eucharistic prayer Sacramentary of Vich simply
        assigns the entire Gregorian Nuptial Mass]

—Mass as usual until the Lord's Prayer/pre-communion
  dismissal
—Nuptial Blessing
—Veiling and Binding of Couple (head of bride/shoulders of
  groom)
—Call to Prayer
—Prayer: Biblical images/Blessing with series of "Amens."
—Veiling of the Bride (She was already veiled!)
—Lord's Prayer (Possibly inserted to satisfy Roman censors in
  1065)
—Blessing (3-fold?)
—*The Priest "gives" girl to the man, admonishes them about
  continence that night . . .*
—Holy Communion
—Dismissal
—Exit Chant
—Final Blessing

Not only does the Visigothic rite provide the earliest evidence for the
use of two rings, the indication that the priest "gives the girl" to the
man as a matter of course will prove to be influential for later
developments in the Western rites of marriage.

IV. The Anglo-Norman Synthesis

In 1012, a provincial synod held at Rouen promulgated the following
canonical regulation:

> Marriages should not be contracted secretly, nor after dinner. But the
> bride and groom should fast and be blessed by a priest, who should
> also be fasting, in a monastery. And before they are joined in
> wedlock, diligent inquiry is to be made concerning their family lines
> (*progenies*). If there is any consanguinity within 7 degrees they
> should be sent away, as also if either of them is divorced. Any priest
> acting contrary to this regulation is to be deposed.[67]

The context and significance of this canon in the history of marriage
rites cannot be exaggerated. For some two hundred years, the Roman

Nuptial Mass in its Gregorian form had been widely known in France and England though its use was sporadic and an optional addition to the more widespread domestic rites: the blessing of the bedchamber and perhaps a blessing of bread and wine in the course of the wedding banquet. This new regulation in effect would lead to the end of the domestic liturgy of marriage. Requiring couple and priest to be fasting and in a monastery was also a way of ensuring that the nuptial Mass would be celebrated since the fast was, from ancient times, broken by the celebration of the Eucharist now celebrated almost universally at 9:00 a.m. This regulation was also an effective way to prohibit clergy from giving blessings during the course of the customary revelries, late at night in the midst of guests who were usually overfed, drunk and less than shy about what should be done only in private.[68] Finally, the careful investigation of bloodlines would lead very soon to the requirement that the "banns" be read in public in order to establish the public character of marriage and to prevent incest. It was a short step to ritualize the essential *consensus nuptialis* to a statement of consent or a response to questions asked by the priest.[69]

In summary, eleventh-century Normandy proved to be the matrix for a synthesis of several factors:

- the Roman Nuptial Mass tradition
- the Gallican/Anglo-Saxon domestic blessings tradition;
- the long-standing theological and canonical stress on consent;
- Ecclesiastical and civil concerns for public character of marriage.

Marriage thus became a public civil/ecclesiastical liturgy rooted in the traditions of the people, of Christianity, of local law as well as the lives and histories of the couple, and was subjected to public scrutiny. Marriage gradually moved from the control of the family or clan to the jurisdiction of the church, and the priest gradually assumed the responsibility which traditionally rested with the heads of families.[70]

The new amalgamation of Roman church rites and Gallican/ Anglo-Saxon domestic rites, with strong canonical influence produced a new form of marriage *in facie ecclesiae*:

- priest meets couple at church doors to preside at and witness the consent

- turns and leads the wedding party into the church for Mass and nuptial blessing.
- blessing of bedchamber either before or after Mass
- blessing of bread and wine or of wine alone after Mass (remembrance of Cana)

A classic example of the Anglo-Norman synthesis is found in a Missal written at Bury St. Edmunds (ca. 1125–1135) and later used at Laon:[71]

   I. Before Mass at the church doors
- ring-blessing
- consent (rubric only, in Latin)
- giving
  —settlement and other gifts
  —*traditio puellae*, by relative
- exchange of rings with Trinitarian formula
  —giving of gold, silver and contract with formula: *de isto anulo te sponso...*
  —gesture of obeisance
- prayers
  —psalmic verses
  —prayer
  —Raguel blessing
- Entrance procession carrying lighted candles
  —Priest leads procession singing Ps 127

  II. Prayer over bowed heads before the altar (choice of texts)

  III. Mass[72]
- as usual until the Peace
- Nuptial Blessing
  —as in the Gregorian Sacramentary but with plural endings
  —a new blessing based on Raguel
- Kiss of Peace (given to groom who 'passes' it to his bride)
- Communion

  IV. Blessings after Mass
- Prayer over couple
(Then in the home)
- Blessing over the cup

- Blessings in the marriage chamber
- Blessing of the room
  —Incensation of the room
- Blessing of the couple sitting or lying on the bed.

The texts which are used in Bury St. Edmunds remain fairly consistent in the eleventh–twelfth centuries, but rubrics, when present at all, vary considerably. What mattered was the local consistency of custom, not uniformity from place to place.

A generation after the Battle of Hastings (i.e., beginning of twelfth century) the domestic Anglo-Saxon rite we saw in Egbert, Robert and Canterbury was replaced by the Norman rite *in facie ecclesiae* and was very soon carried by the Normans into Ireland, Scandinavia, the Rhineland, and Southern Italy, where the Normans set up the Kingdom of the Two Sicilies. It was from Southern Italy that the Norman rite would wield its influence on the ritual produced after the Council of Trent (1614).[73]

Meanwhile, a second type of ritual developed in Southern France: (1) The nuptial Mass was preceded by just two prayer formularies borrowed from the Visigothic *Arrhas* rite; (2) the Gregorian Nuptial Mass with its blessing before the *pax* included the veiling and use of the *iugale* (cord) as in the Visigothic rite; (3) after Mass there were two prayers and the joining of hands with the famous Raguel blessing; and (4) then at home: a blessing of the bedchamber based clearly on that of the *Liber Ordinum*.

The thirteenth and fourteenth centuries produced an enormous variety of marriage rites.[74] One of the most interesting appears in a ritual from the Abbey of Barbeau,[75] a Cistercian foundation in the diocese of Sens (central France). The *Officium Matrimonii* includes the entire marriage rite with full texts of prayers and rubrics from initial betrothal to blessing of bedchamber. In the following outline, the texts that are read/spoken in the vernacular are marked with an asterisk (*):

I. Betrothal
- *Pledge of marriage ". . .within forty days, if holy Church agrees."
- *Blessing and initial hand-joining

II. At the Doors of the Church
- *banns read final time
- *consent established
- *vows exchanged
- ring blessed
- *ring and coins given
- blessing of the couple

Procession into church, priest leading bride and groom by the
        hand to the altar

III. Mass
- with Gregorian blessing before the Peace.
- Groom receives Peace from priest and passes it on to all the
        people.

IV. Home
- At the door of the house
   —Bread blessing and sharing
   —Wine blessing and sharing
- Priest leads couple by the hand into the house
   —Banquet (?)
- Wedding chamber blessed in evening

Barbeau's rite provides some of the earliest evidence for the use of
the vernacular but even more important is the clear leadership of the
priest and the permission of 'Holy Church.' The role of the priest in the
joining, already seen in proleptic form in the Visigothic rite, becomes
even more pronounced as theologians and canonists continued to argue
about the essence of the sacrament and the proper minister of
marriage.[76]

V. 'Ego Vos Conjungo' and the Council of Trent

For the first time in 1455, the priestly joining formula, *"Ego vos
conjungo in matrimonium, in nomine Patris et Filii et Spiritus Sancti,"*
appeared in a ritual from Rouen bringing to a climax the evolution of
the Church's involvement in marriage in the West.[77] The formula
became very well known throughout Normandy and the rest of France

in the next 50 years and made its way to the Norman settlements in Southern Italy. In some places, the priest took the end of his stole and wrapped it around the hands of the couple as he recited "*Ego vos conjungo. . . .* " This joining formula was included in the *Liber Sacerdotalis* of Alberto Castellani (1523) and was quoted during the debate on marriage at the Council of Trent by those who favored the view that the priest is the minister of the sacrament but opposed as an innovation by those who felt the bride and groom are the true ministers and were anxious to keep their own local customs, rites and formulae. A compromise was reached: the formula was to be used as an example but it was not to be required as was the verbal consent of the couple.[78]

The Council of Trent's reform of the marriage rite was published in two books: (1) the *Missale Romanum* (1570) which included a *Missa pro Sponso et Sponsa* where the texts from the votive Mass of the Trinity were replaced by the chants, prayers and readings from the Gregorian tradition's Nuptial Mass; and (2) the *Rituale Sacramentorum Romanum* (1614) under the title *Ritus Celebrandi Matrimonii Sacramentum*.

The latter is not as much a "rite" as it is a collection of formulae for securing the consent of both parties and the public nature of marriage as taught by the Council of Trent.[79] The rubrics direct that the banns are to be published on three feast days before the wedding and expects the celebration to be held in church. Even if it takes place at home, it must be in the presence of the *parochus* (parish priest) assisted by a cleric and at least two or three witnesses. (1) The *parochus* begins by asking each "about their consent to the marriage, using the vernacular tongue and the following form: 'N. will you take N., here present, to be your lawful wife/husband, according to the rite of holy mother Church?'" There is no mutual giving or taking of pledges, *arrhas* or other remnant of the betrothal rite. (2) Assured of the consent of each, "the priest orders them to join their right hands and says: '*Ego vos conjungo in matrimonium, in nomine Patris † et Filii, et Spiritus Sancti, Amen*' or other words may be used according to the received rite of each province. Then he sprinkles them with holy water." (3) There follows the blessing and exchange of the rings with the priest reciting "*In nomine Patris † et Filii, et Spiritus Sancti, Amen*" as the groom places the wedding ring on the ring finger of the bride's left hand. (4) A series of litanic invocations follows with the Lord's Prayer, and the opening collect from the ancient nuptial Mass. The final rubrics are worth noting in full:

6. When all this is done, and if the marriage is to be blessed, the parish priest celebrates the *Missa pro Sponsa et pro Sponso* as found in the Roman Missal, observing everything prescribed therein.

7. Moreover, if besides the above, some provinces are accustomed to using other laudable customs and ceremonies in the celebration of the sacrament of matrimony, the holy Council of Trent desires that they should be retained.

8. When everything has been completed, the parish priest enters in the register of marriage, in his own hand, the names of the couple, of the witnesses and other things required; and that he, or some other priest designated either by him or by the ordinary, has celebrated the marriage.

The reforms of the Council of Trent were not intended to replace the great variety of local customs and rites but to be integrated into them in order to ensure stricter discipline. If used alone, the rite outlined in the *Rituale Romanum* constituted a great impoverishment since it was concerned with the disciplinary rather than the theological or spiritual content of marriage. Later editions of diocesan rituals were strongly influenced by the *Rituale Romanum*, especially with regard to the rubrics, inquiries, prayers, and requirement that the marriage be held in church.[80] (It was only much later that it began to replace local rituals entirely, but, some of the ancient and medieval customs survived until the twentieth century).

VI. Conclusion

Until the Council of Trent, the shape and content of the liturgy of marriage was as much a reflection of evolving laws and customs of peoples and nations as it was the product of theological reflection and canonical discipline. The differences from one province to the next, the blending of customs from different families or nations, a blessing or prayer borrowed from here or there, as well as the need to say something appropriate to the occasion led to the development of one of the most creative ritual traditions in the West. The texts of prayers and formulae are for the most part the work of anonymous and long-dead pastors whose apt invocations in the context of marriage survived to accompany, to interpret and perhaps to transform the old, inherited way of doing things. The Fathers and the moralists like Jerome may have had negative views of sexuality and marriage[81]; the assembled families may have had specific economic goals or social ambitions in mind in marrying off their children. [82] In their presence, and before this young, often barely pubescent couple, what was a pastor to say? As Mark Searle wrote in the conclusion of *Documents of the Marriage Liturgy*:

> Liturgy is always a moment of decision, when the theorizing has to end and the ideal has to yield to the practical: something has to be said and something has to be done. These documents witness to what nameless believers have found to say about marriage in the concrete, about the life and relationship that is opening up before this couple, and about the *sacramentum*. The *sacramentum* of matrimony—using the term in a broader sense than Augustine—is what holds the order of faith and the order of experience together. It is not an ideal, but a given reality. At a wedding it may be more or less clearly evoked, more or less overlaid by the social or even the erotic; but it is never moralizing. It is what it is. In the liturgy of marriage it draws the couple and the attendants—more or less wittingly, more or less willingly—into its ambit. Over against all forms of dualism, these texts bear witness to the struggle of Christians to hold the two dimensions of the Christian life together in all their wholeness. Holism is the heart of catholicism. These documents of the liturgy show, more than the writings of the theologians, and more than those who romanticize the erotic, a balanced and forward-looking vision of how the mystery of marriage can be understood and lived.[83]

As W.B. Yeats asked in the poem with which this chapter began, "How but in custom and ceremony Are innocence and beauty born?" The liturgies of marriage evolved in response to the need to mark "with custom and ceremony" one of life's most significant transitions; one with consequences that are inevitably personal, social, political, economic, ecclesial, spiritual and even cosmic.

Notes

1. See A. van Gennep, *The Rites of Passage*, Eng. trans. (Chicago: University of Chicago Press, 1960) esp. 116–145. In Christian initiation these correspond to enrollment in the catechumenate, the catechumenate itself, and the rites of initiation which include Baptism, Confirmation and Communion.

2. Ibid.

3. Tertullian bears witness as well to the *iunctio manuum* and the kiss as part of the betrothal.

4. The description of Roman marriage customs is based on J. Carcopino, *Daily Life in Ancient Rome* (New Haven: Yale University Press, 1945), 77–100; Suzanne Dixon, *The Roman Family* (Baltimore: Johns Hopkins, 1992), chapter 3, 61–84 and most importantly, Susan Treggiari, *Roman Marriage: Iusti Conjuges from the Time of Cicero to the Time of Ulpian* (Oxford, 1991), 16–28.

5. The *tabulae nuptiales* are mentioned by Tertullian (d. 220) and were apparently common by the time of Augustine (d. 430). See Tertullian, *Adversus Marc.* I.29 (CSEL 47, 331, 1. 4–6) and the *Vita S. Augustini*, c. 24 by Possidius, ed. M. Pellegrino, *Vita di Agostino Introduzione, testo critico, versione e note*, Edizioni Paoline, 124, line 3 s.

6. In ancient Rome, a wheat cake was not part of this ceremony but was the last thing shared between the bride and groom before being led into the wedding chamber.

7. Ritzer, Korbinian, *Le marriage dans les églises chrétiennes du Ier au Xie siècle* (Paris: Cerf, 1970), 81–94 = French translation of *Formen, Riten und religiöses Brauchtum der Eheschliessung in den christlichen Kirchen des ersten Jahrtausends*, Liturgiewissenschaftliche Quellen und Forschungen 38 (Münster: Aschendorff, 1962, repr 1982), 81–104.

8. *Epistle to Diognetus* 5:6–8 (c. 130); see Ritzer, 91 and note 164.

9. Stevenson, 13–20, notes on p. 216. There are some indications that the bishop may have had a more active role in arranging the marriages of Christians, e.g., Ignatius of Antioch (c. 110), *Letter to Polycarp* 5:2: "It is proper for men and women who wish to marry to do so with the consent of the bishop so that their marriage is in accord with God's will and not the prompting of lust. Let everything be done to the greater glory of God." See the discussion in Ritzer, 97–104, and in Stevenson, *Nuptial Blessing* (London: SPCK, 1982), 13–32. Ritzer, 97–104, discusses the more extensive role of bishops and presbyters in arranging marriages for orphans entrusted to the church or as marriage brokers. But this active role of pastors in arranging marriages did not last. Its practice in the West is only attested by those who wanted to put an end to it. Jerome thought it unworthy of presbyters to arrange marriages. Ambrose

and Augustine thought it imprudent "since spouses, when they have conflicts, often curse those who brought them together."

10. In his Montanist period, Tertullian insisted that the ideal marriage was "arranged by the church, strengthened by the Sacrifice [= Mass], sealed by the blessing at which the angels are present and to which the Father gives his consent." *Ad Uxorem* 28.6–9; quoted in full in Stevenson, *Nuptial Blessing*, 17.

11. *Vita S. Augustini* by Possidius, Chs. 24 and 27; Ritzer, 114–115, notes 254–256.

12. Even Tertullian allows for this as long as the Christians do not take part in the sacrifices.

13. After the Peace of Constantine, bishops or presbyters would inevitably be invited to weddings as we know from several fourth-century synods which tried to regulate the presence of clergy at such celebrations. Basically, the clergy were directed to bless the couple the day before the wedding but by no means were they to stay for the party!

14. Dennis of Alexandria was rescued during the Decian persecution by wedding guests who were attending an all-night celebration; reported by Eusebius, *Ecclesiastical History*, VI, 40, 6; see Ritzer, 95, n. 178. The *Dextrarum iunctio* is depicted on Christian wedding cups from fourth and fifth centuries and by a fragment of a sarcophagus from Villa Albani in Rome. We have already mentioned the evidence from Tertullian (note 5, above) that North African Christians signed *tabulae nuptiales* in the third century.

15. *Philosophumena* IX 12, 24;references in Ritzer, 93, n. 170.

16. Ritzer, 105–123; Stevenson, 3–32.

17. On the spread of the Roman liturgy see among others, John Brooks-Leonard, "Traditions, Liturgical, in the West, Pre-Reformation" in P.E. Fink, ed. *New Dictionary of Sacramental Worship* (Collegeville: Liturgical Press, 1990), 1282–1293.

18. These texts are provided in English translation in Mark Searle and Kenneth Stevenson, *Documents of the Marriage Liturgy* (Collegeville: Liturgical Press, 1992), 40–54 (hereafter = Searle/Stevenson). See Cyrille Vogel, *Medieval Liturgy: Introduction to the Sources*, trans. and revised by W.G. Storey and N.K. Rasmussen (Washington: Pastoral Press, 1986), 38–134 for an introduction to the content and use of these liturgical books.

19. This collection of *libelli missarum* is often referred to as the Leonine Sacramentary but it is neither Leonine nor a sacramentary; see the introduction in the Vogel *Introduction* mentioned in the preceding note. The marriage prayers are in L.C. Mohlberg, L. Eizenhöfer, P. Siffrin, eds. *Sacramentarium Veronense*, Rerum Ecclesiasticarum documenta; series maior: Fontes 1 (Rome: Herder, 1965), 139–141; reproduced in Ritzer, 240 and 421–424; discussed in Stevenson, 35–37; and translated in Searle/Stevenson 40–44.

20. That is, the *pronuba* had brought the bread and wine which was set aside at the Offering to be used for the Mass; it was the custom for centuries that everyone brought bread and wine and other food for the poor that was collected by the deacons at the beginning of the Liturgy of the Faithful, from these offerings, some was set aside and presented on the altar for the Eucharist. The *Canon Missae* was the central and for the most part invariable prayer of the Mass; in addition to the Preface, two of the sections within the prayer itself (those which began with the words *Communicantes* and *Hanc igitur,* respectively) also varied according to season, feast, or occasion.

21. The veiling of bride and groom is mentioned in the *Wedding Ode* (Carmen XXV) written by Paulinus of Nola (353–431) for the marriage of a church lector, Julian, son of Bishop Memor of Capua, to Titia, possibly the daughter of another bishop named Aemelius; text and commentary in Searle/Stevenson. The veiling of bride and groom was known as well in the Visigothic/Mozarabic marriage rite.

22. Siricius (384–399), answering a letter which Himerius of Tarragona had written to Pope Damasus (d. 384), informed Himerius that the bride is to be veiled and this veiling is to be joined closely to the priest's blessing; and the blessing was not to be given in religiously mixed marriages, *Epistola ad Himerium* I, 4 (*PL* 84, 632); see Ritzer, 230–231.

23. Ambrosiaster, *Commentarium in Ep* I ad Corinthos 7, 40 (*PL* 17, 238A) *Comment. Ep I ad Tim 3,* 12, and 5, 3 (*PL* 17, 497A and 502D) and *Liber Questionum novi et veteris Testamenti* (CSEL 50, 400, lines 11–14).

24. *Hadrianum* (Cambrai, Bibliothèque municipale, *codex* 164 (*olim* 159); Cambrai, copied directly from the original in 811–812). The *Hadrianum* is a Gregorian type of sacramentary which means that it was compiled originally for the papal stational liturgy of Rome. A copy was sent from Hadrian I to Charlemagne between 784–791 to become the *urtext* for Charlemagne's liturgical reforms in his kingdom (cf. Vogel, 79–82). Critical edition is J. Deshusses, ed. *Le Sacramentaire grégorien: ses principales formes d'après les plus anciens manuscrits.* Spicilegium Friburgense 16 (Fribourg: Éditions universitaires, 1992, 3rd edition), 308–311; translation of Gregorian texts provided in Searle/Stevenson, 45–49.

25. Searle/Stevenson, 45.

26. Ibid., 45–46.

27. Christian writers elaborated on the ring as symbol of fidelity, e.g., an antiphon for the feast of St. Agnes: *Annulo suo subarrhavit me Dominus meus Jesus Christus, et tamquam sponsam decoravit me corona* is used at the consecration of virgins in the tenth-century Romano-Germanic Pontifical. Consecrated virginity as betrothal to Christ is mentioned already in the sixth-century *Passio S. Agnetis* and in a sermon of the fourth century attributed to

Ambrose or to Maximus of Turin "since by her blood she was betrothed to Christ." See R. Metz, *La consécration des vierges dans l'église romaine. Étude d'histoire et de la liturgie* (Paris, 1954), 65, note 105 and R. D'Izarny, "Mariage et consécration virginale au IVe siècle," *Supplément de la vie spirituelle* 24 (1953), 92–118.

28. Ritzer, 218 with note 6.

29. That Nicholas I (d. 867) in his *Letter to the Bulgarians* had written, "*consensus* alone suffices," was a very influential ruling that made its way into Gratian's decretals (1148) and later canon law; quoted with sources in Ritzer, 219 and discussed in Stevenson, 1982, 44–45.

30. *De Viduis*, 9, 59; "Suasimus, fateor, ut vestem mutares, non ut flammeum sumeres" (*PL* 16, 625B); Ritzer, 219.

31. Letter of Gelasius I to Hostilius, ed. P. Ewald, *Neus Archiv für ältere deutsche Geschichtskunde*, 5, 562; Ritzer, 219.

32. *Monumenta Germaniae Historica,* Legum sectio, Leges nationum germanicarum, 5 vols. (Hanover: Hahn [imprint varies] 1835–1962), is the usual source for the Germanic codes, though German translations of many have appeared in the series, *Germanenrechte Texte und Übersetzungen* (Weimar, Göttingen: Akademie für deutsches Rechte, 1934), and good English translations are readily available for a few: *The Burgundian Code,* trans. K.F. Drew (Philadelphia: U Penn Press, 1949, reprint 1972); *The Lombard Laws*, trans. K.F. Drew (Philadelphia: U Penn Press, 1973); *The Laws of the Alamans and Bavarians*, trans. T.J. Rivers (Philadelphia: U Penn Press, 1977). See also James A. Brundage, *Law, Sex, and Christian Society in Medieval Europe* (Chicago: U Chicago Press, 1987), 126 n. 3 for a more complete list.

33. Ritzer, 220–222; Brundage, 124–128.

34. MGH Leg. Sect. 1.17–156, 1.2; Ritzer, 267–272.

35. Ritzer, 268–270.

36. Ibid., 270 and note 185.

37. Ibid., 271, notes that later, the French still had the expression: "Au coucher la femme gagne son douaire."

38. Synod of Verneuil (755): "ut omnes homines laici publicas nuptias faciant tam nobiles quam ignobiles;" cf. Orleans (541) canon 24, et al. subseq. Ritzer, 272.

39. ". . . Ingressus thalamum cum rege posuit manum suam supra capita amborum et dixit: 'Deus Abraham, Deus Isaac, Deus Jacob, benedic adulescentes istos . . . pro utilitate didicerint hoc facere cupiant per Iesum Christum, recupertorem . . . saecula saeculorum.'" Quoted in Ritzer, 274, note 200.

40. Ritzer, 274–276.

41. Caesarius had visited Pope Symmachus in 510 to consult him on various matters; he was given the pallium (the first non-Italian to receive it) and named papal vicar for Gaul and Spain.

42. Ritzer, 276–278.

43. Paris, BN lat. 13246; eighth-century copy of sixth-century text, is a mixture of Gallican, Visigothic, Ambrosian, and Roman elements; see E.A. Lowe and J. Wickham Legg, eds. *The Bobbio Missal: A Gallican Mass Book*, Henry Bradshaw Society 53 (London, 1917) and the marriage prayers in Searle/Stevenson, 100–102; discussed in Ritzer, 277 and 299 and in Stevenson, 56–57. There is no indication of how the marriage actually took place or whether there was a nuptial Mass.

44. H.M.J. Banting, ed. *Two Anglo-Saxon Pontificals*, HBS 104 (London, 1989); Ritzer, 312–318; Stevenson, 63–64 and Stevenson *To Join*, 36–37.

45. Searle/Stevenson, 113–114. Canterbury contains only the blessings given by a bishop; see the discussion in Stevenson, 64–65.

46. Ritzer, 430–431; Searle/Stevenson, 115–116; discussed in Stevenson, *To Join*, 37–38.

47. Alcuin may have had a copy older than the *Hadrianum* sent to Charlemagne's court from his home in York, which would mean the Gregorian tradition had made its way to England as early as the eighth century; see the discussion in Deshusses, *Le sacramentaire grégorien* and in Vogel, *Introduction*.

48. H.A. Wilson, *The Benedictional of Archbishop Robert*, HBS 24 (London, 1903), 149–151; Searle/Stevenson, 107–112. Jumiéges was Archbishop of Canterbury from 1051–1052. The benedictional probably was compiled for Robert of Rouen, edited in England, used in Normandy, preserved at Rouen.

49. Stevenson, 66–67; Ritzer, 311ff.

50. See H.G.J. Beck, *The Pastoral Care of Souls in South East France During the Sixth Century* (Rome: Herder, 1950), 232–233.

51. Ritzer, 281–288.

52. Ibid., 289–290.

53. This rescript is the first evidence of the influence of Eastern betrothal practices on Roman law.

54. Ritzer, 290–292.

55. Ibid., 292–293.

56. Ibid., 293–294.

57. For a long time, the Roman *Annulus pronubus* or engagement ring was not distinguished from the *arrha;* the *Lex Visigothorum* II, 1 (681) expressly mentions the rings as *arrhae.*

58. Ritzer, 294–297.

59. The Mozarabic liturgy continued to be celebrated in one small chapel in the cathedral at Toledo until modern times. See "Traditions, Liturgical, in the West, Pre-Reformation" in *New Dictionary of Sacramental Worship*, 1286–1288.

60. Epistola 1, 4; quoted in Stevenson, 26.

61. *De Ecclesiasticis Officiis* II: 20, 5–8 (*PL* 83, 810c–812b); Ritzer, 432–433; Searle/Stevenson, 117–119.

62. Ritzer, 299: "Le rite Mozarabe présente un développement particulièrement riche de la liturgie nuptiale."

63. 3 mss, Silos/Cogolla; eleventh century. M. Férotin, *Le Liber Ordinum en usage dans l'Église wisigothique et mozarabe d'Espagne du cinquiéme au onziéme siècle*. Monumenta eccles. Liturgiae 6 (Paris, 1904), 433–443; Ritzer, 298–305; Stevenson, 48–53; Stevenson, *To Join*, 45–49; Searle/Stevenson, 120–134.

64. León, tenth century. J. Vives, A. Fabrega, L. Brou, eds. *Antifonario visigotico mozarabe de la Catedral de Léon*. Monumenta Hispaniae sacra, 5/1. Madrid-Barcelona 1959, 454–455.; Ritzer, 298–300; Searle/Stevenson, 135–138.

65. Vich, eleventh century. A. Olivar, ed. *El sacramentario de Vich*. Monumenta Hispaniae sacra. Series Liturgica, IV (Barcelona, 1953), 208–210; Ritzer, 257–259; Stevenson, 54–56; *To Join* 45–46; Searle/Stevenson, 139–147. Vich is a Romano-Mozarabic hybrid that includes many elements from the Gregorian tradition, including the Nuptial Mass.

66. Catalonia, tenth–eleventh century. See Jordi Pinell y Pons, "La liturgia nupcial en el antiguo rito hispanico," in G. Farnedi, ed. *La Celebrazione cristiana del matrimonio* = Studia Anselmiana 93; Analecta 11 (Rome: Pontificio Ateneo S. Anselmo, 1986), 87–106.

67. Provincial Synod of Rouen (1012), canon 13; Bessin, ed. *Concilia Rothomagensis provinciae* I (Rouen, 1717), 56; cited in R. Besnier, *Normania* 7 (1934), 79, note 3 = canon 14 in Mansi XX 34; Ritzer, 390–391.

68. Ritzer, 391.

69. The earliest interrogation by a priest appears first in the early twelfth century Magdalen Pontifical; ed. H.A. Wilson, *The Pontifical of Magdalen College* (London, 1910), 221–225.

70. Ritzer, 395–397.

71. Laón, Municipal Library, ms 238, 165v–167v; ca. 1125–1135; See J-B Molin, P. Mutembe, *Le rituel du mariage en France du XIIe au XVIe siècle* (Paris, 1974), 289–291; Searle/Stevenson, 148–151.

72. The rubric indicates that on Sundays the chants and prayers from the Votive Mass of the Holy Trinity are to be used, and on weekdays those from the Mass, *Invocabit me* (= Mass from the first Sunday of Lent!); the priestly

prayers from the nuptial Mass would be said in addition at the appropriate places.

73. *Rituale Sacramentorum Romanum,* 17 June 1614. See the discussion below.

74. See the discussion of French, British, Scandinavian, German, and Italian rites in Stevenson, 71–94.

75. Melun, Municipal Library, ms. 13, 54v–68v, late fourteenth century; Molin/Mutembe, 305–308; Searle/Stevenson, 156–162.

76. Theodore Mackin, *What Is Marriage?* (New York: Paulist, 1982), 248–293. On the whole question of the role of the liturgy in theological and canonical discussions, see Cyrille Vogel, "Les Rites de la célébration du mariage: leur signification dans la formation du lien durant le haut moyen âge," in *Il Matrimor `o nella societá alto medievale. Settimane di studio del centro italiano di studi sull'alto medioevo* 24, 22–28 Aprile 1976 (Spoleto: Presso la Sede del Centro, 1977), 397–472.

77. See the discussion in Joanne Pierce, "A Note on the 'Ego Vos Conjungo' in Medieval French Marriage Liturgy," *Ephemerides Liturgicae* 99 (1985), 290–299.

78. See the Documents of the Council of Trent, *Decree on the Reformation of Marriage* (Promulgated 13 October 1563).

79. Much of the debate at the Council of Trent can only be understood in light of the reformulations and positions taken by the leaders of the Reformation. For the marriage rites proposed by Luther, Calvin, the Book of Common Prayer and the later Protestant denominations, see the overview in Stevenson, 125–168.

80. A case study of this post-Tridentine development is presented by John Brooks-Leonard, "Another Look at Neo-Gallican Reform: A Comparison of Marriage Rites in Coutances," *Ephemerides Liturgicae* 98 (1984), 458–485.

81. On the early Christian attitudes towards marriage and sexuality, see Mackin, *What Is Marriage?*, 80–111. See also Vogel, *Introduction,* 38–134, for a fine introduction to these liturgical books and their contents.

82. See Brundage, *Law, Sex, and Christian Society,* as mentioned above in note 32.

83. Searle/Stevenson, *Documents,* pp. 262–263.

ISSUES IN LITURGY

THE SONG OF THE ASSEMBLY
IN MEDIEVAL EUCHARIST

Edward Foley

INTRODUCTION

The history of medieval worship music in the Christian West is often presented as a history of music for the specialist. Whether the topic is Gregorian chant, organum, rhythmic modes, or some other aspect of this wide-ranging musical era, the ordinary focus of most inquiries into music of the medieval Church is music produced or performed by the music professional. Such an approach can give the impression that from the end of the late patristic period until the sixteenth-century Reformation, the laity had no significant role in the church's worship.

Such a perspective is problematic from two viewpoints. First of all, it overlooks the significant role that the song of the laity has enjoyed in the worship of the Church. This oversight is often the result of a second problem, that is, the narrow definition given to worship or liturgy in medieval Christianity. While it is true that twentieth-century Roman Catholicism provides clear distinctions between the official liturgy and popular devotions,[1] such distinctions did not exist either in the official legislation or the religious imagination of the medieval period. While it is true that the role of the faithful was significantly diminished in the Mass and Office as the medieval period progressed, it appears that in many situations the people were never completely silenced even in these central liturgical acts. Furthermore, the explosion of new forms of worship throughout the medieval period insured that the song of the people would find a voice in what they at least considered to be significant and important ecclesial worship.

There is no single contemporary resource which adequately maps the breadth of congregational singing in Christianity through the Middle Ages in the West. In an attempt to fill part of that lacuna, this article will consider the musical role of the assembly in the Eucharist. While this was certainly not the only type of worship event which occurred in Western medieval Christianity, it appears that it was yet the central genre of liturgy for that place and era. The survey nature of this presentation will not allow for an in-depth study of the various aspects of congregational song noted here, nor will it allow for much musicological consideration of the various musical forms presumed by such congregational performance. As a general principle, this study will be "text-driven," i.e., tracing the role of the people in worship according to the texts in which they musically engaged. Given this organizing principle, we will consider the sung role of the laity in the Eucharist according to a three-fold division of Mass texts: 1) the texts of the ordinary, 2) the texts of the proper, and 3) other texts.

While there are innumerable ways to define the "medieval period," a liturgical perspective suggests a time frame commencing with the death of Gregory the Great (d. 604), who could be considered the last great patristic author, and ending with Luther's "publication" of the 95 theses in Wittenberg in 1517, a convenient date for the onset of the Reformation.

THE ORDINARY

General Responses

While not frequently considered in the context of the "ordinary of the Mass," various dialogues such as that before the Preface, the versicle-response *"Dominus vobiscum—Et cum spiritu tuo"* and the closing "Amen" to various orations constitute an indexical part of the Mass and are very much an "ordinary" and unchanging component of its celebration. Some of our earliest witnesses to worship in the West note that these responses were the prerogative of the laity.[2] That they continued as such in the patristic West is clear from the testimony of writers such as Jerome (d. 420) and Augustine (d. 430),[3] as well as numerous local synods.[4] As will be noted frequently, the Carolingian reform witnessed a kind of "rebirth of the popularity of congregational singing in sacred worship."[5] This seems to have included numerous general responses such as "Amen," *"Et cum spiritu tuo,"* and the responses to the preface dialogue. Sources indicate that the assembly shared in these general responses, especially North of the Alps, well into the late Middle Ages.[6] While it is not always clear to what extent these were strictly "musical" elements of medieval worship, to the extent that they were proclaimed if not sung in public worship, they can be considered at least lyrical if not properly musical elements.

Kyrie eleison

While predating Christianity, the *Kyrie* first appears as an acclamation in Christian worship at the end of the fourth century of the common era.[7] Its origin as an acclamation in Roman imperial cult,[8] as well as its employment in litanic form in Christian worship,[9] underscores its role as a response of the people. This was also true at the time of Gregory the Great.[10] By the time of *Ordo Romanus* I (c. 700), it appears that the choir alone is singing the *Kyrie*.[11] It is probable, however, that as Jungmann notes, "in simpler surroundings and under . . . conditions [other than a pontifical Mass], the *Kyrie* still remained the people's song."[12] Thus the decree of Herard, Bishop of Tours, in 888, who ordered that *"Gloria Patri ac Sanctis, atque credulatis, et Kyrie eleison reverenter canatur."*[13] The trend announced in OR 1, however, eventually eliminated the laity from joining in the Kyrie: a development apparent in the musical elaborations (both monophonic and polyphonic) of this text.[14]

Gloria in excelsis

Written in imitation of the psalms of David, an early form of this *psalmus idioticus* appeared in the *Apostolic Constitutions*.[15] It was eventually to become a standard element in Eastern matins.[16] The *Gloria* was introduced into the Roman Mass at Christmas by the beginning of the sixth century and, by extension, was employed on Sundays and feasts of martyrs, but only when the bishop presided.[17] Originally priest presiders were allowed to employ it only during Easter night and on the day of his ordination.[18] Beginning in the eighth century, however, it began to be employed in the Frankish kingdoms on Sundays and feasts regardless of who presided.[19]

Most authors believe that the *Gloria* was originally a congregational chant, although this conclusion is more by inference than direct evidence. Some draw this conclusion from the nature of the oldest surviving melodies which are easily singable by a congregation.[20] Jungmann concludes that the *Gloria* was a congregational song because in OR 1.9 the bishop is described as turning toward the people to intone the *Gloria*, "just as he does at the *Dominus vobiscum* or *Pax vobis*, [which] is an indication that originally the entire congregation was called upon to sing this hymn."[21] There is also evidence that the *Gloria* was popular even outside of Mass in the Carolingian period: accordingly, when Charlemagne invited Leo III to Paderborn in 799, the people sang the *Gloria*.[22] Amalarius of Metz (d. 850/1), notorious for his liturgical allegorizations, does provide an enticing commentary on the *Gloria*: noting that just as on the first Christmas, first a single angel and then the entire heavenly choir appeared, so in the same way does one bishop begin and then the entire church echoes praise to God.[23] Finally, there is limited and late evidence that, outside of the pontifical Mass, the people did sing the *Gloria*.[24] Given the various restrictions concerning when the *Gloria* might be sung,[25] its ordinary setting within pontifical celebrations where a schola[26] and other assembled clerics dominated the music, and the length of the text, it is understandable that the *Gloria* was one of the less employed congregational chants in the medieval west.

Credo

What came to be known as the *Credo* in the West, emerged as a complete text in the acts of the Council of Chalcedon (451).[27] It first appeared in the eucharistic liturgy in the West in sixth-century Spain, where it was employed before the *Pater noster* as a preparation for communion.[28] The *Stowe Missal*—written between 792 and 812, but whose archetype dates back to the early seventh century[29]—testifies to the fact that the *Credo* was employed in Ireland soon after its appearance in Spain. Charlemagne (d. 814) seems to have introduced the creed into the Eucharist at his palace chapel at Aachen in the last decade of the eighth century, where it was sung after the gospel.[30] Rome did not introduce the *Credo* into its eucharistic liturgy until 1014.[31]

Because of the *Credo*'s evolving role as a litmus test for the orthodoxy of all believers in the West, there is little doubt that—at least when first introduced into the Mass—it belonged to the entire congregation. As previously noted, Bishop Herard of Tours calls for the singing of the creed along with the *Gloria Patri, Sanctus* and *Kyrie* by all.[32] Similarly, Walter of Orleans in 871 decrees "*Ut Gloria Patri et Filio et Spiritui Sancto et Credo in unum Deum apud omnes in missa decantetur.*"[33] Amalarius clearly assigns the *Credo* to the people.[34] Few writers after the ninth century, however, report the *Credo* as a congregational event.

While there is little doubt that the creed once belonged to the eucharistic assembly in the West, there remains the question whether that assembly sang or recited the text. Jungmann holds that, contrary to the practice usual in the Orient, the *Credo* was sung in the West.[35] Thus, to the extent that the text belonged to the community, he contends that it was sung by the community. Few others hold this position.[36] Maybe it is more effective to consider the congregational proclamation of the creed in the same genre as the general responses, considered above, i.e., to the extent that they were proclaimed if not cantillated in public worship, could the *Credo* be considered at least a lyrical if not properly musical element of the medieval Mass?

Sanctus-Benedictus

This ancient element of the eucharistic liturgy is also one which endured longer than any part of the ordinary as a congregational song. Reliant upon Jewish precedents,[37] a primitive form of the *Sanctus* is already quoted in Clement's *Epistle to the Corinthians*[38] (c. 96 CE), although it is by no means clear that there was any fixed liturgical use of this text by Christians in the first or second century of the common era.[39] By the third century there is a relatively clear reference to the use of the *Sanctus* in the Eucharist by Origen (d. c. 254),[40] and the fourth century provides many more attestations from the East, including the eucharistic prayer of Serapion (d. c. 360)[41] and the eighth book of the

Apostolic Constitutions (c. 375).[42] Despite the assertion of the *Liber pontificalis* that it was "Pope" Sixtus (d. c. 127) who added the *Sanctus* to the Roman liturgy,[43] the first evidence of the *Sanctus* as part of the Mass in the West comes from around the year 400 from the north of Italy.[44] Further evidence from Africa in the late fifth century and Gaul from the early sixth century,[45] testifies to the widespread employment of the *Sanctus* in the West by the dawn of the Middle Ages.

That the *Sanctus* was sung by all the people is attested, first in the East,[46] and by virtually every early source in the West.[47] Even the previously cited entry in the *Liber pontificalis*—while asserting that the *Sanctus* was introduced into the Roman liturgy in the second century, more properly serves as a reliable witness to early sixth-century Roman practice[48]—notes that "*ut intra actionem, sacerdos incipiens, populo hymnum decantare: Sanctus.*"[49] OR I, in discussing the *Sanctus*, does not explicitly relegate the singing of this acclamation to the schola, as do other texts about music in that ordo,[50] which leads Jungmann to suggest that even in the pontifical Mass at Rome, the people yet joined in this hymn:[51] a plausible interpretation, given the previous evidence from the *Liber pontificalis*. In the Frankish kingdoms the *Sanctus* clearly belonged to the people, even before the Carolingian reform. Thus Caesarius of Arles (d. 542) complains about those who leave church before the singing of the *Sanctus*,[52] and one manuscript (St. Gall 349) from OR XV, while describing pontifical worship [!], notes: ". . . *inclinant iterum subdiaconi, proclamantibus omnibus clericis vel populo cum tremore et reverentia: Sanctus.*"[53] It is notable that, as Jungmann points out, during the Carolingian reform it was not necessary to insist that the people sing the *Sanctus*, but rather that the priest join in singing the whole of the hymn before continuing with the canon.[54] Literary evidence demonstrates that the *Sanctus* continued to be the song of the people in some places well into the twelfth century.[55] Musicological support for this late ownership of the *Sanctus* by the congregation could be found in the fact that, while polyphonic settings of the ordinary develop in the thirteenth century, the *Sanctus* is seldom set polyphonically, and tenaciously holds on to its chant settings. Ultimately, it was not the onset of polyphony which eliminated the *Sanctus* as the song of the people. Rather, it was the growing tendency, already apparent in the late eighth century, to recite the canon silently.[56] This move effectively separated the assembly from the priest, who no longer had to wait to sing the *Sanctus* with the people but who could continue with the canon while attending clerics or a schola sang the angelic hymn.

Agnus Dei

What might be considered one of the more functional elements of the rite, the *Agnus Dei* is a unique textual element in the ordinary of the Roman liturgy. From the beginning, the breaking of the bread had been an essential element in the emerging Christian Eucharist.[57] As the size of the community grew, this took an increasingly longer period of time, and thus it became appropriate to accompany this action with music. In the Byzantine liturgy this was the *Koinonikon,* and in the Milanese liturgy it was the *Confractorium,* but the Roman liturgy was silent during this ritual action.[58] There is general consensus that the *Agnus Dei* was introduced into the Roman liturgy by the Syrian pontiff, Sergius 1 (d. 701).[59] Drawn from New Testament imagery,[60] this introduction of "lamb" imagery is sometimes explained as an allusion to the sanctified bread which, in the oriental liturgy with which Sergius was acquainted, was designated as the "lamb."[61] It is also possible that the use of "lamb" language was an explicit reaction to the Trullan Synod of 692, which forbade employing lamb symbolism for Christ.[62] It should be noted, however, that the *Gloria in excelsis*, introduced into pontifical liturgy at Rome by the sixth century, not only contained the title *Agnus Dei* but also a "mini-litany" built around the phrase "*qui tollis peccata mundi*."[63] The same combination of phrases also occurs in a litany for the Holy Saturday vigil in the old Gelasian sacramentary[64] which, while copied in the middle of the eighth century, was reliant upon a text which could go back to the first quarter of the seventh century.[65]

Such litanic precedents underscore that, from its introduction into the Roman liturgy, the *Agnus Dei* presumed the engagement of the assembly, at least on the "*miserere nobis.*" The *Liber pontificalis* is clear about this role of the assembly.[66] OR I does not mention the assembly but only the schola.[67] This does not necessarily exclude the assembly from this litany but could simply underscore the leadership of the schola here. The participation of the assembly in the *Agnus Dei*,

even in Roman pontifical Eucharist, is further bolstered by the awareness that such a litany needed to be extended until the fraction was
completed,[68] often being troped.[69] It is unlikely that the people would
not engage in this constantly repeated phrase as the bread was broken
and the wine poured.

With the introduction and ultimately the requirement for
unleavened bread in the West[70] and the move from domestic bread to
hosts as well as the withdrawal of the cup from the people,[71] the length
of the fraction rite was severely contracted. In some places by the ninth
century, and more generally by the tenth century, the *Agnus Dei* no
longer served its original purpose and began to migrate as a song
accompanying the *pax* or communion.[72] In a parallel development, this
expandable litany was eventually curtailed to only three verses—in
some places, already by the ninth century.[73] By the twelfth century this
metamorphoses was complete: not only with the reduction to three
repetitions but also with the transformation of the last refrain to "*dona
nobis pacem*" or, in the case of a Mass for the dead, "*dona eis
requiem*."[74] As the text was diminished, so was the assembly's role in
this chant, which was eventually taken over by the choir or recited by
the presider.[75]

THE PROPER

Introit

The ancient eucharistic liturgy in the West did not have any
introductory chant. Even at the time of Augustine, the liturgy in Hippo
began with a greeting, silence, and the readings.[76] While the *Liber
pontificalis* is often interpreted as demonstrating that Celestine I
(d. 432) introduced psalmody into the entrance rite of the Roman
liturgy,[77] more recent studies have demonstrated that Celestine
probably introduced responsorial psalmody at the readings rather than
any introit psalmody.[78] The oldest reliable witness for an entrance song
in the Roman liturgy is the old Gelasian sacramentary,[79] which could
reflect worship practice at the end of the first quarter of the seventh
century in Rome.[80] OR I provides a fuller description, noting that the

chanting accompanied the pontiff through a relatively complex series of maneuvers which take him from the *secretarium* to the altar.[81]

There is no evidence that the antiphon is repeated between verses of the psalm during the entrance procession,[82] which would have been the logical entry for the assembly into this song. Thus it is difficult to imagine the assembly sharing in any part of this song, unless they joined in the *Gloria*. When the entrance psalm migrated into the Carolingian empire, the antiphon apparently was repeated after each verse of the psalm.[83] This feature, along with the imperial injunction that the people should sing the "*Gloria Patri*,"[84] suggests that the Frankish assemblies had a more consistent role in this entrance song. Such was not to last very long, however. The abbreviation of the introit into a single psalm verse, between a repeated antiphon and the *Gloria Patri* was already occurring in the ninth century.[85] This, combined with the increasing complexification of the chant and growing dominance of musical specialists, meant that the engagement of the assembly in the entrance song was only a short-lived phenomenon of the Carolingian reform.

Gradual/Tract

The introduction of a musical response to the readings in Christian worship was a development of the patristic period.[86] Tertullian could be the earliest witness to this practice,[87] and one of the earliest witnesses to the use of Davidic psalmody in Christian worship.[88] The practice of singing psalms after the reading is established in the East by the fourth century,[89] and in the West by at least the fifth if not the fourth century.[90] As previously noted, it appears that this practice was introduced into the Roman liturgy by Celestine I before 432.[91]

The engagement of the congregation in this responsorial form is presumed from the moment of its appearance in the liturgy. While some do not believe responsorial forms were employed in the psalms anywhere before the third century,[92] such a conclusion seems to draw too sharp a distinction between responsorial forms that employed only a single word (e.g., "Alleluia") and those that employed phrases, half verses or full verses as the response. Furthermore, as Cattin suggests "the global scale of subsequent developments is such that the argument [against the existence of the responsorial psalm before the third century] *ex silentio* seems very weak, the more so because the Biblical precedents for psalms with a refrain are particularly notable . . . even if their plan is not exactly that of the Christian responsorial psalm."[93]

After Ambrose, Augustine, and Celestine I, evidence that the people responded to the psalm after the first reading is yet found in the writings of Leo the Great (d. 461).[94] Beyond the middle of the fifth century, however, there is exceedingly sparse testimony about the role of the assembly in this chanting. The evidence of OR I—which, as in so many other situations, gives no evidence of the people's participation in this chant[95]—does not appear to be offset by testimony about the sung response of the people in non-Roman or non-pontifical worship. Carolingian sources, for example, provide virtually no documentation which would suggest the people's engagement in the response to the readings. Jungmann suggests—and many others concur—that the "enemy of the ancient responsorial technique" in the West was musical art; with the musical elaboration of the *responsum*, the role of the assembly was eclipsed by trained singers.[96]

A final caution about the role of the congregation in the chants between the reading is provided by Terrence Bailey, who notes that all early references to chants between the readings might not be references to the responsorial form of the gradual. Rather, they could refer to solo chants without refrains, in which there was no responsorial engagement of the assembly. Rather, these could have been psalms "sung by the soloist on behalf of all those present." Eventually a refrain could have been incorporated into these *psalmi in directum*, with little difficulty. Such a refrain, however, was not necessarily an original element.[97]

Alleluia

What evolved as a separate part of the Proper of the Mass, originally may have been indistinguishable from the other psalmody between the readings. Such was true because one of the forms of psalmody, known already in Judaism, was the chanting of the psalm by a soloist with the congregation singing "Alleluia" after each verse.[98] "Hallelujah" already appears as a *kurze Lobsprüche*[99] in the New Testament,[100] consistently appears in the "Odes of Solomon,"[101] and clear evidence of Davidic alleluiac psalmody appears in the writings of Tertullian and Hippolytus.[102] Jerome, describing worship in Bethlehem, seems to know "Alleluia" as a psalm refrain between the readings at Eucharist[103]—a Palestinian practice further reflected in the old Armenian lectionary of the early fifth century, which notes the use of the Alleluia and psalm 39 before the gospel at the Easter vigil.[104] The placement of alleluiac psalmody immediately before the gospel is noted in the Greek text of the apocryphal *Martyrium Matthaei* (fourth or fifth century).[105]

It is possible that Augustine's famous text about the employment of the Alleluia, once used here and there but now universally employed during Easter,[106] indicates its usages before the gospel during this season.[107] Despite the assertion of Gregory the Great that Damasus I introduced the Alleluia into the Roman liturgy under the influence of Jerome,[108] solid evidence for the eucharistic employment of the Alleluia in Rome does not exist until the sixth century. John the Deacon could provide the first testimony that an Alleluia was sung—probably before the gospel—in the Roman liturgy on the Sundays of Easter.[109] Gregory the Great admits the use of the Alleluia—again, probably before the gospel—outside of the Easter season.[110] By the time of OR I the placement of the Alleluia before the gospel is indisputable.[111]

As to the role of the assembly in the singing of the Alleluia, it appears that the distinction between alleluiac psalmody and the Alleluia as an independent element in the Roman liturgy also delineates the difference between the Alleluia as a refrain of the community and its existence as a special piece for the trained singers. Augustine's comments about melismatic song already signal that florid melismas were entering the community's worship.[112] When the Alleluia entered the Eucharist of the West as an independent chant before the gospel, it seems to have appeared as an independent, relatively florid piece of chant. Cassiodorus (d. c. 580) seems to know the Alleluia as such a solo,[113] and Anglès suggests that such comments indicate that, already before the time of Gregory the Great, the Alleluia was already quite melismatic, which would have excluded the people's participation in its singing.[114] Consequently, it appears that the assembly never had a role, properly speaking, in the Alleluia as a chant before the Gospel in the medieval West.

Offertory

It is possible that a chant at the offertory was introduced by Augustine, first in Carthage and later in Hippo.[115] It appears that the role of this chant was to accompany the procession of gifts by the laity at the offertory which had been introduced into North African worship by the time of Augustine.[116] Previous to this, it does not appear that the people were engaged in any liturgical procession of gifts during the Eucharist either in the East or the West but rather brought their gifts prior to the beginning of the worship, which were in turn transferred to the altar by the clergy.[117] How long it took for the practice of an offertory chant to spread beyond North Africa is not clear. Some believe that this chant may have passed to Rome already in the fifth century.[118] The first decisive evidence for an *offertorium* chant in Rome is an enigmatic notice in OR I which reports that at the end of the offertory, "*pontifex . . . respicit scolam et annuit ut sileant.*"[119] Outside of Rome, the presence of a chant at the offertory (called the *sonus*) in Gallican worship seems to have been in place since the sixth century.[120] Parallels are also found in the Old Spanish (*sacrificum*) and Milanese (*offerenda*) rites.[121]

It is very difficult to substantiate any role for the laity in this chant as it emerged in the West.[122] While Augustine seems to give us evidence for music at the offertory, there is no indication that the people took part. Nor does it seem that the laity in Rome had any role in this chant. Wagner suggests that initially at Rome the offertory chant was a psalm, performed "antiphonally"[123] by two halves of the choir. By the eighth century, however, it appears that this "choir-chant" became a highly developed "solo-chant."[124] The latter consisted of an antiphon, two or three verses, and a refrain (often a repetition of the end of the antiphon) after each verse.[125] Apparently the *Gloria Patri* was never appended to the verses of this chant.[126] While it is theoretically possible that the people responded during this chant with the refrain, as Jungmann theorizes, "by this time there was obviously little interest in such participation of the people in responsorial chanting."[127] Outside of Rome the equivalent chants in the Old Spanish and the Milanese rite were similar in structure and melismatic composition,[128] which would seemingly rule out congregational roles in those rites at the offertory as well. The one exception to this could be the old Gallican chant at the

offertory, which concludes with a threefold alleluia.[129] If this entered
Gallican worship under the influence of Eastern worship, in which the
Alleluia could have served as a refrain to the chant at the Great
Entrance,[130] it is possible that Gallican chant as well could have
allowed for a community's alleluiatic response to an offertory psalm. In
general, however, it seems that the people ordinarily had no role in the
singing of the offertory chants in the Eucharist of the medieval West.

Communion

A cluster of witnesses from both the East and West demonstrate that a
communion chant entered Christian worship in the second part of the
fourth century. In the East, for example, both the *Apostolic
Constitutions* and the *Mystagogical Catecheses* of Cyril of Jerusalem
note the singing of Psalm 33 during communion,[131] and John
Chrysostom knows Psalm 144 as a communion psalm at Antioch.[132] In
the West, the previously cited text from Augustine's *Retractiones*[133]
demonstrates that psalmody was sung at communion time in
Carthage—a practice which Augustine may have known from his time
in Milan.[134] Jerome reports that communion psalmody was known in
Rome and in Spain,[135] and Aurelian of Arles (d. 541) notes in his rule
that there is singing during communion.[36] That these chants were not
always composed of psalms is evident from the work of Severus of
Antioch (d. 538) who composed several hymns for communion.[137]
Such early and widespread evidence suggests that the communion
chant was one of the earliest established chants of the so-called
"proper" throughout Christianity.

Not only was a communion chant widespread throughout worship
of the patristic era, it also appears that the people participated in this
chant in East and West. For example, in his careful study of the Eastern
material, Thomas Schattauer concludes that Chrysostom's exposition of
Ps 144 suggests that the faithful joined in a responsorial singing of
Psalm 144 with a cantor.[138] Jerome seems to indicate that the
congregation also had a response to the communion psalm,[139] and the
so-called *Canons of Basil*, possibly dating from the early fifth century,
also note the engagement of the congregation in responsorial singing at
communion time.[140] While written for monastic communities,

Aurelian's rules also indicates that the people sang while going to communion.[141] Jungmann suggests that in the Old Spanish rite as well as in certain oriental liturgies, Alleluia was the people's response to the communion psalm.[142] Besides these few tantalizing references to sing-ing by the people during communion, one must also reckon with the consistent use of Psalm 33 as a communion psalm in both East and West, facilitating the engagement of the people on a consistent and accessible refrain such as the very popular verse 8: "Taste and see how good the Lord is."[143]

As with other parts of the Mass, however, the people's role in the communion song was not to continue. As to be expected, OR I gives no role to the assembly for the communion chant.[144] The pattern of OR I does not appear to be the exception for the West, however, but quickly becomes the rule. While it is possible that the people may have joined in on the *Gloria Patri*,[145] which seems to have been a part of the Gallican communion chant (*trecanum*),[146] even Carolingian com-mentaries—which often, in exception to Roman practice, noted the singing of the congregation—presume that the assemblies hear rather than chant the communion song.[147] Eventually, the communion chant became the sole domain of the schola and ultimately even migrated to a position after communion, with the *Agnus Dei* becoming the real communion song.[148]

OTHER TEXTS

Besides the ordinary and the proper of the Mass, there evolved other moments of alternative chants within and around the Mass which allowed for the engagement of the assembly. Often, in contrast to the ordinary and the proper, these newer forms were in emerging vernacular languages, which facilitated their congregational access. While not an exhaustive list, some of these other chants include:

Processional Chants

One eucharistic medium for the musical engagement of the congregation outside of the ordinary and proper of the Mass could have been the processional chant. There are innumerable sources from the Middle Ages which demonstrate that, outside of Eucharist, popular religious songs were employed in religious processions. For example, English carols [both monophonic and polyphonic] were sometimes employed as processional songs; [149] Italian *laude* played an important role in popular religious processions; [150] German *Geisslerlieder* accompanied the processions of the flagellants; [151] and across Europe during the Middle Ages, the great pilgrimage movements to shrines like Canterbury, and especially Santiago de Compostela, spawned an entire repertory of pilgrim songs. [152] While these extra-eucharistic models— virtually all of which included some kind of refrain—do not prove that such popular forms were employed during the processions at Mass, they do set the context for such conjecture.

It is probable, for example, that some popular religious songs sometimes occurred during the opening processions at Mass. While these would not have replaced the introit, this first song of the proper had been so abbreviated, already in the ninth century, that it would have been unable to accompany adequately an extended procession, especially on great feasts or the high holy days. Certain carols, for example, have rubrics such as *"in die nativitatis."* [153] Could these have been employed as a processional chant on Christmas? Or would at least some of the *laude*, so integral to the processions of the *laudesi* companies of Tuscany, worked their way into the opening processions of the grander eucharistic celebrations or requiems sponsored by these groups? Or could not some of the *Leise*, [154] which were sung by shepherds driving cattle, employed in litanies, used as a refrain in battle and chanted during the installation of bishops, [155] also have been used in Mass processions? [156] While such was not the ordinary pattern, it does seem that such popular processional pieces did appear in the eucharistic liturgy. This is probably at least one of the reasons why diverse diocesan and provincial synods in the late Middle Ages ordered that the Latin chants of the Mass must neither be truncated nor abandoned in favor of the German chants. [157] And, as Paul Bradshaw rightly notes, such legislation "is better evidence for what it proposes to prohibit than for what it seeks to promote." [158]

Sequences

Clearer evidence exists for congregational engagement during and around some of the sequences. This medieval accretion, which evolved into a special type of hymn which was chanted after the Alleluia on special occasions, seems to have developed in the ninth century.[159] The popularity of this form was demonstrated in the thousands of texts which emerged during the late Middle Ages.[160] While some sequences survived in the particular liturgies of religious communities or local churches,[161] only five sequences were retained in the Missal of Pius V (d. 1572), published in 1570 for "universal" usage following the Council of Trent (1545–63).[162]

While sequences were ordinarily in Latin and sung by musical specialists, vernacular paraphrases developed in some places alongside the official texts, allowing for the engagement of the assembly. Sometimes the parallel vernacular text was interpolated into the sequence, with the congregation singing a strophe after each Latin strophe.[163] In other situations, the vernacular text was performed after the sequence.[164] Many well-known texts arose from the popular appropriation of sequences.[165] The intimate link between sequences and emerging vernacular hymnody is continued even after the Latin Mass is abandoned in the sixteenth-century reform. Thus, the reformer Martin Luther (d. 1546) employed the Latin sequences as one of the bases for his chorales.[166] While such texts written in imitation of sequences eventually took on a life of their own, both in Protestant and Roman Catholic worship, their original medieval function seems to have been to engage the assembly within an "official" part of the eucharistic celebration itself.

Homily[167]

A third "soft spot"[168] in medieval Eucharist in the West, which allowed for the insertion of popular vernacular song, occurred after the homily. When it took place,[169] the homily was virtually always a vernacular event, even when the rest of the worship was not.[170] Consequently, the homily often precipitated responses from the assembly, as in Hippo where Augustine's congregation alternately cheered, sighed, laughed or audibly beat their breasts when the great bishop preached. [171]

Probably less because of ancient precedents and more because of natural response, there is evidence from at least the tenth century in the Germanic territories that a brief acclamation of one or two lines (*Ruf*) was sometimes sung after the homily at Mass. [172] There is also evidence from a later period that longer *Leisen* such as *"Christ ist erstanden"* and *"Mitten wir im Leben sind"* were sung after the homily. [173] While there is less hard evidence for their eucharistic usage, it is also possible that various *laude* with their congregational refrains were sung after the homily in thirteenth and fourteenth-century Tuscany. This conjecture is based on the undeniable linkage between the *laude* and mendicant preaching. [174] While *laude* ordinarily were sung in special *laudesi* services, their intimate connection with mendicant preaching [175] suggests that, at least on some occasions when such mendicants preached to the *laudesi* within the context of Eucharist, *laude* would have been sung there as well. [176]

Besides the *Ruf*, *Leise* or *lauda*, it also appears that various forms of the refrain *"Kyrie eleison"* were sung by the assembly after the sermon. This ubiquitous refrain—which sometimes was even sung by the people during the creed[177]—appeared after the sermon on at least some occasions as a relic from the old prayer of the faithful, which disappeared from the Roman liturgy but survived in various forms in the West. [178]

Eventually a kind of vernacular office attached to the sermon evolves, which incorporates aspects of the old prayer of the faithful, song and announcements. While a nascent form of this prône (*pronaus*) already appears in the late ninth century, [179] evidence for what could be considered a full prône service does not appear until almost 400 years later. [180] Some of these services are explicit about the inclusion not only of the *Kyrie*—which could have been recited—but of other hymns or antiphons hymns, which were presumably sung by the congregation. [181]

SUMMARY

At the dawn of Christianity, to the extent there was music in Christian Eucharist, one could suggest that such music belonged to the community. While there is some evidence of solo or specialized singing—even in the early period—the norm seems to have been community song in Christian Eucharist. With the complexification of Christian beliefs, community structures and a parallel complexification of eucharistic worship during the patristic period, musical specialists emerged: first to share musical roles with the Christian assembly, and eventually to dominate and virtually usurp these roles. This was especially apparent in pontifical worship at Rome which drew heavily upon the courtly etiquette of imperial ritual.

Eucharistic worship at the beginning of the medieval period still allowed for the song of the assembly, especially North of the Alps. The Carolingian reform—and maybe the Gallican instincts which lay behind the reform—even seem to have encouraged the assembly to join in certain musical moments of the Eucharist. The vocal instincts of the increasing numbers of Germanic Christians also could not be suppressed within the Eucharist. Increasingly, however, these instincts or wishes for congregational song were relegated to non-essential elements of the rites. Most elements of the proper as well as the ordinary of the Mass disallowed for congregational engagement by the end of the millennium. While certain exceptions could be found, and various authorities expressed the opinion that ordinary people should be engaged—especially in elements of the ordinary of the Mass—this became more the exception than the rule.

In the second millennium of Christianity the explosion of devotional forms gave many ordinary believers a forum for their song. It appears, however, that the growth of popular religious music in the second millennium is almost in reverse proportion to the vocal engagement of the ordinary assembly in eucharistic worship. It was this situation that the sixteenth-century Reformation was to challenge and ultimately reverse.

Notes

1. For example, the 1958 Instruction of the Sacred Congregation of Rites, *De musica sacra*, notes: "'Liturgical services' [*actiones liturgicae*] are ... those sacred actions which have been instituted by Jesus Christ or the

Church and are performed in their name by legitimately appointed persons according to liturgical books approved by the Holy See, in order to give due worship to God, the saints, and the blessed. Other sacred acts performed inside or outside the church, even if performed by a priest or in his presence, are called 'pious exercises' [*pia exercitia*]," n. 1; as translated in R. Kevin Seasoltz, ed., *The New Liturgy* (New York: Herder and Herder, 1966), 257.

2. Justin Martyr (d. c. 165), *First Apology* 65.3 notes the people's "Amen" to the eucharistic prayer = Migne, *Patrologia Graeca* [hereafter, PG] 6:428; Hippolytus (d. c. 225), *Apostolic Tradition* outlines an early preface dialogue between bishop and people = Bernard Botte, ed., *La tradition apostolique*, 2nd ed., Source chrétiennes [hereafter, SC] 11bis (Paris: Cerf, 1984), 48.

3. In his commentary on Paul's letter to the Galatians, Jerome notes how, in Rome, the "Amen resounds so that it crashes like heavenly thunder" (*ad similitudinem coelestis tonitrui Amen reboat*), *In Ep. ad Gal.* 2, prefatio = Migne, *Patrologia Latina* [hereafter, *PL*] 26, 381; for further references to the use of the "*Amen*" in patristic sources and the Christian West, see Dennis Krouse, "The Historical Experience: A Review of the Great Amen in Christian Tradition," *Chicago Studies* 16:1 (1977), especially pp. 142–148.

4. e.g., the second Synod of Braga (563) notes, "*Item placuit, ut non aliter episcopi et aliter presbyteri populum, sed uno modo solutent, dicentes: Dominus sit vobiscum . . . et ut respondeatur a populo: Et cum spiritu tuo,*" c. 3 = Mansi 9:777.

5. Higini Anglès, "The Various Forms of Chant Sung by the Faithful in the Ancient Roman Liturgy," *Scripta Musicologica*, 3 vols., ed. Joseph López-Calo (Rome: Edizioni di Storia e Letteratura, 1975), 1:73. A number of medieval ecclesiastical sources note how the Germanic peoples loved to sing. See the references in Philipp Harnoncourt, "Le 'Kirchenlied' dans les églises d'Allemagne," *La Maison-Dieu* 92 (1967), 84.

6. These are well documented in Josef Jungmann, *The Mass of the Roman Rite: Its Origins and Development*, 2 vols., trans. Francis Brunner (New York: Benzinger, 1950), 1:236–237.

7. For an introduction to its history and development, see John Baldovin, "Kyrie Eleison and the Entrance Rite of the Roman Eucharist," *Worship* 60:4 (1986), 334–347.

8. Franz Dölger, *Sol Salutis: Gebet und Gesang im christlichen Altertum*, Liturgiewissenschaftliche Quellen und Forschungen 4/5 (Münster: Aschendorff, 1925), 77–82.

9. e.g., *Apostolic Constitutions* 8.6.4 in *Didaskalia et Constitutiones Apostolorum*, ed. F.X. Funk, 2 vols. (Torino: Bottega d'Erasmo, 1964), 1:478.

10. *"Kyrie eleison ... apud nos autem a clericis dicitur et a populo respondetur,"* Ep. 9.12 = *PL* 77, 956.

11. *"scola, vero, finita antiphona inponit Kyrieleison,"* Ordo Romanus [hereafter, OR] I.52 = Michel Andrieu, *Les Ordines romani du haut moyen âge,* Spicilegium Sacrum Lovaniense 23 (Louvain: Spicilegium Sacrum Lovaniense, 1960), 2:84; also, OR 4.20 = Andrieu 2:159.

12. Jungmann 1:343.

13. as cited in Anglès, p.73.

14. Polyphonic Kyries already appear in the eleventh century.

15. 7.47–49 = Funk, 1:454–458.

16. Robert Taft, *The Liturgy of the Hours in East and West* (Collegeville: The Liturgical Press, 1986), 45.

17. Louis Duchesne, *Le Liber pontificalis, texte, introduction et commentaire,* 2nd ed., ed. Cyrille Vogel, 3 vols. (Paris: E. de Boccard, 1955–57), 1:253, 263.

18. OR 39.27 = Andrieu 4:285.

19. OR 15.124 = Andrieu 3:121.

20. Peter Wagner, *Introduction to the Gregorian Melodies,* Vol. 1: *Origin and Development of the Forms of the Liturgical Chant up to the End of the Middle Ages,* rev. 2nd ed., trans. Agnes Orme and E.G.P. Wyatt (London: Plainsong and Medieval Music Society, 1901), 69; more recently, David Hiley, *Western Plainchant: A Handbook* (Oxford: Clarendon Press, 1993), 157.

21. Jungmann 1:358; for a different interpretation of this positioning, see Mario Righetti, *Manuale di storia liturgica,* Vol. 3: *L'Eucarestia* (Milan: Ancora, 1949), 176–77.

22. Johannes Emminghaus, *The Eucharist: Essence, Form, Celebration,* trans. Matthew J. O'Connell (Collegeville: The Liturgical Press, 1978), 123.

23. *"Non unus solus angelus cantavit, sed unus primo adfuisse dicitur, et subito cum eo factam esse multitudinem angelorum laudantium Deum. Sicque modo unus episcopus inchoat et omnis ecclesia resonat laudem Deo."* Amalarius of Metz, Missae expositionis (codex 1), 3.2, in J.M. Hanssens, ed., *Amalarii episcopi opera liturgica omnia,* 3 vols., Studi e testi 138–140 (Vatican City: 1948–1950), 1:258.

24. Sicard of Cremona (d. 1215) in his *Mitrale seu de officiis ecclesiasticus summa* notes *"solus sacerdos alte incipit, ad orientem conversus, quam populus concinendo recipit laetabundus,"* 3.2 = *PL* 213, 97.

25. A question that persisted at least into the eleventh century, as evidenced in the writings of Berno of Reichenau (d. 1048), *De quibusdam rebus ad missae officum pertinentibus,* c. 2 = *PL* 142, 1058–1061.

26. On the emergence of the *schola cantorum*, see Stephen van Dijk, "Gregory the Great, Founder of the Urban *Schola Cantor*," *Ephemerides Liturgicae* 77 (1963), 345–356.

27. Council of Chalcedon, *Expositio fidei concilii habiti in Nicea* = Mansi 6:957; a simpler form can be extracted from catechetical lectures 7–18 of Cyril of Jerusalem, which appears almost a century earlier (= MG 33:606–1059); and a more complete version in the *Ancoratus* of Epiphanius (d. 403) from 374 (c. 119 = MG 43:232).

28. 3rd Synod of Toledo (589), c. 2 = Mansi 9:993.

29. Cyrille Vogel, *Medieval Liturgy: An Introduction to the Sources*, trans. and rev. William Storey and Niels Rasmussen (Washington, DC: The Pastoral Press, 1986), 38.

30. Jungmann 1:469.

31. Berno of Reichenau, *De quibusdam rebus ad missae officum pertinentibus*, c. 2 = *PL* 142, 1060–1061.

32. see above, n. 13.

33. as cited in Jungmann 1:471, n. 61.

34. *Missae expositionis* (codex 1), 8.1–2 = Hanssens 1:261–2; also *Eclogae de ordine Romano et de quattuor orationibus episcoporum sive populi in missa* 19 = Hanssens 3:248; and, *Ordo missae a sancto Petro institutus cum expositione sua* 9 = Hanssens 3:305.

35. Jungmann 1:472.

36. Hiley is typical, ". . . in the early Middle Ages it was sometimes recited by the congregation, sometimes sung by the clergy," p. 169.

37. See Bryan Spinks, "The Jewish Sources for the Sanctus," *Heythrop Journal* 21 (1990), 168–179.

38. Clement 34 = J.B. Lightfoot, *The Apostolic Fathers*, Part 1: *Clement of Rome*, 2 vols (London: Macmillan, 1890), 2:105.

39. Similarly, Tertullian (d. c. 225) offers this relatively oblique reference to the *Sanctus*: "*Cui illa angelorum circumstantia non cessant dicere: Sanctus, Sanctus, Sanctus. Perinde igitur et nos . . . jam hinc coelestem in Deum vocem et officium futurae claritatis ediximus.*" *De Oratione* 3 = *Corpus scriptorum ecclesiasticorum latinorum* [hereafter, CSEL] 20:182.

40. Origen, *De principiis* 1.3.4, also 4.3.14 = SC 252, 1:148 and 3:394.

41. Which has neither the "*Hosanna in excelsis*" nor the "*Benedictus*" as part of the text; *Preces Missae Euchologii Serapionis* 13.10 = Johannes Quasten, *Monumenta eucharistica et liturgica vetutisima*, Florilegium Patristicum 7, eds. Bernhard Geyer and Johannes Zellinger (Bonn: P. Hanstein, 1935), 61.

42. Also without the "*Hosanna*" but with an abbreviated "*Benedictus,*" *Constitutiones Apostolorum* 8.12.27 = Funk 1:504–6.

43. *Liber pontificalis* 1.128.

44. Chavoutier, "Un libellus pseudo-ambrosien sur le Saint-Esprit," *Sacris erudiri* 11 (1960), 189. Chavoutier concludes that it was Pope Damasus (d. 384) who introduced the *Sanctus* in Roman liturgy, a conclusion based on the fact that Damasus exchanged a series of letters with Jerome dealing with the Trinitarian sense of the corresponding text in the prophet Isaiah. Ibid, pp. 183–84, as cited in Robert Cabié, *L'Eucharistie*, Vol. 2 of *L'Église en prière*, ed. A.-G. Martimort (Paris: Desclée, 1983), 112.

45. Victor of Vita, *Historia persecutionis Africanae provinciae* 1.2.100 = CSEL 7:70–1; also, the Council of Vaison (529), c. 3 = Mansi 8:727.

46. Gregory of Nyssa (d. c. 395), *De baptismo* = PG 46:421; also, John Chrysostom (d. 407), *In Is. hom.* 1.1 = PG 56:97–99.

47. Both the previously cited pseudo-Ambrosian *libellus* from North Italy as well as the Council of Vaison specifically note that the people join the priest in singing the *Sanctus*.

48. The earliest form of the *Liber pontificalis* appears to have been written during the pontificate of Boniface II (530–32) by a Roman presbyter.

49. *Liber pontificalis* 1.128.

50. "*Et subdianoni regionarii, finito offertori, vadunt retro altare, aspicientes ad pontificem ut quando dixerit Per omnia secula, aut Dominus vobiscum, aut Sursum corda, aut Gratias agamus, ipsi sint parati ad respondendum stantes erecti usquedum incipiant dicere hymnum angelicum, id est Sanctus, Sanctus Sanctus.*" OR 1.86 = Andrieu 2:95.

51. Jungmann 2:129, n. 6.

52. *Hom.* 12 = *PL* 39, 2276; Caesarius also is an early Western source for the text of the *Benedictus*.

53. OR I 5.38 = Andrieu 3:103; this ordo dates from the middle of the eighth century, probably from southwestern Gaul.

54. Jungmann 1:129; thus the *Admonitio generalis* of 23 March 789, n. 70 = *Monumenta Germaniae Historica* [hereafter MGH] *Legum* 2, *Capitularia Regum Francorum*, ed. Alfred Boretius (Hanover, 1883), 1:59; Herard of Tours, c. 16 of his synadodal statutes = *PL* 121, 765; and, Rabanus Maurus (d. 856), *Liber de sacris ordinibus* 19 = *PL* 112, 1182.

55. e.g., Hildebert of Lavardin (d. 1133), *Versus de mysterio missae* = *PL* 171, 1182; and, Honorius of Autun (fl. early twelfth century), *Gemma animae* 1.42 = *PL* 172, 556.

56. OR 15.39, speaking of the onset of the canon after the *Sanctus*, notes "*Et incipit canire dissimili voce . . . ita ut a circumstantibus altare tantum audiatur*" = Andrieu 3:103; OR 5.58 (c. 850) demonstrates the shift by noting that the text is now proclaimed so that even those standing around the altar

cannot hear: "*Quae dum expleverint, surgit solus pontifex et tacito intrat in canonem*" = Andrieu 2:221.

57. So much so that "the breaking of the bread" could be considered one of the earliest, if not the earliest name for Christian Eucharist, i.e., Acts 2.42; also, Johannes Behm, "kláo," *Theological Dictionary of the New Testament*, ed. Gerhard Kittel, trans. Geoffrey Bromiley (Grand Rapids MI: Eerdmans, 1965), 3:730.

58. Righetti 3:410.

59. *Liber pontificalis* 1:376.

60. e.g., Jn 1.29 and Rev 5.6–14.

61. Thus Jungmann 1:334; also, Ludwig Eisenhofer and Joseph Lechner, *The Liturgy of the Roman Rite*, trans. A.J. and E.F. Peeler (Edinburgh-London, 1961), 325.

62. This is the opinion of Duchesne; see Trullan Synod, c. 82 = Mansi 11:977–980.

63. "*Domine Deus, Agnus Dei, Filius Patris. Qui tollis peccata mundi, miserere nobis. Qui tollis peccata mundi, suscipe deprecationem nostram.*"

64. "*Et incipit clerus laetania et procedit sacerdos de sacrario cum ordinibus sacris. Veniunt ante altare stantes inclinato capite usquedum dicent Agnus Dei, qui tollis peccata mundi, miserere.*" Liber Sacramentorum Romanae Aeclesiae ordinis anni circuli, ed. Leo Mohlberg, Rerum Ecclesiasticarum Documenta, series maior 4 (Rome: Herder, 1960), n. 425 = p. 68.

65. Vogel, *Medieval Liturgy*, 69.

66. "*Agnus Dei qui tollis peccata mundi miserere nobis a clero et populo decantetur,*" *Liber pontificalis* 1:376.

67. "*Et archidiaconus, evacuato altare oblationibus, preter particulam quam pontifix de propria oblatione confracta super altare reliquid, quid ita observant ut, dum missarum solemnia peraguntur, altare sine sacrifio non sit respicit in scolam et annuit eis ut dicant Agnus Dei et vadit ad patenam cum ceteris,*" OR 1.105 = Andrieu 2:101.

68. "*Diaconibus vero fragentibus in patena, vertit se archidiaconus ad scolam, ut incipiant Agnus Dei, quod tamdiu cantatur usquedum complent fractionem.*" OR 3.2 = Andrieu 2:131.

69. See Charles Atkinson, "The Earliest *Agnus Dei* Melody and Its Tropes," *Journal of the American Musicological Society* 30 (1977), 1–19; for an edition of *Agnus Dei* tropes, see Gunilla Iverson, ed., *Tropes de l'Agnus Dei*, Corpus troporum 4 (Stockholm: University of Stockholm, 1980).

70. Alcuin (d. 804) offers one of the first testimonies for this change in his *Letter to the Brothers in Lyon* (c. 798): "*Panis qui in Corpus Christi*

consecratur, absque fermento ullius alterius infectionis, debet esse mundissimus." = *PL* 100, 289.

71. Already in eighth-century Rome, the people no longer handle the cup but are required to drink through a tube, OR 1.111 = Andrieu 2:103.

72. See the extensive references to these two phenomena in Jungmann 2:337, nn. 30 and 31.

73. Jungmann 2:338, n. 36.

74. John Beleth (d. 1165), "*Agnus Dei ter canitur . . . bis dicitur cum Miserere nobis, tertio cum Dona nobis pacem . . . sed horum neutrum adjungitur in missa pro defunctis, verum ter cum Dona eis requiem.*" John Beleth, *Rationale divinorum officiorum* 48 = *PL* 202, 55.

75. The Dominican Ordinary of 1267 is one of the earliest texts noting that all chant texts must be read by the presider. Francis M. Guerrini, ed. *Ordinarium iuxta ritum sacri ordinis Fratrum Praedicatorum* (Rome: Angelicum, 1921): Kyrie, n. 47 = p. 285; *Gloria*, n. 49, = p. 236; *Sanctus*, n. 76 = p. 241; *Agnus Dei*, n. 93 = p. 243.

76. Augustine, *De civitate Dei* 12.8 = Corpus Christianorum, Series Latina [hereafter, CCL], 48:826.

77. "*Hic constituit ut psalmi CL David ante sacrificium psalli,*" *Liber pontificalis* 1:89.

78. Peter Jeffery, "The Introduction of Psalmody into the Roman Mass by Pope Celestine I (422–432)," *Archiv für Liturgiewissenschaft* 26 (1984), 165.

79. ". . *postquam antephonam ad introitum dixerint, data oratione adnuntiat pontifex in populo dicens: Auxiliante domino deo . . .* " n. 20 = Mohlberg, p. 24.

80. see above, n. 65.

81. OR I.44–52 = Andrieu 2:81–84.

82. The text of OR 1, to the contrary indicates that only after the *Gloriam* does the scola return to the antiphon ("*Scola vero, finita antiphona, inponit Kyrieleison,*" OR 1.52 = Andrieu 2:84).

83. Jungmann 1:325.

84. "*ut 'Gloria Patri' cum omni honore apud omnes cantetur,*" *Admonitio generalis*, n. 70 = MGH, *Legum* 2, *Capitularia Regum Francorum*, 1:59; in the following century such congregational involvement was still presumed in the decree of Herard of Tours, see above n. 13.

85. Hiley, p. 109.

86. The theory that the responsorial psalm was a practice borrowed from the synagogue is no longer tenable.

87. Speaking of the Sunday morning Eucharist, he writes ". . . *prout Scripturae leguntur aut psalmi canuntur aut allocutiones proferuntur aut*

petitiones delegantur," *De Anima* 9.4 = CSEL 20:310; for a general discussion of the role of psalmody in the liturgy as reflected in the writings of Tertullian, see E. Dekkers, *Tertullianus en de geschiedenis der Liturgie* (Brussels-Amsterdam: Desclé de Brouwer, 1947), 31–36.

88. The only reliable earlier evidence comes from the apocryphal *Acta Pauli* (c. 190 Œ), ed. and trans. Wilhelm Schubart and Carl Schmidt (Hamburg: J.J. Augustin, 1936), pp. 50 and 51, line 11; for a further discussion of the role of psalmody in primitive Christian worship, see my *Foundations of Christian Music: The Music of Pre-Constantinian Christianity* (Nottingham, England: GROW/Alcuin Publications, 1992).

89. *Apostolic Constitutions* 2.57.6 = Funk 1:161.

90. Augustine is clear that responsorial psalmody during the Liturgy of the Word was employed in Hippo, e.g., *Sermo 176* = *PL* 37, 950; it is also possible that a comment from Augustine's *Confessiones* 9.7 = CSEL 33:208 suggests that such a practice—in imitation of Eastern practice—already existed in Milan at the end of the episcopate of Ambrose. See Helmut Leeb for his close reading of this text in *Die Psalmodie bei Ambrosius*, Wiener Beiträge zur Theologie 18 (Vienna: Herder, 1967), 91–98.

91. See above, n. 78.

92. Ernest Moneta Caglio suggests that the first incontestable evidence is found in the work of Athanasius (d. 373), *Apologia de Fuga Sua* 24 (= PG 25:676), Athanasius' language suggests that this responsorial practice is somewhat older, though Caglio would not want to push it much earlier than the end of the third century. Ernest Moneta Caglio, *Lo Jubilus e le origini della salmodia responsoriale*, Jucunda Laudatio 14–15 (1976–1977), 58–59.

93. Giulio Cattin, *Music of the Middle Ages* I (London: Cambridge University Press), 10; also, Leeb who, reiterating the stance of Jungmann, holds that responsorial psalm singing was the only form of psalm singing known to the Church until the middle of the fourth century, p. 17.

94. *Serm.* 3.1 = *PL* 104, 145;

95. OR 1.57 = Andrieu 2:86.

96. Jungmann 1:426; or, as Hucke summarizes, "instead of the popular refrain there is a choral 'respond' which precedes the verse of the soloist and which is also repeated after the verse. . . . This substitution must have occurred after the second half of the 5th century." Helmut Hucke, "Gradual," *New Grove Dictionary of Music and Musicians* [hereafter, NGDMM], ed. Stanley Sadie (New York: W.W. Norton, 1980), 7:599. On the emergence of the specialized singer in the Christian tradition, see my "The Cantor in Historical Perspective," *Worship* 56 (1982), 194–213.

97. Terrence Bailey, *The Ambrosian Cantus*, Musicological Studies 47 (Ottawa: The Institute of Mediaeval Music, 1987), 35.

98. The various forms of psalmody in ancient Judaism are well outlined in Hanoch Avenary, "Formal Structure of Psalms and Canticles in Early Jewish and Christian Chant," *Musica Disciplina* 7 (1953), 3–6; it should be noted, however, that the emerging Christian community probably did not borrow this practice from the Synagogue, as much as from Temple and domestic usage of the Hallel psalms. See, for example, Mark 14.26 and Matt 26.30 which most scholars accept as references to the singing of the second half of the Passover *Hallel* (Pss. 114 or 115 to 118).

99. See Reinhard Deichgräber, *Gotteshymnus und Christushymnus in der frühen Christenheit* (Göttingen: Vandenhoeck & Ruprecht, 1967), 24–59.

100. e.g., Rev 19.1–6.

101. "Halleluia" concludes every one of these *psalmi idiotici*, which Charlesworth calls the "first Christian hymnbook" and could date from the end of the first or beginning of the second century of the common era. See *The Odes of Solomon*, ed. and trans. James H. Charlesworth (Missoula MT: University of Montana Press, 1977).

102. *De Oratione* 27.17 = CSEL 20:198; and *Apostolic Tradition* 25 = Botte, 64–66.

103. *Tractus de psalmo* 7 = CCL 78:19; such is the opinion of A.-G. Martimort, "Origine et signification de l'alleluia de la messe romain," *Kyriakon: Festschrift Johannes Quasten*, 2 vols., ed. Patrick Granfield and Joseph Jungmann (Münster: Aschendorff, 1970), 2:818, n. 47.

104. Athanase Renoux, *Le Codex arménien Jérusalem 121*, 2 vols., Patrologia Orientalis [hereafter, PO] 163 & 168 (Turnhout: Brepols, 1969 & 1971), n. 44ter = 168:308–9.

105. *Acta apostolorum apocrypha*, eds. R.A. Lipsius and M. Bonnet (Leipzig: Mendelssohn, 1898), 2:252–3, as cited in Martimort, "Origine," 2:820.

106. *Epist.* 55.32 = CSEL 34:207; for further references to its usage during the Easter season, but outside of Eucharist, see Jacques Froger, "l'Alleluia dans l'usage romain et le réforme de saint Grégoire," *Ephemerides Liturgicae* 62 (1948), 31–40.

107. This position could be bolstered by another sermon of Augustine in which he indicates that the Alleluia was sung at two different services on the same day, e.g., morning prayer and Eucharist. *Sermo* 252.9 = *PL* 38, 1176. Such is suggested by James McKinnon, *Music in Early Christian Literature*, Cambridge Readings in the Literature of Music (Cambridge: Cambridge University Press, 1987), 162.

108. *Epist.* 11.12 = *PL* 127, 976.

109. *Epistola ad Senarium* 13 = *PL* 59, 406.

110. *Epist.* 11.12 = *PL* 77, 956; it is also widely held that Gregory introduced the "Alleluia verse" to the practice of singing the Alleluia before the gospel (see Martimort, "Origine," 2:834); it is also possible that Gregory did not simply "extend" the use of the Alleluia outside of the Easter season, but actually cut back on its more widespread usage beyond this season (see Hiley, p. 502).

111. *"Ad completionem autem Alleluia vel responsorii, parant se diaconi ad evangelium legendum,"* 1.58 = Andrieu 2:87.

112. *In Ps.* 99.4 = CCL 39:1394.

113. *"Hinc ornatur lingua cantorum; istud aula Domini laeta respondet, et tamquam insatiabile bonum tropis semper variantibus innovatur,"* In Psalm 104 = *PL* 70, 742.

114. Anglès, p. 70; also, Jungmann 1:426.

115. *"Hymni ad altare dicerentur de psalmorum libro, sive ante oblationem, sive cum distribueretur populo quod fuisset oblatum,"* Retractiones 2.37 = CSEL 36:144; for an examination of this text, see Joseph Dyer, "Augustine and the *Hymni ante oblationem*: the Earliest Offertory Chants?" *Revue des études augustiniennes* 27 (1981), 85–99. Dyer concludes, "The 'traditional' interpretation of these *hymni* as the earliest offertory chants cannot be excluded, though henceforth it must not be considered a certitude," p. 99.

116. In one of his epistles Augustine refers to women who are able *"ferre oblationem ad altare Dei vel invenire ibi sacerdotes per quem offerant Deo,"* Ep. 111.8 = CSEL 34/2:655.

117. In his study of the Great Entrance in the liturgy of John Chrysostom, for example, Robert Taft concludes that "there is no convincing evidence that there was ever an offertory procession of the faithful in the East." *The Great Entrance*, Orientalia Christiana Analecta 200 (Rome: Pont. Institutum Studiorum Orientalium, 1978), 11.

118. e.g., Jungmann 2:27 and Righetti 3:257; for a different view, see Johannes Brinktrine, "De origine offertorii in missa Romana," *Ephemerides Liturgicae* 40 (1926), 15–20.

119. OR 1.85 = Andrieu 2:95; OR 38.83 = Andrieu 3:409, on the other hand, notes that the *offertoria* (as well as the *Agnus Dei* and *communio*) is not sung at the Easter vigil. While the archetype of this ordo was composed around the year 800, it is possible that OR 38 could harken back to an earlier tradition when no offertory chant existed in the Roman liturgy. Walafrid Strabo (d. 849) was of the opinion that the ancient practice in the West was that reflected at the Easter Vigil, i.e., a practice without chant. *De ecclesiasticarum rerum exordiis et incrementis* 21 = *PL* 114, 948.

120. *Expositio antiquae liturgiae Gallicanae*, which could have been the work of Germanus of Paris (d. 576), knows this chant; see the edition of E.C.

Ratcliff, Henry Bradshaw Society 98 (London: Harrison and Sons, Ltd., 1971), 10; on the question of the authorship of this text, see A. van der Mensbrugge, "Pseudo-Germanus Reconsidered," *Studia Patristica* 5 (1962), 172–184.

121. It is also possible that the *antiphona post evangelium* in Milanese worship played some role in the offertory rites in Milan.

122. In the Byzantine liturgy, on the other hand, it is clear that the congregation had a role in this chant, known as the *Cherubikon*. Taft believes it is probable that the *Cherubikon* was an earlier refrain of an antiphonally executed psalm at the Great Entrance. See Taft, *The Great Entrance*, pp. 78–83, 86–98.

123. He probably means "alternately"; on the nature of antiphonal psalmody, properly speaking, see Robert Taft, "The Structural Analysis of Liturgical Units: An Essay in Methodology," *Worship* 52:4 (1978), 321–324.

124. Wagner, p. 95.

125. Giacomo Bonifacio Baroffio and Ruther Steiner, "Offertory," NGDMM 13:514.

126. Jungmann 2:29.

127. Ibid.

128. Hiley, p. 500.

129. Expositio antiquae liturgiae Gallicanae = Ratcliff, p. 11.

130. Taft, *The Great Entrance*, p. 98.

131. 8.13.16 = Funk 1:518; and SC 126:168–170.

132. In *Ps. 144* = PG 55:464.

133. see above, n. 115.

134. In his mystagogical catechesis, delivered about 391, Ambrose gives the impression that psalm 23 is chanted during communion. *De Sacramentis* 5.12 = *PL* 16, 468.

135. *Epist.* 71, *ad Lucinum* 6 = CSEL 55:7; also, for Rome, see Cassiodorus, In *Ps.* 33 = *PL* 70, 234–5.

136. *"psallendo, omnes communicent," Regula ad monachos = PL* 68, 396.

137. *Octoechos* = PO 7:678.

138. Thomas Schattauer, "The Koinonicon of the Byzantine Liturgy: An Historical Study," *Orientalia Christiana Periodica* 49 (1983), 117; this is also the opinion of McKinnon, p. 82.

139. In *Is.* 2.5.20 = CCL 73:77; such is the opinion of McKinnon as well, p. 144.

140. Canon 97, as cited in McKinnon, p. 120, n. 266.

141. Both his *Regula ad monachos* and *Regula ad virgines* contain the text *"psallendo, omnes communicent," PL* 68, 396 and 68:406, respectively.

142. Jungmann 2:393.

143. This chant could have almost considered part of the "ordinary," since it was in such widespread use as a communion psalm; see some of the reports of it usage in Henri Leclercq, "Communion," *Dictionnaire d'archéologie chrétienne et de liturgie*, eds. Ferdinand Cabrol and Henri Leclercq, 15 vols. (Paris: Letouzey, 1907–53), 3:2428–29, 31–33; also, the comment in Wagner, pp. 102–3.

144. OR 1.117 = Andrieu 2:105.

145. See above, n. 13.

146. *Expositio antiquae liturgiae Gallicanae* = Ratcliff, p. 16; also, Jungmann's comment, 1:395–6.

147. e.g., *Expositio Primum in ordine (before 819)*, which notes *"et dum ipse a fidelibus percipitur, dignum est, ut communio sacramenti modulationis lenitate aures accipientium mulceat ut ociosa quaeque minus recordari . . . cordaque eorum ad conpunctionem ejus amoris, quae accipiunt, excitentur"* = *PL* 138, 1186.

148. Jungmann outlines these developments, 2:397–8.

149. John Stevens, "Carol," NGDMM 3:805.

150. Blake Wilson, *Music and Merchants: The Laudesi Companies of Republican Florence* (Oxford: Clarendon Press, 1992), 15, 34, 47, 60, etc.

151. Walter Salmen, "Geisslerlieder," NGDMM 7:221.

152. A useful introduction to the expanse of this music is the recording *In Gottes Name fahren wir: Pilgerlieder aus Mittelalter und Renaissance*, ODHECATON (Köln) FCD 97208.

153. Especially those found in the Ritson manuscript, as noted in Stevens, p. 805.

154. "A *Leise* is a non-polyphonic folk-hymn that ends with a melodic formula whose text is 'kyrie eleison,' 'kyrio leis,' 'kirleis,' or 'krles.'" Johannes Riedel, *Leise Settings of the Renaissance and Reformation Era*, Recent researches in the Music of the Renaissance 35 (Madison: A-R Editions, Inc., 1980), vii.

155. See Walter Wiora, "The Origins of German Spiritual Folk Song: Comparative Methods in a Historical Study," *Ethnomusicology* 8:1 (1964), 4–5.

156. It appears, for example, that a Christmas *Leise*, *"Sei willkommen Herre Christ"* was sung by the people before the Introit. See Johannes Janota, *Studien zu Funktion und Typus des deutschen geistlichen Liedes im Mittelalter* (München: C.H. Beck, 1968), 112–113.

157. For example, Basel (1435), Eichstätt (1446) Schwerin (1492) and Basel (1502), as cited in Harnoncourt, p. 85.

158. Paul Bradshaw, *The Search for the Origins of Christian Worship* (New York: Oxford University Press, 1992), 68.

159. The early history of the sequence and the impetus behind its origin is disputed. See the balanced summary of the various opinions in Hiley, pp. 185–189.

160. An accessible collection of these texts is found in various volumes of *Analecta hymnica medii aevi*, eds. Guido Maria Dreves, Clemens Blume and Henry Marriott Bannister, 55 vols (Leipzig: Reisland, 1886–1922), vols. 7–10, 34, 37, 39–40, 42, 44, 53–55.

161. For example a sequence for the Feast of St. Francis continues to be employed today by many Franciscan communities. See *Franciscan Lectionary*, English-Speaking Conference of the Order of Friars Minor (New York: Catholic Book Publishing Co., 1975), 66–67.

162. These were *Victimae paschali* for Easter, *Veni, Sancte Spiritus* for Pentecost, *Lauda Sion* for Corpus Christi, *Stabat Mater* for the Feast of the Seven Sorrows of the BVM (September 15), and *Dies irae* for the Mass for the Dead. The *Dies irae* was dropped from the Missal of Paul VI (d. 1978), published in 1969 following the Second Vatican Council (1962–65).

163. For example, a *Schulordnung* from 1480, notes that "*Item circa alia festa resurreccionis ascenssionis et corporis Christi habentur plures canciones convenientes cum sequencys: videlicet in sequencias "Victime pascali laudes' Christ ist erstanden circa quoslibet duos versus etc. regulariter fit.*" The ordo goes on to illustrate how "*Erstanden ist der heilig Crist*" was to be interpolated into "*Surrexit Christus hodie*," and notes that the "*wlgaris prosa*" "*Crist fuer gen himel*" could similarly be inserted into the Ascension sequence "*Summi triumphum,*" and how "*Kum heiliger geist, herre got*" could be employed with the Pentecost sequence "*Veni sancte spiritus.*" W. Crecelius, "Craislheimer Schulordnung von 1480 mit deutschen geistlichen Liedern," *Alemannia* 3 (1875), 251–52.

164. For example, according to the *Ordinarium inclitae ecclesiae Sverinensis* (1519), the *Leise* (which is how Riedel classifies it, p. xii) "*Gelobet seistu Jesu Christ,*" was sung at Christmas Mass after the sequence "*Grates nunc omnes.*" Franz Magnus Böhme, *Altdeutches Liederbuch,* 3rd ed. (Leipzig: Breitkopf & Härtel, 1925), 616–617.

165. For example "*Nun bitten wir den heiligen Geist*" based on "*Veni Sancte Spiritus.*"

166. See Konrad Ameln, *The Roots of German Hymnody of the Reformation Era* (St. Louis: Concordia, 1964), 3–19.

167. While there are a variety of genres of preaching [i.e., "sermons"], the homily, properly speaking, is a liturgical event.

168. Robert Taft, "How Liturgies Grow: The Evolution of the Byzantine 'Divine Liturgy,'" *Orientalia Christiana Periodica* 43 (1977), 357.

169. While ordinarily a part of the eucharistic celebration in the early church, there were numerous situations where the homily dropped out [e.g., OR 1] or even was forbidden [see the various articles in *Preaching in the Patristic Era*, ed. David Hunter (New York: Paulist Press, 1989)]; there was a resurgence of preaching during the Middle Ages [*see De Ore Domini: Preacher and Word in the Middle Ages*, eds. Thomas Amos, Eugene Green and Beverly Mayne Kienzle (Kalamazoo: Western Michigan University, 1989)].

170. Various Carolingian councils, for example, explicitly ordered that the homily should be in the language of the people, even when those homilies were read from the Fathers of the church, e.g., the Synod of Rheims (813) notes "*Ut episcopi sermones et homilias sanctorum patrum, prout omnes intelligere possit secundum proprietatem linguae praedicare studeant*," c. 15 = Mansi 14:78; similarly the 3rd Synod of Tours (813)) c. 17 = Mansi 14:85.

171. See the wonderful summaries of these reactions in F. van der Meer, *Augustine the Bishop*, trans. Brian Battershaw and G.R. Lamb (London-New York: Sheed and Ward, 1961), pp. 138. 140, 143, 339–340, 414, 421, 427–432 and 522. The most dramatic evidence of congregational response to Augustine's preaching occurred on 26 September 426, on the occasion of the election of Eraclius as coadjutor and successor to Augustine. The record of the event notes over 200 shouts and acclamations on the part of the assembly during and after the sermon. Van der Meer well summarizes, pp. 270–273.

172. Volker Mertens, for example, provides examples of various *Ruf* sung by the people after preaching on the feast of All Saints, Christmas, Masses for the dead, etc. "Der Ruf—eine Gattung des deutschen geistlichen Liedes im Mittelalter?" *Zeitschrift für deutsches Altertum und deutsche Literatur* 104 (1975), 70–74.

173. Janota, p. 74.

174. Thus Blake Wilson suggests that various strophes of some laude may have been heard as a sermon-like expansion (p. 23) and summarizes that "many laude looked two ways—towards heaven as sung prayer, and to the confratelli as sung sermon," p. 24.

175. "There was rarely an occasion in the various *laudesi* services when preaching and *lauda* singing were not closely juxtaposed," Wilson, p. 28.

176. For example, in the context of Masses for deceased *laudesi*—a common occurrence since the *laudesi* societies operated to a certain extent as burial societies for their members and required that their members offer and attend Masses for deceased members. Wilson, p. 34.

177. Testimony for such comes from Honorius of Autun, *Gemma animae* 1.19 = *PL* 172, 550; Sicard of Cremona, *Mitrale* 3.4 = *PL* 213, 113; and William Durandus (d. 1296) *Rationale divinorum officiorum* 4.25.14 (e.g., Strasbourg: Jordanus, 1488), 69v; there is no standard edition of Durandus'

work, although a critical edition is currently in preparation under the direction of Anselme Davril). It appears that some *Ruf* also occurred more as "*Credo*-songs," Mertens, p. 71.

178. Jean-Baptiste Molin, "*L'oratio fidelium*, ses survivance," *Ephemerides Liturgicae* 73 (1959), 310–311.

179. Regino of Prüm (d. 915), writes "*Oportet ut in diebus festis vel dominicis post sermonem intra missarum solemnia habitum ad plebem sacerdos admoneat ut juxta apostolicam institutionem orationem omnes in commune pro diversis necessitatibus fundant ad Dominum pro regibus et rectoribus ecclesiarum, pro pace, pro peste, pro infirmis qui in ipsa paroechia lecto decumbunt, pro nuper defunctis . . . ,*" *De ecclesiasticis disciplinis*, c. 190 = *PL* 132, 224–25.

180. A. Gastoué, "Les prières du prône à Paris au 14e siècle," *Questions liturgiques et paroissiales* 12 (1927), 240–249.

181. For example, two fifteenth and one early century-century texts from England note the singing of the *Ave regina caelorum* (or in Easter time the *Regina caeli*) toward the end of the "bidding prayers." Thomas F. Simmons, ed., *The Lay Folks Mass Book*, Early English Text Society, 71 (London: N. Trübner & Co., 1879), pp. 66, 72, and 79.

THE MIND'S EYE:
THEOLOGICAL CONTROVERSY AND
RELIGIOUS ARCHITECTURE IN THE
REIGN OF CHARLEMAGNE

Susan A. Rabe

Over the last thirty years scholars have become increasingly aware of a variety of ways in which religious architecture responded to the development of religious policy in the Carolingian period. Ann Freeman's studies of the authorship of the *Libri Carolini* for example, have brought to light the probable relationship between Theodulf of Orléans' church at Germigny-des-Prés and the refutation of *iconodulism* in the Libri.[1] Walter Horn and Ernest Born's monumental study of the Plan of Saint Gall has argued that this archetypal monastic plan reflected a powerful debate over the nature and role of monastic spirituality in the reign of Louis the Pious.[2] Similarly, Werner Jacobsen's recent study of general tendencies in church architecture during the reign of Louis has illuminated the practical effects of the reform program of Benedict of Aniane and its legislation in the Aachen councils.[3]

One of the richest periods for such cultural debate was the period from about 785 to 810, when Carolingian scholars spilled much ink over what they saw to be theological issues of critical importance: Adoptionism and the nature of Christ, the *filioque* and trinitarian theology, and the meaning of religious images. The extent of the debate and the vigor with which it was engaged reflect precisely the lack of clear consensus on how to articulate the central beliefs of the faith.

Of special interest in this context is the fact that three of the participants in the clarification and promotion of the Carolingian position also built churches during these years. The first, already noted, is Theodulf of Orléans. The second, Benedict of Aniane, is usually studied for his later monastic reforms and buildings at Inde, but there is telling evidence of his first monastic church at Aniane which was built while Benedict was campaigning against Adoptionism in Septimania. The third is Angilbert of Saint-Riquier who built this monastery at the same time that he was serving as Charlemagne's representative to the Pope on the religious controversies. The evidence that we have for these architectural programs is uneven; we know much more about Angilbert's buildings and intent than about the others. Nevertheless, a comparison of the three within the broader and specific context of the theological controversies is illuminating. Despite their apparent relationship to the christological, trinitarian, and image debates all three programs were distinct. They reflect, then, both the liveliness of the cultural debate and a variety of ways in which religious architecture was understood to be meaningful.[4]

THE THEOLOGICAL CONTROVERSIES

We may begin with a cursory overview of the theological issues. Scholars have generally viewed these controversies separately as discrete issues. Yet the theological claims impinged upon each other, and Carolingian scholars came to view Adoptionism, images, and the *filioque* as integrally related to each other. They need to be viewed in this light, then, both to see the relationships between them and the reason why they became so threatening to Charlemagne and his theologians.

The quarrel with Spanish Adoptionism which began in the 780s focused on what Carolingian scholars felt to be a misrepresentation or misunderstanding of the relationship between divine and human in Jesus.[5] Spanish theologians such as Elipandus, Archbishop of Toledo and Primate of Spain and especially Felix, Bishop of Urgel (in Carolingian territory), used the ancient terminology of adoption to signify the Word become flesh. Working within an indigenous tradition of exegesis, the Adoptionists used Philippians 2:7 as the foundational authority on the incarnation, which said that Christ, "though he was in the form of God, emptied himself and took the form of a slave."[6] In their exegesis, the self-emptying of Christ and his adoption of the flesh from Mary was essential to the accomplishment of salvation. It was precisely the paradox of the slavery represented in the Word's adoption of the flesh that was important to the Adoptionists: through it the Son became a son by grace—the human condition—as well as by divine nature. This paradoxical adoption established a familial relationship between Christ and sinful humans who now could also be adopted into salvation. In this way, Adoptionism stressed a familial paradigm of salvation, rather than the unique mediatorial role of Christ as Redeemer delineated in Chalcedonian formulations. Christ was the "elder brother" of those saved by grace.[7]

From its earliest appearance, however, this language of adoption stimulated serious criticism. As early as 785 and again in 793 Pope Hadrian interpreted the Adoptionist formulation as a "new Nestorianism" separating the human Jesus from the divine Christ."[8] Working from a Chalcedonian basis Hadrian interpreted the terminology of slavery as a degradation of the second person of the Trinity and a denial of the integrity of God and human in Jesus. The charge of Nestorianism was a stigma that Adoptionism never lost.

The Chalcedonian formulation as a starting point for christological reflection led to three primary arguments by Carolingian theologians against the Adoptionists: first, a stress on the essential unity of the Trinity as revealed in certain actions of Jesus; second, a clear distinction between the status of Jesus as Redeemer and those he has redeemed, underscoring his unique mediatorial role; and third, new theological consideration of the significance of Mary as Mother of God.

Unaware of or ignoring the Adoptionist use of Philippians 2:7, Alcuin and Paulinus of Aquileia, the two who wrote the anti-Adoptionist treatises, used instead a variety of texts emphasizing the special status of Jesus as the Son of God, different from other humans, including the Annunciation and the Nativity, the Baptism of Jesus, and the Crucifixion, Resurrection, and Ascension.[9] They used other texts including John 10:29, 14:9–10, and 17:6 to prove the likeness of Father and Son. John 20:21–22, Jesus' breathing the Holy Spirit upon the disciples, stressed his relationship with both Father and Spirit, as did Matthew 28:18–19, stressing the redemptive activity of the Trinity as a whole.

Opposing the terminology of adoption of the flesh, Carolingian writers spoke instead of the Word's assumption of the flesh at the moment of incarnation in the womb of Mary. It was this mystery of personal unity that made Christ true redeemer of humankind in a mediatorial sense, not in the seemingly blurred familial distinctions of elder and younger brothers. The position of Mary as Mother of God, not merely mother of the man Jesus who was adopted as God, was a crucial corollary of this christological stance, as it had also been against Nestorius.[10]

At about the same time that Adoptionism came to the attention of Charlemagne a different challenge arose from another quarter. It was probably in 789 that the decrees of the Second Council of Nicaea against Iconoclasm reached the Frankish court from Rome. As is well known, the Council had brought an end to the policy of the destruction of religious images.[11] Iconoclasm had been based upon a theology that said that a material image could in no way resemble its prototype, a spiritual reality, and therefore was unworthy of veneration. The Council reaffirmed the spiritual character of icons, and pronounced them worthy of veneration *(proskynesis)*. The decrees were sent to Rome along with a statement of faith, where they were translated into Latin and disseminated. However, the Latin translation was so poor that it grossly misrepresented the Greek position as "worship" *(adoratio)* of images.[12]

In addition to this, the Byzantine credal statement did not include a phrase which had become traditional in Western usage: the *filioque.* This was, of course, the phrase that had been interpolated into the Nicene Creed in Spain, which stated that the Holy Spirit "proceeded from the Father and the Son." Carolingian scholars were fully aware that the *filioque* phrase was an interpolation. However, arising in tandem with the Adoptionist christological challenge, such an omission by the Greeks took on serious dimensions. Although the Greeks never spoke of the veneration of images and the nature of art as a trinitarian issue, the Carolingian response, the *Libri Carolini* did make such a connection, claiming that because the Byzantines misunderstood the very nature of God, they also worshipped images.[13] Such confusion over the nature of the divine inevitably led to idolatry, worship of things that were not divine. The *Libri* went on to deny any spiritual character to images, claiming an essential difference between an image and the prototype to which it referred. An image was a likeness *(similitudo)* of the transcendent spiritual reality but was not in itself and could never be that reality.

The response of Charlemagne and his circle of scholars to the emergence of these challenges to the faith was immediate. Once the errors of the Byzantine decrees were identified, Theodulf of Orléans undertook the writing of the *Libri Carolini* in response. The list of chapters, or *reprehensia*, were ready by 792. In the same year, Felix of Urgel, the most sophisticated defender of Adoptionism and Bishop of the Carolingian see of Urgel, was called before the Synod of Regensburg to explain his views. Felix was condemned, and Angilbert of Saint-Riquier was commissioned to take him to Rome to make his recantation before the Pope. Angilbert also carried with him the *reprehensia* for papal approval.[14]

Despite his recantation Felix again took up his Adoptionism when he returned to Spain. He was again called to the court to explain his views, this time before the general Council of Frankfurt in 794, which again condemned him. The Council produced two synodal letters containing the scriptural and patristic refutations and included a strong anti-Adoptionist letter from Pope Hadrian. This letter made an explicit connection between the procession of the Holy Spirit and the true Sonship of Jesus in an argument which would subsequently be more fully developed by Alcuin and Paulinus:

> Over whom do you judge that the Holy Spirit descended in the form of a dove, over God or over man, or, on account of the one person of Christ, over the Son of God and of Man? For the Holy Spirit, since he is inseparably of both, namely of the Father and the Son, and proceeds essentially from the Father and the Son *(ex patre filioque)*, by what means can he be believed to have descended over God, from whom he had never withdrawn and from whom he proceeds always ineffably? For the Son of God, according to that which is God, because the Father was never withdrawing from him, sent the Holy Spirit in an unspeakable way; and according to that which is man, received the one coming over him.[15]

The Council also took up the question of images, and anathematized the claim that images should be worshipped just as the Trinity. It did not, however, formally promulgate the *Libri*. Pope Hadrian's response to the *reprehensia* had arrived in 793 and had rejected the *Libri's* theological position, claiming, rightly, that it was a misreading of the Greek view. Thus, formal work on the treatise was brought to an end, though the statement was still made politically through the Council.[16]

Despite his second condemnation, Felix of Urgel continued to refine his Adoptionist arguments in further teachings. In 796 Paulinus convoked the Synod of Friuli to clarify trinitarian and christological doctrine. He defined the *filioque* as the critical component in trinitarian belief, arguing that the very oneness of the Trinity demanded the simultaneous procession to affirm the equality of Father and Son.[17] With Alcuin, Paulinus now promoted the Creed as the most effective tool for teaching the faith, which became a permanent part of the Mass by 798 in Carolingian lands. In response to Felix's increasingly strident writings, a final anti-Adoptionist assault was undertaken, and Felix was condemned at Aachen in 799 to be held under house arrest in Lyons until his death.[18] Theodulf and Benedict of Aniane continued the campaign in Septimania, succeeding finally in eliminating Adoptionism there.[19]

As this summary will show, the Carolingian participants in these battles perceived an inherent connection between correct belief in the Trinity and Christ, the *filioque,* Marian theology, and the nature of religious art. Theodulf, Benedict, and Angilbert were all involved in this campaign. Let us turn now to the churches they built during these years.

THE CHURCHES AND THEIR RELIGIOUS ART

Theodulf and Germigny-des-Prés

We may begin with the most well-known program, Theodulf of Orléans' little church at Germigny-des-Prés. The church at Germigny seems to have been a chapel attached to Theodulf's villa. The current building is a reconstruction, since the original chapel was destroyed; unfortunately the reconstruction is not faithful to the original. Only the apsidal area and its mosaic remain from Theodulf's structure.[20] These, however, reveal a great deal about Theodulf's vision and interests.

The apse was decorated only with stucco borders surmounted by the Ark of the Covenant held by two angels and two cherubim. As a motif placed directly over the altar this was a subject unique in Western iconography. The traditional presentation would have been the Ark borne by Levites in a narrative sequence along the base of the apse. The placement and the iconography thus express the dogmatic and symbolic character rather than the narrative character of the subject.[21]

There are close parallels between the stuccos and mosaic on the one hand and the illuminations of Theodulfian Bibles on the other, and these underscore the aesthetic principles put forth in the *Libri Carolini*. They express what has been called a fundamental artistic iconoclasm, at least in religious art.[22] This austere decorative program, centered on the Ark of the Covenant, represented a principal element of Theodulfian spirituality: the primacy of the Word over the Image.[23] This particular choice of motif is significant, since the Ark of the Covenant was explicitly mentioned in the *Libri* as a special case in religious art. The *Libri* distinguished certain types of sacred art that, because consecrated, were of a particular character and effect. These were *res sacratae*: the Eucharist, liturgical vessels, the Cross, Scripture, and the Ark of the Covenant. Because these objects were blessed by God, they had a direct contact with the holy. Because they received the operation of divine grace, they either mediated that grace to humans, as in the Eucharist and the liturgy, or reminded believers of spiritual mysteries, such as the Cross and the Ark of the Covenant.[24] Thus, although a variety of iconographical interpretations have been advanced stressing the importance of Old Testamentalism for Theodulf, the central concern expressed in Germigny's mosaic is closely and specifically related to the image controversy and the issues set forth in the *Libri Carolini*. This mosaic, with its simple, severe, and unambiguous portrayal, denies the ability of images or material symbols in any way to express spiritual truths. As a *res sacrata*, the Ark focuses the viewer on one overriding mystery: the binding power of the Word of God expressed through ineffable grace.

Benedict's Aniane

The few scholars who have studied Benedict's program at Aniane have also stressed the Old Testamental character of his iconography.[25] Given the fact that Benedict founded Aniane at the time that he was involved in the anti-Adoptionist effort, however, the evidence warrants a fresh consideration.

Benedict's disciple and biographer, Ardo Smaragdus, tells us that Benedict founded Aniane on his family patrimony in Septimania, probably sometime around 782. It was precisely at this time that Adoptionism became a serious challenge in Septimania.[26] By 786 Adoptionist numbers were so strong in the territory that Pope Hadrian thought it necessary to condemn the teachings of Elipandus of Toledo in a letter.[27] Benedict seems to have completed the building of his monastery in the early 790s, because Charlemagne granted Aniane an immunity which brought the abbot to court in 792 at the same time that the Synod of Regensburg was investigating Felix's theology. Subsequently, Benedict was one of the primary agents of the anti-Adoptionist effort in Septimania. As Heil has pointed out, it was due primarily to the work of Benedict, both through his anti-Adoptionist campaign and through the spread of his monastic reform, that Adoptionism was defeated in Septimania.[28]

Despite his pragmatic focus Benedict did write two anti-Adoptionist treatises: the *Opuscula*, an argument from Scripture on the coequality, coeternity, and consubstantiality of the Trinity, and the *Disputatio adversus Felicianam impietatem*, which presented the scriptural authorities on christology.[29] These were probably written in the late 790s during the final campaign against Adoptionism after the condemnation of Felix at the Synod of Aachen.

Ardo provides a description primarily of the liturgical furniture of Benedict's church. According to his account there was already near the site a preexisting church that the monks rededicated in honor of Mary the Mother of God.[30] Ardo described the main church of the cloister in great detail, in a passage worth quoting in full:

> Indeed the venerable father Benedict, surpassing in pious consideration, determined to consecrate the aforesaid church not in the dedication of any saints whatsoever, but to use, as we have already said, the name of the sacred Trinity. So that, I say, it might be recognized in clear daylight, he resolved that three altars be placed under the main altar, which is understood to be the principal one, so that in these the persons of the Trinity might be understood to be signified symbolically. And this is a marvelous arrangement, that in three altars the undivided Trinity and in one high altar the Deity

constant in essence might be shown. Indeed that high altar is solid on the outside, but hollow on the inside, so that what Moses built in the desert earlier, containing the small dwelling place of God, was clearly prefiguring where the reliquaries are kept enclosed on ferial days, with the various relics of the Fathers. Let these words about the altars suffice. Let us continue on succinctly to the vessels of the church, by what order and number they are arranged. Indeed, all vessels which are kept in that church we know to be consecrated to the septenary number. There are, namely, a seven-branched candlestick made wondrously by the workman's art, from whose trunk proceed branches and small spheres and lilies, reeds and goblets in the manner of nut-trees made, namely, in the likeness of that which Beseleel put together with wondrous skill. Before the high altar stand seven lamps, magnificent and most beautiful, made with inestimable effort, which are said by those who are experienced in such matters and who long to see them, to have been cast in the manner of Solomon. Other silver lamps in the manner of crowns, just as great, hang in the choir, which receive small ladles all around on rings inserted in themselves; and by special custom on festal days, filled with oil, they are lit; and these having been lit, the entire church glitters both day and night. And finally, three altars are dedicated in that same basilica: namely, one in honor of Saint Michael the Archangel, another in veneration of the blessed Apostles Peter and Paul, the third in honor of the soul of the protomartyr Stephen. In the church, truly, of Blessed Mary Mother of God, which was founded earlier, are seen to be kept the altars of Saint Martin and moreover of Blessed Benedict. And that which stands founded in the cemetery is distinguished as consecrated in honor of Saint John the Baptist, him whom no one born of women has risen up greater, as divine oracles attest. It pleases to consider with how much humility and reverence this place must be held in awe, which is known to have been protected by so many princes as these. Indeed the Lord Christ is Prince of all princes, King of kings and Lord of lords; truly his same blessed Mary Mother of God is believed to be Queen of all virgins; Michael is praised of all angels; Peter and Paul are the heads of the apostles; Stephen the protomartyr holds first place in the choir of witnesses; Martin truly shines forth as the jewel of protectors; Benedict is father of all monks. And in the seven altars, in the seven-branched candlestick and in seven lamps is understood the septiform grace of the Holy Spirit.[31]

Bloch has cited this passage as evidence of Benedict's Old Testamental spirituality. Ardo's citation of Moses, of Solomon, and of the seven-branched candlestick and other utensils in groups of seven is proof for him that the essential impulse behind Benedict's work was to recreate in new form the Temple of Solomon. Even being mindful of the multivalence of symbolism and of the inclusiveness of Carolingian spirituality which sought legitimacy in many kinds of authority, Ardo's words express a rather different impulse.

First, Ardo took pains to stress the fact that Benedict chose to consecrate his church "not in the dedication of any saints whatsoever, but of the sacred Trinity" *(non in alicuius sanctorum pretitulatione, set* [sic] *in deificae Trinitatis)*. It was for that reason *(quod ut)* that he placed three small altars *(tres aras)* in the main altar *(in altare, quod potissimum ceteris videtur)*, "so that in these the persons of the Trinity might seem to be signified symbolically" *(ut in his personalitas trinitatis typice videatur significari)*. Ardo likened this great altar to the Ark of the Covenant which Moses built only to say that the Ark was its prefiguration *(illud videlicet prefigurans, quod Moyses condidit in heremum)*, in the sense that just as the Ark contained the small dwelling place of God *(hostiolum)*, so this altar contained reliquaries with various relics of the Fathers *(quo privatis diebus inclusae tenentur capsae cum diversis reliquiis patrum)*.

Ardo then went on to describe the holy vessels and utensils in the church, "consecrated in the septenary number" *(in septenario numero consecrata noscuntur)*. When he cited Solomon, he did so by way of pointing out the beauty and majesty of the lamps (which he distinguished from the seven-branched candlestick): "Before the altar hang seven wondrous and most beautiful lamps, made with inestimable effort, which are said by those who are experienced in such matters and who long to see them, to have been cast in the manner of Solomon" *(Ante altare etiam septem dependunt lampade mirae atque pulquerrimae, inaestimabili fusae labore, quae a peritis, qui eas visere exoptant, Salomonaico dicuntur conflatae)*. Here the Old Testament references are meant not so much to invoke an exact identity as to describe an appearance or character. Ardo did, however, invoke an exact identity: adding up the total number of altars, the candlestick, and the lamps, he described the repetitious use of the number seven in the following terms: "Therefore, in the seven altars, the seven-branched candlestick, and the seven lamps is understood the septiform grace of the Holy Spirit" *(In septem itaque altaria, in semptem candelabra et in septem lampades septiformis gratia Spiritus sancti intelligitur)*. Thus, in the arrangement of his church Benedict repeatedly used the numbers three and seven with the intention of stressing symbolically the Trinity and the Holy Spirit.

Angilbert's Saint-Riquier

Like Benedict, Angilbert's contributions to the resolution of the theological controversies were pragmatic rather than theoretical. A close confidant of Charlemagne and prominent in the administration of the court of Pavia under Pepin in the 780s, Angilbert became Charlemagne's representative to the Pope on these theological issues. He was probably present at the Synod of Regensburg in 792 when it condemned Felix. In that year, Angilbert conducted Felix to his recantation in Rome. Angilbert also carried with him the *reprehensia* of the *Libri Carolini*.

In the same years, the early 790s, Angilbert was also rebuilding the old Frankish abbey of Saint-Riquier, to which he had been appointed as abbot by Charlemagne sometime around 789.[32] Founded originally in the seventh century in honor of Saint Richarius, a local Frankish holy man, Saint-Riquier had become an important royal monastery by the eighth century, given by Pepin to Widmar, one of his chancery secretaries. It had taken part in the prayer confraternity established by Chrodegang of Metz, as Widmar's signature of the acts of the Council of Attigny attests.[33] Angilbert razed the old buildings and built in their place a new and striking complex of three churches, joined by an arcade that gave the monastery the general shape of a triangle. According to his own description of the new buildings and the liturgy celebrated there, Saint-Riquier housed three hundred monks divided into three *laus perennis* choirs.[34] The monastic churches contained a total of thirty altars; in those of two of the churches, the relics were arranged three by three, that is, the relics of three saints included in each. These are just some of many such numerical references Angilbert makes.

While many scholars have noted the prominent imagery of the number three, none have taken it at face value as indicative of

Angilbert's intent in rebuilding the abbey.[35] Yet he described his purpose in just these terms:

> So that, therefore, all the people of the faithful should confess, venerate, worship with the heart and firmly believe in the most holy and undivided Trinity, we, with God cooperating and my aforementioned august lord helping, have been zealous to found in this holy place three principal churches with the members belonging to them, according to the program of that faith in the name of almighty God.[36]

Angilbert went on to say that this "program of the faith" would be expressed both "in marble buildings and in other decorations ... and also in the praises of God, in various teachings and in spiritual songs."[37] This reveals a program both rich and comprehensive, in which architecture and liturgy were tightly and intentionally integrated to achieve the fullest possible symbolic value.

Three elements particularly illustrate Angilbert's purpose. The first is the conceptual structure of the main basilica. The second is the abbot's integration of Marian concerns into the monastic complex. The third is his carefully orchestrated involvement of the local laity in the program. Let us turn first to the architectural conceptualization of the Basilica of Saint-Riquier and the Holy Savior.

Scholars have traditionally studied the basilica as the first prominent example of a westwork church (a church with a western, as well as the traditional eastern, apse), the prototype not only of Carolingian westwork churches but also of subsequent Romanesque monumental facades. Recent excavations of the Carolingian level of the basilica have revealed that the western end of the church was not a true westwork, but rather a monumental polygonal tower with *augmenta* somewhat smaller than the eastern transept.[38] Nevertheless, the new emphasis on the western end of the church and its liturgical integration into the complex were innovative.

This western structure functioned as a second church, and Angilbert refers to it as a church in his account.[39] This was a two-story polygonal tower with a chapel on the second floor. The chapel contained the altar of the Holy Savior, one of the three principal altars of the monastery (along with the altar of Saint Richarius in the eastern apse, and the altar of Mary, Mother of God in the Mary chapel). Thus this altar was covered by a stone canopy. The eastern transept and apse were dedicated to Saint Richarius, whose relics along with those of Frichor and Chaidoc lay in the crypt below. The altar of the saint, also covered with a stone canopy, lay in the square apse beyond the transept. The eastern and western facades of the basilica were mirror images: the transepts surmounted by a massive tower with a three-tiered lantern, each tower, in turn, flanked by two narrow towers *(cocleae)*. Thus there was a continual rhythmic architectural pattern of threes.

This numerical pattern seems to have been carried through the organization of the basilica's interior space. The available dimensions and arrangement of piers within the church suggest a modular structure similar to and predating that at Saint Gall. Modularity characterized Carolingian ecclesiastical architecture. Churches were organized spatially according to square dimensions based upon the transept crossing.[40] The crossing provided the basis from which all other proportions of the building were developed, the module from which the nave, aisles and apse were calculated. While we do not have exact dimensions for Angilbert's basilica, the module of the transept crossings was ten meters square, or thirty by thirty Carolingian feet.[41]

Other elements of the interior decor were also innovative. The basilica contained four reliefs that were unique in their time. They served as the focal points of liturgical celebrations and of the decoration of the church. Angilbert described the reliefs as the Nativity, the Passion, the Resurrection and the Ascension.[42] The biblical texts of these events were key elements of the anti-Adoptionist treatises.[43] As can best be reconstructed from the liturgical prescriptions, the Nativity stood at the entrance of the basilica. The Passion probably stood over the central nave at the entrance to the eastern transept. The Resurrection and Ascension seem to have stood over the side arches of the nave, just before the Passion. The liturgy of the office of the Dead also indicates that the important altar of the Holy Cross, repeatedly a focal point for specific liturgical celebrations, stood in the center of the nave before the relief of the Passion and between the Resurrection and the Ascension.[44]

Within this physical space a carefully structured liturgy unfolded. The daily liturgy consisted of the office, Masses, and processions between the basilica, the Mary church, and the chapel of Saint Benedict. Each office was sung antiphonally between the three choirs at the basilica, one choir at the altar of the Holy Savior, one at the altar of Saint Richarius, and one before the relief of the Passion. At the completion of Lauds and Vespers, the choirs lined up *(ordinabiliter)* before the Passion. Ten cantors from the choirs remained at that spot while the rest, chanting, processed through the atrium and the western part of the cloister to the Mary chapel, where they prayed the seasonal prayers. They then continued to the chapel of Benedict in the eastern part of the cloister and returned to the basilica where they again formed three choirs.[45] In this way the daily celebration of the Office involved the entire monastic complex and community in a liturgy that repeatedly stressed trinitarian imagery.

The festal liturgies took place in the locations evoked specifically by the day. Most important were the Easter celebrations, which centered liturgically on the Church of the Holy Savior (not, it should be noted at the altar of Saint Richarius, which normally would be considered the principal altar of the basilica). Let us examine a portion of this liturgy.

On Palm Sunday the vigil offices were sung as usual in the basilica. However, the monks sang Tierce at the Mary chapel, distributing palms and branches and then processed to the basilica together with the local community who had gathered at the monastery. There all stopped before the relief of the Nativity where they said prayers, and all then climbed to the Church of the Holy Savior where mass was sung. On Good Friday adoration of the Cross was celebrated at the altar of the Holy Cross in the basilica in the presence of the local populace. Three crosses were adored, one by the monks themselves, one by the schola of boys at the monastery, and the third by the *populus*.[46]

Only the monastic community celebrated the liturgies of Holy Saturday. The Office took place entirely in the basilica. At the completion of Vespers the choirs sang the litany of the saints and prayers at the baptismal font *(ad fontes)*. While the *schola cantorum* sang in the Church of the Holy Savior, the ministers prepared for Mass which they celebrated in the same church. The Mass included three sets of litanies: those repeated seven times, those repeated five, and those repeated three. Finally, all three choirs sang Compline and Matins at the Church of the Holy Savior.[47] On Easter Sunday, the monks celebrated a special procession, Mass, and Office. The townpeople *(populus)* attended the Mass at the Church of the Holy Savior and participated in communion with the monks. Angilbert repeatedly stressed the paramount importance of the common worship of the entire community together:

> But while the brothers and the rest of the clergy receive communion from that priest who shall have sung the Mass on that day, let two other priests with two deacons and subdeacons give communion, one to the men, the other to the women in that same church (the Holy Savior), so that the clergy and the people, having received communion at the same time, can likewise hear the benediction or the completion of the Mass. When this is finished, let them exit at the same time, praising God and blessing the Lord.[48]

It is worth noting that, although we no longer have the texts for the liturgies of Christmas, the references in the Paschal texts indicate that they were very similar to those of Easter. Thus, on the two greatest feasts of the year, the Birth and the Passion and Resurrection of Christ, the ritual celebration brought together "all the people of the faithful" in a very specific and symbolic ritual space. The central redemptive mysteries of the Incarnation and the Passion, of Christ as God and Man, were celebrated at the western altar of the Holy Savior, while the adoration of the Cross was at the altar of the Holy Cross before the sculptural reliefs of the Passion, Resurrection, and Ascension.

The second aspect of Angilbert's program which is significant in the context of the theological controversies is his integration of Marian theology into the monastic complex. As has already been noted above, the Mary chapel was an important element of the daily processional liturgy at Saint-Riquier. The church, whose foundations have been entirely excavated by Honoré Bernard, was a central form dodecagonal church with a basilican entrance in the west. The dodecagonal body of the church contained an ambulatory and an inner wall or pillars and arches meant probably to support an upper story. The dodecagonal structure was about eighteen to twenty meters in diameter, and the nave of the basilican entranceway approximately eight meters long and nine meters wide.[49]

The central altar was dedicated to Mary, Mother of God *(Sancta Maria Dei Genetrix)*, containing her relics and those of nine virgin martyrs. As one of the three principal altars of the cloister, it was surmounted by a stone canopy. This altar was, in turn, surrounded by twelve altars, one on each wall of the church. Each of these contained three sets of relics, those of the Apostle to whom the altar was dedicated and those of two other saints.[50]

The liturgies celebrated in this church were as evocative and specific as those of the Holy Savior. As may be expected, the monks celebrated the liturgies of the Marian feasts here. These included the Assumption, the Nativity, and the Purification of the Virgin.[51] More important, however, was the celebration of the feast of Pentecost. This was the only day in the calendar of Saint-Riquier, as least as far as can be known, that the Masses took place here. Thus, the Mary chapel held special meaning with regard to this feast.

According to the biblical account, on Pentecost the disciples were assembled in the Upper Room with Mary.[52] Angilbert's architectural arrangement of the Mary altar surrounded by the altars of the Apostles parallels a somewhat later illumination of the scene which may help us interpret his iconography. The mid-ninth-century Bible of Charles the Bald presents the Pentecost scene as occurring in a polygonal Upper Room in which Mary is seated in the center, surrounded by the Apostles who sit on benches along the walls. What is striking in both versions is the inclusion of Mary, since in extant earlier-ninth-century examples such as the Drogo Sacramentary and ivory book covers only the Apostles are included in the Pentecost event. While in Byzantine representations the inclusion of Mary was common, it was not so in Carolingian portrayals. Thus, Angilbert's architectural iconography stressed the central importance of Mary's presence at the moment of the fullest revelation of the trinitarian faith, the descent of the Holy Spirit.

Angilbert's involvement of the local laity in the liturgy and architectural iconography of the monastery was essential given his stated purpose to create an architecture and liturgy that would inspire the correct faith in believers. The participation of the *populus* in the Easter and Christmas liturgies has been discussed above. These were focused on a symbolism of place. Angilbert invoked an even more striking symbolism of number in his celebration of Rogations, in which the "program of the faith" was carried through liturgical symbolism to the towns surrounding Saint-Riquier.[53]

Rogations were, of course, the annual ritual of prayers, litanies and processions for reconciliation with God that took place immediately before the feast of the Ascension. Angilbert's prescriptions followed the Gallican tradition of three days of penitential processions (rather than the Roman one-day celebration). His was an elaborate ritual that incorporated not only the local townspeople of Saint-Riquier but the populaces of the seven neighboring towns, each of which was to send a procession and a processional cross.

Angilbert choreographed his Rogations processions in minute detail. On the first day, all participants convened in the atrium of the basilica, before the Nativity, and began with prayers. They then processed in the following order: those carrying three vases of holy water, three censers, and seven crosses from the monastery with the cross of the Holy Savior in the middle. Seven reliquaries followed with the great reliquary of the Holy Savior in the center, followed by seven deacons, seven subdeacons, seven acolytes, seven exorcists, seven lectors, seven porters, and the rest of the monks in ranks of seven by seven. The lay participants followed in the same ordering by sevens, according to their hierarchical ranks. They processed around the monastery chanting specified prayers. The monks sang psalms, and the others sang the three creeds (Apostle's, Constantinopolitan, and Athanasian), the Lord's Prayer, and the general litany. All then sang together three litanies, the Gallican, the Italic, and the Roman. After prayers, the monks celebrated Mass at the Church of the Holy Savior. On the second and third days, the participants followed the same procedures. On the second day they processed to two neighboring towns, finishing with Mass at the Church of Saint Richarius. The third day they visited two other towns, and the monks returned for Mass at the Mary church while the people returned for Mass at their own churches.

Two elements of this liturgy must be noted. First, the singing of three creeds by all of the laity is significant. No such practice is recorded in general Rogations ritual, which comprised the chanting of litanies of supplication, the reading of set passages from the Old and New Testaments, specific prayers, and the Constantinopolitan Creed. Angilbert's prescription of three creeds and the Lord's prayer echoes directly the frequent injunctions of Charlemagne's capitularies that the laity be able to recite these four *memoriter*.[54] It also echoes Paulinus's campaign for the creed as the key to teaching the faith. The constant repetition of the formulae of the faith, and especially of the three creeds, underscored Angilbert's concern that the monastery lead the faithful to correct belief.

The second notable element is the strict ordering of the processions in ranks of seven. Rogations processions were so ordered in Rome, where they represented the seven regions of the city. But Angilbert's own intention was doctrinal: "And we determined for this purpose to walk seven at a time, so that in our work we reveal thanks for the septiform grace of the Holy Spirit."[55]

THE NATURE OF RELIGIOUS SYMBOLS

Angilbert's emphasis on numerical symbolism was consistent with what Benedict also established at Aniane. The incorporation of the numbers three and seven in the churches of both monasteries—as well as the dedication of individual churches within those monasteries to Mary Mother of God—are understandable within the context of the theological controversies over Adoptionism and the *filioque*. Liturgy was a primary vehicle by which the truths of the faith were to be expressed and through which participants were united with that truth. Even the iconoclastic *Libri Carolini* valued certain liturgical symbolism as such a vehicle. A number of references in the theological texts of the anti-Adoptionist and image struggles illuminate the climate of thought in which these men were working.

The opening lines of the *Libri Carolini* stressed the inherent relationship between correct faith and liturgy, and especially the role of the liturgy in expressing the trinitarian faith:

> The Church sets forth through the parts of threefold prayer the mystery of the holy Trinity, while its words must be grasped by the ears of the divine majesty, that is, it prays the melody of psalmody, which it displays without ceasing, and it also prays out with a devoted heart the acclamation which must be understood, that is, the love of the heart, which is received wonderfully not with fleshly ears, but with the ineffable hearing of divine majesty; and it entreats that the voice of its prayer be stretched forth so that it might declare, namely, that this is perfect prayer which inflames the love of a burning heart. And although it intermingles our senses with words changed metaphorically, nevertheless it believes that the divine nature does

not separate the things that are to be separated with the parts of its members, but goes through all things with one power, who hears all things that are seen by us and sees into that which we have thought and are going to think; nor is anything able to hide from this ineffable light. For indeed, to grasp words, to understand the sound, to strain toward the voice of prayer although they be brought forth again and again under a variety of words through that type of speech which is called *metabole* by the rhetoricians, nevertheless the threefold repetition signifies one and the same thing. Even while it says in the invocation of both the King and the Lord God: "Because I will cry to you O Lord my King and my God," it demonstrates that it believes in and confesses three persons and one substance in divinity, because it interposes to the invocation of three names not plural, but singular words.[56]

The meaning of the threefold prayer was direct. The repetition three times of the same prayer confessed the Trinity, *("tres personas et unam substantiam in divinitate)*, "Three persons and one substance in divinity." Liturgy had a double purpose and effect. It was to "seize the ears of divine majesty" *(auribus divinae maiestatis percipienda)*, and to "inflame the love of a burning heart," *(mentis affectus ardentis inflammat)* as the inspiration and expression of the believer. In this way the threefold prayer, which the *Libri* defined as the heart of the liturgy, created a real bond between God and the believer. As *oratio perfecta* it assured a hearing from God, and it inspired desire for God in the heart of the believer.

There was a deeper meaning beneath the sensate effect: the intention and desire of the believer, "the acclamation which must be understood, that is, love of the heart, which is received wonderfully not with fleshly ears, but with the ineffable hearing of divine majesty" *(clamorem intelligendum, id est cordis affectum, qui non auribus carnalibus, sed ineffabilibus divinae maiestatis auditibus mirabiliter excipitur)*. Love of the heart was the internal commitment of the one who prayed. Thus, Theodulf understood liturgy which expressed the Trinity to be critical to the growth of the internal conviction of faith. This revelation was in fact the Church's function: "it reveals unceasingly through the parts of threefold prayer the mystery of the holy Trinity" *(quae incessanter per partes trinae orationis mysterium sanctae Trinitatis exponit)*.

Angilbert expressed a similar view of liturgy but one which placed a much greater weight on material symbols:

> Since our churches have been elegantly ordered and ornamented by these and other of the diverse and aforementioned relics of the saints mentioned above, as we were able to do, Lord granting, we have begun with diligence of heart to treat how, Lord granting, we were able to persist, so that just as in marble buildings and the rest of the decorations churches shine forth for human eyes so also they grow more clearly in the praises of God, in various doctrines and in spiritual songs, in our own and future times, in the strengthening increase of faith, God helping, today and unto eternal salvation.[57]

Indeed, liturgical symbolism and its relationship to correct belief had emerged as an issue in the Adoptionist controversy, over the question of Adoptionist baptismal practice. As a consequence of the long struggle with Arianism, the Visigothic Church came to practice single-immersion baptism, but there is no evidence whatsoever that Visigothic or Adoptionist baptismal practice was heterodox.[58] Alcuin, however, drew such a conclusion. Baptism, and especially biblical texts about the baptism of Christ had become an important christological proof, and both Alcuin and Paulinus cited these texts repeatedly. Alcuin addressed the question of the symbolism and liturgy of the sacrament in a letter to the monks of Septimania attacking Adoptionist single immersion. Here he drew an absolute relationship between the liturgical symbolism and the quality of belief:

> And indeed, a third question from Spain—which was once the mother of tyrants, but now of schismatics—has been brought down to us against the universal custom of the holy Church on baptism. For they say that one immersion must be performed under the invocation of the holy Trinity. The Apostle, however, seems to be against this observation in that place where he said: "For you are buried together with Christ through baptism." For we know that Christ . . . was in the tomb for three days and three nights. . . . Three immersions can symbolize the three days and three nights . . . For it seems to us . . . that just as the interior man must be reformed in the faith of the holy Trinity into its image, so the exterior man must be washed by the third immersion, so that that which the Spirit works invisibly in the soul the priest should visibly imitate in the water.[59]

Alcuin's opinion was unequivocal. The symbolic action of the liturgy brought about a change in the recipient of the sacrament, and that symbolic action grew from or concretized the *fides recta* of the believer. One could not be altered or manipulated without destroying the other two. Thus the effect of the perverted dogma of Adoptionism extended to the very moral condition of each Adoptionist, who could not be washed clean of sin in baptism if neither believing nor praying correctly. Alcuin drew the distinction even more finely in another passage from the same letter in which he considered the interior, spiritually catalytic effect of the symbol:

> To us, however, according to the meagerness of our paltry talent, it seems that just as the interior man must be reformed into the image of his Creator in the faith of the holy Trinity, so the exterior man must be washed with the three-fold immersion, so that, that which the Spirit invisibly effects in the soul, the priest visibly imitates in the water. For original sin is worked in three ways: by desire, consent, and act. And so, because all sin is accomplished either by desire, or consent, or doing, so the three-fold ablution seems to accord with the triple nature of sins. . . . And rightly is the man, who was created in the image of the holy Trinity, renewed into that same image through the invocation of the holy Trinity: and he who fell into death by the third degree of sin, that is, by the work, lifted from death rises into life through grace.[60]

There is no empty formalism in this explanation. Alcuin's concern is the regenerative or recreative potency of the symbol of baptism and Trinity-invoking triple immersion.

This far Theodulf, Benedict, and Angilbert could come together. Yet both Aniane and Saint-Riquier were architectural programs strikingly different from that of Theodulf, whose reluctance to accept the expression of spiritual truths in physical symbolic terms permeated the *Libri*. The expressive liturgy of Saint-Riquier and the numerical arrangements of liturgical implements at Aniane represent the strongest possible contrasts to the symbolic reticence of Germigny-des-Prés. We have only Ardo's account of Aniane, which gives us little further insight into Benedict's aesthetic understanding. Ann Freeman has convincingly suggested that Theodulf's spirituality was rooted in a Hebraic conservatism characteristic of Visigothic Spain and that this explains the conservatism of his understanding of symbols. What accounts for the sensuous character of Angilbert's program?

We have a glimpse into Angilbert's aesthetic understanding through a dedicatory poem that he wrote in 796 for a manuscript of the *De doctrina christiana* which he was offering as a gift to Louis the Pious when Louis was King of Aquitaine. In this poem, Angilbert revealed a deep awareness of Augustine's theory of symbols and of the material world as ordered by "number, measure and weight."[61] While much of the poem is taken up with praise of King Louis, the rest reveals two fundamental elements of Angilbert's aesthetic philosophy in describing Augustine's. The passages here follow:

I

Primus enim narrat Christi praecepta tenere,	For the first explains how to keep the teachings of Christ
Quae servare Deus iussit in orbe pius:	Which God, the Righteous One commanded us to observe on earth:
Rebus uti saecli insinuans praesentibus apte	suggesting how to use the present goods of the world well
Aeternisque frui rite docet nimium.	It also rightly teaches how to enjoy eternal goods to the utmost.
Edocet ex signis variis secundus,	The second instructs by different signs and objects
Qualiter aut quomodo noscere signa queant.	How and in what way signs can be known.
Tertius ex hisdem signis verbisque nitescit:	The third glitters with these same signs and words:
Quid sint, quid valeant quaequevitanda, canit	It sings about what they are, what their power is, and which must be avoided.
Tunc promit quartus librorum dicta priorum:	Then the fourth sends forth the teachings of the prior books:
Quid res, quid signa, quid pia verba docent,	That very book intones with a great expression, what objects, what signs, what pious words teach,
Qualiter et possint cuncta intellecta referre	And how they can refer to all intuited things. . . .
Magno sermone intonat ipse liber. . . .	

II

Haec perlecta pii,	Continually and devotedly
lector doctrina patroni,	pour out as kind praises, reader,
In primis domino,	These teachings of the pious
totum qui condidit orbem,	patron, thoroughly grasped
Devote laudes iugiter	To the Lord who in the beginning
perfunde benignas,	founded the whole earth,
Qui mare fundavit, caelum	Who poured the sea, who
terramque creavit,	created heaven and earth,
Omnia qui numero, mensura	Who enclosed everything by
ac pondere clausit,	number, measure and weight
Per quem cuncta manebunt,	remain and through whom all
	will remain,
Quae sunt, quae fuerant,	That are, that were, that
fuerint vel quaeque	have been and that will be.
futura.	

The lines in part I, summarizing the content of Augustine's four books, stress above all that truth is to be found in forms abstracted from concrete things. Those forms, eternal truths, are intuited from material reality and refer to the eternal world behind the signs: *quid res, quid signa, quid pia verba docent, qualiter et possint cuncta intellecta referre* (lines 16–17). In the second section of the poem, Angilbert teaches that such abstraction is possible, and the eternal world is objectively knowable, because the essence of the created world, the structure that underlies everything, is number: *omnia qui numero, mensura ac pondere clausit* (line 5). These words express the fundamental conviction that Creation is ordered by arithmetical truths. That order is divine, available to both sense and reason, and so it lifts the believer into the realm of the abstract. By feeling the proportionate harmonies and striving to comprehend the internal structures of things, the mind moves toward the truth of right belief in the eternal, unchanging Form that is God. The mind's eye perceives the truth. Even more striking is the fact that Angilbert's God is expressed as a number in the last line of the poem: "God who is reigning in the threefold name, alone above all things." (*nomine qui trino regnans super omnia solus*). God is the numerical form, the Three-in-One, the essence of both unity and multiplicity who gives and guarantees form in numbers to all things which are, have been, and will be, *quae sunt, quae fuerant, fuerint vel quaeque futura* (line 7). Thus signs and the very order of the universe point to the Creator behind them, and both give birth to and nurture correct and salvific faith.

Within this interpretive framework, the emphases of Angilbert's architectural symbolism become clear. Angilbert put into visual terms the association between number, Wisdom, and the vision of the threefold God that he described in his poem. His architecture, especially in conjunction with its liturgy, made explicit the great truths implicit in Creation. Angilbert embodied the number three everywhere. Three churches stood in a triangular cloister. Three main altars designated by three stone canopies were the sites of the main liturgies. Worshipers entered the basilica through three portals. There were three aisles in the basilica and three lecterns. Three towers surmounted the basilica at the west end, and three at the east. Three-tiered lanterns capped the towers. The modular dimensions of the basilica were compounds of the number three. There were thirty altars in the monastery. Three altars in the chapel of Saint Benedict each contained the relics of three saints. In the Mary chapel, the central altar contained the relics of three times three saints, and the Apostle altars each held the relics of three saints. Three hundred monks in three choirs chanted the Office. Three crosses were adored on Good Friday. Three crosses were followed with three holy water vases and three thuribles during three-day processions, and three creeds were sung at Rogations. Here were the physical traces which, in Augustinian terms, mediated a mystery. Without this insight there could be neither recognition of nor participation in divine truth which was the threefold name of God.

In this way Angilbert countered on every visual level the most fundamental challenge represented by the three theological controversies, the denial of the Trinity. Similarly the numerical repetition of the number seven, always with the reference in the texts to the septiform grace of the Holy Spirit, not only represented the Wisdom of the Spirit given to the true believer, but the proper belief in the Spirit challenged by the emerging *filioque* controversy. That challenge was, however, ultimately christological, as was Adoptionism, and the other innovations of Saint-Riquier address and underscore the Carolingian christological position. Angilbert expressed this in the ritual space of the Church of the Holy Savior and in the four reliefs of the basilica. Dedicated to Christ, and the place of celebration for the Nativity and Paschal mysteries, the Church of the Holy Savior stood in stone and prayer as the symbol of Christ himself. Incarnate as God-human on Christmas and as Redeemer in the Paschal Triduum, this was the mediatory Christ of the Carolingians against the Adoptionists.

The four reliefs strengthened the christological symbol. Their doctrinal clues were highly concentrated. Worshipers stood between the Passion and the Church of the Holy Savior, with the altar of the Holy Cross in the center as the sign of Christ's redemptive action. The proof of Christ's unique status as God-human stood in the reliefs of the Resurrection and the Ascension.

The dogma of Christ as truly God and truly human appeared yet again in the vocable of the Mary chapel: *Sancta Maria Dei Genetrix et Apostoli.* The incorporation of this chapel fully into the daily and festival liturgies of the monastery underscored the centrality of the doctrine of Mary as Mother of God for the christological argumentation against the Adoptionists. The celebration of Pentecost at this church expressed the fullest manifestation of the Trinity in its richest symbolic and theological expression.

Thus, church architecture became a principal means of combating the perceived theological aberrations which arose in the 780s and 790s for the Carolingians. In his concern to combat error in the worship of icons and misunderstanding of the Trinity Theodulf rejected the possibility that architecture could symbolically express divine truths, even while he upheld some of the evocative meaning of liturgy. Angilbert and Benedict embraced architectural symbols, and Angilbert integrated this tightly with his liturgy, as a way of teaching doctrine and enabling the mind's eye to see more clearly. In this way religious architecture became the teacher of the faithful, whether for what it said or for what it did not say, creatively forwarded as a source of authority for Carolingian culture in formation.

Notes

The author wishes to thank the University of Pennsylvania Press for permission to use materials from chapters 2, 4, and 5 of *Faith, Art and Politics at Saint-Riquier: The Symbolic Vision of Angilbert*. (Philadelphia: University of Pennsylvania Press, 1985).

1. See "Theodulf of Orléans and the *Libri Carolini*," *Speculum* 32 (1957), 663–705; "Further Studies in the *Libri Carolini* II," *Speculum* 40 (1965), 203–289; "Further Studies in the *Libri Carolini* III," *Speculum* 46 (1971), 597–611; and "Carolingian Orthodoxy and the Fate of the *Libri Carolini*," *Viator* 16 (1985), 65–108. The authorship of the *Libri* has been highly controversial. Cf. Paul Meyvaert, "The Authorship of the *Libri Carolini*: Observations Prompted by a Recent Book," *Revue Bénédictine* 89 (1979), 29–57. The traditional order and dating of events surrounding the *Libri* was established by Wolfram von den Steinen, "Entstehungsgeschichte der *Libri Carolini*," *Quellen und Forschungen aus italienischen Archiven und Bibliotheken* 21 (1929–30), 1–93. On Alcuin's proposed authorship of the text, see Jaffé, the editor of Alcuin's works, in the *Monumenta Alcuiniana*; Dümmler, who edited the *Libri* for the same collection; and more recently Luitpold Wallach in *Alcuin and Charlemagne, Studies in Carolingian History and Literature* (Ithaca, NY: Cornell University Press, 1959), Chapter 9 and *Diplomatic Studies in Latin and Greek Documents from the Carolingian Age* (Ithaca, NY: Cornell University Press, 1977), parts 2 and 3. For an important interpretation of the text within the larger context of Theodulf's thought, see Elisabeth Dahlhaus-Berg, *Nova Antiquas et Antiqua Novitas: typologische Exegese und isidorianisches Geschichtbild bei Theodulf von Orléans* (Cologne/Vienna: Böhlau, 1975), Chapter 4.

2. Walter Horn and Ernest Born, *The Plan of Saint Gall*, 3 volumes (Berkeley: University of California Press, 1979).

3. See "Allgemeine Tendenzen im Kirchenbau unter Ludwig dem Frommen," in Peter Godman and Roger Collins, editors, *Charlemagne's Heir: New Perspectives on the Reign of Louis the Pious* (Oxford: Clarendon Press, 1990), 641–654.

4. For an extensive discussion of these issues and a detailed analysis of the sources, see Susan Rabe, *Faith, Art, and Politics at Saint-Riquier: The Symbolic Vision of Angilbert*. (Philadelphia: University of Pennsylvania Press, 1995).

5. What follows on Adoptionism is based upon the following sources: Beatus and Etherius *Adversus Epipandum libri II*, Bengt Löfstedt, editor, CCCM 59 (Turnhout: Brepols, 1984); Elipandus *Epistula in Megetium* (*CSM* 1, pp. 67–78). *Epistula ad Alchuinum* (*CSM* 1, pp. 96–109), *Epistula ad Fidelem*

(*CSM* 1, pp. 80–81), *Symbolum fidei* (*CSM* 1, pp. 78–80), and *Epistola ad Carolum Magnum* (*MGH Epistolae* 4, number 182); Alcuin *Adversus Felicem lirbi VII* (*PL* 101, 127–230), *Liber contra haeresim Felicis*, Gary B. Blumenshine, editor, *Studi e Testi* 285 (Vatican City: Biblioteca Apostolica Vaticana, 1980), *Adversus Elipandum libri IV* (*PL* 101, 243–300), and *Epistolae* 23, 137, 139, 148, 149, 166, 200ff. (*MGH Epistolae* 4); and Paulinus of Aquileia *Contra Felicem libri III,* Dag Norberg, editor, CCCM 95 (Turnhout: Brepols, 1990) and the doctrinal statement from the Synod of Friuli of 796 (*MGH LL* 3, *CC* 2, pp. 180–189).Two secondary studies are indispensable; most important for a sensitive reassessment of the issues is John Cavadini, *The Last Christology of the West* (Philadelphia: University of Pennsylvania Press, 1993). Also important is Wilhelm Heil's closely argued chronology in *Alkuinstudien,* Volume 1 (Düsseldorf: Schwann, 1970), and "Der Adoptianismus, Alkuin und Spanien," in Wolfgang Braunfels, editor, *Karl der Grosse, Lebenswerk und Nachleben,* Volume 2: *Das geistige Leben* (Düsseldorf: Schwann, 1965), pp. 95ff. Cf. Knut Schäferdiek, "Der adoptianische Streit im Rahmen der spanischen Kirchengeschichte I und II," *Zeitschrift für Kirchengeschichte* 80 (1969), 291–311, and 81 (1970), 1–16; Jesus Solano, S.J., "El Concilio de Calcedonia y la controversia adopcianista del siglo VIII en España," in Aloys Grillmeier and Heinrich Bacht, *Das Konzil von Chalkedon,* Volume 20: *Entscheidung um Chalkedon* (Würzburg: n. pub., 1952), pp. 841–871, and Ramon Abadal y Vinyals, *La batalla del adopcionismo en la desintegración de la iglesia visigoda* (Barcelona: n. pub., 1949).

6. See Cavadini, p. 33, and Jaroslav Pelikan, *The Christian Tradition,* Volume 1 (Chicago: University of Chicago Press, 1971), 256–259; Elipandus *Epistola episcoporum Hispaniae ad episcopos Franciae* (*MGH LL* 2, 118).

7. Cf. Cavadini, p. 35.

8. *Codex Carolinus* 95; *Epistola Hadriani Papae ad episcopos Hispaniae directa* (*MGH LL* 3, *CC* 2, pp. 122–130). Cf. Cavadini, pp. 73–77.

9. On the biblical authorities and their use in the treatises, see Rabe, pp. 44–48.

10. Especially important here is Paulinus, *Contra Felicem* 1.8, 10–19, 23, 32–33, and 3.26 (Norberg, pp. 13–26, 28–9, 37–40, 115); and Alcuin, *Adversus Felicem* 2.11 (*PL* 101, 155). Cf. Rabe, p. 43.

11. On this controversy and the chronology of events, see note 1 above; the *Libri Carolini* have been edited in *MGH LL* 3, *CC* 2, *Supplementum.* Cf. Celia Chazelle, "Matter, Spirit, and Image in the *Libri Carolini,"* *Recherches Augustiniennes* 21 (1986), 163–184 for a sensitive interpretation of Theodulf's aesthetic philosophy.

12. This information comes from Anastasius Bibliothecarius. See *Sancta synodus septima generalis Nicaena secunda* (*PL* 129, 195).

13. The correct faith, including discussion of the *filioque,* is the subject of Book 3 of the *Libri.* Cf. Rabe, pp. 29–30.

14. See notes 5 and 11 above. See also *Annales qui dicuntur Einhardi* (also known as the *Annales regni francorum,* revised version), 792 (*MGH Scriptores* 1, p. 179) for the Synod of Regensburg.

15. *Epistola Hadriani I papae ad episcopos Hispaniae directa* (*MGH LL* 3, *CC* 2, p. 128): Super quem putatis spiritum sanctum, in specie columbae descendisse, super Deum ad super hominem, an propter unam personam Christi super Dei hominisque filium? Spiritus namque sanctus, cum sit inseparabiliter amborum, patris videlicet et filii, et ex patre filioque essentialiter procedat, quo pacto credi potest super Deum descendisse, a quo numquam recesserat et a quo ineffabiliter semper procedit? Dei enim filius secundum id, quod Deus est, sanctum spiritum cum patre numquam a se recedente inenarribili modo mittit et secundum id, quod homo est, super se venientem suscepit.

16. See especially Freeman, "Carolingian Orthodoxy," pp. 89ff.

17. This was, of course, the reason for the original interpolation of the *filioque* into the creed in the struggle against Arianism. For the Synod of Friuli see *MGH Leges* 3, *Concilia* 2, pp. 180–184. See also Bernard Capelle, "L'Origine antiadoptianiste de notre texte du Symbole de la messe," *Recherches de théologie ancienne et médiévale* 1 (1929), 7–20, and "Introduction du Symbole à la messe," *Mélanges Joseph de Ghellinck, S.J.,* Volume 2 (Gembloux: J. Duculot, 1951), 1010–1025.

18. This included Felix's introduction of a new term, *nuncupativus* or "by appellation only," into the debate. Thus, he said that Jesus was *Deus nuncupativus,* "God by appellation only," and Mary was *nuncupativus genetrix,* or "Mother of God by appellation only." This seemed more than ever to stress Nestorian dualism. See Paulinus *Contra Felicem* 1.15; it was against this new turn in the argument that Paulinus wrote this treatise. See also Alcuin *Adversus Felicem, Adversus Elipandum,* and *MGH Epp* 4, 139, 146, 148, 149, 160, 166, 171 and 172; and Cavadini, pp. 89ff.

19. See Heil, "Adoptianismus, Alkuin, und Spanien," pp. 106–7, and an untitled poem of Theodulf lauding the monks of Benedict at Aniane (*MGH PL* 1, pp. 520–522).

20. See above, note 1, for the references on the *Libri Carolini* and Germigny. On Germigny, see Jean Hubert, "L'église de Germigny-des-Prés," *Congrès Archéologiques de France* 93 (1930), 534–538, and *L'art pré-roman* (Paris: n. pub., 1938), pp. 76, 114, 141–2; A. Khatchatrian, "Notes sur l'architecture de Germigny-des-Prés," *Cahiers archéologiques* 7 (1954), 161–169; May Vieillard-Troiekouroff, "L'architecture en France du temps de

Charlemagne," in Wolfgang Braunfels, editor, *Karl der Grosse, Lebenswerk und Nachleben,* Volume 3: *Karolingian Kunst* (Düsseldorf: Schwann, 1965), pp. 336–368. On the parallels with Theodulfian bibles, see Otto Homburger, "Eine unveröffentlichte Evengelien-Handschrift aus der Zeit Karls des Grosse," *Zeitschrift für schweizerische Archeologie und Kunstgeschichte* 5 (1943), 149–165; and May Vieillard-Troiekouroff, "Tables de canons et stucs carolingiens," *Stucchi e mosaici alto medievali, Atti dell'ottavo congresso di studi sull'arte dell'alto medioevo* (Milan, 1962), 154–178. On other interpretations of this mosaic and its sources, see H. Del Medico, "La mosaïque de l'apside orientale a Germigny-des-Prés," *Monuments Piot* 39 (1943), 81–102; André Grabar, "Les mosaïques de Germigny-des-Prés" *Cahiers archéologiques* 7 (1954), 171–183; and Peter Bloch, "Das Apsismosaik von Germigny-des-Prés: Karl der Grosse und die Alte Bund," *Karl der Grosse,* Volume 3, *Karolingische Kunst,* pp. 234–261.

21. This is the insight of Freeman, "Theodulf of Orléans and the *Libri Carolini,*" p. 699.

22. For this term, see Freeman and Vieillard-Troiekouroff.

23. See Dahlhaus-Berg, *Nova Antiquitas,* Chapter 4.

24. *Libri Carolini* 2.27–30, 3.24. Cf. Rabe, pp. 28–9.

25. Most students of Benedict of Aniane have focused their attention on his later work at Inde/Cornelimünster. The primary study of Aniane is Peter Bloch, "Siebenarmige Leuchter in christlichen Kirchen," *Wallraf-Richartz Jahrbuch* 23 (1961), 55–190.

26. On Benedict's life and involvement with Adoptionism see Ardo Smaragdus *Vita Benediti abbatis Anianensis et Indensis (MGH, SS* 15, part 1, pp. 199–220); Heil, "Adoptianismus," pp. 133ff; Abadal, pp. 29–36; and Philippe Wolff, "L'Aquitaine et ses marges," in *Karl der Grosse,* Volume 1: *Persönlichkeit und Geschichte,* pp. 296ff.

27. *Codex Carolinus* 95 (*MGH Epp* 3, p. 637).

28. See "Adoptianismus," pp. 133–4.

29. *PL* 103, 1381–99 and 1399–1411. Cf. Heil, "Adoptianismus" p. 134.

30. Ardo *Vita* 3 and 17 (*MGH SS* 15, part 1, pp. 203, 205).

31. Ardo *Vita* 17 (*MGH SS* 15, part 1, p. 206).

32. *MGH Epp* 4, number 9.

33. Like Angilbert later, Widmar was Pepin's ambassador to the Pope, Paul I, between 761 and 766. See *MGH LL* 3, *CC* 2, part 1, pp. 72–73, and Rosamond McKitterick, *The Frankish Kingdoms Under the Carolingians, 751–987* (New York: Longmans, 1983), 37.

34. Angilbert's text has been published in two separate sections. Georg Waitz has edited his description of the buildings; see *De perfectione Centulensis ecclesiae,* in *MGH, SS* 15, part 1, pp. 173–179. The best edition of

his liturgical prescriptions, entitled *Institutio de diversitate oficiorum*, is by
Hallinger, Wegener, and Frank, *CCM* 1, pp. 283–303. Also important is the
eleventh-century *Chronicon Centulense* of Hariulf, edited by F. Lot, *La
chronique de l'abbaye de Saint-Riquier, Collection de textes pour servir à
l'étude et l'enseignement de l'histoire*, Volume 17 (Paris: Alphonse Picard,
1894). Hariulf's chronicle is the source of the famous eleventh-century picture
of Saint-Riquier. For critical analysis of the sources, see David Parsons, "The
Pre-Romanesque Church of Saint-Riquier: The Documentary Evidence,"
Journal of the British Archeological Association 130 (1977), 21–51; and Rabe,
pp. 12–20.

    35.   For a full discussion of the historiography on Saint-Riquier, see Rabe,
Chapter 1. Among the most important studies of the architectural and liturgical
program are Wilhelm Effmann, *Centula-Saint-Riquier* (Münster-in-Westfälen:
Aschendorff, 1912), the *locus classicus;* Alois Fuchs, "Entstehung und
Zweckbestimmung der Westwerke," *Westfälische Zeitschrift* 100 (1959), 227–
291; Kenneth Conant, *A Brief Commentary on Early Medieval Church
Architecture* (Baltimore: Johns Hopkins University Press, 1942) and
Carolingian and Romanesque Architecture, 800–1200 (Baltimore: Penguin
Books, 1959); Jean Hubert, "Saint-Riquier et le monachisme en Gaule à
l'époque carolingienne," *Il monachesimo nell'alto medeoevo e la formazione
della civilta occidentale. Settimane di studio del Centro italiano di studi
sull'alto medioevo,* Volume 4 (Spoleto: Sede del Centro, 1957), pp. 293–309;
Carl Gindele, "Die gallikanischen 'Laus Perennis'-Kloster und ihr 'Ordo
Officii'," *Revue bénédictine* 69 (1959), 33–48. The most important recent
studies are those of Carol Heitz, *Recherches sur les rapports entre architecture
e liturgie à l'époque carolingienne* (Paris: S.E.V.P.E.N., 1963); "Architecture
et liturgie processionnelle à l'époque préromane," *Revue de l'art* 24 (1974),
30–47; *Architecture et liturgie à l'époque carolingienne* (Paris: Alphonse
Picard, 1980); "De Chrodegang a Cluny II: cadre de vie, organisation
monastique, splendeur liturgique," *Sous la règle de saint Benoît. Structures
monastiques et sociétés en France du Moyen-âge à l'époque moderne* (Geneva:
Librairie Droz, 1982), 491–497. Honore Bernard has excavated the Carolingian
level of the monastery and published the results in a series of essential studies:
"Les fouilles de l'église de Notre-Dame à Saint-Riquier," *Bulletin
Archéologique du Comité des travaux historiques et scientifiques,* n.s., 1 and 2
(1965–66), 24–47 and 219–235; "Premières fouilles de Saint-Riquier," in *Karl
der Grosse,* Volume 3: *Karolingische Kunst,* pp. 369–373; "Un site prestigieux
du monde carolingien: Saint-Riquier," *Cahiers archéologiques de Picardie* 5
(1978), 251–254; "L'abbaye de Saint-Riquier: évolution des bâtiments
monastiques du IXe au XVIIIe siècle," in *Sous la règle de saint Benoît,* pp.

499–526; and "Saint-Riquier: une restitution nouvelle de la basilique d'Angilbert," *Revue du Nord* 71 (1989), 307–361.

36. *De perfectione* 1 (*MGH SS* 15, p. 174): Quia igitur omnis plebs fidelium sanctissimam atque inseparabilem trinitatem confiteri, venerari et mente colere firmiterque credere debet, secundum huius fidei rationem in omnipotentis Dei nomine tres aecclesias principales cum menbris [sic] ad se pertinentibus in hoc sancto loco, Domino cooperante, et praedicto domino meo augusto iuvante, fundare studuimus.

37. *MGH SS* 15, p. 178: sicut in aedificiis marmoreis et in ceteris ornamentis . . . ita etiam in laudibus Dei, in doctrinis diversis et canticis spiritualibus.

38. See Bernard, "Saint-Riquier: une restitution nouvelle."

39. Note in particular *Institutio* 8 (*CMM*, pp. 295–296).

40. See Walter Horn and Ernest Born, "On the Selective Use of Sacred Numbers and the Creation in Carolingian Architecture of a New Aesthetic Based on Modular Concepts," *Viator* 6 (1975), 351–390.

41. The Carolingian foot as computed by Walter Horn was 33.37 centimeters. I have reached these dimensions for Saint-Riquier by using the dimensions recorded in meters by Bernard, multiplying by 100 to obtain the measurement in Carolingian feet.

42. *Institutio* 1, 6, 9, 11, 15, 16, 17 (*CMM* 1, pp. 292–3, 294, 296, 299, 300, 301–303). Cf. Anscher, *Vita Angilberti* (Lot, p. 127) on the fact that these were stucco; and Conant, *Carolingian and Romanesque Architecture*, pp. 11–13.

43. See Rabe, pp. 44–48.

44. *Institutio* 16, 17 (*CMM* 1, pp. 301–3).

45. *Institutio* 1 (*CCM* 1, pp. 292–3).

46. *Institutio* 6 (*CCM* 1, p. 294).

47. *Institutio* 8 (*CCM* 1, p. 295).

48. *Institutio* 8 (*CCM* 1, p. 296).

49. See the references to Bernard in note 35.

50. See Rabe, p. 115.

51. *Institutio* 13, 14 (*CCM* 1, p. 301).

52. See *Institutio* 12 (*CCM* 1, p. 301); the biblical references are Acts 1:12–14 and 2:1–4.

53. See *Institutio* 9 (*CCM* 1, pp. 296–7). For the origins of the Gallican Rogations triduum, see *Liber historiae Francorum* 16 (*MGH SSRM* 2, pp. 266–7. Cf. *DACL* 14, part 2, cc. 2459–2461, and 9, part 2, cc. 1550–1553.

54. See for example *MGH Capitularia* 1, p. 103 number 30, p. 110, numbers 9 and 13.

55. *Institutio* 9 (*CCM* 1, p. 297): Et idem eos septenos ambulare decernimus, ut in nostro opere gratiam septiformem sancti Spiritus demonstremus. Cf. Heitz, "Liturgie processionelle," pp. 35–6; and Hubert, p. 293–309.

56. *Libri Carolini Praefatio* (*MGH LL* 3, *CC* 2, *Supplementum,* p. 2). Cf. Rabe, p. 86.

57. *De perfectione* 3 (*MGH SS* 15, p. 178).

58. T.C. Akeley, *Christian Initiation in Spain, c. 300–1100,* (London: Darton, Longman and Todd, 1967), especially pp. 64, 69, 131–133.

59. *MGH Epp* 4, number 137.

60. Ibid.

61. This is the edition of Ludwig Traube, *O Roma Nobilis: Abhandlungen der königlichen-bayerisch Akademie der Wissenschaft* (1891), 322–331. See the extended discussion in Rabe, pp. 76–81 and 91–99.

SICUT SAMUHEL UNXIT DAVID: EARLY CAROLINGIAN ROYAL ANOINTINGS RECONSIDERED

Paul A. Jacobson

Pippin[1] was elected king according to the custom of the Franks, and was anointed by the hand of Archbishop Boniface of blessed memory, and elevated by the Franks as king in Soisson. Childeric, who was called a false king, was tonsured and sent to a monastery.[2]

This rather modest entry in the history of the Franks reveals what would in due time be seen as a turning point in the history of governance—the creation of the first Carolingian king.[3] Pippin and his brother Carloman had succeeded their father Charles Martel "The Hammer" [d. 741] as Mayors of the Palace under the Merovingian kings of Gaul.[4] Following Frankish custom, Charles Martel had split the administration of the kingdom between the two brothers. In 747, Carlomann retired to pursue the contemplative life,[5] leaving Pippin as the sole Mayor of the Palace.[6] In 750 Pippin sent an embassy to Pope Zacharias to ask if the one who "had the title but not the reality of kingship" should be supplanted.[7]

It now happened that with the consent and advice of all the Franks the most excellent Pippin submitted a proposition to the Apostolic See, and having first obtained its sanction, was made king, and Bertrada queen. In accordance with that order anciently required, he was chosen king by the Franks, consecrated by the bishops and received the homage of the great men.[8]

The election and elevation of Pippin were clearly Frankish customs.[9] What was new was the anointing. Why introduce the rite of anointing? Why now?[10]

We must also ask what texts might have been used at Pippin's anointing. The oldest true *Ordo* of regal texts is the *Ordo* of Judith,[11] assembled for the marriage of Judith, daughter of Charles the Bald to the Anglo-Saxon king Ethelwulf in 856, and her subsequent coronation. Some of the Gallican sacramentaries[12] and benedictionals[13] contained various prayers and blessings for kings, but these were not organized into *ordines*. While we cannot be certain what prayers were used at the first Carolingian anointing in 751, these regal blessings suggest themselves as possibilities.[14] As our concern here is Pippin's anointing, we will focus on blessing 89 from the Friesing Benedictional, *Unguantur manus istae*:

> May these hands be anointed with holy oil, whence kings and prophets were anointed, *as Samuel anointed David* as king. So you are blessed and constituted king in your kingdom, because the Lord your God has given to you rule or governance over these people.[15]

What did the anointing of Pippin in 751 mean? The prevalent view holds that Pippin's accession to the Frankish throne was a natural occasion for innovation,[16] which consisted in giving liturgical form to Old Testament precedents of regal anointing.[17] The Old Testament warrant was thought to be found in the use of the phrase *sicut Samuhel unxit David* [as Samuel anointed David]. Other proposed solutions to these questions have included Papal inspiration; using the model of earlier royal anointings in Spain and England; and, borrowing from the emerging rites of presbyteral and episcopal ordinations. Others have been less enthusiastic in their endorsement of the 751 anointing as either essential to Pippin's reign,[18] or driven by ecclesiastical political maneuvers.[19]

As we approach these arguments, we must keep in mind that our view of the events of 751 is clouded by two things: the paucity of primary, contemporary sources, as we have seen; and the towering figure of Hincmar of Rheims (*ca*. 806–882). In the late ninth century Hincmar synthesized the formula in which ecclesiastical sanction, replacing the *mores Francorum*, became the foundation of medieval theocratic kingship:[20]

> the dignity of pontiffs is so much the greater than that of kings, since kings are anointed into the royal office by priests.[21]

We must keep in mind that this is 130 years after the first anointing at Soisson and avoid placing Hincmar's theology in the minds of the clerics of Pippin's entourage.

Let us briefly consider each of the accepted arguments. The assumption that the Carolingians were simply imitating the example of Samuel and David[22] cannot be wholly satisfactory. Gregory I (Pope from 590–604) and Isidore of Seville (*ca.* 560–636) had already written on the example of Samuel and the sacramental nature of regal unction, fully a century or more before any Frankish ruler was actually anointed.[23] Besides, the Old Testament also shows that it was not only Samuel who anointed kings but also the men of Israel.[24] As Marc Bloch has warned, "We should not be warranted in deducing from a biblical quotation the existence of an institution which might be justified by the quotation."[25]

Pippin's anointing has often been seen as the substitution of one kind of magical sanction for another and thus a protection for the Carolingian usurpers.[26] After all, papal permission for this usurpation had been required by Pippin. The Samuel-David formula was seen as particularly apt, as Pippin (David) replaced Childeric (Saul).[27] Kingship as an office in Gaul was constructed out of war lordship and Roman administrative techniques.[28] Whatever pagan sacrality there may have been[29] was transmitted through heredity or blood-right (*Geblütsrecht*).[30] The Merovingian king-making ritual was centered around an enthronement in the midst of the assembly of nobles.[31] The Carolingians continued to use traditional Merovingian procedures,[32] and the anointing was simply added as the new mark of legitimacy.[33] The *reges critini* were replaced by the *reges christiani*.[34]

It is also doubtful that the sanction for anointing Pippin came from Rome, even though Rome had approved the usurpation of the Merovingian kings.[35] Nothing about Pippin's accession or anointing was recorded in the *Liber pontificalis*. Surely, if the idea had been Roman, it would have been recorded here.[36]

Might Pippin's consecrators have drawn on any more recent examples of regal anointing? The first unequivocal example was that of the Visigothic king Wamba in 672. Julian of Toledo's *Historia Wambae* is quite precise in its description:

then while kneeling the oil of blessing was poured onto his head by
the hand of the blessed bishop Quiricus, and many blessings were
seen.[37]

The anointing was accompanied by the appearance of a column of
smoke-like vapor from which sprung forth a bee—a portent of good
fortune. Julian's exactitude was impressive, but, in the end,
meaningless for the Franks, as it is not likely that the *Historia Wambae*
was known in eighth-century Gaul.[38]

Was there an insular example of regal anointing for the Carolingians to imitate? The *Collectio canonum Hibernensis* (*ca.* 690–725)
was perhaps known to Pippin. Book 25, *De regno*, dealt with the ethical
and legal concepts of kingship. The *Collectio* also contained the story
of Aidán's sacring by Columba. Virgil of Salzburg, an Irish religious,
was in Pippin's entourage and was in correspondence with Pope
Zacharias. Thus, the legend of Aidán might not have been the
proximate cause for Pippin's own anointing, but it certainly added to
the mix.[39]

Another avenue of exploration has been liturgical transpositions
from other status-changing rituals, especially presbyteral and episcopal
anointings. The anointing of the priest's hands first appears among the
Aquitanian Visigoths of Gaul in the beginning of the eighth century.[40]
The prayer for presbyteral anointing from the Missale Gothicum
(seventh-, eighth-century) is quite similar to the regal anointing prayer
(cf. note 15, *supra*).[41] The Gellone sacramentary (790–800),[42] bears
witness to the anointing of a new bishop's head, utilizing the Samuel-
David formula.[43] The Angoulême sacramentary (*c.* 800)[44] echoes the
same practice as the Gellone. The hallowing of bishops with oil spread
more rapidly than did the anointing of priests.[45] Whether regal
anointings preceded clerical anointings, or vice versa, has long been
argued. Such debates, generally centered in legal and political history,
miss the point.[46] There must certainly have been mutual relationships
between regal and clerical anointings, but the search for a causal
relationship between the two is doomed to failure.[47]

SOURCES OF ROYAL ANOINTING

Rites of Initiation

If the impetus for Pippin's anointing was not biblical imitation, or papal inspiration, or earlier royal anointings, or ordinations, where might we look? By now it is clear that the study of medieval kingship requires the opening of a Pandora's box of various kinds of history. Since none of the previous arguments are sufficient, I suggest that we examine the issue as a liturgical question. From a liturgical perspective the most obvious derivation of regal anointing was the rite of baptism and it related anointings.[48] An affinity between baptismal and regal anointings has been noted by others, notably Deshmann,[49] Nelson,[50] and de Pagne,[51] but sidestepped by others, notably Ullmann.[52] The point needs to be pressed further than a simple affinity, though. I want to suggest that the fountainhead for Carolingian royal anointing[53] was the practice of Christian initiation as it came to be practiced in early medieval Gaul. The particular points of connection were the post-baptismal anointing and its relationship to the person and office of the bishop. To show this relationship, we must examine a fairly wide range of material: the Frankish Church under the late Merovingians; the gradual Romanization of the Frankish liturgy as shown in the extant liturgical books; the place of the bishop in the postbaptismal rites in Gaul; and, the various theologies of pre- and postbaptismal anointings. With all these lenses in place, we will then be able to adopt a clearer view of the origin of Frankish regal anointings.

Under Merovingian rule, the Franks, nominally Christian since the baptism of Clovis in 496, had not been completely converted from paganism.[54] During the seventh century the Austrasian (East Frankish) magnates, especially the Carolingians [so named for Charles Martel, the first of the Arnulfing aristocracy to bear the name of Charles], provided protection for and encouragement to Irish Gallic missionaries, such as Boniface and Willibald. Most importantly, from our point of view, they reintroduced bishops into dioceses which had been abandoned by the Merovingians.[55] The restoration of unbroken successions in dioceses and abbeys gave new life to the church in Gaul, as long vacancies had solicited spoliation.[56] The new bishops and abbots came not from Merovingian but from Carolingian families, and the fate of the church was yoked to that of its benefactors.[57] Boniface, made a bishop by Gregory II in 722,[58] recognized the essential nature of this link:

> I am not able to prevent heathen customs or the sacrilege of idolatry in Germany without the orders of and the fear inspired by the prince of the Franks.[59]

This is not to say that the Carolingians' relationship with the church was entirely cordial or supportive. Charles Martel had been ruthless in his acquisition of Church lands and revenues for the prosecution of war, especially against the Moorish invaders of southern Gaul, whom he finally defeated on the plain of Poitiers in 732.[60] These triumphs were seen as Christian victories and a new sense of identity as a chosen people, the *gens Francorum*, began to develop in the Franks.[61]

In the process of restoring their religious life, and of concocting a new, national identity, the Carolingians also searched for distinctive spiritual patronage. St. Martin of Tours had been the patron of the Merovingian dynasty for over two centuries, but the Carolingians looked toward Paris and Rome. St. Denis and St. Peter would soon overshadow the venerable Martin in the eyes and prayers of the Franks.[62] Pippin would

> clear away the uncontrollable and suffocating influence of the innumerable Gallic and Frankish saints whose worship had covered with rank growth the Christian faith in Merovingian Gaul and that with his new measures had cut right through the jungle of sovereign saints.[63]

By 741, a new day seemed to have dawned. The iconoclastic Emperor Leo III died in June, and Pope Gregory III died in November, preceded by Charles Martel in October.

> When the temporal kingdom of glorious Duke Charles was finished and the sovereignty of his sons Carloman and Pippin waxed strong, then indeed, by the help of the Lord God and at the suggestion of St. Boniface the archbishop, the testament of the Christian religion was confirmed, and the synodal institutions of the orthodox fathers were established in proper form among the Franks, and all was amended and cleansed by the authority of the canons.[64]

Boniface urged Carloman to reestablish the much neglected convocation of episcopal councils as the best path to reform. [65] Boniface felt that through the canons of such councils, the Frankish people would be delivered "from the baleful beguiling of the crooked serpent," and "the wisdom of spiritual learning might be disclosed and the knowledge of Christianity come, while the snaring of souls was averted." [66]

Four synodal councils were held, where there gathered together bishops and priests, deacons and clerics, and all ecclesiastical ranks, whom Duke Carloman of illustrious memory caused to be summoned under the sovereignty of his kingdom. [67]

The first of these national Germanic councils was held on 21 April 742. [68] Its decrees, published by Carloman, included:

- priests are subject to the bishop of the diocese in which they live;
- annually during Lent priests will render an account to the bishop of his ministry, including baptisms, prayers, and the order of Mass;
- on Holy Thursday priests are to ask the bishop for freshly conse-crated oil;
- synods will be held annually, "so that in our presence the canonical decrees and the laws of the Church may be re-established and the Christian religion purified." [69]

All of the Germanic councils under Boniface's presidency sought to restore ecclesiastical discipline which had decayed in the early eighth century. [70] Boniface was likewise concerned to expand the episcopal organization of Gaul. [71] He persuaded Pope Zacharias to establish Cologne as a metropolitan see [72] and name archbishops to three other provinces: Rouen, Sens and Rheims. [73] A national group of bishops provided an organizational solidarity which the lay aristocracy could not match and which evoked in the bishops themselves a sense of responsibility for the leadership of the whole society. [74] Although the canons of the new Germanic councils were not concerned with the amendment of the liturgy, *per se*, [75] the quantity of Boniface's lively correspondence with Rome concerning baptism tells us that the manner in which the Church was to be carved out of the still-pagan north very much concerned him.[76]

The late seventh and early eighth centuries, in addition to being a time of political upheaval and social unrest, were times of liturgical anarchy in the West, especially in Gaul.[77] The ecclesiastical provinces were not coherent enough to allow any kind of control,[78] and it is easy to understand the disorganization of liturgical life in this period. As Vogel commented, "It is not an exaggeration to say that about the end of the seventh century, the liturgy was celebrated practically [according] to the will of each."[79]

A large part of the reason for such variety in practice was the fact that an entire library was needed to perform the liturgy: sacramentary, antiphonary, gradual, epistolary, and evangelary. Besides all these, an ordo was required, especially if a newly obtained sacramentary supposed a different style of celebration than that which was common locally.[80] The secularization of monasteries under Charles Martel had interrupted the output of books by scriptoria and workshops, which helps to explain the paucity of extant sources for the Gallican liturgy.[81]

The conciliar reforms of the early eighth century, combined with the Carolingian desire to replace Martin with Peter as the realm's patron, had had the effect of bringing the Frankish church closer to Rome.[82] Thus it seemed only logical for the Frankish church to turn to Rome for some assistance in harmonizing its liturgy. In a letter to Decentius of Gubbio (416), Innocent I had required all the churches of the known Western world to conform to Roman liturgical usage.[83] There does not seem to have been be very much evidence that such a concern was shared by the churches of Gaul until the sixth century.[84] The council of Vaison (529), under the presidency of Caesarius of Arles, was the first to propose adopting a particular Roman liturgical custom, the singing of the Kyrie, precisely because it was Roman.[85] Innocent's claim notwithstanding, even the popes themselves had not seemed particularly eager to promote the liturgy of Rome outside of the city before the middle of the eighth century.[86]

The reign of Pippin marked a divide between the two periods of Roman influence. Before Pippin, the emergence of Roman usages in Gaul was the result of uncoordinated private initiatives.[87] Since the time of Clovis, Frankish pilgrims had made their way to the tomb of St.

Peter, bringing back relics and mementos.[88] Among those souvenirs, Roman books were in high demand for those that could afford them.[89]

Pippin favored a move toward liturgical uniformity through the imposition of the Roman rite.[90] Lowering the liturgical barriers between Gaul and Rome created a stronger relationship with Rome, and Pippin became the defender of the *iustitia sancti Petri*.[91] Disputes with the iconoclastic Emperors in Constantinople (especially Leo III who had removed Sicily and much of southern Italy from Rome's jurisdiction)[92] may have been another motive for using the Roman rite to foil any new Byzantine influences.[93]

By the 750s the liturgy in Gaul was neither completely Roman nor uniform, but it was certainly on the way. Older liturgical books had not been eliminated as copying them was simply too expensive. Between 700 and 850 an incredible variety of Roman, Gallican, and mixed liturgical books existed side by side in Gaul.[94] The ritual result was a hybrid liturgy which was different from the actual liturgy of Rome.[95]

The prayer book of this hybrid liturgy was the eighth-century Gelasian Sacramentary.[96] No archetype for this type of sacramentary exists,[97] but its primary descendants are the Gellone and Angoulême sacramentaries. Andrieu[98] articulated a principle of "Progressive Romanization" in the development of the eighth-century Gelasians. This principle proved that the idea of a "Sacramentary of Pippin" bringing an end to liturgical chaos in Gaul was false. In fact, the introduction of the eighth-century Gelasian sacramentary only accentu-ated the liturgical bedlam of the time.[99] After all, it did not replace those books of earlier types still in use.[100]

More than the Sacramentaries, though, and even before the reign of Pippin, the *Ordines Romani* contributed to the Romanization of the liturgy in Gaul.[101] The *Ordines* contained the rubrics, or ceremonial directions for the liturgy, and thus formed an indispensable complement to the Sacramentaries. Without the *Ordines*, Roman sacramentaries were all but useless in Gaul.[102]

Let us now consider how the place of the bishop himself came to be defined, especially in relation to Christian initiation. Aidan Kavanagh[103] has argued that the ancient *missa* of baptism, the coming under the bishop's hand after baptism and its presbyteral anointing, became more and more separated from the baptismal act itself, often no longer performed by the bishop.

The second stage of this process was typified by Innocent I. In his letter to Decentius of Gubbio, Innocent expressed his pique at priests who assumed the right of consignation. A priest could anoint a newly baptized Christian, but only with chrism consecrated by a bishop, and only *in capite* (on the top of the head), not *in frontem* (on the forehead, or brow). [104] Pope Gelasius (492–496) was also opposed to priests who dared to consecrate chrism or consignate. [105] Thus its appears that Roman postbaptismal anointing, or chrismation, was separate from the bishop's consignation, which in turn could be detached from baptism itself. [106]

The final stage was

> accomplished by the gradual adoption of Roman elements into Gallican liturgies over a span of some three centuries, [which] forced out older Gallican practices of "confirmation" and placed their Roman successor more and more subsequent to the baptism itself— separated first by the baptismal Eucharist, then by Easter week, and finally by the time it took for a circuit-riding Gallic bishop to make his rural rounds. [107]

In Gaul, the firm connection of bishops to the application of chrism[108] was illustrated in the actions of church councils, particularly those in south Gaul. In 439, the Council of Riez allowed a certain Armentarius to confirm neophytes even though he had been consecrated as a bishop illegally and was later deposed. [109]

Canon 2 of the first council of Orange (441) stated that:

> None of the ministers who has received the office of baptizing shall ever proceed without chrism, for we have agreed that the anointing should be done at once; however, in the case where someone, for whatever reason, has not been anointed at baptism, let the bishop be reminded of this in confirmation; as for the chrism itself, there is in every case but one blessing, not to prejudice anything, but so that a repeated chrismation not be considered necessary.[110]

The third council of Arles (between 449 and 461) differentiated between the roles of bishop and abbot. The bishop had the power to ordain, give chrism and confirm neophytes, now apparently something apart from baptism. [111]

The Roman model of postbaptismal anointing had emphasized its sealing aspect—the bishop's acceptance of the neophyte into the community. In fifth century Gaul, the Roman idea of *consignatio* was modified into a *confirmatio*, a completion of the baptismal act and a strengthening of the baptismal commitment.[112] Since this action was no longer a simple postbaptismal salving, the personal agency of the bishop was required. The Roman mode of Christian initiation was naturally of interest to the Frankish bishops who were promoting Roman liturgical practice. It bore the stamp of papal approval and, at the same time, enhanced the liturgical role of those very bishops.[113]

Unlike the councils of southern Gaul, the Gallican sacramentaries which have come to us from the north (e.g., Gothicum, Bobbio, Gallicanum Vetus), do not indicate a special episcopal anointing or imposition of hand.[114] The structure of the postbaptismal rites is nearly identical in all three of these sacramentaries. The Gallicanum Vetus and the Gothicum reflect two slightly different traditions, the Bobbio serving as a bridge between the two.[115] The same is true of the chrismation itself. The Gothicum has a simple signation, while the Gallicanum Vetus and the Bobbio feature an infusion.[116] The Gallican sacramentaries disclose a single postbaptismal anointing, performed by whomever was performing the baptism.[117] Rome, however, had become accustomed to a double anointing as well as a distinct laying on of the hand.[118] In Gaul a separate rite of imposition of the hand was limited to the reconciliation of heretics.[119]

Ordo Romanus XI is a directory for the liturgy of baptism which probably appeared in the second half of the seventh century.[120] Its rubrics tell us that after the neophytes were baptized and anointed by the presbyter, they were taken to the pontiff who gave them stole, chasuble, chrismal cloth and 10 coins.[121] There was a consignation *in frontem*, but no episcopal imposition of hands.[122] Bishops were warned not to neglect this act as each baptism had to be confirmed.[123]

The baptismal rite in the eighth-century Gelasian sacramentaries began to appear independently of the Easter Vigil and the episcopal presence, with the rubrics for presbyteral baptism becoming more explicit. The prayers of various sacramentaries combined with the rubrics of Ordo XI to provide a basic framework that was adapted to local circumstances.[124] The Gellone Sacramentary has a postbaptismal rite at the Easter Vigil like the Gelasianum but with more ritual remarks, showing the influence of the *Ordines*. On the other hand, the postbaptismal sequence of the Angoulême sacramentary is even closer to that of the Gelasianum, with no trace of Ordo XI's rubrics. [125] The sacramentary of St. Amand (*ca*. 800), clearly shows two separate rites. The postbaptismal anointing is done by the presbyter, the consignation by the bishop. [126] The point to be made here is simply that baptismal practice, especially the postbaptismal rites, continued to evolve in Gaul in the seventh and eighth centuries.

As the episcopal postbaptismal rite began to detach itself from baptism, a new rationale for the rite developed, i.e., the necessity of confirmation for completing the Christian life. [127] This theological shift can be detected already in fifth-century Gaul, in the Pentecost homily of Faustus of Riez. [128] Faustus distinguished between baptism which was Christic and confirmation which was Pneumatic. In baptism one was born to new life and confirmed for battle in confirmation, [129] like a soldier preparing for war. [130] Winkler has noted two "fateful shifts in meaning" here: 1) baptism had been loosed from its moorings in the pneumatic imagery of John 3:5; [131] and 2) the character of the post-baptismal rite had been limited to strengthening. [132]

A theology of strengthening was not new to the baptismal rites, but it had tended to be associated with the prebaptismal anointing and exorcism. Ambrose wrote that through unction one was made an athlete for Christ. [133] John Chrysostom saw the anointed catechumen as an athlete entering the arena. [134] It comes as no surprise, then to see the same theology in the prebaptismal prayers of the Bobbio Missal:

> Effeta, the sacrifice is complete, unto the odor of sweetness. I anoint
> you with sanctified oils, *as Samuel anointed David to be king and
> prophet*. Perform your work, creature of oil, perform your work that
> no unclean spirit may lurk here, neither in limbs nor in the inward
> parts nor in the whole frame of the body: may the power of Christ,
> the Son of the most high God, and of the Holy Spirit, work in you
> throughout all ages. [135]

A curious transposition of these prayers is found in the Stowe Missal. The third prayer ["Perform your work"] is said after the post-baptismal anointing with chrism. [136] Such a placement puts the chrismation in a distinctly different light. The postbaptismal anointing gave new Christians the strength to live their new lives in Christ.

With the beginning of conciliar activity of south Gaul in the fifth century we can see the "onset of a problematic evolution focused on the ministers of initiation" which required the bishop to intervene in person to ratify the baptismal rite.[137] Boniface had been preparing for just such a confirmation tour when he was killed.[138] This strongly juridical concept of the postbaptismal rites was to combine with the concept of *confirmatio* as a strengthening and was to exert an enormous influence over the entire Western Church.[139] In the seventh century, the permissible locations and occasions of baptism began to be limited.[140] In the middle of the eighth century, two conciliar decrees again reinforced the episcopal claim—baptism was incomplete without the laying on of a bishop's hand.[141]

Images and Theology of Chrism

Let us now investigate the images and theology connected with the matter of the episcopal postbaptismal rite—chrism. Regal imagery has long been connected with the use of oil, especially in baptismal anointing. The *Apostolic Tradition* tells us that if someone offered oil, thanks was given over it thus:

> as you give health to those who are anointed and receive that with which you anointed kings, priests and prophets.[142]

The association of priests, prophets and kings with the Christian life was found already in the New Testament, particularly 1 Peter 2:9: "You are a chosen people, a royal priesthood." Theologians such as Ambrose of Milan (*ca.* 339–397),[143] and Maximus of Turin (d. 408/23)[144] make clear the Old Testament precedent for baptismal anointings in the early church. The same theological tradition is seen in the writings of Isidore of Seville (*ca.* 560–636):

> So now not only pontiffs and kings, but the whole Church is consecrated with the unction of chrism, because it is a member of the eternal king and priest. Therefore, because we are a priestly and royal nation, after baptism we are anointed that we may be called by the name of Christ.[145]

The oil used for prebaptismal anointing was common olive oil, but the postbaptismal anointing required chrism. Chrism was olive oil mixed with expensive balsam and perfumes, thus set apart, at least by its odor of sweetness, as something special.[146] Janet Nelson has suggested that a permanent "oil-crisis" in the early medieval West[147] heightened the oil's value, making it a potent and scarce commodity.[148]

In fifth- and sixth-century Gaul, the chrism was blessed during Lent, when approaching Easter.[149] By the beginning of the seventh century, the time became more fixed, e.g., diocesan synod of Auxerre (561–605) on the Fourth Sunday of Lent.[150] According to Ps.- Germanus [end of seventh century], the chrism was blessed on Palm Sunday.[151] Under the influence of the Roman liturgy, the blessing of chrism was eventually moved to Holy Thursday, as found in the Gallicanum Vetus and Gelasian sacramentaries. This placement became customary in the eighth-century Gelasians and was legislated by councils in the course of the ninth century.[152]

The oldest Frankish reference to chrism in a sacramentary is the postbaptismal prayer in the Missale Gothicum:

> I anoint you with the chrism of holiness, the garment of immortality which our Lord Jesus Christ first received from the Father, that you may bear it entire and spotless before the judgment seat of Christ and live unto all eternity.[153]

The Missale Gallicanum Vetus[154] contains a Mass formulary on Holy Thursday for the blessing of chrism,

> [with] which you once poured over kings, priests and prophets, flowing from the horn of your beloved.

In the Gelasian sacramentary, the preface for the Chrism Mass on Holy Thursday combined the sense of regal/priestly inheritance of the Gallicanum Vetus and the expression of chrism as clothing found in the Gothicum:

> so that being imbued, as your sacrament shows, with royal and priestly and prophetic honor, they may be clothed with the garment of your perfect gift.[155]

In the Gelasian Chrism Mass the oil of the sick [*oleum ad unguendos infirmos*] is blessed during the Canon, as we saw in the *Apostolic Tradition*:

wherewith you have anointed priests, kings, prophets and martyrs.[156]

Later, after the Lord's Prayer, but before communion, the chrism was blessed, using the form of a preface, with its characteristic dialogue and first line *Vere dignum et iustum est*. The images of David, Moses and Aaron, and Jesus' baptism by John were evoked, and the Holy Spirit was called down upon the chrism:

Infuse it with the power of your Holy Spirit, through the power of your Christ, from whose holy name chrism took its name, whence you have anointed priests, prophets and kings.[157]

Chavasse has demonstrated that this chrismal preface was Gallican in origin[158] and has proposed that we might imagine the earlier existence or organization of a Chrism Mass in Gaul, before the influence of the Roman Holy Thursday Mass was felt too much, in which the preface for the canon was constituted by the present Gelasian chrismal preface. The Chrism Mass of both the Gallicanum Vetus and the Gelasian represent intermediate steps in the development. The Gelasian is more advanced, with more Roman elements than the Gallicanum Vetus, but the ancient Gallican chrismal preface is retained.[159] This Gallican prayer continued to be used in the Gregorian Hadrianum.[160] As always, these developments were not without irregularities.[161] The blessing of the oils would gradually be restricted to bishops, and the formulas would disappear from sacramentaries altogether.[162]

The Gothicum gives us another glimpse of regal images in the postbaptismal collects:

For those who are baptized, who seek the chrism, who are crowned in Christ, to whom our Lord has been pleased to grant a new birth, let us beseech Almighty God that they may bear the baptism which they have received spotless unto the end.[163]

Besides its regal symbolism, [164] chrism was also allotted apotropaic powers. In *Ordo* XI, after the priest blessed the font, the water was chrismated and the people were sprinkled. Then they could take some of the blessed and oiled water home to sprinkle vines and fields. [165]

CONCLUSIONS

So, what do all these observations mean about the introduction of Frankish regal anointing? We have examined the development of the Frankish church and its liturgy as witnessed by conciliar canons and sacramentaries. The Gallican councils of the fifth century built up the authority of the episcopal office in the sequence of Christian initiation. The juridical aspect of the postbaptismal *confirmatio* was reinforced with a new theology of strengthening, now transposed from the prebaptismal rites. The Germanic councils of the mid-eighth century and the sacramentaries illustrate the increasing tilt of the Frankish liturgy toward Rome. This development coincided with the Carolingian replacement of Martin with Peter as the dynastic patron. We have also traced the existence of regal imagery in the baptismal rites, and in the blessing and use of the chrism itself. It was in this milieu that the anointing of Pippin arose.

Regal anointings, like all liturgical acts, are multivalent, and admit of multiple interpretations. It is clear that by the time of Hincmar, the anointing was seen as a direct imitation of the Old Testament unction of kings. Yet even Hincmar had not lost sight of the intimate connection between postbaptismal and regal anointings. At the coronation of Charles the Bald (869), Hincmar claimed that the church at Rheims had preserved the chrism with which Clovis had been baptized and anointed into kingship. [166] While this is certainly an anachronistic, if pious, claim by Hincmar, it further illustrates the point I am trying to make. By looking carefully at liturgical developments before 751, a strong case can be made that Pippin's anointing was an understandable application of the strengthening aspects of the postbaptismal rites, now firmly held in the hand of the bishops, to the new king. [167]

Due to our lack of sources, we cannot tell how the unction of Pippin was perceived by contemporaries. [168] Since regal anointing was a novelty for the Franks, they had only their previous experience of other anointing rituals to draw upon. The Frankish *optimates* did not have to look very far for a ritual pattern. Old Testament kings were represented, but not in an abstract sense, merely to be imitated. The example of David was before their eyes precisely because David was present each and every time someone was anointed. The regal image of David was likewise completely intertwined with the Messianic figure of Jesus, a concept perpetuated in the baptismal liturgy itself.[169]

Modern historians have wanted to see in the event at Soisson the first step on the road to ecclesiastical control of the monarchy,[170] and, it is true, the problems of theocratic kingship would come to occupy many thinkers in the Middle Ages. I think that here, though, we must be comfortable with a bit more ambiguity. Pippin's anointing was a trial run for both the new royal house[171] and the newly organized order of bishops.[172] The new royal house and the new episcopal *ordo* were part of the emerging *gens Francorum*. The salving of a king by a bishop at this early stage was an act of *confirmatio*,[173] performed by the only person whose authority it was to confirm[174]—and with chrism, that substance with which all Christians were anointed as priests, prophets and kings.

Notes

1. Note that the first Carolingian king is variously known as Pippin, Pepin, P~. the Short, and P~. III. I have chosen to regularize references to the latinzied Pippin in this study.

2. Frederick Kurze, ed. *Annales regni Francorum* (Hannover, 1895), 10–11, 752. *Pippinus secundum morem Francorum electus est ad regem et unctus per manum sanctae memoriae Bonefacii archie-piscopi et elevatus a Francis in regno in Suessionis civitate. Hildericus vero, qui false rex vocabatur, tonsoratus est et in monasterium missus.* On Boniface's participation in these proceedings, cf. K.-U. Jäschke, "Bonifatius und die Königssalbung Pippins des Jüngeren," *Archiv für Diplomatik* 23 (1977), 25–54. Childeric III had been placed on the throne in 743. The problem of his precise fate is fully discussed by Krusch, ed., *Monumenta Germaniae Historica (MGH)* Script. Rer. Mero. VII, pp. 508 ff. Pippin was actually anointed twice, in 751 at Soissons, and again in 754 at the Abbey of St.-Denis by Pope Stephen II, during an unprecedented papal journey north of the Alps. On the second

anointing, cf. the so-called *Clausula de unctione Pippini*. *MGH* Script. rer. Mero. I, p. 465. For the extensive literature on the *Clausula*, cf. Wattenbach-Levison, *Deutschlands Geschichtsquellen im Mittelalter, Vorzeiten und Karolinger* II (Weimar, 1953), 163.

3. Germain Morin, "Un Recueil gallican inédit de bénédictiones épiscopales," *Revue Bénédictine* 29 (1912), had suggested, from the evidence in a late ninth century MS, that Pippin might not have been the first Frankish king to have been anointed. The literature on medieval kingship is enormous, and one is best advised to consult some of the standard reference works on the topic for bibliographic information beyond the scope of this study. For example, cf. the following: Percy Ernst Schramm, *Kaiser Könige und Päpste. Gesammelte Aufsätze zur Geschichte des Mittelalters* (*KKP*), 4 vols. in 5, (Stuttgart: Anton Hiersmann, 1968). C.A. Bouman, *Sacring and Crowning: The Development of the Latin Ritual for the Anointing of Kings and the Coronation of an Emperor before the Eleventh Century* (Gronigen: J.B. Walters, 1957). J.H. Burns, ed., *The Cambridge History of Medieval Political Thought c. 350–c. 1450* (Cambridge: Cambridge University Press, 1988), s.v. "Kingship and Empire" by Janet L. Nelson. J.M. Wallace-Hadrill, *Early Germanic Kingship in England and on the Continent* (Oxford: Clarendon Press, 1971). Ernst H. Kantorowicz, *Laudes Regiae: A Study in Liturgical Acclamations and Mediaeval Ruler Worship* (Berkeley: University of California Press, 1946). *Idem*, *The King's Two Bodies: A Study in Medieval Political Theology* (Princeton: Princeton University Press, 1957). Also, of course, the extensive writings of Walter Ullmann.

4. The Merovingian house was greatly weakened in the late seventh century by a series of royal minorities and two assassinations. The Merovingian kings were little more than figureheads from about 717 onwards. Cf. Nelson, "The Lord's Anointed and the People's Choice: Carolingian Royal Ritual," in David Cannadine and Simon Price, eds., *Rituals of Royalty: Power and Ceremonial in Traditional Societies* (Cambridge: Cambridge University Press, 1987), 141.

5. Carloman also relinquished the claim to the Mayoral title of his son Drogo. Cf. J.M. Wallace-Hadrill, ed. *The Fourth Book of The Chronicle of Fredegar and Continuators (Fredegar)* (London: Thomas Nelson and Sons, 1960), chap. 30; *Annales regni. Francorum,*. 746, p. 6; Raymond Davis, ed., *The Lives of the Eighth-Century Popes (Liber pontificalis)* (Liverpool: Liverpool University Press, 1992), Zacharias, chap. 21, p. 46.

6. Cf. *Annales regni Francorum*, 750, pp. 8–11 on the resolution of the competing claims of Pippin, Carloman, Drogo, Griffo and Childeric.

7. *Annales regni Francorum*, 749, p. 8. *Burghadus Wirzeburgensis episcopus et Folradus capellanus missi fuerunt ad Zachariam papam,*

interrogando de regibus in Francia, qui illis temporibus non habentes regalem potestatem, si bene fuisset an non. Et Zacharias papa mandavit Pippino, ut melius esst illim regem vocari, qui potestatem haberet, quam illum, qui sine regali potestate manebat; ut non conturbaretur ordo, per auctoritatem apostolicam iussit Pippinum regem fieri. J.M. Wallace-Hadrill, *The Barbarian West: 400–1000* (Oxford: Basil Blackwell, 1985), 92, has argued that the Merovingians did not "peter out but were violently displaced. And it was Rome that pushed Pippin over the precipice that otherwise he might not even have seen."

8. Fredegar, chap. 33. *Quo tempore una cum consilio et consensu omnium Francorum missa relatione ad ses apostolica auctoritate praecepta praecelsus Pippinus electione totius Francorum in sedem regni cum consecratione episcoporum et subiectione prinipum una cum regina Bertradane, ut antiquitus ordo deposcit, sublimatur in regno.* The continuator here is Count Childebrand, Pippin's uncle. Cf. chap. 34..

9. Cf. J.M. Wallace-Hadrill, *The Long Haired Kings, and Other Studies in Frankish History* (London: Methuen, 1962), and R. Schneider, *Königswahl und Königserhebung im Frühmittelalter* (Stuttgart: Anton Hiersemann, 1972), 187–239. Cf. also Nelson, "On the Limits of the Carolingian Renaissance," in Derek Baker, ed., *Renaissance and Renewal in Christian History* Studies in Church History 14 (Oxford: Basil Blackwell, 1977), 58. Cf. also *Eadem*, "The Lord's Anointed," 151, where she points out that the Continuator of Fredegar places the consecration of the bishops on a parallel with the recognition of the princes.

10. Charles Martel had engineered for the Merovingian throne to remain empty for four years after the death of Theuderic IV in 737. Childeric III was placed on the throne only after the death of Charles himself in 741. Cf. Wallace-Hadrill, *The Barbarian West*, 86.

11. Cyrille Vogel, *Medieval Liturgy: An Introduction to the Sources.* Trans. and rev. by William Storey and Niels Rasmussen (Washington, DC: Pastoral Press, 1986. Original Version 1981), 185. Cf. pp. 185–186 for a list of the extant royal ordines. Cf. also Nelson, "The Earliest Surviving Royal *Ordo*: Some Liturgical and Historical Aspects," in Brian Tierney and Peter Linehan, eds., *Authority and Power: Studies on Medieval Law and Government Presented to Walter Ullmann on His Seventieth Birthday* (Cambridge: Cambridge University Press, 1971).

12. A. Dumans, and J. Deshusses, eds., *Liber Sacramentorum Gellonensis* Corpus Christanorum Series Latina (CCL), 159, 159A. (Turnholt: Brepols, 1981), nos. 2091–2094, pp. 296–298: *Benedictio regalis.* P. Saint-Roch, ed., *Liber Sacramentorum Engolismensis* CCL 159C (Turnholt: Brepols,

1987), nos. 1857–1858, pp. 278–279: *Regalis benedictio quoando elevatur in regno*.

13. Robert Amiet, ed., *The Benedictionals of Friesing,* Henry Bradshaw Society 88 (Maidstone, Kent, 1974), nos. 89–92, pp. 100–102. The Benedictionals are sets of blessings given by the bishop before communion. This was a custom of the Gallican church which was very much criticized by Rome. There were four distinct sets of regal blessings here: *Benedictio. regis in regno*; *Benedictio. regie*; *Item alia benedictio. super regem et populum*; *Item benedicito regis*.

14. Bouman, *Sacring and Crowning,* 108. "The formula *Unguantur* provides the only indication of how the ceremony of royal anointing was performed during the first stage of its history in the Frankish realm." Cf. pp. 90–93 on the development of the accession/ anointing rituals. E. Eichmann, "Königs- und Bischofsweihe," *Sitzungsber. Münchener Akad*. (1928), Abh. VI, pp. 29ff, considered that the Friesing formulae could be referred to as the "Coronation Ordo of Pippin." Cf. also *idem,* "Die sog. römische Königskronungsformel," *Historische Jahrbuch* XLV (1925), 545 ff. On the significance of the incorporation of prayers *pro rege in tempore sinodi* into the earliest royal *ordines*, cf. Nelson, "National Synods, Kingship as Office and Royal Anointing: An Early Medieval Syndrome," in G.J. Cumings and Derek Baker, eds., *Councils and Assemblies* (Cambridge: Cambridge University Press, 1971), 58.

15. Amiet, ed. *Benedictionals of Friesing*, pp. 100–101. *Unguantur manus istae de oleo sanctificato, unde uncti fuerunt reges et prophetae, sicut unxit Samuhel David in regem: ut sis benedictus et constitutus rex in regno isto, quod dedit tibi Dominus Deus tuus super populum hunc ad regendum vel gubernandum.*

16. Thus Nelson, "The Lord's Anointed," p. 142. Cf. also p. 149, "Frankish consecrators were innovators in an age when all men sought legitimation by looking to the past."

17. J.M. Wallace-Hadrill, "The *Via Regia* of the Carolingian Age," in Beryl Smalley, ed., *Trends in Medieval Political Thought* (Oxford: Basil Blackwell), 28, speaks of a "revived interest in liturgifying biblical parallels and putting them to what we should call political use." On symbolizing tendencies, cf. also Nelson, "The Lord's Anointed," p. 150; Robert Deshmann, "The Exalted Servant: The Ruler Theology of the Prayerbook of Charles the Bald," *Viator* 11 (1980), 410; Kantorowicz, *Laudes Regiae*, 56; Bouman, *Sacring and Crowning*, xii.

18. François L. Ganshof, *The Carolingians and the Frankish Monarchy: Studies in Carolingian History,* trans. Janet Sondheimer (Aberdeen: Longoman,

1971), 397. Pippin's anointing, "though something special, was not indispensable."

19. Roger Collins, "Julian of Toledo and the Royal Succession in Late Seventh-Century Spain," in P.H. Sawyer and I.N. Woods, eds., *Early Medieval Kingship* (Leeds: University of Leeds, 1977), 35. "Arguments about the development of early medieval kingship that seem to suggest virtually a clerical conspiracy to seize control of, ritualise, christianise, whatever you like, institutions and practices that 'simple lay folk' would have been happy to leave in their old, immemorial, unreformed way are particularly prevalent."

20. On the coronation of Charles the Bald at Orléans in 848 as the "birth of the fully-fledged sacral-theocratic kingship in Western realms," cf. Walter Ullmann, *The Carolingian Renaissance and the Idea of Kingship,* The Birbeck Lectures 1968–9 (London: Methuen, 1969), 62–4, 80–1. For Carolingian ruler theology, cf. H.H. Anton, *Fürstenspiegel und Herrscherethos in der Karolingerzeit,* Bonner historische Forschungen 32 (Bonn, 1968).

21. Synod of Fismes (881) canon 1. J.P. Migne. *Patrologiae cursus completus, Series latina PL* 125, 1071.

22. Cf. Kantorowicz, *Laudes Regiae*, 57: "'Jerusalem wandered to Gaul; the only Biblical pattern of a hallowed tribe, Israel, helped to shape the tribe that was to shape Europe. Pippin's anointment after the pattern of Israel's kings is the keystone of this evolution and at the same time the cornerstone of medieval divine right and *Dei gratia* kingship."

23. I Samuel 10:1: *Tulit Samuhel lenticulum olei et effudit super caput ejus.* Gregory I, *In I. Regum Expos.,* IV. 5. I. *PL* 79, 278: *quia vero ipsa unctio sacramentum est.* Isidore, *Quest. in Vet. Test.: in Gen. 29:8. PL* 83, 269: *sacramenta mysticae unctionis.* Ullmann, *Carolingian Renaissance,* 74, remarks that Gregory and Isidore were all the more remarkable because of the absence of actual regal anointings. "This needs to be stressed, since the Old Testament always remained in the pattern of royal anointings of kings, and the sacramental character attributed to it by these two outstanding sources of medieval theology, could all the more easily be absorbed."

24. II Samuel 2:4; 5:3; II Kings 11:12; 23:30; I Chron. 11:2; 29:22. In Judges 9:8,15 the very trees anoint their own king. On human agency in Old Testament anointings, cf. Martin Dudley and Geoffrey Rowell, eds., *The Oil of Gladness: Anointing in the Christian Tradition* (London: SPCK, 1993), 38.

25. Marc Bloch, *The Royal Touch: Sacred Monarchy and Scrofula in England and France.* Trans. J.E. Anderson (London: Routledge & Kegan Paul, 1973 English edition of *Les Rois thaumaturges*, 1923), 268. Cf. also Michael J. Enright, *Iona, Tara and Soissons: The Origin of the Royal Anointing Ritual,* Arbeiten zur Frühmittelalterforschung, vol. 17 (Berlin: Walter de Gruyer,

1985), 120. "Not only were the Franks disinterested in the Old Testament idea of royal unction, they were also unimpressed by biblical kingship in general."
26. Ullmann, *Carolingian Renaissance,* 75–77. "The reason for administering unction on Pippin seems clear enough: a substitute had to be found for his lack of blood charisma, and that substitute was to legitimize the coup d'état." Cf. also Nelson, "National Synods," 50.
27. Eichmann, "Königs- und Bischofsweihe," 29ff. This theory was taken up by Erich Caspar in "Das Papsttum unter frankischer Herrschaft," *Zeitschrift für Kirchengeschichte* 54 (1935), 136, n. 8.
28. Wallace-Hadrill, "The *Via Regia*," 22.
29. Nelson, "The Lord's Anointed," 141. If such sacrality ever existed, "it is very unlikely to have survived the powerful impact of Christianity on Frankish royal ideology and practice in the sixth and seventh century." Cf. also Pierre Riché, *Education and Culture in the Barbarian West,* trans. J.J. Contreni (Columbia, SC: University of South Carolina Press, 1976).
30. Nelson, "Kingship and Empire," 214. "The appeal to the pope in 750 meant the replacement of Germanic kin-right by 'Christian principles,' of supernatural sanctification drawn from 'old pagan mythical roots' by an equally supernatural but Christian sanctification."
31. On the "physical and purely human" foundation of Merovingian kingship, cf. Walter Ullmann, *Carolingian Renaissance*, 8–10, 53–5, 59, 95–6, 163.
32. Enright, *Iona, Tara and Soissons,* 122, argues that Pippin grasped at anointing as a short-term solution to bridge the dynasties.
33. On the identification of the Merovingian kings as *reges critini* [long-haired kings], cf. Gregory of Tours, *Historia Francorum,* 3:18, 6:24, 8:10 as examples.
34. David Harry Miller, "Sacral Kingship, Biblical Kingship, and the Elevation of Pepin the Short," in Thomas F.X. Noble and John J. Contreni, eds., *Religion, Culture, and Society in the Early Middle Ages,* Studies in Honor of Richard E. Sullivan (Kalamazoo, MI: Medieval Institute Publications, 1987), 131. "What changed was the religious definition of the sacral character of that kingship." Cf. also Wallace-Hadrill, *Early Germanic Kingship*, 100.
35. Enright, *Iona, Tara and Soissons,* 79, argues against Angenendt's idea that it was the Pope who was primarily responsible for Pippin's decision to be anointed. Cf. Arnold Angenendt, "Rex et Sacerdos: Zur Genese der Königssalbung," in Norbert Kamp and Joachim Wollasch, eds., *Tradition als historische Kraft* (Berlin: Walter de Bruyter, 1982), 100–118.
36. Although it is always difficult to argue from silence, the *Liber pontificalis* does make a point of recording Carloman's monastic vocation. Cf. *Liber Pontificalis* Zacharias 21, p. 46.

37. J.N. Hillgarth, ed., *Sancti Iuliani Toletanae sedis episcopi opera. I.* CCL 115 (Turnholt: Brepols 1976). *Historia Wambae,* cap. 4, pp. 218–20. *Diende curbatis genibus oleum benedictionis per sacri Quirici pontificis manus vertici eius refunditur et benedictionis copia exibetur. Nam mox e vertice, ubi oleum ipsum perfusum fuerat, evaporatio quaedam fumo similis in modum columnae sese erexit in capite, et e loco ipso capitis apis visa est prosilisse, quod utique signum cuiusdam felicitatis sequuturae speciem portenderet.*

38. J.N. Hillgarth, *Visigothic Spain, Byzantium, and the Irish* (London: Variorum Reprints, 1985), 446, n. 2. Pierre Riché, *The Carolingians. A Family who Forged Europe,* trans. Michael Idomir Allen (Philadelphia: University of Pennsylvania Press, 1993), 68, argues that Visigothic refugees would have brought the canon law collection *Hispania,* containing the account of Wamba's anointing, to Gaul with them. For Visigothic influence on Pippin's anointing, cf. E. Müller, "Die Anfänge d. Königssalbung," *Historisches Jahrbuch* 58 (1938), and R. Kottje, *Studien zun Einfluss des A.T. auf Recht und Liturgie des frühen M.A.* (Bonn, 1964).

39. On the importance of the *Collectio canonum Hibernensis* as propaganda in Gaul as well as England, cf. Enright, *Iona, Tara and Soissons,* 85–105.

40. Gerald Ellard, *Ordination Anointings in the Western Church before 1000 A.D.* (Cambridge, MA: The Medieval Academy of America, 1970. Reprint of 1933 edition), 28. N.B., this source contains no anointing for the bishop. On the origin of this formula, cf. H. Boone Porter, Jr., *The Ordination Prayers of the Ancient Western Churches* Alcuin Club Collections No. 49 (London: SPCK, 1967), 37. Porter points out that although the anointing of priest's hands appears in eighth-century Gallican sacramentaries, it was not originally Gallican, as it did not appear in the *Statuta Ecclesiae antiqua.* On the lack of this practice in Rome, cf. Ellard, *Ordination Anointings,* 16f. "From first to last, from the third century to the ninth, there was nowhere a trace of an anointing in connection with Roman ordinations."

41. Leo Cunibert Mohlberg, ed., *Missale Francorum* (Rome: Herder, 1957) #34, p. 10. *Unguantur manus istae de oleo sanctificato et crismate sanctificationis: sicut uncxit Samuhel David in regem et prophetam, ita unguantur et consummentur in nomine Dei Patris et Filii et Spiritus sancti, facientes imaginem sanctae crucis salvatoris Domini nostri Jesu Christi, qui nos a morte redemit et ad regna caelorum perducit. Exaudi nos, pie Pater, omnipotens aeterne Deus, et praesta quid te rogamus et oramus: per.*

"May these hands be anointed with hallowed oil and the chrism of holiness. As Samuel anointed David to be a king and prophet, so be they anointed, and perfected, in the name of God the Father, and the Son, and the Holy Spirit, making the image of the holy Cross of the Savior Jesus Christ our Lord, who redeemed us from death and leads us to the kingdom of heaven. Hear us, gracious Father, almighty eternal God, and grant what we ask and pray of you; through. . . . "

42.   A. Dumas, and J. Deshusses, eds., *Liber Sacramentorum Gellonensis,* CCL 159, 159A. Turnholt: Brepols, 1981.

43.   Cf. Ellard, *Ordination Anointings,* 30f.

44.   P. Saint-Roch, ed., *Liber Sacramentorum Engolismensis,* CCL 159C. Turnholt: Brepols, 1987.

45.   Cf. Ellard, *Ordination Anointings,* table on p. 44.

46.   Cf. Nelson, "Kingship, Law and Liturgy in the Political Thought of Hincmar of Rheims," *The English Historical Review,* No. 363 (April 1977), 262. Kantorowicz, *Laudes Regiae,* p 63. The anointing of the bishop's head "followed rather than preceded the ritual of royal anointment. It implied that the bishops, by their unction, became the king's peers."

47.   Cf. Ellard, *Ordination Anointings,* 31.

48.   The consecration of Pippin by bishops certainly implied the use of chrism. Cf. J.M. Wallace-Hadrill, *The Frankish Church* (Oxford: Clarendon Press, 1983), 167.

49.   Robert Deshmann, *"Benedictus Monarcha et Monachus*: Early Medieval Ruler Theology and the Anglo-Saxon Reform," *Früh-mittelalterliche Studien* 22 (1988), 204–240. Idem, "Otto III and the Warmund Sacramentary: A Study in Political Theology," *Zeitschrift für Kunstgeschichte* 34 (1971), 1–20.

50.   Nelson, "The Lord's Anointed." *Eadem,* "National Synods."

51.   Pagne, Jean de. "Doutes sur la certitude de cette opinion que le sacre de Pépin est la première époque de sacre des rois de France," in *Mélanges d'histoire du moyen âge dédiés à la mémoire de Louis Halphen.* (Paris: Presses Universitaires de France, 1951), 557–564.

52.   Especially Ullmann, *The Carolingian Renaissance,* 75. For Ullmann, the theology of the baptismal anointings "remained controversial and is of no real interest to us here."

53.   And clerical anointings as well.

54.   Wallace-Hadrill, *The Barbarian West,* 75–6.

55.   Miller, "Sacral Kingship," 136. Ganshof, *The Carolingians and the Frankish Monarchy,* 205, charges the Merovingians with reducing the Frankish church to impotence.

56.   Wallace-Hadrill, *The Barbarian West,* p. 91.

57.   Cf. Ian Wood, "Kings, Kingdoms and Consent," in P.H. Sawyer and I.N. Wood, eds., *Early Medieval Kingship* (Leeds: University of Leeds, 1977), 24ff, on the importance of bishops, who tended to be drawn from the aristocracy, to even pagan rulers in the early Middle Ages .

58. *Liber Pontificalis*, Gregory II:3, p. 4.

59. Michael Tangl, ed., *Die Briefe des heiliges Bonifatius und Lullus*, *MGH* Epistolae Selectae, Tomus 1 (Berlin, 1916), 130. Epist. 63: *Sine patrocinio principis Francorum nec populum ecclesiae regere nec ipsos paganorum ritus et sacriligia idolorum in Germania sine illius mandato et timore prohibere valeo.* English translation from Timothy Reuter, "Saint Boniface and Europe," in *idem, The Greatest Englishman: Essays on St. Boniface and the Church at Crediton*, 81.

60. To dispose of church property was also considered a royal prerogative by his son and grandson, Pippin III and Charlemagne, a "right which they exercised on a considerable scale." Ganshof, *The Carolingians and the Frankish Monarchy*, 219

61. On the identity of revolutionary nations with the Chosen People, cf. Kantorowicz, *Laudes Regiae*, 15–60; Wallace-Hadrill, *Early Germanic Kingship*, 99. A caution on too zealous an interpretation of the *gens Francorum* provided by Nelson, "On the Limits of the Carolingian Renaissance."

62. Peter "provided the main bridge between the dynasty and the Frankish church on the one hand and Rome on the other." Miller, "Sacral Kingship," p. 137. Pippin III was brought up at the Abbey of St. Denis. Cf. Wallace-Hadrill, *The Frankish Church*, p. 140.

63. Kantorowicz, *Laudes Regiae*, 60. On the Frankish reform of the Litany of the Saints, p. 90.

64. Wilhelm Levison, ed., *Vitae Sancti Bonifatii archepiscopi Mogutini*. Scriptorem rerum Germanicum (Hannover, 1905), 19ff. Cap. 7: *Cumque Carli ducis gloriosi temporale finitum esset regnum, et filiorum eius Carlomanni et Pippini roboratum est imperium, tunc quippe, domino Deo opitulante ac suggerente sancto Bonifatio archiepiscopo, religionis christianae confirmatum est testamentum, et orthodoxorum patrum synodalia sunt in Francis correcta instituta cunctaque anonum auctoritate emendata atque expiata.* English translation in George W. Robinson, ed., *The Life of St. Boniface by Willibald* (London: Oxford University Press, 1916), 71ff.

65. Tangl, ed., *Die Briefe des heiligen Bonifatius*, p. 82. Epist. 50. Boniface wrote to Pope Zacharias in 742: *Franci enim, ut seniores dicunt, plus quam per tempus octuginta annorum synodum non fecerunt nec archiepiscopum habuerunt ne aecclesiae canonica iura alicubi fundabant vel renovabant.* "The old men say that the Franks have held no synod for more than 80 years, nor had an archbishop, nor established or renewed in any place the canon laws of the church."

66. Levison, ed., *Vitae Sancti Bonifatii*, p. 43. *Plebem a perstifera tortuosi serpentis persuasione eripere curavit . . . ut tam praesentibus quam*

posteris spiritalis scientiae sapientiae patesceret et, aversa animarum circumventione, cognito christianitatis innotesceret.

67. Levison, ed., *Vitae Sancti Bonifatii*, p. 41. *Convenientibus in unum episcopis ac presbiteris, diaconibus atque clericis omnique gradu ecclesiastico, quos inclitae recordationis Carlomannus dux sub regni sui imperio adsciscere fecit, quater synodale factum est concilium.*

68. John C. Sladden, *Boniface of Devon: Apostle of Germany* (Exeter: Paternoster, 1980), 137, notes that the method of dating of these councils was new. No longer were they dated "according to the year of an Emperor's reign, but by the year of the Lord's incarnation."

69. Tangl, ed., *Die Briefe des heiligen Bonifatius*, p. 99. Epist. 56. A letter of Carloman to Pope Zacharias: *Statuimus per annos singulos synodum congregare, ut nobis presentibus canonum decrete et ecclesiae iura restaurentur et religio christiana emendetur.*

70. Cyrille Vogel, "Les échanges liturgiques entre Rome et les pays francs jusqu'a l'époque de Charlemagne," In *Le Chiese nei regni dell'Europa occidentale e i loro rapporti con Roma sino all'800.* Settimane de Studi de Centro Italiano di studi sull'Alto Medioevo VII (1960), 225.

71. This would remain a concern of Carolingian monarchs until at least Charles the Bald. Ganshof, *The Carolingians and the Frankish Monarchy*, 209: "The reorganization of the hierarchy, which continued, completed, and improved on what had been achieved or attempted by the Bonifacian reform, stands out as the most important aspect of royal intervention in the matter of church government." Cf. also E. Lesne, *La hiérarchie épiscopale en Gaule et en Germaine de la réforme de Saint-Boniface à la mort d'Hincmar* (Paris, 1905).

72. Tangl, ed., *Die Briefe des heiligen Bonifatius*, p. 124. Epist. 68, October 745: *De civitate namque illa, quae nuper Agrippina vocabatur nunc vero Colonia, iuxta petitionem Francorum per nostrae auctoritatis preceptum nomini tuo metropolim confirmavimus et tuae sacntitati direximus pro futuris temporibus eiusdem metropolitane aecclesiae stabilitatem.* "The city formerly called Aggripina, but now named Cologne, at the request of the Franks and by a decision of our authority, we have confirmed as a metropolis assigned to you and we have sent to Your Holiness the charter of institution of this metropolitan church for all time." English translation fron Ephriam Emerton, *The Letters of Saint Boniface* (New York: Columbia University Press, 1940), 110.

73. Tangl, ed., *Die Briefe des heiligen Bonifatius*, pp. 102–105. Epist. 57. Cf. Emerton, *Letters of Saint Boniface*, pp. 94ff.

74. Nelson, "National Synods," 43ff. Cf. also Walter Ullmann, *The Growth of Papal Government in the Middle Ages*, 2nd ed. (London, 1962), 125ff.

75. Vogel, "Les échanges liturgiques," 194f. Cf. also *idem, Medieval Liturgy*, 148 re: "some rather timid canons on provincial observances."

76. Pope Zacharias continually stressed that the only requirements for baptism were water and the invocation of the Holy Trinity. Even the intention of the Trinitarian formula seemed to suffice. Boniface was rebuked in 746 for ordering the re-baptism of those who had been baptized by a priest ignorant of Latin who said, *Ego te baptizo in nomine patria et filia et spiritus sancti.* [I baptize you in the name of the nation and the daughter and the holy spirit.] Zacharias felt that simple ignorance was "no error or heresy." Tangl, ed., *Die Briefe des heiligen Bonifatius*, p. 141. Epist 68. Cf. Emerton, *Letters of Saint Boniface*, pp. 122ff.

77. Michel Andrieu, *Les Ordines Romani du haut moyen âge* 5 vols. (Louvain: Spicilegium Sacrum Lovaniense, 1931–1961), II: XVII. "La première moitié du VIIIe siècle fut pour l'Église franque une période de désorganisation et de désarroi. La décadence comencée au siècle précédent s'accélére sous l'action de multiples causes." Cf. also Joseph L. Levesque, "Theology of the Postbaptismal Rites in the Seventh and Eighth Century Gallican Church," *Ephemerides Liturgicae* 95 (1981), 5, n. 3 for a good bibliography of the historical material for seventh- and eighth-century Gaul.

78. Vogel, "Les échanges liturgiques," 226.

79. Vogel, "Les échanges liturgiques," 229, 227: "Il n'est pas exagéré de dire que vers la fin du VIIe siècle la liturgie était célébrée pratiquement au gré de chacun." Ellard, *Ordination Anointings*, 18 has pointed out that "the Gallican tendency is everywhere evident, and everywhere acting in a uniform manner: local usages were being constantly overlaid with Roman ones, and these later adapted to suit a non-Roman mentality."

80. Vogel, "Les échanges liturgiques," 227. Also Vogel, *Medieval Liturgy*, 135.

81. Cf. E. Lesne, *Historie de la propriété ecclésiastique en France. IV. Les livres, scriptoria et bibliothèques du commencement du VIIIe à la fin du XIe siècle* (Lille, 1938).

82. Boniface wrote to Cuthbert in 747 about his desire to submit the entire Frankish church to the Holy See. Cf. Tangl, ed., *Die Briefe des heiligen Bonifatius*, p. 163. Epist. 78. *Decrevimus autem in nostro sinodali conventu et confessi sumus fidem catholicam et unitatem et subiectionem Romanae ecclesiae fine tenus vite nostre velle servare; sancto Petro et vicario eius velle subici.* Cf. also Wallace-Hadrill, *The Barbarian West*, 91.

83. Epistola ad Decentium 2. *P.L.* 20:552. *Quis enim nesciat aut non advertat, id quod a principe Apostolorum Petrum Romanae Ecclesiae traditum est, ac nun usque cusdodiatur, ab omnibus debere servari; nec superduci aut*

introduci aliquid, quod auctoritatem non habeat, aut aliunde accipere videatur exemplum? praesertim cum sit manifestum, in omnem Italiam, Gallias, Hispanias, Africam atque Siciliam, et insulas interjacentes, nullum instituisse ecclesias, nisi eos quos venerabilis apostolus Petrus aut ejus succesores contituerint sacerdotes.

84. Vogel, "Les échanges liturgiques," 193, felt that the council of Vienne (463) was the first to propose any correlation between uniformity of ceremony and unity of faith. Cf. C. Munier, ed., *Concilia Galliae: A. 314–A. 506*. CCL 148 (Turnholt: Brepols, 1963), 155. Canon 15: *Rectum quoque duximus, ut vel intra provinciam nostram sacrorum ordo et psallendi una sit sonsuetudo, et sicut unam cum Trinitatis confessione fidem teneamus; vel varaita observatione in aliquo devotio nostrao discrepare credatur.* The council of Agde (506) adjusted the placement of the *collectio post antiphonam* to conform with "universal" usage (*ecclesiae ab omnibus aequaliter custodiri*). Cf. ibid., 206. Canon 30: *Et quia convenit ordinem ecclesiae ab omnibus aequaliter custodiri, studentum est ut, sictu ubique fit, et post antiphonas collectiones per ordinem ab episcopis vel presbyteris dicantur et hymnos matutinos vel vespertinos diebus omnibus decantari et in conclusione matutinarum vel vespertinarum missarum post hymnos capitella de psalmis dici et plebem collecta oratione ad vesperam ab episcopo com benedictione dimitti.* "Manifestly, liturgical unification and imitation of Roman usage do not appear to have been a problem preoccupying the bishops of Gaul." Vogel, "Les échanges liturgiques," 194.

85. C. Munier, ed., *Concilia Galliae: A. 511–A. 695*, CCL 148A (Turnholt: Brepols, 1963), 78. Canon 3: *Et quia tam in sede apostolica, quam etiam per totas Orientales adque Italiae provincias dulces et nimium salubres consuetudo est intromissa, ut Quirieleison frequentius cum grandi affectu et conpunctione dicatur.*

86. An exception to this was Pope Zacharias in 751, railing to Boniface against the Frankish solemn episcopal blessing before communion (*benedictiones quas faciunt Galli*). Epist. 13 ad Bonif., *PL* 89, c. 951–2. The Benedictional of Friesing contained just such blessings. Zacharias seemed more concerned about their placement than their content. Nevertheless, they persisted well into the following century. Cf. Vogel, "Les échanges liturgiques," 197.

87. Vogel, *Medieval Liturgy*, 70. Both liturgical and non-liturgical books (hagiographies, letters, collections of conciliar decisions) served to bring Roman ideas to the north. Cf. Vogel, "Les échanges liturgiques," 188.

88. Vogel, "Les échanges liturgiques," 189.

89. Queen Brunhilde (597), Gertrude, abbess of Brabant (626–659), Amand, the bishop of Maastricht (c. 647–684), Gregory of Utrecht (c. 530–2)

were but some of the recorded collectors of Roman books. Cf. Vogel, "Les échanges liturgiques," 189 et seq.

90. Vogel, *Medieval Liturgy*, 147. This effort was not to prove successful until at least the reign of Charlemagne. One cannot help but be reminded here of the various Acts of Uniformity under the Tudor monarchs.

91. Vogel, "Les échanges liturgiques," 235. Cf. also A. Baumstark, *Vom geschichtliche Werden der Liturgie* (Freiburg/Br., 1923), 61–64.

92. Vogel, "Les échanges liturgiques," 236.

93. Vogel, *Medieval Liturgy*, 149ff.

94. Vogel, *Medieval Liturgy*, 64.

95. Vogel, "Les échanges liturgiques," 204.

96. Vogel, "Les échanges liturgiques," 238 et seq. Cf. also Bernard Moreton, *The Eighth-Century Gelasian Sacramentary* (Oxford, 1976). Anton Baumstark, *Missale Romanum. Seine entwicklung, ihre wichtigsten Urkunden und Probleme* (Eindhover-Nijmegen, 1929), had called the eighth-century Gelasian a *sacramentarium Bonifatium*, but the presence of prayers for Thursdays in Lent makes this dating impossible. Lenten Thursdays were without a liturgy in Rome until Pope Gregory II, so the date of redaction must be placed under Pippin. Cf. *Liber pontificalis*, Gregory II:9, p. 8 Vogel, "Les échanges liturgiques," 241ff, indicates that any more precise dating is not possible and cites the theories of Mohlberg, Andrieu, and Klauser.

97. The now-lost Sacramentary of Flavigny, or Frankish Gelasian Sacramentary. Cf. Vogel, *Modern Liturgy*, 71.

98. Michel Andrieu, "Quelques remarques sur le classement des sacramentaires," *Jahrbuch für Liturgiewissenschaft*, XI (1931), 46–66. Cf. also A. Chavasse, "Le sacramentaire gélasien du VIIIe siècle," *Ephemerides Liturgicae* 73 (1959), 249–298.

99. On official requests for Rome to send books to the north, cf. Vogel, *Medieval Liturgy*, 80ff; *idem*, "Les échanges liturgiques," 228.

100. Cf. Vogel, "Les échanges liturgiques," 261–265, on other Frankish efforts to import Roman liturgical customs (e.g., in the Office), and further unify the Frankish liturgy. The reluctance of popes to comply with Frankish requests for liturgical books may be a reflection on the poor state of the library in Rome at the time. Paul I would send only an antiphonary and a responsory to Pippin: *libros quantos reperire potuimus i.e., antiphonale et responsale. MGH* Epist. mero. et karol. aevi I, p. 529.

101. Cf. Michel Andrieu, *Les Ordines Romani*.

102. Vogel, "Les échanges liturgiques," 217.

103. Aidan Kavanagh, *Confirmation: Origins and Reform* (New York: Pueblo, 1988).

104.   Epistola ad Decentium III: 6. *PL* 20, 554–555. *De consignandis vero infantibus manifestum est, non ab alio, quam ab episcopo fiere livere. Nam presbyteri licet secundi sint sacerdos, pntificatus tamen apicem non habent. Hoc autem pontificium solis deberi episcopos, ut vel consignent, vel paracletum Spitirum tradent, non solum consuetudo ecclesiastica demonstrat, verum et illa lectio Actum Apostolorum, quae asserit, Petrum et Joannem esse directos, qui jam baptizatis traderunt Spiritum sanctum. Nam presbyteris, sive extra episcopum sive praesente episcolo cum baptizant, chrismate baptizatos ungere licet, sed quod ab episcopo fuerit consecratum, non tamen frontem ex eodem oleo signare, quod solis debetur episcopis, cum tradunt Spritum paracletum.*

105.   Gelasius, *Epistola* 9, 6. *P L* 59, 50: *Nec minus presbyteros ultra modum suum tendere prohibemus; nec episcopali fastigo debite sibimet audacter assumere: non conficiendi chrismatis, non consignationis pontificalis abhibendae sibimet arrigere facultatem; no praesente quoibet antistite, nisi fortasse jubeantur, vel orationis, vel actionis sacrae supplendae sibi praesummant esse licentiam; neque sub ejus aspectu, nisit jubeantur, aut sedere praesumant, aut veneranda tractare mysteria.*

106.   Nathan Mitchell, "Dissolution of the Rite of Christian Initiation," in *Made, Not Born: New Perspectives on Christian Initiation and the Catechumenate* (Notre Dame, IN: University of Notre Dame Press, 1978), 56. "To write the story of the dissolution of Christian initiation is to write about the emergence of episcopal confirmation as a rite separated from baptism."

107.   Kavanagh, *Confirmation*, 67–8.

108.   The development of calling this act Confirmation is explored by Eugene M. Finnegan, *Origins of Confirmation in the Western Church*, STD dissertation, Trier, 1970; Kavanagh, *Confirmation*; and Gabriele Winkler, "Confirmation or Chrismation? A Study in Comparative Liturgy," *Worship* 58 (1984), 2–16.

109.   Canons 3, 4 of the Council of Riez. CCL 148, 67–8.

110.   CCL 148, 78. *Nullum ministrorum, qui baptizandi recipit officium, sine chrismate usquam debere progredi, quia inter nos placuit semel chrismari. De eo autem qui in baptismate, quamcumque necessitate faciente, non chrismatus fuerit, in confirmatione sacerdos commonebitur. Nam inter quoslibet chrismatis ipsius nonnisi una benedictio est, non ut praeiudicans quidquam, se ut non necessaria habeatur repetita chrismatio.* The translation is that of Gabriele Winkler, "Confirmation or Chrismation," 9.

111.   Council of Arles (449–461). CCL 148, 133: . . . *idest ut clerici atque altaris ministri a nullo nisi ab ipso vel cui ipse iniunxerit ordinentur, chrisma nonnisi ab ipso speretur, neophyti si fuerint ab ipso confirmentur.*

112.   On the development of postbaptismal rites in fifth-century Gaul, cf. L.A. Van Buchem, *L'Homélie Pseudo-Eusebienne de Pentecôte. L'origine de*

la confirmatio *en Gaul Meridionale et l'interpretation de ce rite par Fauste de Riez* (Nijmegen, 1967).

113. J.C.D. Fisher, *Christian Initiation: Baptism in the Medieval West,* Alcuin Club Collections No. 47 (London: SPCK, 1965), 52–77. Cf. also Leonel Mitchell, *Baptismal Anointing,* Alcuin Club Collections No. 48 (London: SPCK, 1966), 125.

114. M.P. Vanhengel, "Le Rite et la formule de la chrismation postbaptismale en Gaule et en Haute-Italie du IVe au VIIIe siècle d'apres les sacramentaires gallicans," *Sacris Erudiri* 21 (1972–1973), 161. These sacramentaries contain the only three rituals known or identified as Christian initiation in Gaul. Cf. also Levesque, "Theology of the Postbaptismal Rites," 41. Cf. n. 48 for a list of the councils. Cf. also Finnegan, *Origins of Confirmation*, 257, and Mitchell, *Baptismal Anointing*, 125.

115. Vanhengel, "Le Rite et le formule," 167f. Cf. 199 for the comparison of the three formulae. The pertinent sections are: Leo Cunibert Mohlberg, ed., *Missale Gothicum* (Rome: Herder, 1961), 261, 262, 265. E.A. Lowe, ed., *The Bobbio Missal [Text]* Henry Bradshaw Society 58 (London, 1920), 251, 252, 253, 254; Leo Cunibert Mohlberg, ed., *Missale Gallicanum Vetus* (Rome, 1958), 175, 176, 177.

116. Vanhengel, "Le Rite et le formule," 168, 202. Vanhengel finds that the structure of the rites in the Gallicanum Vetus is "manifestly more primitive," but that the Gothicum represents the ancient liturgy of Gaul, p. 219. Cf. ibid., 202–204 on the relation of the Gallican infusion of chrism to the rites of the *Apostolic Tradition* and Tertullian [*De baptismo*, VII]. Infusion was not a practice of Roman, Ambrosian or Mozarabic liturgies for postbaptismal unction.

117. Winkler, "Confirmation or Chrismation," 8.

118. Winkler, "Confirmation or Chrismation," 11.

119. These were those who had been baptized into Arian Christianity. Cf. the second council of Arles, Canon 17. CCL 148, 117. *Bonosiacos autem ex eodem errore venientes, quos sicut Arrianos baptizare in Trinitatem manifestum est, si interrogati fidem nostram ex toto corde confessi fuerint, cum chrismate et manus impositione in ecclesia recipi sufficit.* On the reception of heretics into the church, cf. Van Buchem, "L'Homélie pseudo-Eusebienne," 169, et. seq.

120. Vogel, *Medieval Liturgy*, 164–5. Andrieu, *Les Ordines Romani*, II, 409–413.

121. OR XI, #98–99.

122. OR XI, #101.

123. Cf. Finnegan, *Origins of Confirmation*, 314. OR XI #102 in Andrieu, *Les Ordines Romani,* II, p. 446. Despite the change in nomenclature from

consignatio to *confirmare*, the actions described in the Hadrianum and in Ordo XI are virtually identical. Cf. Finnegan, *Origins of Confirmation*, 316.

124. Vogel, *Medieval Liturgy*, 165, presents both arguments concerning the precedence of Ordo XI and the Gelasian sacramentary. Andrieu thought that Ordo XI was the source for the Gelasian, and Chavasse thought that it was the other way around. Vogel agreed with Chavasse.

125. Cf. Finnegan, *Origins of Confirmation*, 324ff.

126. S. Rehle, ed., *Sacramentarium Gelasianum Mixtum von Saint Amand,* Textus Patristici et Liturgici Fasc. 10 (Regensburg, 1973), 81–82. #353: *Postea cum ascenderit a fonte infnas signatur a presbitero in cerebro de xrismate.* 358: *Diende consignatur ab episcopo. . . . Postea signas eum in fronte de xrysmate.* Note again that the priest and the bishop anoint different parts of the head. Only the bishop anoints *in frontem*.

127. Finnegan, *Origins of Confirmation*, 334.

128. Van Buchem identifies this author as Pseudo-Eusebius. Winkler, "Confirmation," accepts a Gallic provenance, but not mid-fifth century date. Cf. Finnegan, *Origins of Confirmation*, 501–513 for a good summary in English of Faustus' (or Ps.-Eusebius') theology.

129. Van Buchem, ed., 41. *In baptismo regeneramur advitam, post baptismum confirmamur ad pugnam.*

130. Cf. Van Buchem, ed., 40. *Sicut exigit militaris ordo eit cum imperator quemcumque in militium receperit numerum.*

131. "Truly, truly, I say to you, unless one is born of water and the Spirit, he cannot enter the kingdom of God." [RSV]

132. Winkler, "Confirmation," 14.

133. Otto Faller, ed., *Sancti Ambrosii Opera* VII. Corpus Scriptorum Ecclesiasticorum Latinorum, v. 73 (Vindobonensis, 1955), 17. *De sacramentis,* I.4, *unctus est quasi athleta Christi*.

134. Chrysostom, *In Epist. ad Coloss. cap. 2*, hom. 6, c. 4. PG 64:342: *Ungitur sictu athlete stadium ingressuri. . . . Non solum enim venit ut doceatur, sed etiam ut deceret et exerceatur*.

135. Lowe, ed., *Bobbio Missal*, p. 74 (241–243). 241: *Effeta effecta est hostiam in odorem suavitatis*. 243: *Ungo te de oleo sanctificatio sicut unxit Samuhel David in rege et propheta*. 244: *Operare creatura olei operare ut non lateat hic immundus spiritus nec in membris nec in medullis nec in uno conpagine membrorum esd operitur in te virtus christi filii dei altissimi et spiritus sancti per omnia saecula*. Cf. E.C. Whitaker, *Documents of the Baptismal Liturgy* (London: SPCK, 1970), 211. In the Eastern Church, this act was "intimately connected with the pouring of oil over David's head when he was anointed." Cf. Gabriele Winkler, *Das armenische Inationisrituale. Entwicklungsgeschichte und liturgievergleichende Untersuchung der Quellen*

des 3. bis 10. Jahrhunderts. Orientalia Christiana Analecta 217 (Rome 1982), 138, 409–412, 458–459. eadem, "The Original Meaning and Implications of the Prebaptismal Anointing," *Worship* 52 (1978), 24–45.

136. G.F. Warner, ed., *The Stowe Missal,* 2 vols., Henry Bradshaw Society, 31–32 (London, 1906–1915). The Stowe Missal is a Celtic work from 792–812, but its archetype dates back to the early seventh century.

137. Winkler, "Confirmation or Chrismation," 16.

138. Levison, ed., *Vitae Sancti Bonifatii*, p. 49. Cap. 8: *Sed quia festum confirmationis neobitorum diem et nuper baptizatorum ab episcopo manus inpostionis et confirmationis populo praedixerat ian longe lateque disperso*. Cf. also Van Buchem, *L'Homélie pseudo-Eusebienne*, 102. "On est donc fondé à penser que le premier emploi des mots *confirmare-confirmatio*, de même que la naissance du rite qu'ils indiquent, doivent être vus dans les perspectives particulières de l'initiaion à la campagne."

139. Winkler, "Confirmation or Chrismation," 16.

140. The Synod of Auxerre (561–605), limited baptisms to Easter Day, except in the case of death. CCL 148A, p. 267. Canon 18: *Non licet absque paschae sollemnitatem ullo tempore baptizare, nisi illos, quibos mors vincina est, quos gravattarios dicunt*. The fathers at the council of Mâcon (585) complained that so many parents were having their children baptized on martyrs' feasts that there were only two or three to be baptized at Easter itself. CCL 148A, p. 240. Canon 3: *Relatione quorumdam fratrum nostrorum comperimus Christianos non observantes legitimum diem baptismi paene per singulus dies ac natalis martirum filios suos baptizare, ita ut vix duo vel tres reppereantur in sanctum pacha, qui per aquam et Spiritum sanctum regenerentur*.

141. Concilium Veronese (755), c. 7. *MGH* Capit. Reg. Franc. 1 (1883), 34; and Decretum Compendiense (757), c. 12. ibid., p. 38. Cf. Finnegan, *Origins of Confirmation*, 340

142. Geoffrey J. Cuming, *Hippolytus: A Texts for Students* (Bramcote Notts: Grove Books, 1976), 11. *Apostolic Tradition* 5: . . . *unde uncxisti reges sacerdotes et profetas*.

143. Ambrose, *De mysteriis*, VI, 30. *PL* 16, 415: *Quare hoc fiat intellige, quia oculi sapientis in capite ejus. Ideo in barbam defluit, id est, in gratiam juventutis; ideo in barbam Aaron, ut fias electum genus, sacerdotale, pretiosum; omnes enim in regnum Dei et in sacerdotium unguamur gratia spiritali.* "All of us are anointed into the kingship and priesthood of God by special grace."

144. Maximus of Turin, *De baptismo*, III. *PL* 57, 777: *Impletu enim baptismate, caput vestrum chrismate, id est oleo sanctificationis infunimus, per quod ostenditur baptizatis regalem et sacerdotalem conferri a Domino*

dignitatem. "It is shown to the baptized, through the infusion of chrism, that unto them there has been conferred by God the royal and the sacerdotal dignities."

145. Christopher M. Lawson, ed., *Sanct Isidori episcopi hispanensis de ecclesiasticis officiis,* CCL 113 (Turnholt: Brepols, 1989). *De officiis ecclesiasticis,* II, 26, De crisma: *Sed postquam dominus noster, verus rex et sacerdos aeternus, adeo patre caelesti ac mystico unguento est dilibutus. Iam non soli pontifices et reges sed omnis ecclesia unctione chrismatis consecratur pro eo quod membrum est aeterni regis et sacerdotis. Ergo qui genus sacerdotale et regale sumus idoe post lavacrum unguimur ut Christi nomine censeamur.*

146. For the aromatic ingredients in chrism, see P. Hofmeister, *Die heiligen öle in der morgen-und abendlandischen Kirche* (Würzburg 1948), 25 et seq.

147. Nelson, "Symbols in Context: Rulers' Inauguration Rituals in Byzantium and the West in the Early Middle Ages," in Derek Baker, ed., *The Orthodox Churches and the West* (Oxford: Basil Blackwell, 1976), 118–9. She makes reference to a conciliar fragment from Aix-la-Chapelle (816): *Et quia oleum olivarum non habent Franci, voluerunt episcopi, ut oleo lardivo utantur. MGH* Conc. aevi karol. I, p. 833.

148. Nelson, "On the Limits of the Carolingian Renaissance," 71.

149. Council of Vaison (442), CCL 148, 97. Canon 3: *Per singula territoria presbyteri vel ministri ab episcopis, non prout libitum fuerit, a vicinioribus, sed a suis propriis per annos singulos chrisma petant, adpropinquante solemnitate paschali.* Also in *Statuta Ecclesiae antiqua, ca.* 475, canon 36. *PL* 56, 887: *Presbyteri qui per dioceses Eccleias regunt, non a quibuslibet episcopis, sed a suis; nec per juniorem clericum, sed aut per seipsos, aut per illum qui sacrarium tenet, ante Pasche solemnitatem chrisma petant.*

150. CCL 148A, p. 266. Canon 6. *Ut a media quadragesima presbyteri crisma petant et, si quis infirmitate detentus venire no potuerit, ad archdiacono suum archisubdiaconum trnasmittat, sed cum cristario et lenteo, sicut reliquiae sanctorum deportati solent.*

151. Chavasse, "La benediction du chrême," 117.

152. Chavasse, "La benediction du chrême," 115.

153. Mohlberg, ed., *Missale Gothicum,* #261: *Perungo te crisma sanctitatis tonicam immortalitatis, quam dominus noster Iesus Christus traditam a patre primus accepti, ut eam integram et inlibatam perferas ante tribunal Christi et vivas in saecula saeculorum.* Cf. Whitaker, *Documents of the Baptismal Liturgy,* 162.

154. Mohlberg, ed., *Missale Gallicanum Vetus*, p. 26, #82: . . . *qua quondam reges, sacerdotes, prophetas, cornu a dilectione tua exundante perfusos.*

155. Leo Cunibert Mohlberg, ed., *Liber Sacramentorum Romanae Aeclesiae Ordinis Anni Circuli*, p. 60, #78" *Ut secundum constitucionis sacramentum regio et sacerdotali propheticoquae honore perfusi, vestimento incorrupti muneris induantur.* This sequence of prayers reflects a Gallican "complexification" of a simple Roman rite of blessing chrism. Cf. Gerard Austin, *Anointing with the Spirit: The Rite of Confirmation* (New York: Pueblo, 1985), 103.

156. Mohlberg, ed., p. 61. #382: . . . *[U]nde uncxisti sacredotes reges et prophetas et martyres, chrisma tuum perfectum, a te, Domine, benedictum.*

157. Mohlberg, ed., p. 63, #388: . . . *in sancti spiritus inmiscere virtutem per potenciam Christi tui, a cuius cancte monine chrisma nomen accepit, unde uncxisti sacerdotes reges prophetas et martyres.*

158. Chavasse, "La benediction du chrême," 113ff. He gives three reasons for this determination:

1. it is unknown in books of Roman origin which contain blessings of oils: e.g., Hadrianum, *Ordo* Romanus XXX, *Ordines* Romani XXVII, XXVIII and their common source *Ordo* Romanus XXIV;

2. the use of the phrase *vestimento incorrupti muneris induantur* as in the Gothicum;

3. the place it occupies as a preface on Holy Thursday, the same as in Gallicanum Vetus.

Cf. also Vanhengel, "Le Rite et la formule," 197, 199. On chrismation as garment, cf. also John E. Farrell, *The Garment of Immortality: A Concept and Symbol in Christian Baptism.* Ph.D. Dissertation, The Catholic University of America, 1974.

159. Chavasse, "La benediction du chrême," 115ff.

160. Jean Deshusses, ed. *Le sacramentaire grégorien. Ses principales formes d'après les plus anciens manuscrits,* Spicilegium Friburgense 16 (Fribourg, 1971), 173–4.

161. The final redaction of the Gelasian had confused the formularies for chrism and the oil of exorcism. The mistake was partially rectified by the redactor of *OR* L. Cf. Robert Cabié, "Christian Initiation," in Aimé-Georges Martimort, ed., *The Church at Prayer.* Trans. by Matthew J. O'Connell (Collegeville, MN: Liturgical Press, 1987), v. 3, p. 69, notes 21–22.

162. The blessing of oils would be restricted to Pontificals. Cf. Dudley and Rowell, *Oil of Gladness,* p. 114.

163. Mohlberg, ed., *Missale Gothicum*, p. 68, #265: *Baptizatis et in christo coronatis quos dominus noster a crisma petentibus regeneracione donare*

dignatus est praecamur omnipotents deus ut baptismum quod acceperunt immaculatum ipsum perferant usque in finem per dominum. Cf. Whitaker, p. 162.

164. On chrism as a symbol of incorporation into the Christian community and of delineation within it, cf. Nelson, "Symbols in Context," 177.

165. Andrieu, *Les Ordines Romani*, II, p. 445. OR XI #94: *Haec omnia expleta, fundit crisma de vasculo aureo intro in fontes super ipsam aquam in modum crucis. Et cum manu sau miscitat ipsum crisma cum aqua et aspergit super omnem fontem vel populum circumstantem.* 95: *Hoc facto, omnis populus qui voluerit accipiet benedictionem unusquisque in vase suo de ipse aqua, antequam baptizentur parvuli, ad spargendum in domibus eorum vel in vineis vel in campis vel fructibus eorum.*

166. *MGH*, Cap. Regem Franc., II, p. 340. Avitus of Vienne, a contemporary of Clovis noted that although Clovis remained a long-haired warrior-king, he had a "salvation-giving helmet of holy anointing" placed on his head. Avitus of Vienne, Epist. 46, ed. R. Peiper. *MGH* Auctores Antiquissimi VI (2), p. 75.

167. Thus also Enright, *Iona, Tara and Soissons*, 165: "Pippin did not depend on Old Testament theory to impress the Franks; rather, he chose to rely on the people's profound confidence in the substance with which they baptized children [sic], healed the sick and produced their own homely miracles in times of death."

168. This is true of the Soissons unction. On the 754 unction of Pippin and his sons at Saint Denis by Stephen II, we have the relatively contemporary commentary of the *Clausula de unctione Pippini.*

169. The regal image of the newly baptized was further emphasized in some Eastern Christian traditions with postbaptismal acclamations and coronations. Cf. Thomas Michels, "Die Akklamation in der Taufliturgie," *Jahrbuch für Liturgiewissenschaft* 8 (1928), 76–85. Cf. also Kantorowicz, *The King's Two Bodies*, 490.

170. Cf. Ullmann, *The Carolingian Renaissance*, 109. "It was the sacrament of unction which performed an invaluable service in the process by which any kind of medieval royal absolutism was from now on effectively prevented." *Contra* this, cf. M. Wallace-Hadrill, "The *Via Regia*," 29: "Carolingian consecrations were surely not designed as a series of wily counter-checks on royal absolutism, nor were they based on an acknowledged principle of contract between a king and his consecrators. His contract was with God."

171. NB the importance of Pippin's family here. In 751 Bertrada was anointed as queen alongside Pippin. In 754 Stephen II re-anointed Pippin and Bertrada, and anointed their two sons. Cf. *Annales regni Francorum* 754, p. 12.

172. Nelson, "National Synods," 49. She points out that the "rite of royal anointing made its appearance in each of these four national churches [Visigothic Spain, East and West Francia, England], at the same period as the upsurge of synodal activity." Ibid., 56f.

173. At least at this early stage and not, as Ullmann claimed, a rebirth. Ullmann, *The Carolingian Renaissance*, p. 71: "Like a child reborn in the font, Pippin was reborn as king—a new man with a changed and indelible character." He bases this contention on I Samuel 10:6: "Then the spirit of the Lord will come mightily upon you and you shall prophesy with them and be turned into another man." [RSV] *et insiliet in te spiritus Domini et prophetabis cum eis et mutaberis in virum alium.* I think that Ullmann's not wanting to distinguish various strains of baptismal theology [cf. note 52, *supra*] manifests itself. Whether or not chrismation confers an indelible character is outside the scope of this discussion. What is clear is that everywhere in the Christian tradition one is reborn through water and the Spirit [*ex aqua et spiritu*]. The font, not the anointing, was the womb of new birth.

174. Cf. Wallace-Hadrill, "The Via *Regia*," 27: "Whether consecration made a king or confirmed him or admitted him, it bore witness to a link between king and God."

INDEX